JOURNALS

1982–1986

Anthony Powell

JOURNALS
1982–1986

Anthony Powell

With an introduction by
VIOLET POWELL

Heinemann : London

First published in Great Britain 1995
by William Heinemann Ltd
an imprint of Reed Consumer Books Ltd
Michelin House, 81 Fulham Road, London sw3 6rb
and Auckland, Melbourne, Singapore and Toronto

This paperback edition published 1996 by William Heinemann Ltd

The extract from Evelyn Waugh's letter to Bobby Roberts (1929)
is quoted by permission from Peters Fraser & Dunlop.

Thanks are due to the following for providing photographs
(all photographs not credited come from the Powell
family albums):

1. © Lewis Morley/the Akehurst Bureau; 2. 11. 14. 16 National
Portrait Gallery; 4. © Alistair Morrison/IPC; 5. Sir Nicholas Henderson;
8. Alice Boyd; 22. 24. 26. 27. 28. 29. Hulton Deutsch Collection;
23. Marcelle Quinton; 31. 32. Tom Hustler.

A CIP catalogue record for this title
is available from the British Library

ISBN 0 434 00304 2

Typeset by Deltatype Ltd, Ellesmere Port, Wirral
Printed and bound in Great Britain by
Clays Ltd, St Ives PLC

Contents

For Tessa
With
Many Thanks

I wish to thank Tessa Davies for transcribing these *Journals*, Christopher Falkus for his editorial assistance, and my wife, Violet Powell, for helpful suggestions and advice.

Introduction

The idea of keeping a journal appealed to Anthony Powell as bridging a gap when a novel was not in immediate production, though *O, How the Wheel Becomes It!* and *The Fisher King* both came to be written in the years covered by this volume. He had never before kept any diary more detailed than an engagement calendar.

In fact, and quite fortuitously, the five years covered in these Journals make an effective sequel to the author's Memoirs, the last volume of which was published in 1982, the year the Journals begin. There are, however, considerable differences in approach and style between Memoirs and Journal. Most obviously, perhaps, a diarist, however reflective, is primarily concerned with day-to-day events. Again, the diarist writes with an intimacy and confidentiality which will not occur in the more literary framework of an autobiography. In so far as practicable, the Journals are printed exactly as they were written down, with all the informality and shorthand expressions retained.

In the New Year of 1982, the Powells had lived at The Chantry, near Frome in Somerset, since 1952. Tristram, their elder son, had married Virginia Lucas in 1968. Their children, Georgia and Archie, born in 1969 and 1970 had seen a lot of The Chantry, as The Stables in the garden have been made over to Tristram and his brother John, who have between them effected a conversion into an impressive house. The lake and grottoes, frequently mentioned, lie below The Chantry in a wooded valley, the lake having been made in the early nineteenth century by damming a stream.

Visits to London are no longer as regular as they had been in the past, business to do with a fortnightly review in the *Daily Telegraph* being settled over the telephone. When trips to London do take place they are apt to be for social events, combined with sessions in the dentist's chair of Howard Sussman, a recurrent figure throughout the Journal.

The village of Chantry lies at the east end of the East end of the Mendip Hills, the gateway of the West, and near enough to Bath for passers-by to come to meals. Throughout the years, some friends from America appear annually or bi-annually, Alison Lurie from Ithaca, New York, Bob and Liddie Conquest from California, Rosemary and John Monagan from Washington. When Evangeline Bruce, former American Ambassadress in London, comes to England there are meetings at Chantry and in her apartment in Albany. There are many exchanges of meals with Mary and Lees Mayall, retired British Ambassador to Venezuela, near and dear neighbours.

In public life the installation as an Honorary Doctor at the University of Bristol brings with it an unexpected drama. There is also a steady flow of interviews for British, French and American periodicals. The interviewers invariably insist on bringing a photographer with them, although repeatedly told that photographs of the highest quality of the author of *A Dance to the Music of Time* are to be had in abundance. Interviewers appear to feel improperly dressed without a photographer at their side.

When in February 1982 *O, How the Wheel Becomes It!* begins to take shape the Journal, begun to bridge a gap, has already become part of the creative process, and continues as a relaxation from the rigours of novel writing. Roland Gant, a long-time friend and editor at Heinemann, not only appears at unexpected hours of day, but conducts complicated telephone conversations, mixing proof correcting with the intricacies of publishing gossip.

Anniversaries, a seventieth birthday, (Violet Powell, V in the Journal) a golden wedding, and an eightieth birthday (Anthony Powell) are all celebrated with enjoyable parties at The Stables, where grandchildren and great nephews and nieces supply not only an injection of youth, but a waiter service. The rally of friends at the eightieth birthday party brought more than thirty in number and they came from as far afield as Oxford and London, braving a December night of storm and rain.

The author of the Journals has never adhered to the tedious practice of reading only one book at a time. Books are kept for downstairs reading, bedside reading and books for review are 'inplanted'. Consequently, cross references are frequent. Sometimes these will call to mind an incident from the past which may illuminate a present happening. This gives the diarist the satisfaction of learning the end of a story, which he has described elsewhere as an enjoyable compensation for getting older.

Mrs Thatcher, as Prime Minister, makes more than one appearance, at dinner parties arranged for her to meet historians, philosophers and novelists, and at the Royal Academy Banquet. She shows herself to be less of a philistine than her detractors have sometimes claimed, and with unabated fascination for her admirers. After these evenings, the London Library offers never failing solace.

The *Hudson Review* Award (which is quickly followed by the T. S. Eliot Award) is celebrated at the American Embassy in Grosvenor Square. The lavish luncheon takes place on the first floor, overlooked by a gallery where the work of the Embassy goes on, unheeding of the clatter of knives and forks and the subsequent speeches.

At intervals children and grandchildren of the friends of long ago write to say how glad they are to have their forebears remembered in *To Keep the Ball Rolling*. Particularly charming is a letter from the granddaughter of Castano, the proprietor of Castano's restaurant in Greek Street. This was a meeting place for luncheon patronized for years by Anthony Powell and his friends. Castano's granddaughter has listened to *A Dance to the Music of Time* on the radio, and has then gone on to read *To Keep the Ball Rolling*.

The Journal comments, 'It should be made clear to all authors when they set out on writing . . . if they put someone in a book . . . the persons involved, or their relations, friends, enemies will get round to it.'

The last year of this volume, 1986, happens to have the most entries. *The Fisher King* was published in April, for which Heinemann gives a luncheon at Claridge's with a mélange of guests to suit all tastes. The guest of honour makes a speech on the theme of the hymn 'Lord behold us with thy blessing once again assembled here', with stress on how much he has owed to Roland Gant for his help and enthusiasm. (It must be added that this tribute was made with no knowledge of how few years remained to Roland Gant.)

In September Hilary Spurling arrives to present the portrait by Rodrigo Moynihan, which she had been instrumental in arranging to be commissioned by friends and admirers for Anthony Powell's eightieth birthday.

The year and the volume ends with congratulations to the author of the Journals on being made a Companion of Honour.

Violet Powell
Chantry
1994

JOURNALS
1982–1986

1982

Monday, 22 February

To London. Originally intended to go just for the day to attend Memorial Service for Pam (Berry) Hartwell [wife of Michael Berry, later Lord Hartwell, proprietor of the *Daily Telegraph*] and see Mr Sussman (dentist). The railway strike prevented this, so I went up, for night, arranging various engagements. Anne Lancaster [wife of the famous *Daily Express* cartoonist Osbert Lancaster] had asked us to look in whenever possible to cheer Osbert's bad state, so I lunched at her invitation at 78 Cheyne Court. Surveying the King's Road from top of bus, I was struck how Chelsea still looks more or less as fifty years ago, unlike most of London, if more crowded than formerly; strange women in djibbas leading equally strange dogs, art students, etc. Osbert in poor shape, owing to hardening of arteries. He can only just get from sitting-room to dining-room with a stick. Very depressed. I asked if he had watched *Brideshead* on TV. Osbert said he always thought it a bad book, could only stand one episode of the TV. He said Evelyn Waugh thought that too, and tried to stop the book at proof stage. True Evelyn did turn against *Brideshead* later, tho' at the time he was on record as calling it a masterpiece (unlike most writers, he thought all his books brilliant when written). Part of Osbert's boredom due to inability to take in anyone else's ideas, sunk in his own already formed ones.

First-class steak at luncheon, bought by Anne for her neighbour, she said, who lives near her Newbury cottage. The Lancasters were unable to go to the country that weekend owing to Osbert's health. Stayed on talking until after 3 o'clock. Anne asked what I was going to do, said visit the Army Museum (near in Royal Hospital Road) to buy some postcards, then to The Travellers. She insisted on driving me to The Travellers, no doubt just to get half an hour out of the house, which must be claustrophobic to a degree.

Dined with Evangeline Bruce at Albany flat, she comes over from Washington at regular intervals. Evangeline is the widow of David Bruce, US Ambassador here, and various other diplomatic posts, perhaps the nicest 'man of affairs' I ever met, quiet, intelligent, amusing, Southerner, banker by profession. Evangeline, his second wife (the first a Mellon), is considerably younger, her father also a diplomat, mother English (née Surtees), stepfather a British diplomat. Evangeline opted for being determinedly American, her sister (who writes well under the name of Virginia Surtees) opting for this country. Evangeline is a beauty, well dressed, intelligent, funny, slightly mysterious, perfect Ambassadress, tho' constant late parties at the Embassy fatigued her, so would sometimes retire early to bed. Bob Conquest, historian, specialist on modern Russia, has a theory that an American Ambassador and wife in London should not be persons of great charm, as a wrong impression is given of what their country thinks; theory for which there may be something to be said.

I first met Evangeline at a luncheon party of Pam Berry's where we got on well from the start. There was a stage when V[1] and I seemed not to be asked to the US Embassy (possibly during a Labour Government, when concentration on different social elements may have been thought desirable), then invitations renewed as much as ever. In this occasion Evangeline said she had put off a 'romantic evening' to arrange a dinner party for me, as I was coming to London. It consisted of the novelist Edna O'Brien, quite jolly, battered good looks of very Irish sort; Alistair Horne, journalist, military historian, characteristic figure of that type, now writing life of Harold Macmillan. Splendid Mouton-Rothschild '52, given Evangeline by Philippe de Rothschild. Alistair Horne said that when he was Foreign Correspondent for the *Daily Telegraph* in Germany in 1950, overwhelmed with work, uncomfortable circumstances, having rough time generally, a message came through from the paper saying: Lady Pamela [ie. Pam Hartwell] is engaging two German *au pairs*, do the trains they will catch run, etc, etc? Horne had blown up at that; three weeks later he lost his job.

Talk about Pam, her mania (about which she made no secret) for all those who exercised power. When Ted Heath was PM I remember her saying 'You know, I really think Mr Heath is rather attractive'; on another occasion, when

---

[1] See Introduction. V is shorthand throughout the *Journal* for Violet, Anthony Powell's wife, whom he married in 1934. Violet was the third of four Pakenham daughters: Pansy, Mary Violet and Julia. Their brother Frank, married to Elizabeth, née Harman, became Earl of Longford.

the Israeli General Dayan (patch over one eye) was over here: 'You know sometimes I think I am really a soldier's girl.' When Pam lunched at Chatsworth the thing that really impressed her was that President Kennedy had given the Devonshires a photograph of himself. This languished, unframed, curling, yellow, on the drawing-room chimney-piece like a postcard. Pam could not get over such nonchalance about a US President. Some discussion about *Brideshead* took place, the fucking scene, what individuals found erotic. Evangeline complained that Jeremy Irons's naked back (as Charles Ryder in bed) was spotty. I said I was not excited by any scene in which another man took part. Evangeline laughed a lot at that, said 'I never heard anything so *British*'. I said I had inherited a German *History of Erotic Art* from my father (who had rather a taste for pornography), in which far the most exciting picture was a woman looking through the crack of a slightly open door. Edna O'Brien said 'I can see you're very romantic'.

The following day Evangeline was taking Diana Cooper [famous society beauty, wife of politician and writer Duff Cooper] and Harold Macmillan to Pam Hartwell's Memorial Service at St Margaret's, Westminster, then giving them luncheon at Albany. Owing to conversation rattling on at dinner, we forgot TV police documentary being shown about preventing a burglary at the house of Laura, Duchess of Marlborough, in which Adrian Daintrey (painter and long-standing friend), the historian Arthur Bryant and others, played some part; we only managed to catch just the end of it. V watched at home, and found it funny.

Tuesday, 23 February

Arrived at St Margaret's, Westminster, soon after 11 am for noon, just missing plain clothes men with two huge hounds of the Baskervilles, sniffing through the church for explosives, as the Home Secretary was to be present. I was greeted at the door by Laurence Kelly, an usher, author, married to Linda McNair Scott, niece of Michael Hartwell. He said: 'We're going to meet at dinner tonight.' He wanted to put me in a pew with the Longfords, up in the front, but I persuaded him to find a place about the middle, next to a pillar. Duff Hart-Davis (also a writer, son of the publisher and editor Rupert Hart-Davis) in a British Warm came into the pew in front; John Saumarez Smith (of the Heywood Hill bookshop in Curzon Street) behind, also Alistair Horne again, who showed forgiving spirit in turning up for Pam's service after her ostensible sacking of him.

Church packed. Hymns: *Lead Kindly Light, I Vow to Thee My Country* (Spring-Rice poem), *Fight the Good Fight*, all in their way appropriate. Evangeline,

Diana Cooper, Harold Macmillan, did not turn up. Coming down the aisle on the way out Colin Welch (Dep. Ed. *Daily Telegraph*) said: 'I'd never realized before what a fine poem *Lead Kindly Light* is.' Same idea crossed my own mind while the hymn was being sung. Colin Welch introduced me to Bill Deedes, Editor of the *Telegraph*, whom I don't think I'd met. Said a word to Liz (Longford) outside the church.

I was about to return to The Travellers when a plump figure in a cassock appeared from the Choir, warmly greeting me. It was the Revd Gerard Irvine. I had not grasped he had been taking the service. 'Are you lunching anywhere? No? Then you *must* lunch with me at the Clergy House just round the corner. Got to hear a few confessions as Lent's coming on, then we'll have a drink. I've been given some Figeac. We'll have it for luncheon.' He seized my arm, and we returned to the interior of the church. I hung about for a bit, then we both set off for Gerard Irvine's incumbency, St Matthew's in Great Peter Street, a few minutes away. The church was partly burnt down (arson or faulty fuses, said Gerard as if one were as common as the other) about five years ago.

In the remains, which looked like a ruin one goes on a trip to see, a few persons were praying, very medieval scene. Gerard introduced the curate who took me down several steps into a large vestry, while Gerard heard about parishioners' sins (he is stratospherically High). There was a big stand for hanging up vestments, long table, several chairs, sink, typewriter, bits of church furniture saved from the fire, now under cellophane, piles of books, pamphlets, all deep in dust, several huge cupboards. Everything in utter disorder under a high ceiling, the room lighted at one end by a large ecclesiastical window. There I was left for some time. Then Gerard reappeared, took me by narrow passages into the Clergy House facing on to Great Peter Street.

The house, long low rooms painted dark red, looked 17th century, in fact 1850, built by Comper (church, Gilbert Scott). Here again everything in a fantastic muddle, books on all sides, not a square inch on the wall for an additional picture. Pictures included two large portraits in the dining-room of Gerard's mother, and her father (like her husband, Royal Marine general), another painting, possibly by Piper in the sitting-room, various odds & ends of bric-à-brac, smaller pictures. In the bedroom a white baroque wooden double bed (canopy & putti, crucifix at head), bought for five shillings at Wotton-under-Edge, where the Irvine parents had lived, a house named Under the Hill (after the Beardsley novel) by its former owner, Nineties figure More Adey, boyfriend of Oscar Wilde's friend Robert Ross.

V and I went over Under the Hill when looking for somewhere to live in the country in 1950s, suggesting ourselves to the Evelyn Waughs for two nights, as

Stinchcombe was quite close. We visited the church before arriving at the house, saw Gerard (whom we did not then know) praying. Evelyn said: 'Oh God, make it £10,000.' Under the Hill painted chocolate colour within, as Evelyn truly remarked, 'not the smallest attempt at elegance'. Later in life we met Gerard several times at parties, then he & his sister, and on another occasion his mother, came on Hellenic cruises. Plump, ebullient, strong traces of Maurice Bowra influence at Oxford in speech.

At luncheon Gerard sat at head of a long table, the curate and I on either side of him. The Figeac '71 Gerard had spoken of was excellent. The curate, Draper, an agreeable young man, had his glass barely moistened, and was soon off on clerical duties. Cold beef, nine different sorts of cheese, fruit. Gerard now has the Westminster parish. He conducted the wedding of Pam Hartwell's daughter Harriet. He said he had to remind Pam once or twice the occasion was Harriet's marriage, not her own. The Clergy House was somewhere between a Firbank novel and Cruikshank's illustration of *The Old Curiosity Shop*.

Afterwards I went to London Library with the sudden idea of checking on the unidentified 'Richard Powell of Brilley, esquire', Escheator of Radnorshire, 1560, etc, who was, I am certain, nephew of my forebear Clement Powell of Brilley, but cannot at present prove that. This jigsaw puzzle side of genealogy is always fascinating. Richard Powell's grandmother was of Philip Dorddu's line, therefore might be shown in Bartrum's recently collected *Welsh Pedigrees*. If I could find whom she married, several things would click into place. Dates turned out to be too late for Bartrum's work. Ran into Tony Quinton, Oxford philosopher, in London Library, whom I urged to come over to luncheon at The Chantry some Sunday.

I dined with the Spurlings [close friends, Hilary, the biographer, and John, playwright] at 48 Ladbroke Grove. Guests: Hilary's mother, Mary Forrest, whitehaired lady, very quiet, did not seem to get much of a look in at dinner; Laurence & Linda Kelly (pretty, half a Berry, accounting for Laurence being usher at the Memorial Service); Anne Winder (interviewed me for Kaleidoscope after Heinemann luncheon for *Hearing Secret Harmonies* in 1975). Laurence Kelly said, in St Margaret's, St John-Stevas MP altered place-cards in his pew so that he might be nearer the aisle, therefore more visible.

Before dinner Hilary took me to see Nathaniel and Gilbert (my godson) who had all their toy soldiers out in two different forts. Daughter Amy appeared earlier, not involved in these military operations. Gilbert said: 'What is your favourite country?' Assuming that winning battles was in question, I replied: 'England.' The preference seemed to be accepted. Hilary told me that they have some pacifist friends with whose son Gilbert (passionate militarist) plays soldiers. As the parents disapprove of toy soldiers, she asked how this was managed. Gilbert said, 'We told them they were archaeologists.' Hilary is writing Introduction for life of Beryl de Zoete [mistress of the Oriental scholar Arthur Waley] quite why I could not make out. She is having quite a lot of trouble about it, as Arthur Waley's relicts, mistress and wife, in their various forms, have always quarrelled with each other, everything rather mysterious about Waley's intimate relationships, possibly touch of homosexuality.

John Spurling gave me a copy of his play *The British Empire*, perhaps somewhat diffuse, but the Foreword cleared up a matter I have tried to trace for a year or two: when did circumcision become fashionable among the British upper classes? No medical authority appears to know. In *Daniel Deronda* the hero was not aware he was a Jew until coming to mature years. An American writer recently remarked that Deronda only had to look. John Spurling states that a certain Dr Ramondino brought the fashion in about 1891, after which circumcision no indication of Jewishness in this country, merely belonging to a certain income bracket. This would have been a bit late for Deronda, in whose day no doubt it was rare. Even then, one feels, there must have been medical reasons in certain individual cases; while not everyone compares his private parts with other boys. Belonging to the circumcised myself, I was vaguely aware some boys resembled me, others not, but never devoted much thought to the matter, any more than shape of their noses. I gave the Spurlings pamphlet of Verses celebrating Roy Fuller's Seventieth Birthday, including my own Drinking Song to him. Driven back to The Travellers by Anne Winder, who mercifully turned out to have a car.

Wednesday, 24 February

I saw Sussman, and have to see him again. Howard Sussman is an unusually congenial dentist, good at his job, amusing to talk to. When young he wanted to be composer, write opera about King Arthur. We came to him quite by chance, owing to death of a dentist whose hobby was refereeing rugger. Sussman spoke of railway strike, and used (with apologetic overtones) the phrase 'patient management' (ie. the management of patients).

Sunday, 28 February

Reflected on Pam Berry (Hartwell). Her appearance, demeanour, rather as one imagines Elizabeth I, tho' not much presence, notwithstanding great concern on Pam's part for the rag-trade, she wore on the whole, awful clothes (gold dresses, etc). In spite of her many awfulnesses, I liked Pam. Her view of life was wholly subjective, and would change from one moment to the next when that suited her, without the smallest sense of consistency, shame at abandoning passionately held opinion of minute before, utter selfishness in relation to everyone else, including husband and children. In a tête-à-tête she possessed a kind of individual wit (no doubt recognizable as her father's had one known him), also shrewdness, of her own, not nearly so taken in by things as might appear from her utterances when among a lot of people . . . Pam probably always retained element of prudence in all her dealing, however reckless at the time. Her instinct made her choose Michael Berry as husband, the younger son, which turned out to be absolutely correct, bringing exactly sort of power background she aimed at. I was surprised by the feeling with which Michael replied to my condolence letter ('I hope you believe in the next world, as there doesn't seem much to look forward to in this one'). I heard elsewhere that, to those he thought sent more than polite formalities, he said many unexpected things, such as that Pam had devoted her life to his wellbeing, tho' he knew she had at times preferred other men to himself. Evangeline Bruce produced the two last paraphrases: Gerard Irvine, the distinction Michael Hartwell made between replying to condolence senders. On balance one feels Pam & Michael suited each other pretty well. I remember at one dinner party of theirs Michael saying with admiration: 'Pam, you *are* a bitch.'

Monday, 1 March

I received a letter written in unusual English (for instance beginning 'Her Highness') asking me to contribute an article to a paper in Bilbao called *Apan*, preferably on the British army, on account of the 'clairvoyance, reality and severity' of my 'point of view'. V said the description was just right.

Tuesday, 2 March

I finished Conrad's *The Rover* (1923), not read before. By no means Conrad at his best, at same time his usual mastery of scenes of action. Chief interest of novel (an aspect to which I have never seen attention drawn) is the French plan to deceive Nelson by planting bogus dispatches on captured or dead French naval officer; in fact just what was done successfully during the second war, as described in Duff Cooper's *Operation Heartbreak*, also another book *The Man Who Never Was*. Did the idea come from *The Rover*? There it is represented as emanating directly from Bonaparte himself. In Conrad novel it is only through a series of chances that the dispatches are found on a *dead* man, a PoW having been intended.

Monday, 8 March

I continued to get my novella under way. The sluggish imagination of old age makes giving of reality to characters difficult. The story must be seen from the point of view of a writer's own age group, later life being on the whole thin in action of the kind to give point to novels. Projected outline: Winterwade (a name found in Domesday Book), successful critic in his seventies, twice married, has when young been in love with Isolde Upjohn. Winterwade is also a close friend of Falconer, who produced a few once praised, now forgotten, novels before the Second World War, in which he was killed. A Diary of Falconer's turns up in Australia, written so much in abbreviations, symbols etc, as to be only intelligible to someone who lived in that distant period.

Winterwade reads MS of the Diary for a publisher. He finds to his mortification that, quite unknown to himself, Falconer was also in love with Isolde Upjohn, and spent a weekend with her in Paris. The weekend was a ghastly failure, as she is frigid, but Winterwade is so enraged that, although the Diary is obviously good stuff, he reports unfavourably. He then suffers guilt. His wife goes away for a day or two at a moment when a TV programme is being made about Winterwade by Gerry Craddock, a TV interviewer well known for his bad manners. Just before the camera crew arrives, Isolde Upjohn herself turns up. She has been married to various oilmen, sheiks, etc, and has written her memoirs, which have been accepted for publication. She wants Winterwade to do an Introduction. Point is that although she has had an exciting career, she hopes to emphasize the days when she was young, knew intelligent young men, and especially affair with Falconer, which has become in her mind a great romantic idyll.

As Winterwade was friends with Falconer at the time, Winterwade could help expand that. Craddock arrives, manages to get Isolde Upjohn into the programme about Winterwade, including the Falconer aspect. Possibly Winterwade's wife involved in all this through unexpected return; row which might result in the death of Winterwade. Story might open with his Memorial Service. Problem of getting life into the two literary men, who have no particular models.

Wednesday, 10 March

Rab Butler's death in paper. We were once on Hellenic cruise with him and his wife. About twenty-five years ago the Royal Society of Literature instituted something called a Companion of Literature, which they handed out to various writers, including Evelyn Waugh, who accepted it. Later Evelyn asked what I thought about it. I said I should be quite prepared to be made an Hon. Fellow of the Society (which in fact they don't do), and be given a plastic model, Oscar in some form, or an infinitely small sum of money as a prize, but that I thought an honorific title (in this case one also objectionable because so ludicrously named) appropriate only to the Queen, not a self-constituted body like the RSL. Evelyn said: 'Would you like me to arrange that you are never offered it?' 'Yes.' 'I will see to that.' I take this to mean that Evelyn had a word with Freddie Birkenhead.

That worked for about fifteen years, when the RSL came along with an offer of their Companionship of Literature. I replied politely that I would prefer not, but did not outline reasons in case that sounded pompous. When we were on the cruise with Rab Butler I remembered that he was, or had been, President of the RSL, so took the opportunity, when we were alone together, of explaining my reasons for refusing the thing. Butler listened, and apparently quite understood. Some days later he spoke to V of the conversation, saying: 'Does Tony mean that he would like to be offered the C of L again?' It would be hard to find a better example of a politician being utterly unable to understand private feelings, human motives, for that matter plain English, hopelessly getting hold of the wrong end of the stick (as somebody said, of that sort of figure, the jewelled end of the sceptre). I believe Tom Eliot also refused the Companionship.

Thursday, 11 March

I now habitually end the day with reading Shakespeare (possible another Jacobethan dramatist) in bed, followed by some poetry. This is restful, and sends one off to sleep. I have just finished *The Tempest*. I am struck by the fact that all the action takes place within three hours, so that Ferdinand's labours gathering wood could not have been so dreadfully onerous, as he was later spending time playing chess. Bringing in wood seems to have been the chief problem on the island (fires for cooking, generating power for Prospero's spells?), because Caliban was also chiefly employed in that manner.

Friday, 12 March

Arthur Perry's funeral at Chantry Church. A neighbouring farmer, eighty-six, formerly of Orr Farm, just across the field and to the West. Mr Perry was latterly in an Old Persons' Home in Frome after series of strokes. One of the nicest of men, quiet, intelligent, model (with Ernie Moore of Manor Farm) for Mr Gauntlett in *Dance*. Perry used to live (with his rather bleak wife, no children) in another house in the village, Orr Farm, occupied by his rather strange brother Bob (who had his own perfectly coherent Hardyesque routines), and Harry Rogers who did odd jobs, a now non-existent vocation. Years ago Rogers had been engaged to Miss Perry, but somehow they never managed to bring the wedding off. Mr Rogers, who potters about mending fences and putting up gates in the oldest of clothes, was also great racing man. When he went off in belted mackintosh and a little car to Newbury, he could well have been eccentric race-horse owner.

Ernie Moore contributed rather less to Mr Gauntlett, chiefly his haunted house, murder supposed to have taken place at Manor Farm when whoever lived there was out hunting; whether in the 14th century or 18th century seems impossible to ascertain. Ernie Moore jolly old buccaneer, with strain of bogusness, Breton plates on the wall, the house then in the last stages of tumbledownness and interior muddle. At Christmas we would call on him, when the table in the parlour would be loaded with bottles of every kind, sometimes quite exotic drinks, and hams, brought in to avoid taxable transactions, he told us. Only about forty persons in church at Arthur Perry's funeral. We had expected more. I suppose he had been away from the village too long to be generally remembered. (*The King of Love my Shepherd is, Thine for ever God of Love, Abide with me.*)

Saturday, *13 March*

Tristram gave a party at The Stables[1] for V's seventieth birthday. Champagne. Guests: Percy & Jane Somerset,[2] with daughter, younger son, Francis, and the latter's fiancée; Joff & Tessa Davies (connexions with Frome printers Butler and Tanner) with daughters Lucinda & Mary Anne; neighbours Lees & Mary Mayall, John & Victoria Jolliffe, Michael & Isabel Briggs; Henry & Virginia Bath;[3] Ferdie & Julia Mount[4] who are staying at

---

[1] See Introduction. The Stables is the converted house in the garden of the Powells' home The Chantry, near Frome in Somerset. It is jointly owned by the Powells' sons Tristram and John. Tristram and his wife Virginia live in Stockwell, London, and they and their family are usually called 'The Stockwells' for convenience throughout the *Journals*. The Stockwell children are Georgia and Archie.

[2] Percy, Duke of Somerset, married Jane Collette. Their sons are John, Lord Seymour, and Francis Seymour. Their daughter is Anne, and the family are friends and neighbours of the Powells.

[3] Henry, Marquess of Bath, married to Virginia Tennant, née Parsons.

The Stables with the three children. Percy Somerset typical Officer of the Line of jollier sort, commanded The Wiltshire Regiment's Depot as a major; on retiring said to have done much to pull the family fortunes together. Ferdie agreed Percy was good value as a duke. When shooting with Arthur Duckworth (Arthur and Mary live in imposing house near Frome) at Orchardleigh Percy had burped the National Anthem without being at all pressed to do so. Henry Bath has now given up drink, and although he is quite compos, talking to him is a little as one imagines talking to Lazarus immediately after return from the Dead; perfectly all right, just a touch of needing to get used to an already forgotten condition.

John Jolliffe said he attended Charles Johnston's Pushkin readings. On arrival he saw Clarissa Avon [widow of prime minister Anthony Eden, later Lord Avon] was there. As Jolliffe was prominent in organizing Victims of Yalta Memorial, kept far end of the room. When it came to taking seats, found he had been put next to Clarissa. Nothing was said on the subject of returned Russian PoWs.

Virginia Bath asked about the Horrockses, who had briefly rented The Stables, before their renovation and making over to Tristram & John. She laughed a lot when I told her how General & Lady Horrocks were sunbathing with little or no clothes in the garden (then mostly nettles, old tins, broken glass), when Hussey, a rather grotesque ex-colonial forestry official who appears from time to time to see about cutting down trees, came wandering through at the back of The Stables, thinking the place uninhabited. There seems to have been some sort of explosion from Horrocks, which Hussey later described as the General 'pulling rank'.

The Stockwells dined here. I had just read Ferdie's novel *The Man who rode Ampersand*. It contains a telling picture of his father, Robin Mount, otherwise insufficiently made a hero, having ridden this famous horse. Owned by a character modelled on the well-known racing figure Dorothy Paget, for whom our former excellent cook, Doris Mears, once worked. After that, Doris said, all employers seemed easy. Doris and Irene Mears were two pretty sisters, who worked for Mary, Violet & Julia Pakenham when they were living at Rutland Gate for the end of the lease of their mother's house.

Reread Casanova's *Memoirs*, and was struck, as ever, by his narrative ability, skilful comments on what he was himself feeling like at moment of writing. Casanova supposed he would live three or four years longer than he did which may have affected the rounding off of the *Memoirs*, also reread

---

[4] Julia Pakenham, Violet's sister, married Robin Mount, gentleman rider, in 1938. Their son Ferdinand, novelist, political journalist, and subsequently a member of the government Think Tank, married Julia Lucas, twin of Virginia Powell. Their children are William, Harry and Mary.

Helen Gardner's commentary on *Four Quartets*. She throws much interesting light on Eliot & Hayward as a team. John Hayward obviously had a good ear for words, but was quite without Eliot's sudden bursts of eccentricity, eg. insisting on spelling arras 'aresse', because it was so spelt in Elyot's *The Governour*, the author of which TSE regarded as putative kinsman. Reread Benjamin Robert Haydon's *Autobiography*, most of it immensely boring, but occasional flashes, like Keats not being sober for six weeks on end.

Read for the first time *A Pair of Blue Eyes* (Proust's favourite Hardy novel), opening clearly modelled on Hardy's original meeting with his first wife Emma. Like all Hardy's novels, machinery of narrative improbable beyond words, somehow series of comparatively convincing relationships emerging in spite of that.

There is awkwardness of writing and clichés are recurrent, but something like a group of rustics discussing character of pigs can be splendidly funny, making more certain my theory that Firbank [Ronald Firbank, novelist, 1886–1926] learnt a lot from Hardy.

Monday, 22 March

J. R. Ackerley's *Diaries* being reviewed. Someone (who, I can't remember) introduced me to Ackerley in The Travellers in the 1950s. I did not take to him. He said, 'Ah, yes – you wrote – what was it? – No, don't tell me – novel about an artist.' This seemed the most patent one-upmanship, bearing out what one had heard of him as power-maniac when Literary Editor of *The Listener*. Later he rang up to ask if I would review something for that paper, which for some reason I was unable to do. Sonia Orwell presided over Ackerley's obsequies, as of several other literary figures.

Tuesday, 23 March

Reading Casanova, I am reminded of a remark made by Fluff, retainer of the Harris family, Osbert Lancaster's in-laws, former governess/duenna of Karen Lancaster, Osbert's first wife. Fluff must have been pretty when young, perhaps at one moment on easy terms with Sir Austin Harris, to whom she once rapped out at dinner: 'Don't gobble, Daddy.' She was also famous for her malapropisms. A book called *Casanova Loved Her* (about which mistress I can't remember) was lying on a table in the Harrises' dining-room in Catherine Street, Westminster. Fluff picked up, read the title: 'Karsavina loved her – do you know I never knew she was a lesbian.'

Thursday, 25 March

These spring frosts cause me to wake at 5.30, buzz all over, and feel like hell. Sleep rarely returns, utter gloom takes over until towards 7 o'clock. At 7.30, opening up the house, one begins to feel better, once about my daily business, at least no worse than usual. Nocturnal or early morning low spirits by no means new, now an absolute routine, perhaps from thinning of the blood.

Last night on TV we watched the *Nancy Astor* serial, which we have done intermittently. This instalment was dominated by the homosexual scandal implicating her son by first marriage, Bobby Shaw (well played by Nigel Havers), who became almost hero of story. My memory is that the case involved a trumpeter of The Blues when the regiment was in camp, but here represented as a street pick-up, less picturesque, but perhaps otherwise would have caused difficulties with the Royal Horse Guards.

Good climax to the serial would be the scene witnessed on the night we dined with Diana Cavendish (Boothby/Campbell-Gray/Gage) in Eaton Square some years ago. Diana Cavendish lived in a flat of her own in Lady Astor's house, with a slight understanding that she kept an eye on Lady Astor, by then of fairly advanced years. When we left the flat, the door of the Astor side of the passage was open. In a kind of hall or lobby, Bobby Shaw was sitting on a chair, his overcoat on, Lady Astor, wearing a shawl standing over him. V heard Bobby Shaw say: 'All I want is to get away from *you*.' One of those scenes to be thought contrived in a book or a film.

Wednesday, 31 March

Ronald Bottrall (met for a second or two about thirty years ago, possibly in office of the *TLS*) wrote in 1977 about a poem of his on the subject of *Dance*. A letter from him arrived this morning asking permission to dedicate a poem to me. He related a past year of great disaster for him & his wife: mistakenly imprisoned by the Italian police; wife broke her hip in Portugal; burgled in Rome. He is about my age, his poem *old Age* (like most of them as far as I am concerned) strikes a chord. Bottrall suffered the early handicap of being admired by F. R. Leavis.

Village item, social and gastronomic: Dick & Dolly Blacker's Silver Wedding (she worked here at one time, he, at his own request, patrols the lake with dog & gun, combined keeper & water-bailiff); at the party for their two sons with respective girl-friends: the fare 'take-away' Chinese food, Mateus Rosé.

Saturday, 3 April

A reflection on one aspect of the Argentine invasion of the Falklands: *Dance* supposedly being translated into Spanish by Argentine publisher (said to be more reliable than Spanish publishers), at first El Cid, changed to Adiax. The war must be somewhat awkward for Willy Walton's Argentinian wife, as they are over here for his eightieth birthday, also for the Anglophile Borges. Borges one feels is a nice, rather a great man, tho' I find difficulty in reading his works.

Wednesday, 7 April

I noted in paper a Memorial Service for Bobby Birch (met once, I think), journalist who had seven wives. Appropriately, ceremony held at *St Bride's* Fleet Street.

Thursday, 8 April

The German translator of *Dance*, Dr Heinz Feldmann, came to luncheon to talk about difficulties in doing the work, bringing with him a near-pretty girl named Waltraud Schulzke, described as his 'assistant'. She wore an infinitely German white trouser-suit, broadbrimmed blue hat. Feldmann, tall, fiftyish, teaches English at Münster University. He seemed nice, dedicated to *Dance*, intensely German (father killed in the war). He wanted to debate the nature of translation *a priori*. Eventually I got him on to more immediate matters, like the fact that the Germans have a different word for a grass field, tilled field, and playing field; that 'house', in the boarding-school sense, is untranslatable.

He seemed to think that Germans would find the occultism difficult to understand, though admitted German newspapers carry horoscopes. I find it hard to believe that in the country of Faust they cannot get round to a little fortune-telling. Feldmann had listened to *Dance* on Radio 4, which can be picked up in North Germany, where the smart thing is to intercept TV beamed for British troops stationed there: eg. *Brideshead*, which had much impressed him, especially the picture of Oxford, something utterly unfamiliar in German he said. I withstood the temptation to say it was pretty unfamiliar in English, even if one had been up at Oxford at the time.

Friday, 9 April

Finished with enjoyment A. N. Wilson's *The Laird of Abbotsford*, wondered if I would not make an effort to try Scott again. I read *Woodstock* (at Mr Gibbs's school, I think), attempted *Quentin Durward* at Oxford (recommended for my

French history period), but utterly broke down, got through *Rob Roy* during the vac, retaining one good passage about Highlander getting in rage for no particular reason, making snorting noises. Scott held High Tory views, but seems to have been on easy terms with all social categories. One story about a rebuff Scott received, trying to be matey, recalled the occasion when Frank (Pakenham) leaving a political meeting after the war, said to a dear old lady by the door: 'Goodnight, mother'; to which she replied with considerable feeling; 'I'm not your fucking mother.'

Saturday, 10 April

Nigel Hollis (who lives near, son of Christopher and Madie Hollis) brought advance copy of *The Strangers All Are Gone* [volume four of Anthony Powell's Memoirs *To Keep the Ball Rolling*]. With unbelievable stupidity this has been bound in orange; other three vols of memoirs in black. [Later put right.]

Easter Sunday, 11 April

Nina Lucas (Tristram's mother-in-law, née Grenfell) is staying at The Stables. We had to return a luncheon of Geoffrey & Mary Waldegrave, she a Grenfell cousin of Nina's, took opportunity of having them today, so that Nina, Tristram and Virginia, might be of the party. There were doubts about leaving Georgia & Archie to lunch on their own, then The Stables house-party was increased by Rose Jackson (daughter of Derek Jackson rich, much-married physicist) and her child, so Nina & Tristram came, Virginia & the children looking in later. Prawn-&-egg au gratin; boeuf en daube (M. de Norpois's favourite dish); cherries & cream with gâteau (instead of Françoise's Nesselrode Pudding), Château Picard '71 (St Estephe), the last good.

After some ritual hesitation Geoffrey Waldegrave put fair amount of claret back, considerably loosening up. He is friendly if a touch pompous, she quiet, seems nice. A parson's son, Geoffrey Waldegrave likes to talk about church matters. They live in a house that could well have been a rectory of more spacious C of E days. In origin the Waldegraves are one of the comparatively few noble families who go back in the male line to a relatively distinguished ancestor *temp*. Edward III, having kept their end up pretty well ever since. In that they resemble aristocratic family in a novel, also in possessing interesting Horace Walpole *et al* relics. Unlike what is found in novels, they became somewhat reduced in 19th century, now living modestly enough. Enjoyable party, tho' Geoffrey W. showed signs of disengagement in connexion with The Falklands. Tristram remarked later that Nina said given half a chance

Geoffrey Waldegrave would try to patronize the Grenfells. She thought the luncheon established diplomatic equilibrium.

Monday, 26 April

South Georgia retaken from the Argentines, island discovered by Captain Cook, wholly British, to which Argentina has not the smallest claim. Newspaper headline: *Junta breaks the news gently*, evoking Max Beerbohm cartoon. A young man from *The Times*, Alan Franks, came to interview me. He wrote a tolerable novel, *Boychester's Bugle*, about a provincial newspaper office, to be published by Heinemann. He said his family were of Anglo-Brazilian background, and he had some knowledge of Latin-America. Accordingly, his second novel, already sketched in, by extraordinary fate, is about Anglo-Argentines.

I often wonder how these interviews could be conducted to extract anything of interest from subject. The first step would be to ask no apparently profound questions, which clearly cannot be answered in a word or two off the cuff. Perhaps, as the vast majority of interviews suggest, it is impossible. In this one, only about 1500 words, no more than standard statements brought up to date.

Celia Johnson (widow of Peter Fleming, travel writer and Ian's brother) obit. She was due to appear in an opening night this week, collapsed, it is said, at the bridge-table. Celia played the best Juliet's Nurse (TV Shakespeare) I have ever seen, making sense of a part often mangled. In recalling this I said to V by mistake 'Hamlet's Nurse'. We agreed that Hamlet's Nurse was the omitted key to the play. Ferdie Mount appointed one of Mrs Thatcher's advisers.

Thursday, 29 April

I am engaged on reviewing Martin Seymour-Smith's (quite good) life of Robert Graves, so I have only just had the opportunity to read Billy Chappell's symposium on Ed Burra [artist and stage designer, 1905–76]. Discussing where exactly the parent Burras' house was outside Rye, V recalled our being taken by the Goldsmids[1] to a house which must have been much like it, if not actually the Burras' former residence. It was owned by a tycoon, who (presumably apropos of the Rye colony of sapphists) asked the riddle: Why are lesbians like an unaccompanied church service – because they like playing hymns without an organ.

[1] Sir Henry d'Avigdor-Goldsmid Bart. and Rosemary, née Nicholl. Family friends, the Powells enjoyed a lot of their hospitality both at Somerhill, Kent, and in London.

Wednesday, 5 May

Wrote piece for *Apollo* about the Chappell symposium on Burra. This is a curious memorial to small, in its way rather remarkable group, all at Chelsea Polytechnic and Royal College of Art together. Remember as a child passing the latter in Kensington Gore, seeing a lot of strange characters outside, being told they were 'students', which made a lifelong impression as to what 'students' looked like. Burra, Chappell, Barbara Ker-Seymer, Bumble (Beatrice) Dawson, Hodge (Irene Hodgkins), also a girl called Clover Pritchard, who writes amusingly. Oddly enough I never before heard of her. Apparently she lived adventurously, much abroad. In the late 1920s these people formed the essence of certain sort of party, with ballet-based connotations rather than painting, including Freddie Ashton, now knighted, OM, CH, CBE, who later took to smart life. Ed Burra (dcd) always existed in complete obscurity (his family vaguely county), seeing only a few intimate friends. Ed is now a famous painter, canvases fetching thousands both here and in the US. Chappell, the nicest (by no means least talented), has kept afloat by dancing, stage designing, and theatre directing (now in *Who's Who*), having to work hard to survive in his seventies. Hodge (dcd), pretty, did not do much more than get in love tangles, then married a successful adman called Varley. Varley also married at various times Enid Firminger, Chelsea beauty I once fruitlessly loved in the Twenties, Elizabeth Montagu (of Beaulieu), the last Varley wife, I think, still surviving.

I met Hodge once during the war with old friend Desmond Ryan, and we all dined somewhere. When saying goodbye she embraced me with considerable warmth, told me she had always had a fancy for me and ran off. She and I did not meet again as Hodge died soon after. Barbara Ker-Seymer, gifted, drew well, at one time a good photographer. Unusual personality. Barbara started as a lesbian, then had two marriages (Humphrey Pease, in Pop at Eton, rich, Conscientious Objector; then John Rhodes, twenty years younger). When the marriage bust up John became a tycoon and went into *Encyclopaedia Britannica*. Barbara had various lovers, then presumably lapsed into lesbianism. She ran a Laundrette, keeping up with Billy Chappell, occasionally writes me very funny fan letters, full of go, otherwise withdrawn from any sort of intellectual world. Reading about these people in their early London days is interesting and essentially comprehensible.

In the evening I had a strong sense of contrast with all this, when reading military material, in its way also familiar. Philip Ziegler (of Collins) got in touch at the last moment to say that General Sir David Fraser, in his biography of *Alanbrooke* had quoted without permission about half a page from *The Military Philosophers*, was that all right? It was the passage about the CIGS.

I said it was all right, adding that Alun Chalfont had not bothered so much as to inform me in quoting about a page and a half of my description of the Field Marshal in his book on Montgomery. I said I should like Philip to send a copy of *Alanbrooke*. Fraser turns out to be an extremely competent writer, retired (full) General, Grenadiers, Turf Club, Pratt's. Felt again I knew more or less what the author was writing about, his own point of view, anyway roughly, what the subject's status was when appointed, say, BMRA (Brigade Major, Royal Artillery) to a Division in the first war; just as *mutatis mutandis*, various employments of people in the Burra book.

One supposes the ideal novelist would be at home, plus/minus, in every known society, at least that would help for dialogue. A complicated question. I have always taken the view that it is not necessary for the novelist *personally* to have been through all the stuff written about, but what he has not experienced must be handled obliquely. I have never been drawn to imaginary accounts of being in wartime action in, for instance, Stephen Crane. Stendhal, of course, had operational experience, also Tolstoy, and Lermontov. Kipling, on the other hand, not, tho' on the whole convincing. Pleased that vignettes of Alanbrooke and Montgomery have been reproduced in this way by their respective contemporary biographers, both professional soldiers.

In the afternoon a photographer from Bristol came to take pictures for *The Times*, which has a piece on *The Strangers All Are Gone* (published on Monday) in Saturday number. Photographer, longish hair, small moustache, CND badge in his lapel. He looked like a 'photographic Hartist', of the 1850s or a 'little cove' drawn by Leech in *Punch*. He emphasized several times that he had never heard of me, which always makes relations easier.

Thursday, 6 May

Diana Trilling, in her book about the middle-aged American schoolmistress, who shot dead her diet-doctor lover of even more mature age, ends with a quotation from *Dance* on subject of *crimes passionelles* (their banality), thereby making satisfactory week's pendant to mention in *Alanbrooke* biography.

Saturday, 8 May

Bernard Crick wrote to me saying that he was donating the English rights of his Orwell biography to establish a fund for young writers, to which more would be added by contributors. The trustees of fund would be Crick himself, Barbara Hardy, Eric Hobsbawm, Karl Miller, Julian Symons, Arnold Wesker. He asked if I would allow my name also to be used. Barbara Hardy, female don, who has written on George Eliot, I know nothing about. Miller gets by. Julian Symons perfectly all right, indeed excellent; I am, however, not at all confident that George Orwell would have approved of the antics of Hobsbawm or Wesker, so I said I would not add my name. It seems to me the fund might quite easily be channelled into areas representing precisely what Orwell did not want, ending up by being Communist, or similar, manipulated. I wrote to Symons explaining my position, adding that I thought a stipulation that candidates for fund should have to state why they thought themselves eligible as Orwellian beneficiaries was a mistake.

Orwell liked all sorts of different writers (eg. P. G. Wodehouse, Kipling). I am not at all certain he would approve necessarily of those consciously modelled on himself. Also repeated my perennial admonition that it is in old age, not youth, that writers are apt to need help. Julian Symons replied, very sensibly, that undoubtedly the Orwell Prize would be given to just the sort of crackpot anarchist with whom poor old George would have got himself involved when alive – so there was no point whatever in worrying. I wholly agree. How very sensible of Julian. All the same I felt that, if I could not personally keep an eye on things, it was better to remain out of any committee on the subject.

Sunday, 9 May

Journalist from the *Daily Express* rang saying he understood there was no mention of either Lord or Lady Longford, or Lady Antonia Fraser in *The Strangers All Are Gone*. I said that they had been dealt with in earlier volumes of Memoirs, and argued this was not a family chronicle. He said Frank was thought by some to be model for Widmerpool. I replied that, so far as I knew, Frank himself had put that about. In fact, I think the first person to make any such suggestion was John Raymond (dcd journalist of some, never realized, ability).

When Thomas Pakenham (eldest son of Frank and Elizabeth Longford) was staying here some years ago Frank wrote to him, saying, at one point in the letter, that he was Widmerpool, at another Erridge. I said to Thomas that his father really could not be everyone in the novel. It is characteristic of people who know nothing whatever of novel-writing to suppose that only an individual with a recognizable newspaper *persona* would make a good character. In point of fact I cannot imagine ever even considering Frank as a model, least of all when I began the sequence. Frank uses up all his own 'image' in publicity, leaving nothing in suspension, something essential in creating a novel-character based in real life; apart from the fact that Frank is married, has a large family, is a rampant RC, wellborn, in every other respect different from Widmerpool, except perhaps latterly Frank's phraseology, and verbiage, which in his own books, has developed certain Widmerpoolian overtones, but the books did not exist when Widmerpool first came into being.

When the paragraph appeared in the *Express* gossip-column, Widmerpool was referred to as 'wise and eccentric', the Expressman having admitted he had not read the novel, evidently supposing it would be more or less a compliment to be thought like him on Frank's part. Having disposed of the Longford family he went on to remark that it was interesting what was said about Kingsley Amis. 'He's back with his first wife now, isn't he?' he added. I said that was so in the sense that Kingsley was sharing a house with Hilly (formerly Hilary Amis) and Lord Kilmarnock to whom she was married. This came as complete surprise to the Expressman, tho' the Amis/Kilmarnock establishment has been adumbrated in the column for which his own paragraph is no doubt destined not less than once every ten days. 'It would make a good TV serial, that story,' he mused. All in the best traditions of journalism.

Monday, 10 May

Heinemann's luncheon for *The Strangers All Are Gone*. About thirty guests, all went well. Vidia Naipaul [V. S. Naipaul, Trinidad born novelist] had put off flying to São Paulo ('to interview a couple of dagos') to be there, he told Julian Jebb, [TV producer and grandson of Hilaire Belloc] who was also present. Vidia said we ought to have bombed Buenos Aires right away, now too late. Added that the Argentines liked the kind of government they have, all mere pretence to say anything else. They are vain, aggressive, not amenable to anything but force. I am sure he is right. Roy Fuller's second volume of Memoirs, *Vamp Till Ready*, crossed with mine sent to him. Roy and I just had a word together after luncheon as to why the Royal Navy was known as The Andrew, my research indicating perhaps from the ship *Andromache*, known at the time as the Andrew Max.

Kingsley, having broken a leg falling downstairs coming home from Garrick when tight some months ago, had the limb in a splint. He didn't look at all well, tho' has knocked off all drink. He has also grown a moustache (Philip Larkin, Oxford contemporary of Kingsley's, says a mistake) and seemed in goodish form. In the mêlée I did not have time to tell him about the *Express* enquiry as to his domestic circumstances.

I sat between the American novelist Alison Lurie & Hilary Spurling (subject for painting by Reynolds); V between Roy Fuller and John Spurling.

Alison revealed her next book novel about London. Hilary said, contrary to what I had implied in *Strangers*, it was against etiquette for dramatic critics to discuss a play in the bar. She had only known one case of that during her period doing that job, when all agreed to give a poorish show reasonably kind notices owing to the age of author (Nevill Coghill's *Chaucer*). She agreed that dramatic critics were on the whole ignorant, stupid, philistine, incredibly conceited, and deserving anything that was said about them.

My publisher Roland Gant made a speech, short, appropriate, to which I replied. Food quite tolerable, plenty to drink (this was all in Heinemann's office at 10 Upper Grosvenor Street). Quite a pleasant occasion. When we arrived home we had been in the house about half an hour when a man knocked on the door, asking me to sign all four vols of Memoirs. He had stutter, and said he was in London Transport, by name Mills. I said I did not normally sign books for people I did not know personally, but as he had gone to so much trouble signed one, adding to his name, the words 'under pressure'.

Sunday, 16 May

Wrote in reply to Julian Symons that I perfectly agreed with his view that any Orwell Fund would be likely to hand over money to a series of Lefties, therefore an appropriate manner of commemorating poor old George, perhaps one candidate in a dozen worthy of help; all the same I preferred to remain outside, as I feel one should keep an eye on anything one lends one's name to. In this case I have neither time nor inclination. V and I went to pre-luncheon drinks with the Somersets at Maiden Bradley to celebrate forthcoming marriage of their second son, Francis Seymour. Maiden Bradley grounds are greatly smartened up since Percy inherited. The house as always enjoyable to dine at, good food, drink, even if it falls short of what might be called essentially ducal; just pleasant country mansion in pretty surroundings. Percy and Jane, as always, nice; guests, presumably neighbours, this time rather heavy going.

Tuesday, 18 May

Both of us to London. I saw Sussman, who adumbrated tedious reconstruction plans. Pratt's was having one of the periodical Club cocktail parties, when wives, and mistresses, have chance of seeing its curious two-roomed underground premises. The party takes place to some extent in the first floor room, which so far as I know, is never otherwise used. Osbert Sitwell lived there for a time (he told me) at the end of the first war, when in The Grenadiers. No one present whom either V or I had ever set eyes on before except Kenneth Rose,

Sunday Telegraph gossip-writer, who was moving about like an *affairé* character from a Beatrix Potter story, or *The Wind in the Willows*. He said he was writing a book on George V, that he knew things about Tommy Lascelles (Private Secretary to several monarchs), which would make your hair stand on end, but revealed none of these eye-openers.

He once gave me luncheon at the Guards Club (Rose having served in the Brigade during the war), quite why, I can't remember. A gloomy-looking man was sitting alone at the bar in the room where we were having drinks. Rose asked if I knew him. The reply was negative. It turned out to be Captain Simpson, second husband of the Duchess of Windsor. I was glad to have set eyes on him, even at longish range. I have rarely seen a figure of such infinite sadness.

More recently the Duke of Kent (in some newspaper interview) expressed liking for my books. Accordingly, Rose invited V & myself to what he called (not unreasonably) 'one of my grand cocktail parties', as HRH said he wished to meet me. Guests included Duke & Duchess of Kent, King & Queen of Greece, sprinkling of Cabinet Ministers, all hoping for publicity one supposes. The Duke was perfectly agreeable, not particularly forthcoming, rather like talking to reasonably articulate cavalryman, which in fact he is.

Later Alison Lurie dined with us at the Lansdowne Club. Alison herself in good form, taking steps to share a flat in London for several months of the year with Diane Johnson, another American writer, author of book about Mrs George Meredith. Alison is now going to embark on a London novel. I saw Adrian Daintrey in The Travellers, who said Lady Anne Tree and Mrs Julian Amery were giving party in June for his eightieth birthday. Adrian looking a little extraordinary, wearing (into the club) a large flat cap shaped like a muffin, which he said had been made specially for him by female friend. His manner is also rather strange these days, tho' in a sense that was always so.

Wednesday, 19 May

Pottered about London Library. Reading for review D. H. Lawrence *Letters*, vol I. Struck by Lawrence's friendship with Henry Savage, now totally forgotten, to whom Lawrence wrote many letters. When I was young, and people used to say – as they often did – what an awful place Rye was, with its tarted up antique shops, bogus bohemians, horse brasses, and lesbians, there was always someone to add that Rye was nothing, in such respects, to Winchelsea, which was far worse. Winchelsea then had a kind of shanty town on its outskirts, populated by what would later become to be known as hippies; in those days regarded simply as old-fashioned bohemians at a low level.

The 'uncrowned king' of these dead-beats at Winchelsea, always spoken of with utter horror (even by people not themselves particularly fastidious), was Henry Savage. I had not heard the name for perhaps 55 years. A note in the *Letters* indicated that H. Savage had written a book about a poet quite unknown to me called Richard Middleton, who had committed suicide in Brussels in 1911. I had the curiosity to look this biography up in London Library. Sure enough it was published in 1922, complete rubbish about this notably untalented poet, who wrote more or less in the Nineties manner. All this seemed of interest, as the forgotten man of letters is or was such a favourite character in fiction. Here was a perfect example both in writer & subject.

We returned home. Listened to Kaleidoscope on radio, in which I had been interviewed about *The Strangers All Are Gone*. They also managed to fit in a word about Alison Lurie, who had mentioned doing an interview with me.

Sunday, 23 May

Pusillanimous attitudes in the US about The Falklands recalled Maurice Bowra [the influential Oxford don whose 'circle' included Anthony Powell] being asked by an American paper (before US entry into war) if he had a message for the American People. Bowra said: 'Tell them not to be ashamed of themselves.' This appeared in print as: 'Tell them not to pity us.' One notes the extraordinary sensitiveness of Americans to their own self-esteem. Perhaps more than any other nation. The UK has been abused so much that one almost expects it on all occasions.

Wednesday, 26 May

Checking something in the D. H. Lawrence *Letters*, I referred to Cecil Gray's *Philip Heseltine*, opening on an epigraph from the poems of Richard Middleton above; odd coincidence, perhaps slightly exonerating Middleton from being obscure, if hardly Savage.

Sunday, 30 May

Hugh Lloyd-Jones brought his new American wife to luncheon. Regius Professor of Greek at Oxford, Hugh is all that a don should be, witty, High Tory, keen on good food & drink, immensely scholarly, in fact one of an almost extinct breed to what one finds now in academics. I met him through an invitation to contribute to the volume he edited commemorating Maurice Bowra. David Holloway, Literary Editor of the *Daily Telegraph*, was at

Westminster with Lloyd-Jones and says he was the inky schoolboy to end all inky schoolboys, tho' always enormously clever. Inky schoolboy Hugh somewhat remains. There had been much speculation about the new wife's appearance. We had liked former wife, Frances (who had a curious partly Dutch East Indies background, I think), whom Hugh had watched playing Clytemnestra in some Cambridge production, asked her out to dinner, then proposed the next night.

All known about the new one was that she was an academic, previously married, called Mary Lefkowitz. She has two brothers on Wall Street, the family against her taking up academic life. Hugh, in great form, seems delighted with the marriage. He brought two vols of his own essays, one of his wife's, the latter showing formidable classical scholarship, tinged with feminism (the last not at all to Hugh's taste), which she said was lessening.

Monday, 7 June

To London. Saw Sussman. We talked of circumcision, when it became fashionable? Told him what I knew. He could give no information, but said he would look into the matter. In The Travellers I met Alan Pryce-Jones, formerly editor of *The Times Literary Supplement*, over from the US. He continues to be a kind of Dorian Gray; seeming at most perhaps in his late fifties, hair slightly grey, immensely spruce, full of social activities as if he had never left England. He appears to own three houses in Newport, Rhode Island, flat in NYC (74th & 5th Ave) let to him by a Japanese, who had gone home to get married to girl he had never seen. The Japanese thought this would undoubtedly be a failure, let the flat for a year, which he judged marriage would last, marriage turned out success, so Alan P-J continues in residence. Very characteristic. We spoke of sad plight of many friends; the Laureate [John Betjeman] for instance, taking three people to get him out of a chair. 'Of course it may be all shamming,' said Alan, 'just to attract attention to himself. Alvilde Lees-Milne [wife of James, important National Trust figure. They live at Essex House, Badminton] shouted, "Come on, you're perfectly all right, stop it." That worked on some recent occasion.' Osbert Lancaster also in sad case; John Sparrow (according to Alan) sunk in drink.

That night I arranged to dine in the new Kentish Town set-up of Kingsley Amis & the Kilmarnocks. This improbable ménage seems to be working well. Although at the back of beyond, the house not unattractive, on a corner with a kind of courtyard, small garden, Regency, or early Victorian, not at all unlike what Kingsley & Hilly used to live in at Swansea. They complain it is jerry-built, which is believable. Early stages of evening just like visiting Kingsley & Hilly formerly when they were married.

About halfway through dinner Ali Kilmarnock appeared. He looks a little like Robin Mount (suggestion of horsiness, tho' nothing like as horsy as Robin was), has written a book or two, takes Liberal/SDP politics seriously in the House of Lords. Later he referred to 'the Barony I hold', so I asked him about the Attainder, under which the family fell in Jacobite times. He gave a complicated account of the attainted Earldom, for which, as I understood it, the (rather attractive) son of ten might be eligible under Scottish Law. Were the Attainder reversed, a minimum of £15,000 would be required even to start the business, which is certainly not available. If successful, result might apparently be two Lord Kilmarnocks, an earl & a baron.

Felt it better not to discuss this interesting question too long in the circumstances. Kingsley still had his leg up, looked much improved from time of Heinemann luncheon party. He had been reading *The Strangers All Are Gone*; and produced a book (which he lent me) on the subject of the Irish, Scotch, Welsh, in English plays, which explains why the Spaniard's fart, in Webster's *The White Devil* (which was to have poisoned all Dublin), had reference to breaking wind in Ireland being regarded as a peculiar insult. Enjoyable evening.

Tuesday, 8 June

To the BBC to watch recording of some of last three vols of *Dance* for Radio. They were doing scenes which follow Pamela Flitton being sick in large Chinese vase. V came up this morning. We lunched with Graham Gauld, the producer, at St George Hotel, close by the BBC, having had drinks before with Ronald Mason, head of radio drama, who said stirrings were beginning again about doing *Dance* on TV. Mason joined luncheon party, also the adapter of the book, Freddie Bradnum (Rifle Brigade during the war, commissioned on the field in Norway, later MM, MC, DSO), nice, bright. Also Elizabeth Proud, who played Lady Isobel Tolland in the production. Mason, rather deaf Ulsterman, quite agreeable.

Years ago, in Avignon, a one-legged middle-aged Frenchman asked if he could sit at my table. He talked of life in Avignon, how there was a large colony of Arabs on one side of the town, some of them doing quite well, even becoming officers in French army. Of the last he said: 'Vous savez, monsieur, c'est une belle position pour un indigène.' I have often thought that phrase very generally applicable, for example in the BBC, which abounds with individuals of whom might be said that it was a 'belle position pour un indigène'. V went to see Sussman in the afternoon, later listened to more of the recordings. It must be hard work for an actor, the constant repetition. This instalment was being read through to them when I arrived that morning. It was gratifying (before entering the studio) to hear thirty or forty of the cast in fits of laughter. At luncheon there appeared to be some sort of battle of wills as to which expense account the meal was to be credited. Returned to the country somewhat exhausted.

Thursday, 10 June

W. D. (Bill) Howarth of Bristol University came to tea, to discuss his presentation of the Hon. D. Litt. which the University is conferring on me. Howarth in his late fifties, Professor of Classical French Literature, book on Molière. We talked of writing. Apparently he himself had put up my name for the degree. He said Iris Murdoch [novelist and philosopher, married to John Bayley the literary critic] had described Flaubert as a wax corpse. In the course of all this I mentioned that some years ago, sitting next to John Sparrow at an All Souls (I think) dinner, Sparrow, who was Warden of All Souls, had spoken of Genet. I remarked, 'Genet kissed me when we met.' Howarth thought I meant this had actually happened, had to explain that Genet never had in fact been given an opportunity to jump from the seat he sat in so far as I was concerned. Incidentally, I noted that this Genet joke was recently made by some *Sunday Times* hack just eight years later than spoken to Sparrow at some Oxford feast; interesting time lag.

Thursday, 16 June

To London. Saw Sussman, and tried to make arrangements for him to do whatever he had to do before threatened railway strike. I lunched with Osbert & Anne Lancaster, owing to circumstances reaching there about 2 o'clock. Osbert deaf, unable to take in answers to his own questions, beginning to grumble that he can't hear before you can get a word in. Anne holding up pretty well in trying circumstances. They had dined with Rosie Goldsmid the previous night. Anne's daughter Clare looked in, Anne's son, Max Hastings, much in evidence as war-correspondent in the Falklands campaign.

Later in the afternoon I ran into Ali Forbes [American writer and journalist, educated in Europe] in Piccadilly, who said: 'Your picture of my second wife [Georgina Ward] in your Memoirs was just right. Very good. A bit teasing, and you pulled your punches, but then of course you always do, your books are the greatest pulling of punches.' He began to speak of Evangeline Bruce not having come over from the US this summer (we were just opposite Albany), trailing off into words uttered by Talleyrand, which entailed a long quotation in French. I thought I might miss my train, so extricated myself. Earlier that day, from on top of bus, I saw an old man with a long grey beard, not outstandingly shabbily dressed, rooting about in a rubbish bin. He carried a large black bag, paper or plastic, on the side of which was inscribed the single word MIDAS. Interesting possibilities opened up as to how Midas had got his money.

Thursday, 1 July

David Cheshire, BBC Producer, lunched to talk about projected TV programme. He and his (American) wife, now separated, once stayed with Tristram & Virginia at The Stables, so just met him previously. I had forgotten Cheshire has so manic a personality. He was keen on my saying more in the programme about American side of my books than has been done previously, eg. *AP Communications*, published by West Michigan University, Kalamazoo, and the group in Palo Alto bookshop, who dress up as characters in *Dance*. Also (at Tristram's suggestion) that something might be said about the plays. I had a letter from Peter Wiseman, Professor of Classics at Exeter University, asking me to lecture. In refusing, I went on record to Wiseman, as I had to Cheshire, that I am trying to write a novella which includes a scene where the main character is interviewed on TV, also where he goes to a new university to give a talk.

Owing to the impending railway strike Sussman said he would, if required, drive down here to finish off various jobs already begun in case strike settled down for months, I could not get to London. I suggested he and his wife should come to luncheon on Sunday. When it looked as if strike was to be off, rang to ask if he could fit me in to do a final adjustment. He then said Mrs S would be heartbroken if they did not come to lunch. Sussmans therefore duly appeared.

As it happened V had also something to be done, so the Green Room was turned into a dental surgery, an Early Victorian armchair (the arms of which fade away on each side (*bergère?*), which had never done a day's work in its life, was transformed into an admirable dentist's chair. Mrs Sussman, pleasant and plump, brought a stupendous arrangement of flowers for V. Everyone's teeth were fixed. Most satisfactory occasion all round.

Wednesday, 7 July

Day of the Bristol Hon. D. Litt. ceremony. We arrived in good time. I was robed in the company of Sir Hugh Springer, Barbadian, prominent figure in Commonwealth affairs, also getting Hon. Degree with me at Oxford two years ago. The Chancellor of Bristol is Dorothy Hodgkin, OM, biologist, Left Wing old hag. She made a tendentious speech about 'cuts' saying she hoped a time would come when education would be put before armaments. I cornered her before luncheon, said it would be hypocritical on my part, after receiving an Hon. Degree at her hands, not to tell her that I utterly disagreed with her, that I was all for education, but not before the defence of the country. If the country was not safe there would soon be no education to be protected.

I have rarely seen anyone so surprised. It was only later I learnt that Dorothy Hodgkin was more or less a Communist herself her late husband actually Party Member, I believe, so glad to have said what I did. In other respects I found everything agreeable.

At lunch I sat next to Mrs Kenny, pleasant American wife of Anthony Kenny, Master of Balliol, he was also getting Hon. Degree that afternoon; on the other side the wife of a retired colonel who carries the Bristol Lord Mayor's ceremonial sword, said to date from about 1530. The Lord Mayor looked everything a medieval Lord Mayor of Bristol should.

Dr Closs, Leslie Hartley's Austrian academic friend, an Homeric bore, now in his eighties, ex-member of the Bristol Faculty, was wandering about in a gown, waffling on the subject of some scheme of his whereby he and I should publish a combined volume of L. P. Hartley's Letters. I tried to explain that I never had more than half-a-dozen of these, if that, all of which I had handed over to Penelope Fitzgerald, who is writing Leslie's biography. Closs said David Cecil [scholar and biographer] was against a biography for twenty years, which I could well believe, as revelations likely to be, to say the least, picturesque. Closs wandered off, reappearing from time to time, repeating all this, like a character in a Chekhov play, or perhaps an academic Cheshire Cat, except that he looked desperately worried, not grinning at all. We got back in time for tea, which was satisfactory.

Sunday, 11 July

Tony & Marcelle Quinton came over from Oxford for luncheon, also Mayalls, not having previously met. Tony Quinton perhaps last relic left, anyway as Head of a House (Trinity), of the Bowra tradition; funny, noisy, good jokes, general feeling that things are to be enjoyed. The Mayalls had just come back from Palmyra to find their house impenetrably locked by the plumber. In trying to get in they set off burglar alarm, and the police arrived. When they managed to enter the house found radiators all put in wrong place.

Monday, 12 July

Bob & Liddie Conquest to luncheon. That morning one of the most deafening thunderstorms I have ever experienced, flashes of lightning, sheets of rain, Shakesperian drama-type weather. The Conquests are over briefly from California, where they appear to be building a house, so I suppose Bob proposes to settle there finally. He is to say a word in David Cheshire's BBC programme. Liddie, trying to get a few pounds off her weight to meet a former boyfriend for lunch in London, confused the club (she supposed The Rag, in fact the Royal Commonwealth), boyfriend turned up twice, only finding her a third time. V suggested afterwards it was like Molnar's play *The Guardsman*, really Bob disguised as the former boyfriend to test Liddie.

Sunday, 18 July

Fram Dinshaw looked in for a drink on his way back from visiting some local Hobhouses, several families of them in our neighbourhood. I was first introduced to Fram at Eton years ago by Cyril Connolly, at the School Library celebration for contemporary OE writers. Fram then still in College, running the Eton Literary Society, now don at St Catherine's. Fram said that when Claude Elliot was Head Master, Elliot observing Connolly in the High Street at Eton on some occasion, threatened him with an umbrella: 'We don't want to see your face here.'

Fram described how at a certain nobleman's Memorial Service a few months ago the family asked a middle-aged-to-elderly man in the village, who happened to have a fine voice, to be a member of the choir, perhaps sing a solo. Afterwards it was felt appropriate to give him a present of some sort in recognition of this, bottle of wine, say; in the end, being unable to make up their minds what was suitable, asked the man himself. He replied: 'It had occurred to me you might be kind enough to do this. I have been thinking about what I would like. I've at last decided my preference would be for a woman. I have never had a woman. That would be my choice, if you really want to give me a present I should like.' Fram did not know how the matter was adjusted. He said John Sparrow had become a serious problem, as he gets so drunk if asked to dinner. Sparrow's licence has been taken away, so he has to be driven home. 'But', said Fram, 'I don't know him well enough to undress him.'

Tuesday, 20 July

An American academic, Dale Salwak, came in connexion with a book of interviews of English writers. Kingsley Amis had spoken well of him. He was middle-thirtyish, agreeable, well informed. Kingsley had taken him to The Travellers for an interview two years ago. During lunch a friend had come up. He asked Kingsley, 'Has the Mozart record arrived?' The reply was, 'No.' Had it beeen 'Yes', Kingsley would have explained that he had to leave immediately; a method of safeguard against the possibility of being bored by Salwak, who is at Citrus College, University of Southern California, but comes from the East rather than those parts.

Wednesday, 21 July

We lunched with Mayalls at Sturford, just the four of us. Mary did not look well, I thought. Lees complained that reports from Comprehensive School attended by his grandson are written in illiterate language. The Mayalls are the neighbours (about eight miles) we see most of. Lees, dazzling success at Eton, good-looking, Second Eight (cox), Sixth Form, etc, son of Eton master, Monkey Mayall, unexciting figure who briefly taught me at one moment as a Lower Boy. Lees went into Foreign Service (nicest member of that government office I have ever encountered), inherited comfortable amount of money from an uncle in business in the Midlands. First marriage (one daughter) went wrong, then he married Mary Ormsby-Gore, daughter of Lord Harlech (by David Cecil's sister Mima), Mary's own marriage to Robin Campbell had gone up the spout (two sons). Campbell, who had been in Reuter's, went off with Lady Mary St Clair-Erskine (married to Philip Dunn, son of a Canadian tycoon). Mary Ormsby-Gore, pretty, talkative, sure of herself, with a lively tongue, which not everyone appreciates (see Evelyn Waugh *Diaries*). Lees & Mary produced two daughters and a son, between them.

Lees was a friend in FO of Donald Maclean, indeed the first time I met Lees his leg had been broken by that deplorable figure in some drunken rampage in Egypt. When Maclean & Burgess decamped Lees was probably unnecessarily quixotic in not making any effort to disown former friendship with Maclean, whom we met more than once at the Mayalls', and I always thought ghastly beyond words. This undoubtedly caused Lees professional harm. In the cold for some time, then Lees established himself by doing outstandingly good job as Deputy-Marshal of Diplomatic Corps & Chief of Protocol (putting life into these usually somewhat inert duties), ending service as Ambassador to Venezuela. The Mayalls have been incredibly hospitable to some pretty hard cases.

Sturford Mead, where they live, was the Baths' Dower House, lived in latterly by Henry Bath himself while married to Daphne Vivian. When that marriage terminated Henry B moved to Job's Mill with Virginia (née Parsons) Tennant, whom he had married. Sturford proved hard to sell, biggish without being grand, architecturally undistinguished. It nearly became a factory for making torpedoes, or something of the sort. Then Robin Mount (married to V's sister Julia) persuaded Lees Mayall to buy it. This must be regarded as one of the rare good strokes of business (not in the least in his own interests except as friend of Lees & Mary) accomplished by Robin.

Thursday, 22 July

Lunched with Denys & Cynthia Sutton at Westwood Manor, unfortified early 15th century (I think) house, where they are National Trust tenants. One always writes one's name in the book after going there, as, to say the least, Denys does not encourage stray visitors. Denys has a beard which looks a little like Cézanne's, or perhaps Lenin's (tho' his views are far from Leninesque). He is Editor of the art magazine *Apollo* and knows a great deal about pictures, is generally intelligent and full of international art gossip. He is subject to great hates. Cynthia, also married before (née Sassoon) his third wife, good-looking in manner of a Persian miniature. Slightly mysterious couple, especially as regards previous marriages. The atmosphere of Westwood curious, not to say creepy (as are all houses inhabited over so long a period of centuries), perhaps not lessened in restless tensions by the Suttons. Excellent Pomerol '53, did not get Château.

Saturday, 24 July

John had a house party at The Stables for the weekend: Maggie de Rougemont, Francesca George, with her boyfriend Tim Pearce (Reuters, recently in Zambia, both going to Tokyo). Maggie's husband, Guillaume de Rougemont, is now in Malaysia conducting a tour, which he does professionally. The Chef d'Escadron de Rougemont, French Assistant Military Attaché (Jockey Club, etc), with whom I conducted War Office business at the end of the war, is head of family, now a General. Guillaume's mother was a de Janzé, his uncle Freddie de Janzé, one of the Happy Valley crowd in Kenya, whose two Kenya books Duckworth published (on commission, ie at the author's expense), therefore we met occasionally in the office in 1920s – good-looking, dashing figure, all that might be expected. Freddy de Janzé (Breton family) had had some sort of connexion (perhaps more or less engaged), so I found later, with Osbert Lancaster's sister-in-law Honey Harris. Francesca George rather key personality in publishing. The girls cooked a splendid dinner.

Wednesday, 4 August

Rachel Cecil's funeral at Cranborne. I met Rachel a few times before V & I
were married, but never knew her well. She was daughter of the literary critic
Desmond MacCarthy, who always seemed a nice man on rare occasions I met
him, but I could never see smallest point in the great acclaim paid to him as
critic, in spite of vast amount of incense burnt to MacCarthy by Cyril Connolly,
and Bloomsbury. We were about to set off in new car acquired two days ago,
when it utterly refused to start. In the end we were taken by Virginia in hers,
with a picnic.

Some miles beyond Tollard Royal, where V knew good place, we found her
sister Mary Clive[1] with her daughter Alice Boyd, already picnicking. Extraordinary chance they hit on exactly the same spot. Cranborne Church packed
with Cecils and Cavendishes, powerful family atmosphere to put it mildly,
there was a decided touch of *temps retrouvé*, several people not seen for some time
now fairly battered. Apparently David Cecil slept in same bed as Rachel right
through her illness, taking sleeping draughts, and was woken by the nurse still
holding Rachel's hand, Rachel dead – like the Arundel Tomb in Larkin's
poem. (There now seems some suggestion that the Arundel hand-holding was
effected during a Victorian restoration, even so, if true, the Romantic Revival
overtones are not without their own feeling.)

We were asked up to the Manor, where resplendent tea had been laid out by
the Salisburys. I was taken by the 18th century beauty of Lady Rose Cecil, tho'
with no more contact with her than accepting a slice of bread and butter at her
hands. (Somewhat Praed-like incident.) Andrew Devonshire in church, did
not turn up at house.

Friday, 6 August

V & I were photographed (at instigation of Roland Gant) by Tara Heinemann
(grandniece of founder of the firm), nice girl, if rather vague, jumpy. [She took
a good one of V, which was subsequently used.]

Thursday, 19 August

Jeremy Treglown, Editor of the *TLS* (whom I don't know) rang to say he had
been lunching with Alan Franks (who did the *Times* interview when *Strangers*
came out), who mentioned I was going to review Treglown's *Rochester* but the

---

[1] V's sister, Mary Clive, née Pakenham, married Meysey Clive, Grenadier and Major,
who was killed in 1943. Their children are George and Alice.

book was lost in the post last Christmas. Treglown asked if he could send another copy. This I agreed to and subsequently reviewed it. My agent John Rush rang to discuss the fee for David Cheshire's TV programme (Arena), asked my opinion on the radio *Dance* (good many criticisms, if on the whole acceptable). He said the BBC was still havering about TV *Dance*, Granada was now showing interest.

Monday, 23 August

Roland Gant looked in on way back from seeing the Dorset thriller-writer James Leasor. I sketched in the plot of the novella so far (26,000), which sounded rather flat on my own ears. However, Roland appeared reasonably happy. I am reviewing a tolerable life of Robert Browning. When Browning was a young man he lived in Camberwell. From a start he was marked down to be a success and belonged to a society of local intellectuals, which included the poet Ernest Dowson's grandfather. Interesting literary continuity.

Saturday, 28 August

Julian Jebb staying at The Stables. Julian, Tristram and Virgina, came to dinner. Julian in rather a gloomy state about his work. He is doing a TV programme on Bobby Helpmann, the dancer.

Sunday, 29 August

Lunched with Anthony [bibliographical historian] and Tanya Hobson. William & Mary Seymour there, he, regular, Scots Guards, in Laycock's Commando with Evelyn Waugh. Seymour had also known Guy Burgess, who was brought up in the same village, tho' Burgess somewhat junior at Eton. When Seymour latterly went to Moscow on some semi-official visit Burgess asked him to luncheon. Burgess was living with a Russian miner as boyfriend, the latter supplied by the Soviet authorities. Burgess said: 'Of course I was not a traitor.' Seymour said: 'No, I quite realize that you were a very subordinate figure in the Foreign Office, who didn't have access to any secrets of the least importance.' Burgess was annoyed at that and said on the contrary he was in MI6, and knew everything there was to be known. Tanya's radiation treatment is said to be going well. I gave Anthony a copy of the Roy Fuller Seventieth Birthday presentation of poems pamphlet. The Hobsons had been for some months in Dublin on bibliographical work. They are now going to Oxford for a spell on similar job.

Thursday, 2 September

John & Ros Anderson came to luncheon. He is Lower Master at Eton, with whom I became involved as he is a fan. He asked me to the Masters' Annual Dinner, which I thought might be funny, as indeed it was, tho' I retired before they really began to drink, which has always been a tradition of Eton beaks. Anderson (not a bad old stick, as George Orwell said of his first wife when she died), known by the boys as Jack the Ripper, owing to tendency to 'tear over' exercises in school. V had brilliant idea of asking the Mayalls to meet the Andersons, as Lees's father, Monkey Mayall, when an Eton master, had lived in the house called Weston's, in Weston's Yard (where Lees, as a golden boy, passed an idyllic childhood), now inhabited by the Andersons. This all went with a swing.

Friday, 10 September

Allan Massie to luncheon. He gave *The Strangers All Are Gone* an interesting review in *The Spectator*, so I sent him a line, to which he replied by asking if he could talk about the book he was himself writing on models in novels, principally in books of Waugh, Nancy Mitford, & myself. Massie is in his early fifties, in quiet way very Scotch, house on the Borders (Thisladean House, Selkirk, wonderfully R. L. Stevenson name), seemed intelligent, has written three novels, gave me one, *The Death of Men*, about modern Italy and terrorism, written from an Italian point of view; perhaps touch of *Gattopardo* influence, perhaps Pirandello. Massie was at Trinity, Cambridge, with George Heygate, with whom at one moment he was going to write a book on the author Norman Douglas. Uncle Norman used to take the two Heygate boys, then about five or six, to the Ladder Club, an afternoon drinking haunt off Bruton Street.

Sunday, 12 September

Vidia & Pat Naipaul to luncheon (curry, Chateauneuf, a favourite wine of Vidia's, seems to 'go' perfectly well with curry), fetched by John from Vidia's new Wiltshire house at Salterton. The Naipauls brought with them Ivan Nabokov (son of the musician), Vidia's French publisher (Michel). Vidia in very good form. He had liked Brazil. Nabokov agreeable Russo-Franco-American.

Monday, 13 – Thursday, 16 September

David Cheshire, with TV camera crew, came to do BBC programme (Prod.

Assist., Deborah Hall; Cameraman, Gene Carey; Assist. Cam., Brian Jones; Sound, Michael Turner; Elect., Eric Fever.). David Cheshire (friend of Tristram's) intelligent. Debby Hall, nice girl, whose brother concerned with helicopters on oil rigs, interesting social bracket, a fact which came out by accident. On the last night David Cheshire gave us dinner at a recently opened Frome restaurant, Haligan's in Vicarage Street, where one has to ring the doorbell to get in. A large plump blonde opened the door and served drinks in the bar, apparently wife of the *patron*, who did cooking. The dining-room beyond was pretty empty, food good.

Saturday, 18 September

To Oxford for the Dervorguilla Dinner at Balliol. On arrival I looked in for tea at the (old) Senior Common Room, where six or eight Strullbrugs of fearsome aspect were sitting in gloomy silence facing each other, giving grimmest portents of what was likely to be in store. Sherry party in Master's Lodgings now vacated by Anthony Kenny, with whom I had evaded staying, tho' at Bristol I had found him & his American wife agreeable.

I was introduced to a Communist character called Platts-Mills, slightly junior to me, I believe a New Zealander, rowing-man, personable, interesting variety of one type of Communist, especially of the period. The party was kicked out of pre-dinner drinks in The Lodgings at 7.30. Dinner in Hall was not till 8 o'c., so I sat on a seat in the quad, round which white-haired dinner-jacketed figures circulated aimlessly in semi-darkness. I was joined by one of these, who turned out to be John (Lord) Foot of that terrible brood. He seemed shocked to find that I was senior to him at Balliol. He said he had a flat in Kennington Park Road. I told him I had a son who owned one of the houses there.

At dinner I was set at the High Table, backing on the undergraduate tables, now filled with Dervorguilla guests. On my right was Stanley Wells, of the Oxford University Press, Shakespearian specialist, married to the writer Susan Hill (never met), who sometimes reviews for the *DT*. On my left was Richard Cobb, who arrived only just in time for dinner. He looked very thin, crimson in the face. He was hard to hear as acoustics were bad, and there was a fearful row of chattering.

Richard Cobb, Professor of Modern History, authority on the French Revolution, who sometimes writes his books in French, was formerly a don at Balliol, but now at Worcester. He became a friend through our corresponding from time to time. He writes very funny letters about his life, and must now be well over sixty.

Beyond Cobb sat a ninety-year-old, eminently spry, white-bearded Balliol man called Meyer, some musical affiliation, probably there as the oldest member of the College still on his feet. Opposite me at the High Table, Bill Williams (Balliol Fellow, notable Jugoslav war career), who enquired after V's Margaret Kennedy book; on Williams's right, Denis Healey MP; The Master, Tony Kenny; next to him The Chancellor, Harold Macmillan, eighty-eight, looking every day of it, tho' he began to do that years ago.

Cobb told me had reviewed Graham Greene's book *J'accuse* for the *Sunday Times* at proof stage, then told it could not go in owing to fear of libel. I had wondered why there were no reviews, having thought what had already appeared of the book in serial form to be poor stuff. According to Cobb he had sent his review to the publisher to show what would have been said had that been allowed. In answer to this he received two furious letters from Graham Greene in one day, complaining about the review. I gathered Cobb had complained there was insufficient information in the book to derive any idea of what had really happened. That had certainly been my own impression from serialized sections.

Richard Cobb said – which seems to be generally believed – that the girl married to the crook in the book was the daughter of Graham's established French mistress of some few years, tho' now (from a recent interview with Graham) she does not seem to be living with him any more, anyway not under the same roof in Antibes. As the whole lot, husband, wife, girl, girl's husband, Graham himself, etc, all seem to have been on good terms at one moment – rows about custody of children are by no means uncommon in circumstances quite other than gangster life on the Riviera – a great deal more needs to be explained to make the matters under dispute at all clear, let alone in the least interesting to other people. Cobb said he thought Graham wanted to end his life by being murdered at the hands of a Nice Mafioso. I certainly think Graham has always felt, from his earliest days, that somehow his life is not glamorous enough in the eyes of the public, although he is always doing things to make it sound exciting.

A similar conversation about Graham Greene was taking place between the Master and Denis Healey opposite, Tony Kenny saying that obviously Greene ought to write about the Ambrosiano money scandal at the Vatican, now going strong, a subject no doubt particularly attractive to Kenny, as a former priest. If such a book were to be any good (not sort of Peyrefitte stuff) I think it would take a cooler, better informed, better organized, grasp of public affairs than Graham possesses. Healey, immediately addressing me as Anthony, turned out to be a fan. I remembered then that he had recommended my books, early novels, I think, to my Swedish fan, Ulf Brandell, Foreign Editor of the main Stockholm daily, who comes over here regularly.

Healey brought up alleged resemblance of Widmerpool to Ted Heath, something that never occurred to me, although the Tory group called The Monday Club wrote asking me to address them on 'Heath as Widmerpool', which I declined. Healey said a friend of his in the CID had been investigating suicide (possible murder) of the financier Calvi (concerned with above Vatican money scandals), in London. CID man's first act had been to go to sex shop in Soho, buy a rubber woman, that legendary piece of equipment, now easily procurable (more appropiate word than purchased). I asked if the CID man had carried her away in his arms. Healey said she is packed in a box, and inflated when you got home (presumably with a bicycle pump; otherwise it would leave one with little breath to obtain sexual satisfaction), in this particular case possibly done on the spot, where she was to be used to reconstruct Calvi's death. This seems to add probability to the Frank Brangwyn picture adumbrated by Constant and Maurice Lambert called *Blowing up the Rubber Woman.*

I turned to Cobb to discuss this ingenious expedient (worthy of Sherlock Holmes), to find he was, in fact, sleeping like a child, with his head on the shoulder of his ninety-year-old white-bearded neighbour, who looked across at me, raising his eyebrows in appeal for sympathy, whether for Cobb or himself I was uncertain. I had missed the moment of Cobb's sudden collapse. He equally suddenly revived during The Master's speech. This subsequent recovery was sufficient for him to clap loudly after The Chancellor's speech, and express great enthusiasm to me. It was indeed a good speech, in the characteristic Macmillan manner.

Later we adjourned to the (new) Senior Common Room, a somewhat grim addition to the College. Kenny was talking to Macmillan. By this time feeling like retiring to bed, I touched him on the shoulder, and said goodnight. By an exceedingly adroit movement, Kenny managed to flit off in a flash, leaving Macmillan on my hands, in fact placing bed further off than ever. Macmillan is perfectly coherent when talking, if fairly heavy going vis-à-vis. In his speech he had remarked how difficult it was to know what people were like in 1282, the year the Lady Dervorguilla Balliol (perhaps more correctly Dervorguilla, Lady Balliol, tho' she was a considerable heiress in her own right) confirmed the establishment of Balliol as a College, compared with what he, Macmillan, felt about Classical times.

To bat the ball back, I said I felt reasonably at ease in the Middle Ages (far from the truth), a claim in any case completely ignored by Macmillan, who went pressing on, enlarging his own thesis. He remarked that one would have no difficulty talking to Cicero, 'if he came into Pratt's'. I allowed that Cicero might well have been a member of Pratt's, otherwise full of young Praetorian

Guardsmen. Macmillan then lost interest in the subject, beginning long diatribe against iniquity of pulling down churches and monasteries. 'Now it's the Inland Revenue,' he said. I expressed hearty agreement. At that moment The Master reappeared with another human offering. I escaped swiftly, leaving Macmillan with his new victim. Healey was at the bar. I waved goodnight. Healey replied with a reasonably steady mock military salute.

Saturday, 25 September

John had Guillaume & Maggie de Rougemont staying at The Stables, where we dined, Maggie as usual cooking splendid dinner. Guillaume, in addition to his courier tours in Asia, is also scientifically concerned with study of insects. His travel firm is closing down, so he talks of writing book about his insects. Maggie's literary agency seems going well.

Monday, 18 October

A rather depressing character called Michael Langley, who has occasionally written fan letters in the past, came self-invited to tea. Seventyish, a journalist, he has lived for eighteen years in Milan, and does odd jobs for the British Council. He discovered through *Infants of the Spring* that he was distantly related (shared blood of Turners of Mulbarton, Norfolk). One of the thorns in the crown that genealogists must wear without flinching is genealogical intrusion, sometimes by one's own family. Langley rather parsonic. Also left sense of guilt, as he asked when his taxi should return, I named an hour's time, he laughed, said an hour and a half. I felt afterwards I should have been more hospitable. Lowering incident.

Tuesday, 26 October

Some weeks ago Hugh Thomas (now Lord Thomas of Swynnerton), whom I have known vaguely for some time, wrote to ask if I would be able to 'have a talk with the Prime Minister over dinner'? This came, to say the least, as a surprise. Previous contacts with Mrs Thatcher were: (1) cocktail party given at 10 Downing Street for 'intellectuals' and the like, at which I was impressed with the energy she gave out shaking hands. I managed to tell her later that, three or four years before Kevin Billington (married to Rachel, one of the Longford daughters) and I had agreed she was the Answer. She said: 'Oh, well, it's a battlefield.' (2) At Royal Academy Banquet when she spoke, quoting Guillaume Apollinaire in a speech (something about a man walking blindfold over a cliff), passage I did not recognise, tho' I know Apollinaire's works fairly well. On the way out I mentioned this to Hugh Casson, PRA, who said: 'She hasn't gone yet, you'd better talk to her about it.' I thought she had left, but she was still in the outer hall, so Hugh reintroduced us. Mrs T knew roughly about Apollinaire, a bit vague about quotation (which I still can't find). (3) Clarissa Avon gave a party for Mrs Thatcher. When we arrived I was immediately, without the least warning, put on sofa beside her. She has no small talk, I could think of nothing to say, so rather ineptly returned to Apollinaire, asked if I might send her a copy of his poems, supposing I could easily get Maurice Bowra's *Selection*. She said yes, but hoped it was easy French.

At that point Clarissa interposed another guest for Mrs T to look over (meanwhile V talking to Mr Thatcher about the American Civil War). It turned out that the Bowra edition of Apollinaire impossible to find. In the end, some little time later, I managed to obtain a rather textbook-like volume of Apollinaire's poems, with English on the opposite pages (possibly just as well). Unfortunately it did not contain *La Jolie Rousse*, which was obviously apposite. However, I wrote Mrs T's name in the book with the quotation:

> Ses cheveux sont d'or on dirait
> Un bel éclair qui durerait
> Où ses flammes qui pavanent
> Dans les roses-thé qui se fanent

She wrote quite a civil letter of thanks, saying she would read the poems during the Parliamentary Recess.

On the way to London for the Hugh Thomas dinner party I met Percy Somerset on Westbury platform, who said nowadays he disliked having to make London trip, with which I agreed. In The Travellers I saw Robin McDouall (former Club Secretary), very lame, doddery. I was reading an evening paper, waiting to set out for dinner, when inevitably, Alan Pryce-Jones appeared on one of his London visits from the US; just returned from Greece, the Wexford Festival, etc, slightly less like Dorian Gray than a few months before, plumper, no less remarkable for his age. A good-looking young American then turned up, to whom Alan P-J was giving dinner. The American (called Hudson, like a Henry James character) seemed put out at Alan continuing conversation with me, pouring out a flow of Pryce-Jonesian stories: for instance, that Mrs Thatcher was half-first-cousin of Diana Cooper, because Mrs T's maternal grandmother had been a housemaid at Belton, seduced by Harry Cust (claimed, with some reason, to be Diana Cooper's true father), great womanizer, younger son of the Brownlows. There is not the least evidence that Mrs Thatcher's grandmother was housemaid at Belton or anywhere else; indeed, I think only her parents lived in Lincolnshire, the family before that coming from Northamptonshire. I told Alan that I was dining that night with the Hugh Thomases to meet Mrs T, and would closely examine her likeness to that celebrated beauty of earlier years, Diana Cooper. He said: 'I can tell you who two of your fellow guests will be, Stephen Spender & Isaiah Berlin.'

I set off for 29 Ladbroke Grove, and was looking for the house on the right-hand side of the street proceeding northwards, when somebody passing from the opposite direction muttered as he went by: 'I think we are still too early.' This turned out to be Isaiah Berlin himself. We talked for a moment, then crossed the road. There was a small garden in front of the Thomases' house, the gate of which both Isaiah and I failed to open. At once a figure glided from out of the shadows with the words: 'May I help you, sir?', evidently a security man previously concealed in the bushes. Within the house were gathered together some dozen or so writers of one kind or another: Vidia Naipaul, Tony Quinton, V. S. Pritchett, Tom Stoppard, J. H. Plumb, A. Alvarez, Dan Jacobson, Stephen Spender, Philip Larkin, Nicholas Mosley, a Peruvian novelist called Mario Vargas Llosa, whom I had heard of as Llosa, did not immediately recognize as Vargas in the foreign style with double-barrelled names. Vanessa Thomas was the only other woman who sat down to dinner. We were waited on by Thomas daughters and another nice little girl, to whom I was introduced, but failed to memorize name. It was all rather like the children of a feudal lord acting as pages in the Middle Ages. Before dinner began everyone had a word with Mrs T, who was talking to someone about how much she had enjoyed Helen Gardner's book on Eliot's *Four Quartets* when my turn came, so I followed up on that same subject.

I find Mrs Thatcher very attractive, if not at all easy. In the course of the evening I made covert enquiries as to how others felt in this respect. Physically desirable was the universal answer among all those questioned, including Vidia. At dinner I sat between Alvarez & Jacobson, with neither of whose books was I familiar, tho' I knew about Alvarez to some extent as a poet, poetry critic; Jacobson, as South African novelist. Both seemed agreeable. When dinner was at an end Hugh Thomas tapped on his glass, said something like: 'Prime Minister, you were brought up a scientist, have you ever wished you had been educated as an historian?' This started a general discussion, which broadly speaking led to hearing people's views on Russia.

It was really a kind of seminar. I was, so to speak, 'put on' at one moment. I do not excel on such occasions. This continued until about midnight, not at all without interest, if rather like discussions of various levels of the Joint

Intelligence Committees for 'putting up a paper' on some subject during the war. The Quintons have a flat in St James's Square, so Tony Quinton, owner of a car, offered to drop Isaiah at Albany, and me within a step of The Travellers.

Wednesday, 27 October

Arrived as requested soon after midday for luncheon at the Lancasters, Jock Murray, Osbert's publisher, said to be coming with copies of *The Lady Littlehampton Selection* for Osbert to sign, also bringing a bottle of champagne to celebrate its publication. In fact Jock turned up only shortly before one o'clock, by which time Osbert was well advanced into his first, if not second vodka. I was drinking sherry, which, much as I like fizz for dinner, I prefer in the middle of day. Osbert was rather cantankerous about signing copies. Susie Allison there, nice, widow of doctor who looked after John Betjeman, Kingsley Amis, and various similar hard cases. V went to Allison (through psychiatrist Frank Tate, friend of Lancasters) when John was ill to get something for her own nerves. She met Betjeman there in deep depression in the waiting-room. She told Dr Allison, who said he only wished he could find something to cure his own depression. His widow has now established herself as going round getting things like taxation material in order for Osbert, Kingsley, *et al*, including the now departed (matrimonially) Jane (Howard) Amis. Susie Allison said difficulty was being experienced in Kentish Town to persuade Kingsley to move his bed out of the ground floor sitting-room (where he has been since falling downstairs when returning from The Garrick), although his leg is now pretty well recovered. He lies there, like Lord Marchmain awaiting death in the Chinese Drawing Room, to the considerable inconvenience of the rest of the household.

Monday, 1 November

I received letter from a granddaughter of restaurateur Pietro Castano, asking for a book to be signed, and expressing great delight at what I had said in my Memoirs about the niceness of Castano (known to her as Peter Pop), his daughter and her mother's beauty. Castano's was in Greek Street (one or two doors south of the arch into Manette Street on east side). It was formerly called Previtali. When I first used to go there, it was much frequented by my Oxford generation, for example John Lloyd, known as 'The Widow', and others known to me, for good cheap Italian food. It ceased just before the war, when Castano got into financial difficulties over his gambling (trotting races). I never managed to establish with certainty whether the place in Greek Street (where I used to lunch every day) was the same as that Previtali's, where Gissing and H. G. Wells used to eat. There seems to have been a Previtali in the Strand at much earlier date. Did it move from there? Castano's granddaughter (who lives in the large block of flats over the bookshops in Charing Cross Road) reached the Memoirs through listening to the radio version of *Dance*.

This is an interesting example of how people *always* get round to mention of them, or theirs, in a book, whether favourable, or the reverse. This should be made clear to all authors when they set out on writing. Without fail, if they 'put someone in a book', whether directly or obliquely, the persons involved, or their relations, friends, enemies, will get round to it, however unliterary the milieu or subject. Letter from John Anderson, Eton Lower Master, enclosing school list of this year. This gave details of speeches (recitations by Sixth Formers, twenty in number, on Fourth of June), one of which was the passage about the Monkey Temple from *The Strangers All Are Gone*; rather different from Speeches in my day (Plautus, Racine, etc). I received from Freddie Bradnum questions for the TV Mastermind quiz on *Dance*, which he set. He enquired about possibilities of radio plays from the pre-war novels, which I tried to encourage.

Sunday, 7 November

Clarissa Avon & Jim Lees-Milne to luncheon. Jim rather worried because Alvilde, away on cruise doing Crusader castles, had stepped back when photographing some site, fallen into a pit: uncertain how bad her injuries. Both Clarissa & Jim were interested in *Asquith's Letters to Venetia Stanley*, which I have for review. Clarissa had known Venetia Stanley well. She said, politically speaking, Venetia Stanley was like talking to a man. At Clarissa's party some months ago, when Mrs Thatcher had been present, V had sat for a time with Mr Thatcher. They talked about the American Civil War because he was reading a book on the subject. He complained about this particular work: 'But where were the bloody maps?' V, fairly well up in the Civil War, partly owing to my own interest in it, partly her American Gt-Aunt Mabel Leigh (whose family came from the South, lost their fortune in the war), afterwards reported the conversation to Clarissa. In consequence of this, when Clarissa, who was recently in Washington, was consulted as how best Denis Thatcher could be amused (the Thatchers also on a visit there), Clarissa at once recommended the Civil War battlefields. It appears that Mr Thatcher stood up to the first three or four pretty well, but as a manifestly unending panorama of engagements, from Bull Run to The Wilderness, began to unroll before him, he broke down, begging to be shown no more.

Tuesday, 9 November

To London. While I was getting my ticket to Westbury, Jane Somerset rushed up, said: 'You've left your lights on', most kind, as I was quite unaware of this, something on the car's switchboard catching one's hand with this effect. Saw Sussman, asked why his house was called Fandango; apparently named after a boat he had possessed. Drinks with Evangeline Bruce at Albany: Tony & Marcelle Quinton, Isaiah & Aline Berlin, Nicko Henderson. Tony Quinton, Nicko Henderson & I went on to the Literary Society at The Garrick, where we found Duff Hart-Davis, Michael Howard, Martyn Beckett, V. S. Pritchett, Dick Troughton, Jo Grimond. I sat between Tony Q. & Dick T. Good evening.

Walking back to The Travellers, I was vaguely aware of two youngish girls looking rather lost on the corner of Pall Mall by The Senior (as was). They appeared to be saying goodbye to each other. I crossed the lower part of Waterloo Place and was just by the corner of The Athenaeum, when I found they had run after me, and seemed to want to ask the way. One of them said something about 'business', I thought they were foreign, enquiring how to get an address. I said: 'I don't quite understand where you want to go.' The girl yelled with laughter, said: 'Do you want any business?' They were in fact very young tarts. I said I had a date already. They said: 'Would you like to give us a pound anyway?' I replied in the negative. One of them said: 'Come down there', indicating the Duke of York's steps, whether 'business' would have been transacted on the steps, or in the Park below, I am uncertain. Their age, clothes (rather prim, grey & black), general demeanour, quite unlike what one used to associate with tarts. I passed on up the steps, through the portals of The Travellers. When I told Virginia Bath about this incident she said: 'You were lucky they did not attack you.'

Saturday, 13 November

Roland Gant rang up from his Dorset hide-out, or rather the nearest telephone-box, as he lives in far too primitive conditions when in the country to permit a telephone. He came to lunch, so I was able to give him the typescript of *O, How the Wheel Becomes It!*, V at the same time returning her Margaret Kennedy typescript with suggested emendations completed.

Saturday, 20 November

V & I lunched with Clarissa Avon, arriving first. Then four decidedly comic figures trooped in, called respectively Teddy Millington-Drake; a Greek named something like Stephanides or Stephanotis; a young man with an unruly mop of hair, whose Christian name was Alexander; a middle-aged-to-elderly bald American (rather like a version of the American painter J. O. Mahoney, friend of the Mizeners who have been so hospitable to us when in America), lately living in Athens, now moved to Key West. These were almost immediately followed by Spider, Peter Quennell's former (fourth) wife, apparently staying with this quartet. Spider looked not a day older than twenty years ago; Jill Hare, wife of Alan Hare of the *Financial Times*, who (with her husband) surfaced at Clarissa's before. Cooking was, Clarissa said, done by female painter who earns a living by housekeeping. Her son plays the flute. Luncheon was long delayed, the first course having for some reason gone west. Otherwise the food was perfectly eatable, indeed rather good. I sat between Clarissa & Spider, the latter was still very jolly. Clarissa's time was somewhat taken up in controlling the guests.

Tuesday, 23 November

V & I lunched with Mayalls. Other guests: music critic Desmond Shawe-Taylor; his brother Bryan, young nephew of Lees's named Bennett, whose father married Lees's sister, and invented a new religion, of which he was godhead. I had met Desmond Shawe-Taylor occasionally in the past, never known him at all well. The Widow and his brother Wyndham Lloyd used to call him Operatic Annie, at times varied to Florentine Musical May; the latter name from poster they had seen announcing: 'There will be a Florentine Musical May this year.' We talked again about the *Asquith Letters to Venetia Stanley*. Mary Mayall had met her (by then Venetia Montagu), and liked her.

Virginia (Powell) rang up about 11.30 pm to say her mother had died. Very sad news. Nina Lucas was to have come down to The Stables this Christmas. She had been giving a female friend dinner at her Goudhurst house, gone into the kitchen to fetch the next course, dropped down dead. I suppose she was about seventy-seven. I used to see her, as Nina Grenfell, at deb dances (which she said she attended for fifteen years), but oddly enough we never met. I saw Archie Lucas once or twice in Sligger's room at Balliol, but never talked to him. He was slim, dark, good-looking, moved in the eminently well behaved undergraduate world of David Cecil/Leslie Hartley, etc. Maurice Bowra is said to have had deep unavailing passion for him. Nina was a person the whole family will miss.

Tuesday, 7 December

We set off in foulest weather to lunch with David Cecil at Red Lion House, Cranborne. Fog, as well as sheets of rain, round Tollard Royal. David was holding up pretty well considering what a fearful blow he must have suffered in Rachel's death. A lady has been found to cook for him. She has a good deal of personality, formerly worked for the Rob Walkers (of Nunney, a mile south of us, whose son was at school with John) in Australia. A creditable meal was produced. David, now eighty, remains remarkably unchanged from when I was at Goodhart's [House at Eton] with him. He talked of his time there, and the group of boys sacked from the house just before my own arrival. Said he regards it as quite a tolerable period of his life. I had always noticed a late 18th century portrait of a young man in the drawing-room, never before asked who this was – apparently Pennistone Lamb, Melbourne's (legitimate) older brother, a rake, who died at twenty-six. It was painted by Mrs Cosway, wife of the miniaturist, quite a decent picture. The picture came to David through his mother, appropriately as he wrote a life of Melbourne.

Friday, 10 December

Radio programme on Kingsley Amis, himself good, in spite of the producer's unsympathetic personality. I remarked that Kingsley's school (City of London) had been Asquith's. V said also 'Master Lush's', once famous choirboy songster of the Temple Church. V had talked to Kingsley about Lush, shade older, Kingsley having once sat next to him at Old Boy dinner. V suggested this contact might have given rise to Kingsley's novel *The Alteration*.

Thursday, 16 December

Joanna Head came from the BBC Bristol to talk about Gerald Reitlinger, as they are doing a TV programme on benefactors of The Ashmolean, Oxford. Reitlinger had left to the Museum his collection of oriental ceramics. It is hard to think of anything I have not said about The Squire at one time or another, already in my Memoirs. However, I managed to produce some quite funny photographs of him as Squire of Woodgate. Since the programme was to deal with all Ashmolean benefactors, I pointed out that I was also an authority on John Aubrey, who certainly ought to be remembered as one of the chief benefactors, in his own particular way, in the collection's early days. Inevitably he won't, part of Aubrey's bad luck. The girl seemed reasonably intelligent, but as so many young people appear to one, a trifle devitalized.

Saturday, 18 December

We drove to Oxford for the Master of Balliol's luncheon for Roy Jenkins, as one of the founders of the Social Democratic Party. We had refused the formal invitation, then Roy wrote to ask specially that I should come if I could, as he rarely gets to the Lit. Soc. these days, nor indeed do I. The best to be said for the projected SDP is that it might be less actively harmful to the interests of the country than the current Labour Party has become, and less inane than the Liberals, for those who feel themselves on the Left. This trip will also give opportunity for bringing over to Oxford various books belonging to my great-uncle, D'Oyly Ramsay Jefferson, for the Balliol Library (mostly Eton 'leaving Books', & Prince Albert's German Prize, Goethe, Schiller, etc), which the College seemed to want more than Eton, DRJ having been at both: then going off his rocker as a young man.

Lovely frosty sunny winter day for drive. Luncheon: Tony & Nancy Kenny (our host & hostess); Roy & Jennifer Jenkins; Jo & Laura Grimond; David Astor & his wife; Labour MP Dick Taverne & wife; Andrew Gilmour (son of Tory politican Ian Gilmour) & wife; (Sir?) Ronald Macintosh, civil servant of varied employments. Roy Jenkins spent most of the pre-luncheon period talking to me about *Dance*; most of post-luncheon talking to V on same subject. Among other things he also talked of the *Asquith/Venetia Stanley Letters*.

I told Roy how much Asquith embarrassed Rachel Cecil, as a girl, with his hand under the rug, when she and her mother were travelling in a car with him. Roy pertinently asked if Asquith were fumbling Mrs (Desmond) McCarthy on the other side; a nice idea. Roy said he had been an undergraduate at Balliol just at the moment of outbreak of war in 1939, when personnel of the College was moved into Trinity next door. He said one of the events of his life had been the spectacular rise in his standard of living on exchanging the rigours of Balliol for the comparative luxury of Trinity.

He was a Gunner during the war, characteristically in a smart Yeoman cavalry regiment, transformed into Royal Artillery (the Hertfordshire Dragoons, I think). By one of those extraordinary chances his Battery Commander was R. F. Wilson, sometime Captain of the House at Goodhart's, an odd rather uncomfortable figure. He was the son of the Wilson of the Tranby Croft scandal (when Sir William Gordon-Cumming allegedly cheated at baccarat with Edward VII, as Prince of Wales, present). Robin Wilson was second husband of V's Australian ex-cousin Pat, formerly married to Grandy Jersey. Robin Wilson was killed falling off a jeep turning a corner during the Italian campaign. By that time, I think, Roy Jenkins had become an ADC.

David Astor looked so much older, I did not recognize him, until told who he was by Laura Grimond. Mrs Taverne was quite pretty, one would suspect something of a handful. Laura chattered away as if she had not been allowed out for months. She talked about Malcolm Muggeridge, and asked if he were a humbug. I said yes and no. It was rather like asking if the actor who played King Lear was really so old and upset, as Malcolm believes all he says at the moment of saying it. I suppose the short answer is yes: he is a humbug. I used to imagine the Missionary in Maugham's short story *Rain* rather a contrived figure, but Malcolm could perfectly well have taken part in the whole sequence of events, except he would never have finally cut his own throat. Laura said her mother was just like that, Lady Bonham-Carter (later Lady Violet B-C & finally Baroness Asquith of Yarnbury), really did believe, for instance, that Stanley Baldwin & Ramsay MacDonald were plotting downfall of the country. In deference to Roy's well advertised taste for claret, superlatively good magnums of a '71 wine were produced, the name of which I failed to see. When offered port, Roy said: 'Perhaps if there's any left in that (claret) magnum . . .'

Saturday, Christmas Day

We lunched at The Stables, where Ferdie & Julia Mount staying with their children. Ferdie is now working at 10 Downing Street. He looked rather tired. He 'puts up papers' all the time, sits in Cabinet sub-committees. On such subjects he maintained, as ever in all aspects of his life, an extreme reserve. Tristram brought back an amusing account of filming his TV programme on Philip Roth, the American writer, in the US. Roth lives with Clare Bloom, herself in Tristram's film. Tristram was much impressed by the star treatment American novelists expect, indeed get, in the US. Apparently Clare Bloom developed a cold when the film was to be shot (invariable occurrence with actresses, Tristram says).

Sunday, Boxing Day

Drinks in the morning with Mayalls, Mary Mayall in fact in bed with flu. Gave them paperback of Jocelyn Brooke's *The Image of a Drawn Sword*, copies of which arrived to make suitable hand-out as Christmas presents for those getting something later. Mary Mayall shared with Jocelyn Brooke childhood horrors about book called *Little Detchie Head*, the subject a child whose head was transformed into a cooking pot. Among those present at the Mayalls was Milo (Lord) Parmoor, who lives at Sutton Veny, John says a person of some note in the City, son of White's Club character Freddie Cripps, nephew of Sir Stafford Cripps. The Stables party dined with us.

Monday, 27 December

Drinks at The Stables. Lees Mayall described Moët et Chandon party he attended recently in Bath through agency of Robin McDouall, former Secretary of The Travellers, now in rather tumbledown condition physically, as noted earlier. Two high-powered French chefs had been flown over. The food was marvellous, drink rather indifferent. Twelve guests (in fact only eleven, Mary Mayall having flu) including Percy & Jane Somerset, with their eldest son and his wife, otherwise Lees knew no one. Efforts were made to address the two chefs – summoned for congratulation – in French, when Percy Somerset spoke they had no idea what he was talking about, Lees finally saving situation having considerable command of the language. One of the guests at The Stables party was a schoolmaster from Millfield, who had taught English at Eton. He said the Headmaster of Millfield was bent on transforming whole neighbouring landscape with trees, in an effort to efface all record of Meyer, who founded the school, which now has 1300 pupils, a staff of 150.

Thursday, 30 December

Georgia & Archie came to tea as usual, this time Archie bringing his guitar. He played, sang, very charmingly, unselfconsciously, Georgia lying on the floor, turning the music for him.

Friday, 31 December

Reread Dowson's *Letters*, then Beardsley's *Letters*. These hold up well, especially Beardsley, whose wit, courage facing the world notwithstanding shattering ill health, very appealing. Also in Vol IV of Pepys, never read straight through until now, having bought a secondhand set of the definitive edition. Most people love Pepys. I cannot find him sympathetic in spite of his undoubted taste for the arts, and integrity as a civil servant. It is perhaps the contemporary figure of Aubrey, a gent, even if a broken-down one, as well as intelligent, who diminishes Pepys. Incidentally Pepys never took in Aubrey as a personality, tho' he must have had plenty of opportunity to do so at the Royal Society. I found myself unexpectedly riveted by James Fox's *White Mischief* about Lord Erroll's murder in Kenya in 1940 by Sir Jock Delves Broughton. This is to some extent because I, and/or V, had met quite a lot of the people concerned in the story. Derek Erskine, Rory More O'Ferrall, Bill Allen (last two marginal figures) were actually at Goodhart's (Allen before my time); Fabian Wallace at Eton, not met till Oxford, then not as an undergraduate;

Lizzie Lezard (Lees Mayall says Lezard had to say at the trial he was in a black brothel) met at parties once or twice; Dickie Pembroke (nice P. G. Wodehouse guardsman) often with the d'Avigdor-Goldsmids at Somerhill; James de Vere Allen (Jim) stayed here after John had done his African tour, son of the Chief Gaoler at Nairobi prison, now curator of the Lamu Museum; Freddy de Janzé (uncle of John's friend Guillaume de Rougemont) used to come into Duckworth's when his book *Vertical Land*, & another, was published 'on commission'; just met (Sir) Charles Markham & Mike Lafone (when taken to a party by Olga Vickers); Paula Gellibrand (a fan) at dinner with the Glenconners; 4th Lord Delamere (subsequently married Delves Broughton's wife Diana, mistress of Erroll) in White's during the war; possibly others, the most striking encounter being with the superlatively unpleasant Lord Carbery.

About 1929 I flew back from Marseilles, first time in a plane, which was very small & uncomfortable. After being driven to Marseilles airport in bus, I asked tall apparent Englishman, who got out beside me, whether one tipped the driver. He replied sourly, with a strong American accent, to the effect that you 'gave him a bill of ten francs' (or whatever the appropriate sum was). Something so disagreeable about him caused me to enquire of another passenger if he knew who the tall man was. He said: 'He's Lord Carbery, but he likes to be known as Mr Carbery', as the book explains, owing to his extreme anti-Britishness (he was Anglo-Irish).

I had a seat right up at the front in the plane. Carbery had a somewhat similar type with him, or picked him up on the plane, and, after we came down at Lyons, on returning, I found this couple had taken my seat up by the pilot. It didn't seem much good trying to evict them, so I left it at that. There had been a tremendous thunderstorm raging, with flashes of lightning, etc, since Marseilles. When we came to Paris I decided not to get out in the rain. Carbery & his companion did leave their seats. I took some pleasure in seeing one of those seats taken by an old man boarding on two sticks. When Carbery returned he said: 'These are our seats.' The old man in a loud raucous voice, like an actor registering extreme senility on the stage, almost yelled: 'I'm seventy-eight, sir, and very lame, sir, I'd be exceedingly glad, sir, if you'd leave me in peace.' The Carbery couple, defeated, retired to the back of the plane, where, owing to the storm, rain had already begun to come through badly from a hole in the roof. Between Paris and London this drip increased to something not much short of a bathroom tap, pouring down on both of them, matter of great enjoyment for me. The point of interest, however, is the quite exceptional nastiness of Carbery's personality as revealed by *White Mischief*, which clung round him like an aura.

I have at the moment no idea for a new book, beyond toying with the possibility of a novel in the form of letters, beginning by an author replying more or less formally to a fan-letter, which then develops into some sort of an involvement; alternatively, attempting a ghost story. The New Year will in due course bring proofs of *Wheel* (to appear in June) and the abridged four-in-one Memoirs (published in September). The TV situation about *Dance* is that the BBC have offered to do it in eight, possibly nine, ninety-minute episodes. I am holding out for at least twelve, even twelve inadequate, as demonstrated by radio.

Rereading *Hamlet*, struck by a note in the Arden edition explaining that when Hamlet makes a satirical remark about killing a calf to Polonius (who says he acted in his youth), this clearly ties in with Aubrey saying Shakespeare was a butcher's son, who used 'to kill a calf in great style'. Killing a calf seems to have been a standard Mummers' turn. Shakespeare as young man might well have taken part in mumming, or equally possible that his father was butcher or grazier as well as glover. A curious point, which indicates that, as usual, what Aubrey says is not to be ignored, even when some confusion may have taken place regarding information recorded.

1983

Thursday, 6 January

After Dowson/Beardsley *Letters*, I moved on to Wilde's (superbly edited by Rupert Hart-Davis). Mention there of *Lord Arthur Savile's Crime* (1891) stimulated rereading story. Wilde (as opposed to, say, James, many others) always sounds convincing on aristocratic names. Was Conrad familiar with *Lord Arthur Savile's Crime* when he wrote *The Secret Agent* (1907)? Lord Arthur's visit to Soho, after deciding to blow up his elderly relation, bears distinct resemblances to similar negotiations about obtaining explosives on part of Conrad's anarchists, dealing with The Professor, etc. It is generally said that most of Conrad's terrorist material (so far as England is concerned) came through his Ford Madox Ford connexion, Ford possessing young relations mixed up to some extent with such attitudes; eg. running revolutionary periodical of the kind to be found for sale in Mr Verloc's rubber-goods shop in Leicester Square (on the site, said Conrad, of where the Leicester Gallery stood for many years, but I suspect he was in fact thinking of Lisle Street) where the Greenwich explosion in the book (which actually took place) was planned.

Saturday, 8 January

V & I drove to lunch with Jim & Alvilde Lees-Milne at Essex House, Badminton, a kind of upper-class Cranford village at the gates of the Duke of Beaufort's park (Essex House formerly some kind of Beaufort Dower House), enormously neat within, pretty furniture, odds & ends. Alvilde, daughter of a rather flamboyant first-war general, Tom Bridges, celebrated, when troops' morale was low, for buying a tin trumpet or toy drum, played while marching with Second-in-Command at their head. Alvilde was first married to the musical peer, Lord Chaplin, (one daughter). During the war Jim was invalided out of the Irish Guards early on. Employed by National Trust, which he kept together almost singlehanded during war period, he did an immensely hardworking job, travelling about on a bicycle, and saved many historic houses. This is all described in Jim's *Diaries*, written with real talent for that difficult art. They are particularly readable owing to his job being quite different from anyone else's, also taking him all over the country to places essentially of interest. V knew Jim Lees-Milne long before I did. Jim is always enjoyable to talk regarding gossip and art matters. Alvilde is resplendent, elegant, a wonderful cook. The only other guests at luncheon were the two Jungman sisters (who live in Gloucestershire, perhaps Bristol neighbourhood). I had not set eyes on Zita since staying at Renishaw with the Sitwells in 1929. She was then married to an unexciting guardee, Arthur James (my contemporary at school). Zita at that period was very beautiful, evidently bored to hell, impossible to get a word out of. In light of later knowledge, I imagine the Arthur Jameses had been invited to Renishaw because Sachie Sitwell had a passion (probably platonic in effect) for Zita, as he intended to fall for that sort of exquisite narcissistic beauty (Lady Bridget Parsons, and ballerina Pearl Argyle, *et al*). Zita grateful for any notice she can get; Baby holding up much better, indeed in a manner of speaking looking much as she always did. As it happens I never met Baby in early days. I came across her first about twenty years ago when Bridget Parsons, on the Zoological Society's board, gave a party at the Zoo, which we attended, Baby Jungman was present. She and I got separated from rest of the party for a few minutes while being shown round, when I saw she had considerable charm, and very reasonable for Evelyn Waugh to have been in love with her after breakup of his first marriage (in respect of which one feels it right of Baby not to publish her Waugh letters). Both were RCs, Evelyn not yet clued up about annulments, so all was abortive. An interesting possibility had they married. Frank Pakenham, and several others, were in love with Baby too, at an early date. In the end she married a Canadian Air Force Sergeant (or something of sort) called Cutherbertson, which didn't last, two children, the boy killed in an accident. Baby chatters away agreeably, both at the Zoo, and at the Lees-Milne luncheon party. At the former, when we were being shown the back entrance to cages, I noticed one of the chimpanzees, when nobody else was looking, put his arm at full stretch out of the back-door of his house, and draw inside with him a small broom hanging on the wall, presumably used for cleaning the place. One wondered if he hit the keeper over the head with it when he arrived in the morning. Alvilde as usual cooked splendid luncheon (fish pâté, pheasant in sauce, parsnips, red cabbage, mashed potatoes, crème mousse with almonds). Jim is about to produce another vol of his *Diary* (1947).

Sunday, 9 January

A journalist, Dennis Pitts, lunched at short notice to do interview for *Sunday Express Colour Magazine*, having got in touch through Heinemann. (Journalists do not know about books of reference such as *Who's Who*.) As John (Powell) said, Pitts was an archetypal Fleet Street figure, grey-haired, some of the air of an actor, complexion tanned with long exposure to all climates. He might have been worse. He wanted to talk about 'my friends', but finally agreed not, as an impossible subject to elaborate. Even after all these years I can never really adapt myself to the mechanics of the interview, at which people I know (Kingsley Amis, for instance) are so adroit. [Nothing was ever published, in spite of one or two subsequent telephone calls by Pitts to expand our talk together.]

Sunday, 16 January

V's sister, Pansy Lamb, staying with Helen Asquith, Lord Asquith's sister, at Mells (the mile from which she walks) came over for tea. Rome seems to suit her. Pansy's conversation is incessant monologue, different in subject matter, otherwise close to Mrs Bloom's reflections, spoken aloud. She said Frank sent his biography of Jesus to his (Frank's) son Thomas, who replied this sounded a most interesting man, why had he never heard of him?

Tuesday, 18 January

V to London, among other things to attend the Duff Cooper Prize party, later dine at the Amis/Kilmarnock Kentish Town residence. Down here Walter Cronkite, noted American political commentator, brought a camera crew to interview me for the CBS TV programme on George Orwell. I liked Cronkite, who asked sensible questions, and has a pleasant manner. His grey moustache, general demeanour, make him resemble the Peter Arno *New Yorker* clubman (the one in bed with married couple, saying 'Nice of you two to have me to stay', or the top hatted figure dropping a brassière into a rag-and-bone man's barrow, with the words 'May I?'). The CBS producer, Burton Benjamin, his (British) secretary, Patricia Burny, also made a good impression. They arrived about 11–11.30, did not get through until 2 o'clock. I was struck by the contrast of American and home camera crews; former (as in all work) taking things for granted much more, none of that Dad's Army approach, when getting on with the job. The Americans are not necessarily more efficient (possibly on the whole less), just wholly different. On this occasion there were various crises, lights fusing, etc, had to be put right by the advice of Mr Fricker (positively saintly local electrician) by telephone, only final casuality being one electric kettle. It appears there is much argument taking place in the US as to whether Orwell would now be a 'neo-conservative', or remain a staunch Socialist. My own feeling is that George would never abandon what might be called romantic Leftishness – dislike for anything approaching the conventional formalities of life, evening clothes, or even normally neat male garments, all his far-fetched attitudes about working-class life as it was about eighty years before his own day (anyway how he imagined it). But I think he would have been anti-CND, pro-Falklands Campaign, any other approach would have been appeasing a Latin-American dictatorship, and in favour of certain other policies of the Right, which to some extent he always was. Of course impossible to guess what anyone, let alone George, might think after thirty years or more.

George and I were once talking about the Spanish Civil War. I said, little as I liked Franco, in the last resort I should have supported the Nationalists against the Communists. George said: 'Well, I think whether one was on the Right or the Left in Spain very much depended on which part of the country one was living in at the time.' He certainly agreed that, 'with Europe Red at each end', a Spanish Communist Government would have joined German/Soviet Pact, probably invaded France, which Franco at least refused to do for Hitler. The Orwell programme is to appear in April. I am always doubtful how much of what is shot about oneself will survive after sub-editors have been at it, even if it is shown at all in this country. [About two brief sentences of mine were spoken in the event, of what one saw over here neither of the faintest significance.]

Thursday, 20 January

I have been struck in Wilde's *Letters* how he utterly changed almost from one day to the next, the good-natured hardworking Editor of a women's paper transmuted to the literary lion always harassed for money (only on account of headlong extravagance), evidently beginning to live dangerously. The last happening quite suddenly so far as one can see. *Folie de grandeur* seems to date from the stay in Paris, when Wilde met Lord Alfred Douglas. They started up some kind of affair almost immediately, and soon letters to Douglas show Wilde completely reckless about boys. It has been suggested that Douglas introduced Wilde to the male prostitute habit, which seems convincing; all contemporary with Wilde becoming successful playwright, which (as it so often seems to happen to playwrights) had a very definite, not to say disastrous, effect on Wilde's paranoiac behaviour. The latter in any case didn't need much encouragement to blossom. Meanwhile, there seems to have been no sign of his wife suspecting anything. Did they continue to cohabit? [Richard Ellmann's subsequent biography suggests Wilde avoided that by pleading a return of his syphilitic symptoms, tho' in fact there is no proof that Wilde had syphilis.]

Friday, 21 January

This weekend John was driven down by his lodger, Amina Minns, & her cameraman boyfriend Jeremy Stavenhagen (some such name). Amina, daughter of a former Egyptian Ambassador in Rome, is a Doctor of Anthropology or some related science, pretty, looking very Ancient Egyptian, with a square pageboy bob, like one of those figures navigating boats on the Nile in wooden models found in Pyramid Tombs. One imagines her former Minns husband was probably some connexion of Minns KS in the Eton Society of Arts, perhaps nephew. Minns KS never spoke. Harold Acton told me years later that he was only there because Brian Howard was in love with him. 'My dear, honey on the comb.'

Sunday, 23 January

James Fox, author of *White Mischief*, in consequence of fan letter I wrote him, rang to ask advice. *Burke's Peerage* describes Erroll as 'served in Eritrean campaign 1940 (despatches)'. Fox pointed out in *White Mischief* that Erroll, as Military Secretary to Kenya administration, employed in Nairobi, was in fact murdered the day before the Eritrean Campaign opened. Nonetheless, it appears Erroll did indeed receive a 'mention' between 1939 & 1941. Now Sir Iain Moncreiffe of that Ilk, accomplished genealogist but obdurate *farceur*, has sent Fox a Lawyer's Letter saying his, Moncreiffe's, reputation as genealogist is damaged by a suggestion that he put piece of bogus information into a book of reference; Moncreiffe's first wife being Countess of Erroll in her own right (the murdered man's daughter), Moncreiffe, as her genealogist husband, filling in the entry. (Later they were divorced.)

The only explanation I could offer to Fox was that whole of Kenya might have been officially designated an 'operational area', therefore included in military dispatches, in which the Military Secretary, like any other serving soldier, could be awarded a 'mention' for meritorious conduct. I also drew attention to Moncreiffe having said in letter to the papers that Cyril Connolly had been in love with Erroll (then Hay), who left Eton (sacked) in 1916; Connolly not arriving at Eton until 1917. That, at least, is what the Eton lists seem to show. Although Connolly appears to imply in Fox's book that he knew Hay at Eton, he also says that Hay was shown as 'absent' in lists. Incidentally Erroll was uncle of Ali Kilmarnock, married to Hilly, formerly Amis.

Tuesday, 1 February

A photographer, Ralph Gobitz (who did work for Tristram's Jean Rhys programme) came from the *Sunday Express*. He had two assistants, Carol & Dan. Photography is now sometimes much as in 1850, the photographer putting his head for hours under a black cloth, the subject sitting very still, head practically in a metal clasp. Gobitz continually stood with the cloth draped over his head, sometimes moving about with it on him, which with his beard, made him look like an Old Testament prophet. [As stated earlier, in spite of various ringings up, nothing ever appeared in the *Express Colour Magazine*.]

Wednesday, 9 February

V & I watched TV programme on Ashmolean benefactors. The Reitlinger Collection of Ceramics makes Gerald Reitlinger now one of half-a-dozen greatest of these. The Director, David Piper, told me worth close on £2,000,000 when presented; now no doubt considerably more. I contributed to the programme several photographs of The Squire: one in a fur cap signing his abdication, sitting in an ornate late Empire chair (it was the moment of Edward VIII's abdication), also one of him, almost naked, holding up a candle, cursing the world; both taken in garden of Woodgate House.

Tuesday, 15 February

David Cheshire appeared again to look through our photograph album for his programme. He photographed what he wanted and seemed pleased with photographs available. He talked of the John Updike & Robert Lowell TV programmes in the US. Updike (one of those competent American writers I can't really read) was perfectly agreeable, but the crew was never offered so much as cup of coffee during five days filming. There was a marked *de haut en bas* attitude on the part of American writers, which Tristram commented on with reference to his own Philip Roth programme. David Cheshire had been Robert Lowell's pupil at Harvard, so he knew the subject pretty well. Lowell took his first wife out for a drive with the object of breaking off their engagement, then had so bad an accident that she had to go to hospital for six months. After the accident Lowell felt he must marry her. Soon after her emerging from hospital he hit her on the nose so violently that she had to go to hospital again. When Lowell married to his third wife, Lady Caroline Blackwood, they lived in a flat in Castletown (Ireland's largest mansion, built by an MP called William Conolly, Cyril Connolly accordingly having a fantasy about Castletown being really his). Lowell wrote a note to Caroline saying he had decided to go back to his second wife, Elizabeth Hardwick. He set off to do so, getting lost in the labyrinthine passages of Castletown: a Kafka situation. At last he managed to get back to the US, dying, however, in the taxi before reaching his second wife's place of residence. The sequence recording these things, also the occasion when Lowell struck his father, all included in the Cheshire film, then censored out by a consortium of Lowell wives. Robert Lowell is an interesting instance of the American self-deception as to no class existing in the US; Robert Lowell never on any occasion being mentioned without his precise standing within the Lowell family, as a Lowell aristocrat, albeit a minor one, being gone into.

Thursday, 17 February

Tom Rosenthal, of Heinemann, asked if I would attend the Jerusalem Book Fair to present Vidia Naipaul with the Jerusalem Prize. Much as I admire Vidia, I always feel the Public Orator role far from mine, while in fact to introduce him to the Israelis would not be at all easy. I have already been to Jersusalem (a city I don't really care for), and wouldn't much relish journey these days. Also I am not too keen on exchanging courtesies with the terrorist Begin. In short I refused, but felt rather bad about not doing as much for a friend. Vidia himself has apparently not been told that a British writer will do the presenting. I can't see why such is required. I had a letter from Eric Anderson, the new Head Master of Eton, saying my long campaign for getting *The Eton Register* brought up to date (it only goes properly up to 1799) has at last been put to the Provost and Fellows, something now may really be done. Anderson is the first of many persons I have pestered to grasp that a proper *Register* would be an invaluable document to all sorts of historical, and biographical, researchers; something that Harold Caccia, Martin Charteris (when Provosts), with lots more minor Eton official figures, seemed incapable of taking in.

Tuesday, 22 February

To London to see Sussman. I gave Evangeline Bruce luncheon at the

Lansdowne Club. She seemed at first a bit disorientated, as she was before when she was over here early on, no doubt jet-lag, then cheered up in the course of luncheon, appeared to enjoy herself. I asked if she had been watching the Betjeman TV programmes. She said she had seen the first, not watched the second. She added that a friend of hers turned the latter programme on briefly, and reported Betjeman as being interviewed by a really dreadful Australian, so switched off again. This is very enjoyable, as the dreadful Australian was Barry Humphries doing his act as Sir Les Patterson, Australian Cultural Attaché, and being taken absolutely seriously by the viewer.

Sunday, 27 February

V & I lunched with the Mayalls, Mary is excellent cook in quiet way. It appears that Evangeline's friend was by no means alone in taking Barry Humphries's impersonation seriously. Dozens of people did. Just one more warning of danger of making jokes, especially in public, most of all on television. We watched the Betjeman programme again in the evening. The visit of the poets for John's seventy-fifth birthday was more than a shade grisly, not least a bearded character called Pringle, who did the honours, a figure unknown to me. Some sequences were shown of Penelope Betjeman in India, for instance negotiating a river lying on her front on an inflated buffalo hide, which gave a good idea of Penelope's personality and figure. Elizabeth Cavendish flickered about briefly in the background when the poets were arriving in front of the Betjeman house in Chelsea. Not otherwise.

Sunday, 13 March

We had invited the Mayalls to luncheon; in fact lunched there again, as Lees had to go to Poole on some business about a Member for the Euro-Parliament, so Mary, entertaining David Cecil by herself, wanted help (as relations slightly tricky owing to Mary being David's niece, etc). An enjoyable luncheon. David in good form. He usually spends weekends with his children or going up to Cranborne. That day, for some reason connected with his housekeeper's car, he was driven over, dumped at the Mayalls for the weekend. I reminded him of the occasion when I had been his fag, let his fire out, and he had not had me beaten, which would have been perfectly reasonable. He said that Hugh Lygon (Eton contemporary, fellow member of Eton Society of Arts), like me, had been his fag; like me, let his fire out. It being a cold night David rather scolded him, then saw a huge tear appearing in each of Hugh Lygon's eyes, and roll down his cheeks. We talked of A. N. Wilson, whose book about Scott David too had approved. He had not read Wilson's *Milton*. Wilson apparently wanted to go into the Church, but was found unacceptable by the ecclesiastical authorities. He also made several efforts to get a Fellowship that were unavailing. Wilson is married to a female don (his former tutor, I think) considerably older than himself; I always find A. N. Wilson's journalism worth reading.

Sunday, 20 March

Joanna Hylton [Raymond, Lord Hylton's wife. Raymond the son of Lady Perdita Asquith] rang to say that Quintin Hailsham, the Lord Chancellor, staying at Ammerdown, had asked that I should be invited to luncheon. This, to say the least, unexpected, as I barely know him, tho' when he arrived at Eton as a scholar we were in the same division (up to E. V. Slater, a tiresome beak, with an obsession about cribbing) which I had reached after more than a year at school. We agreed to accept. V as usual went to church at Chantry, where Raymond Hylton and Hailsham turned up. The new Rector, functioning only for the second time, will get an inflated idea of his normal congregation at Chantry Church with a local Roman Catholic peer and the Lord Chancellor attending the service. Luncheon at Ammerdown was fairly odd; Hailsham's daughter, a barrister in her middle thirties but looks younger; Betty Miller-Jones (née Askwith), somewhat chastened from the self-assertive days of her early life.

Hailsham talked intelligently before lunch about the St Oswalds picture, *Sir Thomas More and Family*, which Hailsham is going to unveil. Carbon tests now suggest it is by Holbein, not, as formerly thought, Lockey (a painter I had never heard of). There is a Latin inscription, in a book there depicted, from Boethius, 6th century Roman philosopher, whose execution bears some similarity to More's which makes the Holbein attribution more doubtful.

I sat between Joanna, whom I like, and her mother-in-law Per Hylton (née Asquith). Per came in from a side door for luncheon, retiring through the same exit to some remote part of the house, as in a play. We talked about where to get cheap wine. A rather pretty jolly New Zealand au pair (two au pairs were waiting at table) insisted on my having a second helping of pudding, which she dumped on my plate. This made me laugh. Joanna said she was first introduced at age of fifteen to Evelyn Waugh at a dance. She was thrilled. He said crushingly, 'A little girl like you ought to be in bed at this hour.' Hailsham talked about reform of the House of Lords. He said he was in favour of leaving things as they are. 'If you poke a mummy with an umbrella it disintegrates.' He thought 'The Headmistress' (Mrs Thatcher) felt the same. If Labour came in and abolished the House of Lords, then quickly went out, he was in favour of establishing an elective Second Chamber.

Thursday, 25 March

An American academic, Paul Gaston, came to talk about 'The Extended Novel' (whatever that may be), on which he is doing a piece in one or other of two academic periodicals. Slight, with moustache, South Illinois University, he came himself from the South. He brought a present of a bottle of Tabasco, product of his home State, Louisiana. He had been at the University of Virginia, their Oxford, and seemed reasonably bright. [The Tabasco lasted a long time, turning out extremely useful for flavouring.]

Sunday, 10 April

Hilary & John Spurling to luncheon, with the object of Hilary doing an interview for *Harpers & Queen*. Eggs Mayonnaise, roast beef, cheesecake, two bottles of Latour-de-Mons, Margaux, '75. Hilary looking very pretty, wearing sweeping dress with top boots, rather like lady in a riding-habit on Beardsley's cover for one of the *Savoys*. She did some interviewing in the afternoon, while John Spurling listened to a cassette of *The Garden God* in V's room next door. Hilary said she couldn't say anything about *Wheel* in the *Harpers & Queen* piece, as it was dedicated to her. She wanted to do an article some time about my writing of women, which she thought I did well; an opinion that greatly pleased me, as in my view most male novelists do that quite astonishingly badly. John Spurling, after listening to *The Garden God*, which took just an hour, said it needed half an hour longer for pauses: actors had done little more than read their parts. He suggested a black actor might do Priapus, which seemed a good idea. There is a project Hilary should write my biography, her own suggestion, though she said she would be too embarrassed to ask me any questions. She went into the troubles about the Compton-Burnett rights being held by Gollancz; that firm leaving the novels out of print, while discouraging other publishers from taking them on.

Thursday, 14 April

Andrew Motion, a poet, came to luncheon to talk about book he is writing on the Lambert family: Constant, his father George and son Kit. Motion made a goodish impression, nice, intelligent, much hung with jewellery. W. H. Auden is alleged to have made pass at him as undergraduate, when Auden was taking refuge in Oxford at the end of his life. Motion revealed that Flo Lambert, Constant's first wife, is said now to be doing the cooking for publishing firm of Weidenfeld.

Saturday, 16 April

After considerable demur on the telephone I agreed to photographer, Tim Mercer, coming here for Hilary's *Harpers & Queen* piece, tho' they must possess dozens of pictures of me. Mercer apparently spends his weekends in Frome, where he has some sort of residence. He is better than he sounded on the line. At one moment he said: 'Look quizzical.'

Sunday, 17 April

We lunched Mayalls. Our gt-niece Rebecca Fraser (Antonia's eldest daughter) was staying there, invited by Robert Mayall. Robert works in Rota's bookshop in Long Acre. Rebecca is now in Quartet Books. She is very much the sort of girl publishing is undertaken by these days.

Tuesday, 19 April

To London to see Sussman. He said Dutch dentist made good speech to a group of dentists at a dinner on the subject of Pepys, ending with words: 'Now let us be gay with each other.' We discussed how ludicrous, even disastrous, use of this epithet to mean homosexual. I forgot to ask Sussman what the Dutch dentist said about Pepys, remembering afterwards that Mrs Pepys often suffered from toothache.

Thursday, 21 April

Michael Barber (whose sole distinction that his interview for *Paris Review* was put in, after four or five journalists before him had interviewed me for that periodical, then not published) came from *Books & Bookmen*. An uninspiring figure, to say the least. Like everyone else he had read *Wheel*, although the book is not yet published.

Sunday, 24 April

The Lomers (Dick & Patricia), who have bought Manor Farm, which lies in the hollow bordering us on south, came in for a drink. Lomer went into The

Coldstream during the war, then, I think, remained for time as a regular, leaving to become solicitor, having risen to rank of major, possibly Lieut. Colonel. Big, touch of Robin Mount (not the side of Robin like Ali Kilmarnock), perhaps a little like Whitelaw, the Home Secretary, in physical appearance. Badly wounded, still having lot of health trouble. Both seemed fairly all right. She on the surface more or less the usual army wife of the better kind. She is said to have American family affiliations. They have two sons, one in The Coldstream, at the moment at the Staff College, other doing oil research, on boats where the crew are tough, 'May have to use his fists,' Lomer said.

Wednesday, 27 April

Two Oxford undergraduates, Edward Whitley and David Cantor, endlessly badgered for interview for a book they were doing about Oxford, chiefly The Twenties. Undergraduate interviewers being without exception tedious, I told them they could not come. They continued to press, saying they were seeing everyone of my period at Oxford, royalties were to be given to charity (the Red Cross, something of the sort), so in the end I reluctantly agreed. After being told to arrive at 2.30, they did not turn up. Then one telephoned to say their car boiled, they would be late. Typical undergraduate behaviour. Eventually they appeared about 4.40 and were given tea. Whitley at St Catherine's; Cantor half American, educated in Switzerland; both doing their Finals this year.

They talked a bit about Oxford, then turned their attention to *Dance*, in which they seemed much more interested than Oxford in The Twenties. Whitely asked if it had been easier to write freely after the Chatterley Trial. I replied that was so to some small extent perhaps, especially so far as dialogue was concerned. Otherwise, I thought everything dealt with in the novel could have been expressed, no doubt in a less direct manner, but without missing anything. Whitely, more aggressive and stupider of the two, said: 'But you were quite pornographic before that.' I asked, with some surprise, what passages he had thought pornographic. He said: 'Well, your heroine had affairs with three or four men.' He had not only no idea of what writing was about (impossible to explain to him, which I tried), but he did not even know what commonly used words mean. They were also altogether unable to take in what they were told. Their manner was partly obsequious, partly immensely pleased with their own brilliance, heads stuffed with clichés, *idées reçues*. Really dreadful couple.

Tuesday, 3 May

Nigel Williams came to luncheon to talk about BBC projected Orwell programme. On the telephone he asked if he could bring his 'sister', who had a car, as his wife was using his own car. Tristram had said he knew and liked N. Williams, so when Tristram rang about something, I enquired if he knew anything of the sister. Tristram laughed a lot, and said it was his *'assistant'*. Nigel Williams turned out son of David Williams, who reviewed for the *Telegraph* (we once met in the office), and had just had stroke. [Died two days later.] I liked Nigel Wiliams (said to be Leftish).

It is a permanent mystery to persons who interview me about George Orwell as to why we got on well together. This is, I think, due to hopeless inflexibility of most relatively intelligent people's minds these days, especially those impregnated with Left Wing views, which seem to have a peculiarly stultifying effect in preventing them thinking out anything for themselves. Orwell was an example of the opposite; indeed not easy to describe to someone of a younger generation, so much debris by now accumulated round George, most of it misleading, if not positively incorrect. It was agreed that a good farce could be written round the confusion of 'sister' & 'assistant'. Nigel Williams, author of plays that have been performed, seemed nice bright young man, looking in physical appearance like a comic character in a school story.

Friday, 6 May

Roland Gant & Tom Rosenthal (both of Heinemann's), came to luncheon. My first view of Rosenthal. He is big, flamboyant clothes, quite unlike what I was prepared for, which was something rather on the lines of Weidenfeld (one of those publishers thought never to have read a book in his life). Rosenthal, on the other hand, is full of book-lore, and First Editions, on which he is very keen. He pointed out something I had never noticed, more likely long forgotten, that our Mellstock Edition of Thomas Hardy (bought by my father) is signed. Rosenthal was sent back to Westbury for his train in John's arriving taxi. Roland stayed on for tea, before proceeding to his Dorset hide-out. He brought advance copies of *Wheel* for inscriptions.

Tuesday, 10 May

David Cheshire, with a reduced camera crew, came to take a few additional shots for the programme, including my reading aloud from *Wheel*, a project now abandoned in favour of passages from *Dance*. One gradually develops grasp of special idiosyncrasies of camera crews, 'Sparks' the electrician being as a rule a particularly interesting individual study.

Saturday, 14 – Monday, 16 May

V & I stayed at Whitfield. Guests: John & Iris (Murdoch) Bayley; Mark & Anna (Ford) Boxer. Iris somewhat put out by reviews of her recently published novel *The Philosopher's Pupil*. These might have been thought not too bad, though one knows only too well that reviews look quite different to the author from the impression given to other writers, and the general public. Anna Boxer also disturbed having been sacked in her capacity as Anna Ford from TV/AM. In fact the Boxers were to see Lord Goodman on way back to London regarding alleged libel in this connexion. John Bayley & Mark Boxer both in good form, former one of the best, most sensible contemporary literary critics, often quite surprising in his immediate straightforward definition of the point about any given writer or book mentioned. Mark Boxer, well up in the arts, is much more interested in the power world, and money, although on the whole it is through the arts that he approaches the latter. I remember noticing this when I gave Mark dinner in the 1950s to involve him in *Punch*. Suki Marlow, who has a job on *The Spectator*, and of whom one heard a good deal in the past, another guest. At first I thought her charms rather overrated, but gradually fell under them and liked her very much. The younger Anna Ford, exceedingly pretty, humourless, preoccupied about her work, and her baby, putting up little competition in attraction.

Penelope Betjeman came to tea on Sunday. Her appearance slightly better now she is older, ear-piercing decibels, shattering egotism, unchanged, essence of the sort of buffoon, in this case clowness, the upper classes find amusing, indeed are devoted to. Mary, with V & I, drove Penelope back to her cottage at Cusop, where she lives alone, high on the uplands south of the Wye, looking across to Radnorshire, traditional Powell country for centuries of Llowes, Clyro, Brilley. Enjoyable visit.

Wednesday, 18 May

A Billy Bunter-like character, Jeremy Beadle, came to talk about the Oxford dissertation he is writing for a doctorate on *Dance*. He was recommended by John Bayley, who says Beadle just missed a Fellowship. Nothing much emerged. He knew the books well. Later I saw a photograph about an apparently well-known comedian called Jeremy Beadle, which I sent to John Bayley.

Saturday, 21 May

Stockwells came down. Tristram & Virginia dined. Virginia had attended the Jamie Maclean/Sarah Jansen wedding on the Jugoslav island of Korculla, where a slap-up four-day party was laid on by the Jugs in memory of Fitzroy Maclean's successful efforts during the war to persuade Churchill to ditch Mihailovitch (Resistance leader) and support Tito's Communist Partisans, a very dubious business. Fitzroy Maclean himself was there, wearing Croat-type hat (not particularly appropriate, it might be thought, in the light of Croatian anti-Communist nationalism, tho' style perhaps now regarded as Partisan headgear). Maclean was greatly enjoying this afterglow of local prestige, and showing off. Interesting that a Communist Government should have thought a beano of this sort worth mounting for eighty smart London guests. One still wonders whether British policy as to Tito was really wise; also why Fitzroy Maclean seems to be allowed, for instance, to travel more or less where he likes in the Soviet Union. He is in short a mysterious figure one way and another. Virginia found it all pretty awful, and was glad to get home. She took some notably funny photographs. V tried cooking braised lamb from Arabella Boxer's recipe, great success; Chianti Classico Castell'in Villa, '78, went well.

Monday, 23 May

Bob Boscawen, our MP, came to do pre-Election whistle-stop tour of Chantry, neighbourhood. After we had supported him with our presence when he spoke at Bullen Mead housing-estate in the village, V dropped me off at our gate, or rather just opposite. I stayed for the Boscawen car to pass, which was just behind us. I was waving goodbye when Boscawen stopped. He said: 'Something I've wanted to tell you for ages – I'm trustee of the Widmerpool estate in Nottinghamshire.' Apparently the Widmerpool estate belongs now to heirs of Lady Bristol. Bob Boscawen said a word or two about this. Some of the cars behind were in his own entourage, others not. The latter became an ever increasing queue and began to hoot. Bob treated these with complete disregard, continuing to talk about Widmerpool (subject to which I never supposed he had devoted much thought), an imperturbability showing how he had won MC and could support turmoil of House of Commons.

Thursday, 2 June

Charles Nevin, Mandrake of the *Sunday Telegraph*, came to luncheon for

Guest List for Anthony Powell Lunch
Tuesday 7th June 1983

Literary Editors, critics

Anthony Curtis – Financial Times
Derwent May – The Listener
Peter Grosvenor – Daily Express
Suki Marlow – *The* Spectator

Friends, booktrade etc

Alison Lurie
Mr & Mrs Conquest
Barbara Ker-Seymer
Lady Antonia Pinter
Jilly & Leo Cooper
Mark Boxer
Dorothy Olding – Harold Ober Associates
Bruce Hunter – David Higham Associates
Donald MacFarlan – Penguin
John & Hilary Spurling
John Saumarez Smith – Heywood Hill bookshop
Simon Bainbridge – Hatchards bookshop
Julian Jebb – BBC

Heinemann

Tom Rosenthal
Charles Pick
Roland Gant
Tim Manderson
Brian Perman
Jane Turnbull
Steven Williams

Anthony Powell's Speech at Heinemann Lunch, 10 Upper Grosvenor Street.

Tom Rosenthal has been very kind. This party makes me think of the occasion when a Salvation Army girl rattled a collecting-box in front of Sir George Sitwell, with the words: 'Self-Denial Week.'

Sir George – rather a notably selfish man – did not hesitate for a moment in his reply. As he walked on he said quietly: 'For some people every week is Self-Denial Week!'

I think it must be Self-Denial Week every week for the Directors and Staff of Heinemann's once more to lay on so enjoyable a luncheon for a book of mine.

I should like to take this opportunity of saying a word about book jackets. I am delighted with the appearance of Barbara Ker-Seymer's picture on my own book, which really does look like a girl from The Twenties, not one of the awful travesties of the looks and clothes of that period which are peddled in pictures and on the media.

The more down to earth side of The Twenties is shown in the photograph on the jacket of my wife's biography of Margaret Kennedy that appears in a couple of weeks. That picture suggests The Twenties very well too – in a way that is nearer to the knuckle, if that is the right phrase.

– Finally, I was fortunate enough the other day to pick up for a mere song a First Folio of *Hamlet*. The copy had been overlooked on the shelves of a bookseller – I won't mention which one as several booksellers are present.

The particular interest in this copy is that the text shows certain variations on what is usually to be read or acted. Let me give you an example:

Queen Gertrude says:

> 'Welcome, dear Rosenthal and Gantenstern,
> Moreover that we did much long to see you,
> The need we have to use you did provoke
> Our hasty sending.'

I think this points very clearly to the fact that the Queen had written a novel she wanted published. I have no doubt the Shakespeare experts will suggest this new reading is a forgery, but they may find some difficulty in proving that. It looks genuine enough to me. In any case I will give no opinion. I merely echo King Claudius's words, those which follow close on the Queen's:

> 'Thanks Gantenstern, and gentle Rosenthal.'

interview; gave impression of rather run-of-the-mill journalist. In the event did a friendly piece.

Monday, 6 June

Andrew Lynch requested an interview for a Bristol paper. He turned up with another young man, Nicholas Patterson, to drive him over. Both at Bristol University. Lynch, in fact, asked for the interview on spec to sell to two Bristol papers. He is doing a dissertation on *Dance* (War Trilogy) and seemed reasonably intelligent. He wanted to be journalist on the editorial side, preferably not in London. His father is a retired RAOC officer. Desire to be a journalist out of London seems growing tendency; interesting.

Tuesday, 7 June

We went to London for Heinemann's luncheon party for *Wheel*, given at 10 Upper Grosvenor Street, publishing premises which in general I prefer to a restaurant. We arrived about 11.30. I was interviewed by Anthony Cheevers for Radio 4, then talked with Roland Gant, while V signed copies of her Margaret Kennedy book, which also comes out at the end of month. About twenty-eight people at lunch, including Bob & Liddie Conquest, Barbara Ker-Seymer (who designed the *Wheel* jacket), Antonia Pinter, John & Hilary Spurling, Jilly & Leo Cooper, Suki Marlow, Julian Jebb, together with Literary Editors and business characters of various sorts. Alison Lurie & Dorothy Olding (my US agent) turning out to be in London by chance, also came. I sat between Hilary Spurling & Jane Turnbull of Heinemann's (where she does paperbacks, fixing me up satisfactorily with Donald MacFarlan of Penguin, also present). She is a pretty girl, with whom I discussed possibilities of Collection of my journalism, project on which, in fact, I have hitherto never been very keen. The party went well, the food a bit odd. Mark Boxer had no pudding, because Antonia, sitting next to him, brushed pudding aside, as if Mark, her little boy, was not allowed any either.

Thursday, 9 June

Day of the Election. Have voted at a mobile polling booth by Whatley Church. They are always charming people in charge. In the afternoon Duncan Fallowell came to interview for *Time Out*, something arranged through Heinemann. I told Fallowell I knew little or nothing of *Time Out*, and thought the paper did not have features like literary interviews. He replied that was true, the Editor (or Literary Editor) is a fan of mine. This is the first Fallowell knew of such an assignment. He said *Time Out* was a Left paper, intended to take the place of now intellectually collapsed *New Statesman*. Fallowell seemed reasonably intelligent, greatly pleased with himself, perhaps fairly well off. He talked of living some of the time in the South of France, where his parents have a house.

Tuesday, 14 June

Max Hastings rang up to ask for an interview for the *Standard*. He is coming to luncheon tomorrow. He was followed soon after by Alison Lurie, also invited. In the afternoon a photographer, Mervyn Gilliam, came from Bristol to take photographs for the *Standard* article. He turned out to be a great cat fan, possessing two Siamese, who would jump from his shoulder to his wife's. Trelawney was less intolerant of him than of most photographers, allowing a brief picture.

Wednesday, 15 June

Max Hastings lunched here for an interview. I did not know he did that sort of journalism and had never before met him. Years ago he put all the Penguin row in the *Evening Standard* (I think that was the paper), rather to the horror of his stepfather, Osbert Lancaster. Hastings is big, heavily bespectacled, with a booming manner. We talked about his Falklands reporting, where he had been war-correspondent. He said the army had treated the whole affair rather like the Royal Tournament, but no doubt that would have changed somewhat had things gone on long. After Max Hastings left, Alison Lurie (at one moment coming to luncheon, then altered her plans) turned up on her way back from staying with Diana Melly (wife of George Melly) in Wales. Alison had hired a car in Bath. She talked of her new novel about an American who believes himself descended from a hermit employed to give authenticity to an 18th century English grotto. Apparently Frome is actually mentioned, so identification will not be difficult. I have explained that, although hermits are said to have been employed in that manner, and period, our own grottoes are *c.* 1840, this making no impression. Alison was in good form, she has a flat in Randolph Avenue, Maida Vale, shared with another American writer, Diane Johnson (books about George Meredith's wife and Dashiell Hammett). We discussed advantages, and disadvantages, of publishing collected journalism, the sort of subject upon which Alison's views are worth hearing.

Thursday, 16 June

Nigel Williams, with camera crew, arrived to do BBC/TV George Orwell interview. This (after blowing several bulbs) seemed to go pretty well. Nigel Williams knew (surprising in an interviewer) what I had written about George, which makes things much easier for leading questions. Interviewers more often than not are wholly ignorant on such background stuff. It turned out that a man from Canadian Radio (having, as he admitted, read none of my Memoirs about Orwell, only Bernard Crick's biography) had also been pestering Nigel Williams. Crick remarked when he lunched here that he could not imagine how Orwell and I had ever been friends, which was routine. His biography covered a good deal of ground.

Saturday, 18 June

Tony & Marcelle Quinton to dinner (Tony had been handing out prizes, something of the kind, at Taunton School). They arrived sharp at 4 pm, when conversation began hammer-and-tongs and did not cease until they left at 10 o'clock. We drank Rosenthal's magnum of Pontet-Canet, '70, which he had given us, good if not staggering. Tony Quinton spoke of reviewing A. J. P. Taylor's autobiography; he felt Taylor was a 'base man'. Among many other things we talked of recent biography of Matthew Arnold by American called Honan. I suggested:

> Professor Honan
> Rarely if ever committed the sin of Onan;
> When he felt at all carnal
> He concentrated on Matthew Arnal.

Enjoyable evening.

Sunday, 26 June

We lunched with Joff & Tessa Davies, who had a lot of young people staying at Whatley House for a nuptial ball, including our gt-nephew Benjie Fraser, Antonia's son, who looks exactly like his father, now working for a paper on The Borders. I sat on Tessa's right, her daughter Mary Anne on my right. Halfway through luncheon, while I was talking to Tessa, Mary Anne was exchanged, without my noticing, for Evgenia Citkowitz, daughter of Caroline Blackwood/Freud/Citkowitz/Lowell's second marriage. I thought Mary Anne looked oddly changed when I turned to her, then fell into complete cross-purposes about her getting a job at the Foreign Office. When this was sorted out Evgenia Citkowitz revealed as attractive. She has musical interests, and is about to study drama in New York. She had just been seeing Cressida Connolly, whom she described as very intelligent.

Evgenia Citkowitz had also seen Cressida Connolly's mother Deirdre, and stepfather Peter Levi, whose marriage she reported as doing all right. On the opposite side of table was a tycoon Rudolph Agnew (Consolidated Goldfields and several quarries), and James Pilditch, who told V her autobiography was the best he had ever read; he was also a fan of mine. Joff Davies did not know what Pilditch did, but said he received CBE in the Birthday Honours.

In the evening we watched final instalment of *Brideshead* on the second round. It does not stand up well. The book itself never strikes a suitable mean between a Disraelian romance and a serious novel. This was emphasized in the film. Apart from innumerable period anachronisms, clothes, speech and behaviour, there is an inherent failure to depict upper-class life with any real flavour. Various points: if Mottram were the successful ambitious tycoon-politician represented in the novel (excellently played in the film, one of the best), why was it worth his while to rent a mansion like Castle Howard for his wife & her lover (both poorly played) to live in, apparently never making use of the place himself? How much better if Lord Marchmain really had been in exile for say homosexuality or something of the sort and Sebastian a *pratiquant* queer. That would have made sense, giving the narrative the sinister slant promised at first, the disaster to Flyte family threatened by Blanche but then never brought about.

If Ryder, presented as an obscure young man making his way as a painter, had contracted a smart marriage, then abandoned his wife, Lady Celia, to live with Lady Julia Flyte openly for two years (she being the famous deb described earlier in the book) the whole affair would have been notorious, resulting in all sorts of special circumstances as to their friends and the gossip columns. The idea of men kissing in public – let alone a hetero and homo – would have been unthinkable at that period.

In short the TV version was in many ways disastrous from any point of view as art. Evelyn himself seems latterly to have felt that about the book too. The failure is due really to its insincerities. Good actors, as well as those mentioned above were Anthony Blanche (first-rate), Mr Samgrass (tho' an All Souls don would hardly have taken on the job of being keeper of a drunk), the German légionnaire loved by Sebastian, Bridey (a difficult part very well done), Cordelia (not bad, too pretty), her part could well have been played by the actress who did well as Lord Marchmain's hospital nurse. Lady Celia Ryder (Jane Asher) also well done. Hooper also not too badly cast – in fact the actor (not altogether unlike Evelyn) who played Hooper might have made a more convincing Charles Ryder, as a young painter rising in the social world. I suggest again:

> Hooper
> Never took out a subscription to BUPA
> Accordingly, when years later being treated inside a
> National Health Hospital, he was cut by the (then impoverished)
>   Charles Ryder.

Friday, 7 July

V & I attended Maidie Hollis's Requiem Mass at the RC church in Frome, a building of unusual hideosity. Her son Sam Hollis, an RC priest, took the service, other lay Hollis brothers to some extent participating. At a latish stage of the rites, disturbance was caused by dwarfish figure, who appeared to have entered the church by chance, doing Stations of the Cross on his knees, without regard for ceremony taking place. Afterwards we had a word with Mia Woodruff (widow of Douglas Woodruff, the author) who seems to be holding up pretty well.

Sunday, 10 July

Bibsy & Lennie Colt, daughter and son-in-law of Arthur & Rosemary Mizener [Arthur an old friend, biographer of Scott Fitzgerald and Ford Madox Ford], came to luncheon. We had only once met Bibsy, twenty or more years before, with her parents, dining at The Garrick. She had then for some reason been in very poor form and hardly spoke. She is now quite jolly, also her husband, who is in the packaging industry, his family understood to be more than comfortably off. Bibsy gave up university to get married. She is working for doctorate on the subject of *Dance*. We went round the lake. Bibsy has neat figure like her mother, and resembles both her parents; Lennie, tall, bespectacled, not without humour. His mother, a Borden, must have been fairly closely related to the Lady of the Axe. [Bibsy Colt subsequently sent a copy of her dissertation, which among other things stated that Russell Gwinnett was an entirely unbelievable American type. I had, in fact, received several favourable American fan letters on that subject, including one from a septuagenarian academic, saying a compatriot exactly like Gwinnett had come his way.]

Wednesday, 13 July

Frederick & Judith Tomlin looked in for a drink before they lunched with the Lomers at Manor Farm, Judith Tomlin (second wife) is old friend of Patricia Lomer's. Frederick Tomlin head of the British Council in Japan, when I was there in 1964, made himself most agreeable while taking me round. His first wife went off with an Italian general, it is said. Frederick married the present one eight or nine years ago. She seemed nice, bright, a general's daughter, so keeping up association with that rank; Patricia Lomer also daughter of a general. Frederick, philosopher of some standing; said that he reviewed philosophical books for *The Economist* anonymously, which sounded rather bleak. They both seemed in good shape.

Sunday, 17 July

Juliet O'Rorke, her daughter Sarah and son-in-law John Letts (Folio Books), came to luncheon . . . Juliet now eighty, really didn't look too bad (not without touch of my mother's sister, Aunt Vi); in all than physical respects totally unchanged. This jaunt had been fixed for her as a birthday treat. We had not met for at least forty years. Juliet, very affectionate, nearly burst into tears when we were alone together, the others having gone down to the lake, and she deplored not having kept up with her painting. She certainly ought to have done, as she had a considerable talent as illustrator and decorative artist. She is now gt-grandmother. Sarah is nice, a slightly Augustus Johnish female-type appearance; appropriate in the light of her mother's drawings. Lett seemed a sensible, hard-headed publisher.

Wednesday, 20 July

We watched *The Beggar's Opera* on TV, a good example of contemporary lack of taste, totally missing the point by assuming that certain aspects of supposed realism and sexuality are all important. The opera was theoretically set in a Dickensian 19th century; perfectly admissible so far as that went (tho' one can't see why any change necessary), nevertheless some characters were dressed in three-cornered hats, clothes *ca.* 1730; others as far forward as 1880. The point was rammed home that morals of high society were no better than those of highwaymen and whores, while Gay's satirical insistence that highwaymen and whores at the same time aped the manners of high society, was altogether lost. Polly should have a genuine touch of youthful innocence to give her meaning; instead was played by actress got up as a middle-aged tart, while Peachum (played as Irish) was not nearly sinister enough. Macheath talked in lower-class way, which would have been all right had he attempted a gentlemanly accent, while the essential deference shown him by the gang was never properly indicated. So anxious was the producer to emphasize the whores' dirty underclothes etc, not to mention one of them being then more or less had on the stage by Macheath, that mutual refinement of compliments between whores and Macheath was completely lost. No one could sing with much talent, the tunes were reduced to a minimal number. The performance was of interest as showing the disastrous effect of understandable reaction from playing Gay's characters as Dresden china figures (which the superb 1920 Lovat Fraser production at the Lyric, Hammersmith, at times risked) and in going the way of so much modern disregard of form, historical ignorance, contempt for the past, and love of explicit sex at any price. [Some little time later Jonathan Miller also did a version of *The Beggar's Opera* I thought so good that I wrote him a fan letter. I am far from keen on Miller's productions as a rule, finding his *Alice in Wonderland*, and *Whistle and I'll Come to You* both quite awful. In this case Macheath, played by former pop-singer Roger Daltrey, was much nearer the mark.]

Sunday, 24 July

Fram Dinshaw & Rebecca Fraser looked in for a drink on way back from staying with the Hobhouses at Hadspen. Fram very lively. Talking of the recently published Cyril Connolly *Journal*, he said he hoped in thirty years' time Deirdre (formerly Connolly, now Levi) would leave him the Connolly papers, so that he could write a full biography. That would certainly be appropriate, as Fram Dinshaw was in College at Eton. When I first met Dinshaw as Secretary of the Eton Literary Society (or whatever it is called), Cyril Connolly introduced us, saying I must come down to speak to them, which I did.

The occasion was when various Etonian writers had been asked there for an Exhibition of MSS, in School Library, which the Queen Mother opened. A long time afterwards her Private Secretary, Martin Gilliat, told me that when they had driven up to School Library largish group of boys were standing just outside Weston's Yard. Gilliat was rather surprised at this, as royalty were to large extent taken for granted, owing to the proximity of Windsor. He was even more so when some sort of scuffle took place as carriage drove past, a piece of canvas apparently being rolled up. It transpired later the plan had been on foot to unfurl a banner saying: GOOD QUEEN MUM, SACK MCCRUM (the Head Master). At the last moment hearts failed among those organizing the demonstration. Rebecca seemed a little triste, this country perhaps rather flat after the excitements of the US. Fram said Cressida Connolly is exactly like her father in behaviour; her brother Matthew, on the other hand, is absolutely silent.

Sunday, 31 July

When Andrew Motion lunched here he said he was sharing a cottage at Brixton Deverell, a few miles away, so we thought we might ask him and his partner to luncheon. There was some excitement to see who arrived. Georgie Hammick (author, *People for Lunch* etc) turned out a very personable lady of about forty, living apart from her husband with two or three children, the eldest twenty. Andrew Motion is now 'poetry editor' at Chatto's, where he also does certain amount of routine publishing work. For his book on the Lambert Family he has included an interview with the daughter of the black cigarette-girl (just dcd) at The Nest, with whom Constant had an affair (indeed took her to Toulon), with view to investigating whether the former might be Constant's daughter. That she undoubtedly was not, he established. Andrew was also going to Australia to look into George Lambert's life there, then to New York for material about Kit Lambert. The story of these three generations is a remarkable one. I think Andrew will do it well. He reported that Philip Larkin was having a rough time. His girlfriend Monica Jones is suffering from shingles in the head. Monica has now moved in with Larkin, something never allowed before.

Larkin, one of the most selfish men on earth, now spends all his time running up and down stairs with 'plates of warmed up spaghetti'. This should produce poems, one might think. Andrew had also been to Faringdon to collect Berners material about Constant. The house is now owned by The Mad Boy (Robert Heber-Percy) to whom it was left by Berners. The Mad Boy's boyfriend is a sinister ex-Nazi, grumpy about bringing in tea. Faringdon itself apparently remains unaltered from the days of Berners, doves dyed mauve and wonderful pictures. T. S. Eliot's *Collected Letters* are said to be nearing completion. Enjoyable party.

Saturday, 13 August

Lunched with the Spurlings at their holiday cottage (a highly modernized cowshed) on the Dorset property of friends, a painter John Hubbard & his wife. Other guests were Francis Greene, son of Graham Greene, & Francis Greene's wife Anne. I had not seen Francis Greene since his father asked me to put his son up for The Travellers. Accordingly Greene *fils* lunched with me at the Club some years ago. Then I thought him rather a formidable young man, not at all easy to talk to. When I tried to make conversation about his father, he burst out: 'I hardly know my father.' The only subject he seemed able to delve into was various journeys recently made by him abroad in relatively obscure places. I said (making the assumption on these travels combined with fact that he wanted to become a member of The Travellers, great Foreign Office Club) 'I presume you are going into MI6?' He went crimson, but did not answer. He now has a beard (possibly false?), evidently regards himself as rather a card. His speech, manner, fantastically like his father's tho' certainly true he can have seen little of Graham in early life. Francis Greene, & his wife (rather artily dressed, seemed quite nice) appear to be renovating an Elizabethan house as occupation (perhaps a professional spy's 'cover'). Greene *fils* had the air of expecting to be recognized as a wit, but volunteered no great display of brillance. He refused to be photographed, no doubt another habit entrenched in Secret Service.

Hilary's second Ivy Compton-Burnett volume is to be published next spring. My godson, Gilbert Spurling, is an attractive little boy, other Spurling children seemed nice too, tho' we did not see much of them.

Sunday, 14 August

Jilly & Leo Cooper (who now live in house also called The Chantry at Bisley, Gloucestershire) came to luncheon with the Mayalls. Jilly Cooper is funny, intelligent, not quite like anyone else, least of all other ladies who do her sort of journalism. Leo Cooper, a rugger/cricket-playing publisher, militarily orientated, both professionally and in personal taste. Mary Mayall enchanted Jilly Cooper by saying: 'A priest stayed with the Betjemans, and when he left they found spunk all over his sheets.'

Monday, 15 August

V & I lunched with David Cecil at Red Lion House, Cranborne. David in good form, missing several teeth in front, which gives him a somewhat piratical appearance. Characteristic of him not to have this put right. We talked of Bloomsbury, with which he had fairly close contacts, anyway through Rachel's parents, the Desmond MacCarthys. David made the point that the Bloomsburys, 'although having a quite unjustified contempt for everyone else, did not in fact get on at all well with each other, or only to an extremely limited extent. What they individually knew about was quite different.'

Sunday, 28 August

Driven by John, we lunched with Vidia & Pat Naipaul at their new house, Dairy Cottage, Salterton, near Salisbury. It is a few miles from where they formerly lived on the Wilsford estate owned by Stephen Tennant, eccentric, artistic brother of Lord Glenconner. Wilsford is an Elizabethan-style manor house built in the early 1900s, with various outbuildings, including tiny house occupied by the Naipauls (no doubt arranged through Christopher & Elizabeth Glenconner). Atmosphere of Wilsford, surroundings, very odd, like walking in a dream. Stephen Tennant himself never appeared in public view, as if a character in gothick novel; once in a way sending Vidia a note by hand.

V said Dairy Cottage like the dolls' house in Beatrix Potter's *Tale of Two Bad Mice*. Other guests: Vidia's (female) German translator; his agent, Gillon Aitken and Swedish wife, the latter for some reason (unlike most Scandinavians) difficult to talk to. The Aitkens were perhaps in middle of a matrimonial row. He recently had his licence removed for drunk-in-charge, and there had been some car trouble on way down. Aitken himself seemed pleasant. He started life at Chapman & Hall's in days when Evelyn Waugh was briefly on the firm's board. Vidia was in good form, funny in his best manner about the Pakistan writer called Salman Rushdie (who won Booker Prize), and said something disobliging about Vidia in *Harpers & Queen*, or similar periodical: '. . . I'm sorry . . . I'm very sorry to hear that . . . No respect for his elders . . . He will learn that sort of thing is a mistake . . . People merely think . . .' All perfectly true. I haven't read any of Rushdie's books, but he sounds an ass from interviews. Vidia produced nice red Graves. Pat looked rather harassed, as indeed she probably is. Later read two novels by Rushdie, my instinct correct, characteristic of particular sort of successful bad writing.

Sunday, 4 September

Lunched with Anthony & Tanya Hobson for Anthony's birthday (in fact tomorrow). Other guests Robin Campbell, with his third wife Susan. Robin Campbell (son of ambassador) started life in Reuter's. He first married Mary Ormsby-Gore (now Mary Mayall), had a dashing war career with the Commandos (raided Rommel's HQ, lost a leg, DSO). He left Mary Ormsby-Gore for (Lady) Mary Erskine (then wife of Philip Dunn, newspaper tycoon, a rather awful school contemporary of mine. She is always referred to as 'Lady Mary' by Mary Mayall, a mere Hon.). Robin Campbell became a painter for a time (encouraged by Cyril Connolly), and got job on the Arts Council, then marriage with Mary Erskine bust up, and he married this present wife (art student, I think), good deal younger than him. Campbell himself now somnolent, chastened, well disposed, wants a quiet life; present wife must be admitted to have made good job of dealing with Robin Campbell as a husband. They live in Lymington, she is still doing some sort of work in London. One felt, after all these glamorous wives, and a gallant war career, it was all a bit like Kipling's Troop Sergeant Major, 'whose wife must go charing, and he commissaring', except that Robin Campbell seems to have signed off work, rather than getting a job as a commissionaire, with a limp, covered with medals. William Hobson, now at Lady Margaret Hall (I still get a shock when men are at women's colleges, girls at men's), a nice boy, moderate Mohican haircut; their daughter Emma, very pretty, in Sidgwick & Jackson. Tanya not looking too bad, considering she has been having a rough time with her health. As usual excellent wine, including Corton '70.

Anthony gave an account of his relations with Arthur Waley, Chinese & Japanese literature, a Bloomsbury figure Anthony knew at an early stage through skiing life. Apparently the description given by Mrs Waley (whom Waley married right at the end of his life) of her husband appearing on a snowy peak, and skiing swiftly down to the railway station, where she had just arrived by train, is utterly grotesque. Waley's skiing was no more than utilitarian in skill, without the least style, the railway station quite unapproachable from the mountains. Anthony Hobson comes into Mrs Waley's book, tho' not by name. As a keen bibliographer, he went to see Waley to get some books signed by him, which made Mrs Waley very cross. 'I should sign them Mickey Mouse,' she said. Waley, in his high snubbing Bloomsbury tone, replied 'I don't think that funny.' One can hear Waley saying the words. Mrs Waley also wrote that the Anthony Hobson-figure in her book, and whoever was with him, were shown into 'the library'; later some of the books were missing. Anthony says he did not even know Waley had a library, much less was he taken to see it, nor did he remove any of the books.

Saturday, 10 September

V, John & I dined at short notice with Joff & Tessa Davies at Whatley House. Joff (Godfrey) Davies, chemical-engineer, something of a tycoon, whose work was largely in Persia & the Far East; Tessa, very attractive, 20 or more years younger than husband, is daughter of one of two heiresses of Butler & Tanner, Frome printers, firm of which Joff Davies is now a director. The Davieses had suddenly been confronted with having to give dinner to the Fleet Street figure, Harold Evans (ex-editor of the *Sunday Times*, *Times*, etc), whose 200,000-word book is being printed by Butler & Tanner. He came down to supervise this, which was being done in some secrecy, because contents thought likely to cause trouble, especially in relation to Rupert Murdoch, Fleet Street magnate, proprietor of *The Times*. Murdoch might apply for an injunction, if he had access to Harold Evans's book. The Davieses had never set eyes on Evans, and asked us to dine as only suitably clued-up neighbours they could get hold of at 24-hrs notice.

Harold Evans obviously astonished – delighted – to find us there, evidently expecting something rurally stodgy. I think I may have shaken hands with him in the past at some function, as his face was slightly familiar, but had no recollection of occasion. He wanted to talk about Cyril Connolly (known during *Sunday Times* period), Waugh, Orwell, &c. a chance he probably doesn't often get. Evans is now connected with Goldcrest Films. He enquired about *Dance* & TV. I recited its many ups & downs in the sphere. Evans said his company would certainly be interested. One has seen too much of this sort of thing to expect a great deal. All the same occasion was so strange, Evans showed such excitement about meeting, that there seemed at least a possibility of opening up negotiations again. Also present was a Weidenfeld 'editor', Miss Alex McCormack, a high-powered lady, formerly with Penguin, who has apparently thought of setting up her own publishing house. I exchanged a lot of publishing shop with her.

Evans is a small foxy, intensely lively figure from Manchester, said his grandfather from North Wales, Welsh speaking, illiterate. (Joff Davies's family also from North Wales, his father vicar of Bexhill, and bridge and motoring correspondent of some high-powered paper.)

Talking of cooking, Evans said his first wife was a good cook, his second, Tina Brown (now editing *The Tatler*) did not even know what a shop was, much less able to buy food at one, or cook it. The name of Dennis Potter & Ken Trodd came up in connexion with their running out on *Dance* TV project, the Potter episode, indeed, having buggered up the whole prospect of TV production of *Dance*. An unexpectedly amusing evening. Nice dinner with '71 claret, Château of which I did not get.

Thursday, 15 September

We lunched with Dick and Patricia Lomer. To list the occupants of Manor Farm since we have been here: the octogenarian farmer, Ernie Moore (with Arthur Perry of Orr Farm, model for Mr Gauntlett in *Dance*), in whose day the interior of house looked as if not been touched since, at latest, 17th century, ceilings about to collapse at any moment, lots of little rooms leading into each other. Ernie Moore had considerable charm, at the same time rather bogus old fellow, playing up as Hardyesque stage farmer all the time, quaint language,

Breton plates on walls, etc. Not as truly delightful as Mr Perry. When Ernie
Moore died, Manor Farm was left between several heirs, one in Australia, left
empty for some years and became a real ruin. The fine front door was stolen. A
young surveyor, Roger Wolstenholme, bought the property in spite of some
obscurity as to whom it belonged, and lived there with his newly married wife.
They did a remarkable job renovating the place. The Wolstenholmes then
moved away, and Manor Farm was bought by an unusual ménage, a married
couple named Flint, the husband spending much of his time in Saudi Arabia,
and a friend called Ford, who had developed some tropical disease in Africa.
Ford had been pensioned off by his firm, and lived with Flints. Ford, mostly in
a wheelchair, could drive a car, spent much of his time fishing in the pond there
from a kind of tractor.

It struck me Ford might be The Fisher King, a myth I have always found
interesting. I also had the idea of writing about a man in a wheelchair (novel or
play), germinating from John Hayward, T. S. Eliot's friend, and a bibliographer; and the crowd of pretty women who always surrounded Hayward
at parties. One might somehow combine this with the Fisher King myth.

Manor Farm, which I should judge is at latest 15th century in origin, may
well be earlier. Researches in books about the neighbourhood produced
nothing; Somerset seems badly served in such respects. One theory: that house
was loosely called The Manor locally (although strictly speaking the
Domesday Manor would have been Whatley, where the Manor still exists, a
farm with a fine ancient archway). Then, when the building below us began to
decay, the word 'farm' was added. This breaks down, because early maps
show the house below us simply called Stoney Lane Farm, which is reasonable,
because a 'manor farm' would have a manor attached, and Chantry has no
manor. Neither Chantry, nor Little Elm (which it was formerly called) were
manors. At some stage someone must have named the house that, tho' one
would hardly think it was Ernie Moore. There is a curious sense of peace one is
aware of in the valley. As you reach the foot of the hill, after the small grotto,
just before coming to the lake, this atmosphere of quiet sweeps over you. I have
often spoken of it to V.

Sunday, 18 September

The Stockwells have Jamie & Sarah (née Jansen) Maclean staying at The
Stables. All came up for a drink in the morning. The Macleans are recently
married, Sarah an attractive *jolie laide*. They have bought a Folly on the
Stourhead estate, a few miles from here. Jamie is a friend of John's. He runs a
picture gallery with apparent success. The Folly was previously inhabited by a

naval officer who drank several thousand bottles of wine every year, at least a thousand empties having been already removed as a start to cleaning up. The Folly was nearly taken by the late Robin Fedden, expert on Middle East archaeology, as a love-nest.

Thursday, 22 September

V & I went on a long planned visit to Clevedon Court, the Eltons' house (Tennyson used to stay, his close friend Arthur Henry Hallam's mother being an Elton, and so did many other noted Victorians). We first visited the church on the cliffs, but were unable to gain access to see Hallam's grave within. (On looking up Hallam after returning home I found he was for a time an assistant master at Eton, an Eton beak makes him seem quite different. He had Lincolnshire origins like Tennyson.) We lunched on fish and chips at a fairly horrible glorified pub near the sea. Clevedon town is now large, and abundantly unattractive. Clevedon Court, a short way out, opened at 2.30 pm. Twenty or more persons were already waiting to get in when we arrived.

The house dates back to the Conquest, now mostly late medieval, the Victorian wing having been pulled down. A fine Great Hall with gallery chapel, family portraits, all pretty low grade. One was of Arthur Elton, father of present baronet, by Eve Disher (1933), its style somewhat in the manner of Wyndham Lewis. Arthur Elton, about my age, big, blond (Left Wing, documentary films, railways), was more or less rescued by Eve Disher, a delightful person, but tiny in size who looked after him, as she did many others (she was left Paul Cross's picture collection), in this case living with Elton for a dozen years or more. Elton then married a pretty Canadian-Icelandic girl who made a success of it (which did her great credit), Eve remaining a close friend of the family. The Eltons looked after Eve in now extreme old age (eighty-seven or eight, I think). The House was deeply gloomy, the grounds only just kept going in reasonable state, the motor-way making deafening row all the time as it hurtles past the gates. I had imagined 'Break, break, break' written here; on the contrary, written in Lincolnshire. Interesting jaunt.

Saturday, 24 September

After various attempts to lunch here last year, unsuccessful because trains did not fit in, and they did not command a car, John Russell & his third wife, Rosamond, were due to come to tea, then said they would not be along until 6 o'clock. Peggy, as she was then called, first appeared here twenty-five years ago or more as the wife of a Frenchman named Georges Bernier, with whom she edited a rather good art magazine *L'Oeil*. She is now known as Rosamond and involved in John Russell's various art activities, lecturing, etc. She never draws breath. When she came here before, the Berniers were brought by Sonia (Orwell). Sonia was then married to Michael Pitt-Rivers, living at King John's House, Rushmore, where Cyril Connolly was also staying. Rosamond Russell (then Peggy Bernier) said when they went back to London after that weekend Connolly insisted she must dine with him, as he was feeling depressed. I said, 'I bet you paid.' She said, 'You've guessed the point of my story. We went to the most expensive place, and when the bill came . . .' She had been editress (perhaps assistant-editress) of *Vogue* in London about 1947, when she first met Sonia. She has an odd superficial resemblance to Madge Garland, also a former *Vogue* editress. John Russell, in not at all bad form. He clearly likes living in the US, where his all-purpose coverage of Art & Letters must go down well. He told me that an (unnamed) American bibliographer of eminence had said my talents were such that I had written a very proficient detective story about fifty years ago in the manner of Agatha Christie. John Russell denied this. $50 was bet. The book turned out to be *What's Become of Waring* (1939). John Russell paid up as he had forgotten the plot. I agreed that was being over scrupulous.

John (Powell) had Maggie & Guillaume de Rougemont staying at The Stables. We dined there; excellent dinner, largely cooked by Guillaume, who instructed me in adding small bits of bacon when doing fried potatoes. He was amusing about K. (Lord) Clark, married to his (Guillaume's) de Janzé aunt (daughter of Freddy de Janzé & Alice Silverthorne, then his wife, American, who shot, subsequently married, Raymond de Trafford). K. Clark himself, just before he died, was in favour of his female American biographer whom others deplore. Maggie is a literary agent. There was some question of her joining Higham's, but they are departmentalized and she likes dealing with all aspects of her clients' work. The Rougemonts came to drinks on Sunday morning with Henry, a nice child, now aged two.

Thursday, 29 September

About ten years ago Z (H. D. Ziman, Literary Editor of the *Daily Telegraph*), former Hypocrites Club member at Oxford (in his fourth year when I came up) arranged for me to meet an American publisher friend, Ken Giniger, who wanted to discuss a picture-book illustrating *Dance*, paintings mentioned, period photographs, etc. At the time I thought this project premature, as the sequence itself was not yet finished. Giniger is now back to the charge, lunched

Anne Scott-James (left),
photographed in 1939. Above, her
celebrated husband Osbert
Lancaster. Anne did 'a magnificent
job looking after Osbert who is
completely impossible these days'.

Planting an oak tree on V's 70th
birthday, 13 March 1982.

V on terrace at The Chantry.

AP with Evangeline Bruce, the
'slightly mysterious, perfect
ambassadress'.

Hugh Lloyd-Jones, 'all that a
don should be', at The Chantry
with his wife Mary.

AP receives his Doctorate of Letters at Bristol University from Dr Dorothy Hodgkin.
'I utterly disagreed with her.'

AP with Lees Mayall. Lees and Mary are 'near and dear neighbours'.

Christmas 1982. Virginia Powell,
AP, and Ferdie Mount.

Archie and Georgia Powell. An
impromptu guitar concert at The
Chantry.

George Orwell. 'I think he would have been anti-CND, pro-Falklands Campaign.'

Suki Marlow, whose charms 'I gradually fell under', with Mark Boxer, 'more interested in the power world'.

Max Hastings, 'big, heavily bespectacled, with a booming manner'.

Philip Larkin, 'not really a very nice chap'.

Jilly Cooper, 'funny, intelligent, curious depth of melancholy one would guess', with Mary Mayall, whose risqué story 'enchanted' her.

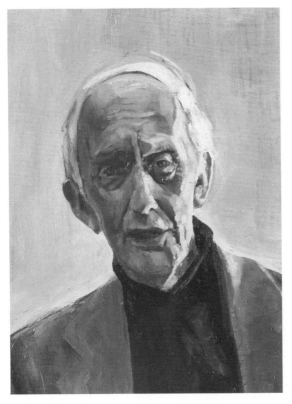

David Cecil, who 'remained astonishingly the same from a boy of 16 or 17'.

here for further discussion, bringing a book of photographs with relevant letterpress dealing with Siegfried Sassoon (US edition, English to follow). This looked quite nice. I still feel uncertain, not wanting such a work to end on Remainder counters (tho', so far as the public goes, people are quite unaware whether they have bought a remainder or a new book). Paul Fussell, who has done the Introduction to Sassoon volume, described Giniger as thinking he looked like a British Guards officer. Giniger has a curly moustache, neatly turned out, but The Brigade would not immediately spring to mind.

After Giniger left, V remarked that she herself would be, if not the only, at least one of the few persons capable of composing such a picture-book properly. The same idea had crossed my own mind, but I was not sure she would want to take on its editing, having already much of her own on hand. The text would be about 20,000 words. Now I have put forward that V might do it. Bruce Hunter, my agent at Higham's, like me, is rather lukewarm about whole project, but will discuss details with Giniger, and report back. Giniger left his hat (rare adjunct these days, perhaps part of his Brigade of Guards image), which V will return next week when she goes to London, as Giniger also stays at the Lansdowne Club.

Sunday, 2 October

We lunched at Westwood Manor with Denys & Cynthia Sutton. Cynthia's son by previous husband there, Andrew Abrahams, black beard, last seen with his brother (now married to a Princess of Sikkim) as little boys handing round dishes at dinner. Andrew Abrahams is in the video business, and said he might find himself in touch with Tristram. He seemed nice. The Suttons are leaving Westwood, as the National Trust is asking more than they want to pay for renewal of the lease, which would include interior repairs, certainly alarming prospect in a building going back to at least the late Middle Ages. A couple named Christopher are taking the place over, they propose to open it up much more frequently (which they could hardly do less than Denys does, latterly even the signpost to 'Historical Monument' mysteriously disappearing on main road). Denys & Cynthia will now live at 22 Chelsea Gardens, probably spend more time on art jobs abroad. Cynthia produced a good Indian chicken dish, the wine as always excellent.

Monday, 3 October

Francie Mount, doing a tour of relations, came to luncheon. She had just been having drinks with the Mayalls (not relations but old friends of Francie's

parents), going on to her uncle, Bill Mount, at Wasing, the Mount seat in
Berkshire, among a nest of other baronets. Francie seemed in fairly good form,
perhaps slightly sad figure (Tristram insists that is not the least so. Francie
perfectly well able to look after herself). She is doing a high-grade horticultural
job (she is a first-class gardener) in Suffolk. Francie used to work at that sort of
thing with the painters Cedric Morris, Lett Haines (Cedric's longtime
boyfriend).

Contact with these two Twenties relics, and with Bobby & Nathalie Bevan
in neighbourhood (Bobby the son of Camden Town Group artist R. P. Bevan),
never seems to have gingered up Francie's life to any visible extent, tho' I am
prepared to believe that is my totally inept judgement. I knew Lett Haines had
married twice, and fathered a son, but not that the son was by yet another
woman to the two wives. Lett had at least one other fairly serious hetero affair.
Odd record for a more or less professional queer, anyway lifelong lover of
Cedric Morris, who certainly never dallied with opposite sex. Lett Haines is
presumably the 'Lett' mentioned by name among the homosexuals at the *bal
musette* party (in fact Ford Madox Ford's), which the narrator attends in
Hemingway's *The Sun Also Rises*. (*Fièsta*.)

Tuesday, 4 October

V & I lunched with Billy Chappell in Bath, where Billy is directing a revue
(this ancient form of theatrical entertainment coming in to fashion again) at
the Bath Theatre. Billy gave us luncheon at the Francis Hotel (not too bad,
tho' Billy grumbled at the food), where Billy, now in his seventies, had
obviously made himself felt. He still looks young for his age, wearing a neat
blue suit, not his former style, if still decidedly camp. He was in pretty good
form, complaining a lot about the people putting on the show not having
faintest idea what a revue ought to be like, because they didn't date back to
period when revues were all the go.

He is editing Ed Burra's *Letters*, which contain descriptions of such scenes as
Brenda Dean Paul staying with Gerald Reitlinger at Thornsdale (Reitlinger's
cottage near Rye, before he moved to Woodgate House), bathing naked in
local stream to the outrage of a local farmer's boy looking through the hedge.
An enjoyable lunch if always rather exhausting to see old friends not
encountered for a long time, both parties raking up fragments of the past. Billy
says he hates showbiz. All the same he doesn't seem to be doing too badly, tho'
overworked. He said 'Sir Fred' [Ashton] is always grousing. When Constant
Lambert & I gave our party at my basement flat, 33 Tavistock Square, in
1929, my old friend Adrian Daintrey said: 'I hope you aren't going to ask

Freddie Ashton & Billy Chappell' (which we did), the former now Sir Frederick Ashton OM, etc, Billy, in his world, well-known Theatre, and Ballet, figure. I remarked to Tristram later that Billy was getting everybody in the hotel on their toes. Tristram replied that anyone who can direct a chorus line can do anything in the power sphere.

Thursday, 13 October

Jeanne Wilkins, visiting friends in Bath, came to tea. When I was just out of the army in 1945, we stayed at Lee, near Ilfracombe, for some months, at one moment renting bungalow there belonging to Jeanne & her husband Geoffrey Wilkins (now dcd, Russian blood, descended from the 17th century Bishop Wilkins mentioned by Aubrey & Pepys). Jeanne's mother was a daughter of Burnand, longtime editor of *Punch*. Jeanne is nice, by chance she had seen Billy Chappell's revue in Bath and reported that some of it was very funny, Beryl Reid carrying the show.

Tuesday, 18 October

Through Heinemann, an American journalist based on London, Jim Fallon, interviewed me for two papers *M* and *W* (*Men* and *Women*), chiefly fashion, gossip, large format like a newspaper, one of these periodicals about to appear for the first time. Fallon and a photographer, Tim Jenkins (British) came to luncheon, both reasonably agreeable young men. Jenkins became perceptibly more upper-class in tone and connexions; as the afternoon progressed, he forgot to use his workaday manner. Once it would have been other way round, he would have tried to seem upper-class, then betrayed by background, manner and accent. The State from which Americans come always of interest, Fallon from Pennsylvania. He said the circulation of his paper is half a million. They took photographs in Park Field, which was rather chilly.

Later Fallon sent copies of paper, kind of *Harpers & Queen*, newspaper size. I was rather put out to find the view attributed to me that I thought the survival of Evelyn Waugh's books was surprising. This is just another example of Americans being unable to understand the difference between the epithets 'successful' and 'estimable', which they almost universally regard as synonymous. I had probably said that, when *Decline and Fall* appeared in 1929, I was surprised that so funny, so original, a book should have achieved such (popular) success. I may also have said that I didn't care for *Brideshead*, a bestseller, but greatly admired *Pinfold*, unlikely to have gone as well in the US. That did not mean that I failed to grasp Waugh's wit, and inventiveness, even if I had reservations, and held different views about what is best, funniest, on the whole not caring for joke worked to death, for instance, in *Scoop*, and *The Loved One*, two of the most popular.

Another example of this American tendency to equate 'successful' with literary approval is illustrated when I said in my Memoirs that Graham Greene would have been 'successful' in any profession he had taken up. American reviewers stated that I was a great admirer of Greene's writing. On the contrary I think Graham's books absurdly overrated. He is prolific, writes good descriptive passages, a capable journalist, usually an interesting literary critic (with reservations), his novels unlike people one has ever come across, filled with self-pity, and a kind of pretentious emptiness when trying to be 'serious', so it seems to me, and enormously unfunny when intended to be funny. Graham himself has a strong personality so far as the public is concerned, while being an odd, unhappy, restless man. In spite of almost literally universal adulation, never somehow seeming to achieve the 'image' he himself wants (whatever that may be), a side shown by ludicrous letters written to the papers, periodic rows, which he goes out of his way to publicize, always seeming to end in shadow-boxing, all perhaps necessary to him to get the adrenalin going. [I got in touch with Fallon, asking for a *démenti* about Waugh to be put in his paper, which he assured me would go in.]

Wednesday, 26 October

David Williamson, Canadian academic, journalist, fan of more than dozen years, has done much to propagate my books in Canada, came to tea with his wife Janice; he quiet, she rather noisy in North American manner, both pleasantly enthusiastic. He thought he might persuade CBC to consider repeat of Cheshire programme.

Thursday, 27 October

John Pickford, BBC World Service, came to interview me about George Orwell. A pleasant young man, but the questions these people put are impossible to answer. One wonders whether the generality of people expected easy answers to the human condition before their minds were rotted by popular journalism, TV, the notion that all life's problems could be answered off the cuff by TV 'personalities', suchlike, in two or three sentences. All the same there is perhaps a faint impression of a person given by the words, demeanour, of a friend. Apparently Bush House (where World Service operates) is a set-up quite separate from BBC Langham Place. Bush House has a slightly Roman Catholic, Jewish, tradition in personnel. Pickford was not born when Orwell died. I tried to think of any literary figure, comparable with Orwell in international reputation, interviewed by oneself in the 1930s, perhaps a friend of Wilde's. These imaginings brought home the utter impossibility of reconstructing any 'literary period' of the past.

Monday, 7 November

To London to see preview of the Cheshire programme. I had a luncheon party at The Travellers before the showing. In first instance the party was to have been: V, I, Tristram, Virginia, John, David Cheshire, Caroline Swift (daughter of Alan Moorehead, travel writer), Roland & Nadia Gant, Hilary & John Spurling, Antonia Pinter. Then Virginia's aunt, Betty Noble, died, and Virginia had to go to Scotland for the funeral. With great agility we replaced Virginia with Charlotte Lennox-Boyd (gt-niece). Then Roland collapsed with the antibiotics administered for some complaint, so Nadia had to look after him. We got Alan Ross, not seen for some time, so welcome, and his girlfriend Elizabeth Claridge (we wanted to meet in any case, as she gave V's *Flora Annie Steel* a good review). She turned out to be a pretty girl in Alan's tradition of elegant, fair-skinned girlfriends' looks. Another crisis took shape when David Cheshire arrived, as the theatre in Soho where the film was to be shown, said at the last moment (for some obscure reason) it was not allowed to show BBC films. The party had to adjourn to BAFTA (British Academy of Film & Television Arts) in Piccadilly, where we had been going first of all, and were diverted because the press would be there. The Press does not like friends, and the public, to observe their going to sleep or making offensive noises when watching previews. There was to be, accordingly, another showing at 4 pm, whether or not the Press turned up, which appeared problematical. BAFTA (apart from the viewing room itself) is an odd place, a kind of club, with staircases going in all directions, like a stage set for a musical, Aldwych farce, or the suites of rooms one wanders through in a dream.

Luncheon at The Travellers was not too bad (fruits de mer, médaillons de veau, pommes Lyonnaises, epinards à la crème, pâtisserie, club hock, the last perfectly drinkable for such an occasion). The meal took place in the library, an unusually pretty Regency room with pillars and a frieze of the Elgin marbles.

Hilary arrived late owing to Gilbert being under an anaesthetic after an accident. I sat between her & Antonia. I mentioned to Antonia that her daughter Rebecca asked us to a party, and V had speculated which of her great-aunts she herself would have invited to that sort of party at the age of twenty-five. I added that in my own case the husband of my only great-aunt (I think) had been described in his obituary as 'one of the first up the ladders at Badajoz', which put her some way back in time, as she had eloped with him when very young. Charlotte is a tall, pretty girl. For a moment Antonia mistook her for her mother (not wholly unreasonable), at once pointing out that was like Jenkins mistaking Jean Templer's daughter for her mother in *Dance*, a good example of Antonia's tact and quick wit. The programme (to be shown BBC 2, Wednesday, when one will get better idea of it) seemed reasonably well done, I thought, with ingenious slottings-in of comments by Kingsley Amis, Bob Conquest (who happened to be over here), Clive James, Alison Lurie and Hilary Spurling, the last being far the most adroit performance. Only howler was for my Powell grandmother's photograph to appear as my mother's mother, than whom no two individuals could have been more different in every respect, physical & moral, though I never knew the latter. V's appearances (looking about thirty-five) were excellent.

Kingsley, after the preview, was captious about James Fox reading from the books. I agree that almost without exception actors read badly, because reading aloud from a novel should not be like acting the characters in a play. If one must have an actor (hard to see an alternative, unless the author always does it), James Fox seemed to me as good, if not better, than most. (Like every actor, Fox will insist on wearing a scarf round his neck all the time, unlike any ordinary human being.) I think this sort of pernicketiness on Kingsley's part is responsible for a good deal of his own difficulties in life (cf. Evelyn Waugh). Otherwise Kingsley was in good form, even if he was complaining that the Kentish Town house is not all it might be, jerry-built and inaccessible.

Tuesday, 8 November

About 3 pm there was knock on front door. A tall man with a greying beard, wearing a tam-o'-shanter, looking in his late fifties, stood on the doorstep, holding a cardboard carton about the size for, say, half a dozen wine bottles. He said: 'I don't want to push myself forward, but I find I live a comparatively short way away, and I admire you so much I want to give you a present.' He then opened the carton, to reveal a clock, perhaps slightly smaller than that hanging in every schoolroom in the country (probably every other country), otherwise identical. He said: 'I made it myself. I have made lots of them. I wondered what to do with it. Then it struck me I should give it to you. I don't want in the least to force myself on you.' I took the clock, attempted thanks. He brushed all gratitude aside, leapt into his car, drove away. The clock, which has an inscription to me with the words 'for a masterpiece', my name round its face, is going, but seems to have no place for winding or adjustment; nor does it appear possible to open at any point. Perhaps the donor has discovered perpetual motion. A letter accompanied this gift expressing warm feelings. We have hung the clock in the billiard room, useful to know the time when watching TV. John explained its working with a battery.

Monday, 14 November

To London for the Balliol luncheon given at Oxford & Cambridge Club, for the eightieth birthday of King Olaf of Norway, Balliol contemporary of mine, tho' we never came across each other there. Lunch was billed as 12.30 for 1 o'clock. When I arrived about 12.40, the King and Prince Harald, were already there. I did not manage to be presented to the Prince, but King Olaf looked much the same, if a good deal plumper than when last seen at Malcolm Bullock's dinner at The Allies' Club for his father King Haakon and himself during the war.

It was then Olaf made his historic remark about Peter Quennell carrying a lily through the quad of Balliol. Olaf produced no conversational gem on this occasion. He seemed to remember Bradders of Military Intelligence Liaison (Major Bradfield, the Norwegian Liaison Officer), when I mentioned him. I also had a word with Richard Cobb, and Roy Jenkins, in the underground room where drinks were consumed before lunch. The row was appalling. This truly awful noise contined in the subterranean dining-room where we ate, making it hardly possible to hear a word spoken, even by the man opposite at table: in my case a somewhat wizened figure, who, apparently aware I was a writer, bawled across the table: 'There's a man here who simply *hates* your books.' He did not reveal who this anti-fan was, when I enquired merely rolling his eyes, possibly to indicate his neighbour. He had spent most of his life in Nigeria, written (among other works) a book called *Nigerian Adventure*, the title of which he inscribed on his place-card, flicking it across: 'You'll enjoy it,' he added.

The High Table was at right angles to where I sat next to Nigel Nicolson. I was interested to meet him, having read his book about his parents, also various entries where he figures as Nigs in Harold Nicolson's *Diaries* (which resulted in V and I always referring to him as Normal Niggs, he being the only normal member of his family). We talked, so far as was possible in the frightful din, at some stage my asking him to look in if ever in our neighbourhood. It at once appeared Nicolson would be lecturing in the Frome area quite soon, so he is lunching at The Chantry on 5 December. He seemed reasonably agreeable, so far as anything could be heard at all. Food & drink were good; Kenny is obviously determined to put Balliol on the map again, after a dynasty of dreary Masters, either dull or actively harmful to the College. One must applaud his attitude.

In the afternoon I went to the Dobson show at the National Portrait Gallery. I found their 17th century pictures not merely enjoyable, but also rather moving: Cavaliers and their Ladies, several characters mentioned by Aubrey, overpowering atmosphere of the period. I returned to The Travellers to have rest before dining with the Stockwells. When I came downstairs I met Peter Fleetwood-Hesketh in the hall (contemporary at school, introduced into MIL by his brother Cuthbert, himself there through Alick Dru, very talented officer colleague of mine in MIL during the war. Bradders, as senior officer of the room, at last told Peter he really must arrive earlier than 9.45 am. To that Peter replied that he was sorry, but he found it impossible to get up earlier. Later, gallantly at his age, Peter was parachuted into France.) He looked thinner, hardly a grey hair, semi-paralysed hand, entertaining to dinner his eldest brother Roger, one of his sisters, his daughter Evrilda. This family concentration was very typical. The last two arriving just as I was leaving with Tristram, who gave me lift to Stockwell. The Cheshire programme was being followed on the box by announcement of Tristram's Philip Roth film *The Ghost Writer*. Very enjoyable dinner. Saw Archie & Georgia in their school uniforms. Tristram ran me back, said they do not like guests walking to the Tube – shades of the good old London suburbs of the Pooters, and *Three Men in a Boat*. But I suppose even then there was the odd garotter of Victorian days – when a young man it never crossed my mind that it might be dangerous to walk home at night.

Tuesday, 15 November

I saw Sussman, who had watched the Cheshire programme, which Mrs Sussman taped. Met V at Child's Bank, having been asked to luncheon there again. Child's (just where Fleet Street reaches the Strand), was founded in the first instance by an ancestor of V's on her mother's side. The previous luncheon was a fairly formal affair, dominated by the strike at *The Times*, whose manager, whatever he is, Duke (Marmaduke) Hussey, who was present, said (as it turned out quite incorrectly) 'all but settled'. The present luncheon was devoted entirely to talking about *Dance*, of which Adam Lee (who invited us), Maurice Davenport, and Bill Dacombe, were all tremendous fans.

An enjoyable lunch, excellent food and drink. It suddenly dawned on me there that I have a certain status in the City as describing an often attacked community in relatively sympathetic terms; somewhat as Pierre Loti (whose biography I have been reviewing) was enormously popular in Turkey, for praising a country rarely spoken of favourably. The Child's Bank luncheon could be seen to link up with that given for me by James Sandilands (member of the eminent stockbroking firm of Buckmaster & Moore) for various City friends, who were fans; and (Sir) Nicholas Goodison, Head of London Stock Exchange, inviting me to Stock Exchange dinner (where I found Roy Fuller, utterly stunned by my presence on such an occasion).

Sunday, 20 November

Derry Moore (son of Garret & Joan Drogheda), a photographer, came to luncheon. We met him at a dinner party some little time ago given by his parents when they had house in Lord North Street, Westminster. He was then introduced as a great fan. Now in his middle forties, he seemed rather different from that occasion; unusual, rather bright, aware of things, particularly in the way of architecture and allied arts. His first wife was American, and he lived in US for some years before they parted. Possible this has left some mark. I was interested in his photographing technique. This included a good deal of measuring, muttering to himself, holding lights in one hand while he took a picture with the other. I mentioned I was pottering about with book that included a photographer, on the subject of which he was both informative and intelligent. One of the curious things about human beings, those who can, and cannot, produce useful facts of their own specialized sort to help one in writing a book.

Sunday, 27 November

Denys & Cynthia Sutton, Clarissa Avon, to luncheon. The Suttons leave Westwood Manor on Tuesday, a parting Denys compared with the close of *The Cherry Orchard*, as the National Trust man had returned to say National Trust poplars would have to be cut down before the new tenants took over. Denys replied: 'Not until we have gone.' Cynthia, as always, enormously well turned out; Denys, with his beard, more than a little resembling one of Cézanne's self-portraits. He reported the Venetian Exhibition at Burlington House was indifferent. Clarissa was in good form, rather exercised as to what happens about letters (chiefly, in her case, one presumes, Anthony Eden's) after death; the subject arising because the Suttons were witnessing V's and my respective wills when Clarissa arrived. There may, of course, be quite other letters written or received by Clarissa, which prompt this interest.

Tuesday, 29 November

Ena Kendall, photographer Tim Mercer, and Mercer's assistant Tessa Marsh, came from the *Observer Colour Magazine* to do a piece on the feature *A Room of My Own*. Ena Kendall was quiet, not bad looking, Mercer previously here for Hilary Spurling's *Harpers & Queen* piece in April. The assistant photographer was rather a nice little girl in a mini-skirt and crimson stockings, who, when looking at the collage in the cloakroom/engine room, asked if she might use the loo, presumably to have a good inspection there too, after satisfying other needs. They worked with quite remarkable speed, arriving just before 2 pm, leaving a few minutes after 3 o'clock.

Sunday, 4 December

Driven by John, we lunched with Leo & Jilly Cooper at The Chantry, Bisley, near Stroud, an area that appears to be something of an intellectuals' colony. The house, said to have medieval parts, is mostly Victorian, not much in front but a pretty view on far side. The Coopers acquired it from Suna Portman, a once famous figure in the gossip columns. Other guests: Stewart Steven (apparently refugee from Germany as a boy), Editor of the *Mail on Sunday* and wife, half-Polish half-Russian; Godfrey Smith, columnist on the *Sunday Times* and wife, she said to be Austrian; Elizabeth Longman, widow of Mark Longman, publisher (both Longmans met when they lived in Wiltshire).

Leo Cooper shares my mania for military matters. He did his service with the East Africa Army Service Corps during the Mau-Mau troubles (white officers with black privates, he said), of which he gave an amusing account. One can only hope they were less awful than most of the RASC officers who came my way when I was in the army. Stewart Steven declared himself a great fan of *Dance*, in spite of early prejudice against. He was converted by a copy bought at Rome Airport, astonishing it should be on sale there, doubt if it would have been at Heathrow, or Gatwick. In case his enthusiasm might raise high hopes, I recall the *Mail on Sunday* as the one paper that carried a paragraph abusing me when among the thirteen 'Best Writers' of the Booksellers Marketing Board. Mrs Steven was a painter, apparently somewhat in the Francis Bacon manner. Not bad looking, talking comparatively intelligibly about painting, which she teaches at the St Martin's School of Art. Godfrey Smith, columnist, big, immensely fat, eating and drinking everything in sight, was fascinated by Cyril Connolly, with whom he worked on the *Sunday Times*, where Smith still writes every week; a good instance of the mesmerism Cyril excited on those who came his way. A pleasant Sunday luncheon of roast beef, every sort of vegetable from the Coopers' garden, successful *bombe* made by the female half of the couple who 'do' for them in London. The latter looked like a soubrette in a Goldoni play. Nice claret, name & year of which I failed to get. Jilly funny, intelligent, curious depth of melancholy one would guess. Enjoyable party (notwithstanding Fleet Street aromas of some pungency). The journey is about forty miles, passing at times through a rather hideous area of Gloucestershire. [January 1986 the *Mail on Sunday* said it was disgraceful that I was not given a knighthood – in fact refused when offered by Ted Heath ten years ago or more in the New Year Honours.]

Monday, 5 December

Nigel Nicolson, staying with Joff & Tessa Davies at Whatley House, while lecturing on Sissinghurst to some local cultural organization, came to luncheon. He was interested only, I think, in his parents, and Sissinghurst, giving out that vague air of ponderous goodwill, without much conviction, that MPs develop, behaving as if everyone they met was a constituent. This has a suffocating effect on conversation. He said Trim Oxford, his near contemporary at Balliol, was then regarded as brilliant, adventurous, in every respect the coming man. This no doubt explains Trim's rather sad air in later life.

I heard from Adrian Daintrey, who has been in a nursing home with bronchial troubles, whence he emerged to go into The Charterhouse (he is in fact a Carthusian), like Colonel Newcome. This seems a good solution.

The Lomers, who lunched here, are bird-fanciers, and have set up various hutches etc in their garden. In spite of that they have already lost two valuable golden pheasants, which managed to get out of confinement, another bird having been killed apparently by fox or mink.

Friday, 16 December

After a certain amount of pressure, I agreed to give a TV interview to NBC (chief rival of CBS) for their Orwell programme. Their London newsman John Cochran, a Southerner from Richmond University Virginia, did this with a crew of three in the Park Field. He was quite tolerable. As promised they arrived at 2 pm, left at 2.45. He asked if Orwell would have enjoyed all the tremendous to-do about his work at the moment. I said I thought not. He liked power, not personal publicity. Afterwards I could not make up my mind whether that was the right answer. George might have liked the fame. I am not sure about vehicles of it, interviews, etc. He tried to suppress so many ordinary feelings and ambitions that they would come out in unexpected ways. Widespread publicity might have turned out one of these shrouded desires. Hard to tell.

I received a sumptuous book about cats inscribed 'thanks for writing' from Robert McNamara, Jr, Oysterville, Mass. I presume this must be the former US Secretary of Defence, and Head of World Bank, much deplored as a political figure by Bob Conquest, who held lowest possible opinion of his capabilities. [This turned out a misapprehension, there being another Robert McNamara, Jr, of about the same age, a publisher, in fact, this one.]

Wednesday, 21 December

My seventy-eighth birthday; at about 12.45 there was a knock on the front door. I found a man on the doorstep, behind a car containing, so far as I could see, a woman. He had a slight stutter, said he was an admirer, tho' he had not read *Dance*, only some of the earlier books. He wanted to give me a present on my birthday. The present turned out to be a poinsettia in a pot. On being asked his name he said it was Mills, that he was in London Transport. He then produced a copy of Snowdon's *Sitters*, and requested me to sign my photograph there, which I did. While all this was going on Trelawney made himself known (as he occurs in the picture) by rushing tumultuously through the door between us.

Tristram, Virginia, Georgia, Archie, to luncheon. A letter from Philip Larkin, to whom I had sent a paperback of my Memoirs *To Keep the Ball Rolling*. He is to get an Hon. D. Litt. at Oxford this year, and says he is dreading the celebrations. V and I watched two Acts of *Madame Butterfly* after dinner. For some reason Pinkerton is made a Marine, when he was, so far as I remember, a sailor; perhaps more glamorous these days. Possibly on thinking it over he was a Marine. Enjoyable. A character in one of Firbank's novels is described as regrettably always humming 'bits from *Madame Butterfly*'.

Saturday, Christmas Eve

About to return through our gates after shopping, V was run into by a car coming too fast from the West. Our own car was badly damaged. We had to borrow Virginia's car (driven by John) to attend Clarissa Avon's luncheon. This was a large buffet party. I sat in the drawing-room most of the time with Lady Congleton, Mrs Juby Lancaster, and an adopted daughter of Michael & Anne Tree, whose name I don't know. I also talked briefly with a woman who had lived in the US for twelve years, and is now staying with a Greek called something like Stefanides, who turns up from time to time at Clarissa's.

Lady Congleton is Norwegian, she said that King Haakon had been very popular. Olaf, not being over bright, had some difficulty in taking over, but had done pretty well in a hard position (the Norwegians are temperamentally Left, and have no aristocracy). Crown Prince Harald is also not over bright. He is married to a girl from a women's underclothes shop, who has fallen excellently into the swing of being royal. Harald's chief quality is ability to drink an immense amount of whisky without showing any change in his metabolism. Mrs Juby Lancaster [niece of Nancy, Lady Astor], now eighty-five, extremely lively, talked of hunting in Virginia, 'Yankees' doing most of it, who arranged neat stone walls to jump over.

The Hobsons were there. I had a brief word with Tanya, whose father, Igor Vinogradoff (now eighty-two) recently rang up to ask if I could get him some reviewing on the *Telegraph*. As it happens I am rereading *The Idiot*, from which Igor (tho' not as the novel's hero) seemed to have walked straight out, when this telephone conversation took place. If Tanya belongs to Turgenev, her father is pure Dostoevsky. I gave Clarissa the abridged paperback of my Memoirs. The party was rather depressing on balance. I seem to have lost such relish as I ever had for smart life, never overwhelming.

In the evening we watched *The Comedy of Errors* on TV. Books & plays about misunderstandings as a rule disturb me, but this (very camp) production was first-rate, especially Roger Daltrey, who doubled the Dromios. Daltrey is a Lincolnshire name, some of them connected with my mother's family, I think.

Sunday, Christmas Day

We lunched at The Stables, where the Stockwells had staying Vicky Feaver (now deserted by her husband), with three daughters and a son, and Julian Jebb. Talked to Julian about Kleist (a competent, if infinitely boring, biography of whom I have for review, there being nothing else over Christmas), in spite of Kleist not being a particularly Yuletide subject. Tristram produced some splendid masks. John had already given me a fine black Carnival mask from the Venetian Exhibition.

Monday, Boxing Day

The Stockwells came to pre-luncheon drinks. At an evening party at The Stables, I talked to Lees Mayall, who spoke of forebodings that they would have to stay at Birch Grove, Harold Macmillan's house, now inhabited by

Maurice Macmillan married to Mary Mayall's sister Katty. Harold Macmillan himself (referred to by Lees as Silver Maggie) now lives in the stables there, with an ex-WinCo, or suchlike, as butler. He insists on coming to dinner, if his son and daughter-in-law have anyone staying with them who he thinks may possibly amuse him.

Tuesday, 27 December

The Stockwells are dining with Joff & Tessa Davies at Whatley, which Julian Jebb could not face, as he is now on the wagon. Also, we think, he really wanted to watch *Dallas* on TV. He came up to talk to us for an hour or so, before we, for our part, watched *The Two Gentlemen of Verona*, which was not bad and does not often get acted. Julian said A. N. Wilson was sacked as Literary Editor of *The Spectator* for altering a review too drastically, which he is much given to doing. This has apparently been a bitter blow, as he enjoyed the job. Julian has seen A. N. Wilson's book on Belloc (his grandfather, whom Julian did not like) and reports it as good.

Thursday, 29 December

Roland & Nadia Gant looked in to tea. Roland handed over Heinemann's presents for us, leather-bound copies *Wheel* and *Margaret Kennedy*. Through John's skilful setting of the radio we managed to hear the World Service on Orwell, in which I said word or two. Nigel Williams's *Orwell* (on Arena) began in the evening, in which Cyril Connolly (from an earlier programme) was certainly the star, tho' much of it fairly amusing.

Saturday, 31 December

Driven by John to Poyntington, we lunched with Rachel & Kevin Billington. Kevin & Ruth Pakenham staying there, the former away shooting with Henry Rumbold. Lots of children. Slight atmosphere of seething from Rachel (not uncommon), chiefly about BBC which commissioned seven plays from her, performed one etc. Then about publishers in general.

1984

Sunday, New Year's Day

Driven by John, we lunched with Jim & Alvilde Lees-Milne at Essex House, Badminton. The other guests were Janet Stone; David & Rosemary Verey. Janet Stone, widow of Reynolds Stone (engraver and typographer). David Verey, Gloucestershire historian, edited several Shell guides (including Central Wales and Radnorshire, about which we talked). Verey belongs in general to Jim's National Trust world. Rosemary Verey turned out to be sister of Sir James Sandilands, chairman of Commercial Union Insurance, father of James Sandilands, my young stockbroker fan, who organized the City luncheon of some years ago for fellow City *Dance* fans. As usual Alvilde produced marvellous food. Asking if one wanted the loo when leaving, Jim remarked that Lady Lloyd, wife of George (Lord) Lloyd, proconsular figure to whom Jim was formerly secretary, used to enquire: 'Do you want to put your hat straight?'

Sunday, 15 January

Anthony & Tanya Hobson, Lees & Mary Mayall, to luncheon. I consulted Anthony about an American who has asked to do my bibliography, now proving himself a bore by bothering Heinemann, saying he wants access to all correspondence about my books. This gets passed on to Roland Gant (up to his eyes in work as it is), the American leaving messages to be rung, then, when Roland rings back, still in bed and not available. Roland and my agent have plenty to do in my interests without being pestered with this sort of thing. My inclination is to put an end to whole business. Anthony Hobson disagreed. He is keen on writers being bibliographized, and says there is a man at Lampeter, Cardiganshire, a librarian, whose name he can't remember, already at work on my bibliography. Anthony will let me know further about this.

Anthony said the Army HQ in which he served was responsible for repatriating the Jugoslav PoWs who fought against Tito, and were later executed by him. The facts were: the orders were given by British Government to send these Jugs back to Ljubliana in a train stated to be going to Trieste, about 4500 of them (not the hundreds of thousands later spoken of) mostly peasants conscripted as Home Guard by the Germans, or Jug collaborators. Only 1500 could be accommodated on the train. They were all machine-gunned by Tito's Partisans on arrival. News came back that this had happened. Accordingly, Field Marshal Alexander, on his own authority, refused to repatriate any more. This gets the story reasonably straight.

Tanya, rather plumper, looks more Russian than ever. I mentioned that her father, Igor Vinogradoff (notable Oxford figure in the generation before my own) recently rang to enquire if any Russian subject reviews available from the *Daily Telegraph*, regarding which I said a word when David Holloway next got in touch. Her father is a fanatical cat-lover. Tanya said when he came to stay he always brought some cat-food as a present.

Lees & Mary gave an account of their visit to Birch Grove, Harold Macmillan's country seat. At dinner Harold Macmillan said: 'I expect I'm the only one here who knows the Sultan of So-and-so [one of the Trucial States in Arabia]. Lees replied that, as it happened, he himself, when in the Foreign Office had been called upon frequently at one stage to negotiate with that potentate about some local matter. Macmillan brushed Lees's words aside. He said: 'I gave him [the Sultan] such-and-such [a neighbouring territory]. Many didn't want me to do it, but I gave it to him.' Lees also supplied the correct version of an incorrect statement made in her book by Diana Mosley to the effect that the British Embassy staff in Paris was forbidden to visit Sir Oswald and Lady Mosley (who incidentally perpetually allows herself to be called Lady *Diana* Mosley by the media. She really ought to know better). Anthony Rumbold (then Counsellor, I think) told the Ambassador, Sir Oliver Hervey (much a 'man of the Left' himself) that he, Tony Rumbold, had received an invitation to the Mosleys and asked if he should accept. Hervey said he saw no objection. Lees (with whom I would heartily agree) said that, for his own part, he did not think it appropriate for Embassy personnel to be seen there. He too had received invitation, was not going. Hervey then said: 'Perhaps you're right. In that case no one had better go to the Mosleys unless they have a good reason.' Enjoyable party, St-Emilion '70 not at all bad.

Saturday, 4 February

The Stockwells, who had Virginia's cousin Christina Noble, with her Indian husband (Kranti Singh) staying at The Stables, came for drinks. Christina by now looks nearly as Indian as her husband, indeed perhaps more. His shock of white hair and heavy black moustache might well be Neapolitan, or suchlike. They run a pony-trekking agency in India.

Sunday, 5 February

Driven by John, we lunched with Andrew Motion & Georgie Hammick at her cottage in Brixton Deverell, a typical Wiltshire cottage, not unlike The Malt House, Chitterne, (where Julia & Robin Mount used to live), if somewhat grander. It is also better situated off the road, big sitting-room, all well done up. Georgie Hammick's sister, Sarah Rivière, also separated from her husband, an academic, staying there. When still married, she had spent a year at Harvard, about which she was quite funny. At dinner an American don had said something to her, to which she replied (one must admit rather an arch comment to make) 'You're flirting with me.' At that the American went scarlet, and stammered: 'No, no, I love my wife.'

Georgie Hammick's former husband seems to have been a Grenadier. We were told by Leo Cooper he was a bookseller, tho' no reason why he should not have combined in the course of his life both professions. I was amused to find myself correct in guessing that Georgie herself was a soldier's daughter, quite how I can't say. She was a little put out by this divination, tho' certainly nothing uncomplimentary implied, rather the contrary. Andrew spoke of John Wain (regarding whom, as poet, novelist, Professor of Poetry at Oxford etc, he holds as low opinion as myself). Wain (whom I have never met in the flesh) insisted on staying with Philip Larkin at Hull University (Larkin librarian there, Motion in some academic employment). Larkin, famous for his meanness, possessed a spare room, but unfurnished. He bought some furniture *ad hoc* for the Wain visit. Wain afterwards naturally wrote a Collins. Larkin complained: 'He thanked me for having him to stay, but gave no thanks at all for there being furniture in the room.' Even if Larkin's stinginess is legendary no doubt this was meant as a joke.

Before we reached Georgie Hammick's cottage we tried another one, where a hawk was tethered on the lawn. The door was opened by somewhat military-looking type, who at once directed us to the right destination. Georgie, when told of this, said he was Major Hope-Johnstone, evidently characteristically eccentric member of that decidedly eccentric family. He was rumoured to refer to his wife as the 'Command Module'. Enjoyable party.

Wednesday, 15 February

To London. I saw the National Portrait Gallery show of 20th century portraits, unexpectedly including blown-up drawing of myself, done some few years ago by Andrew Freeth, not my favourite representation of the subject, tho' flattering to be in those surroundings. The Ten Year Rule, wilting when I was still on the board, must have been abrogated. I bought a pair of gloves for V's birthday, but failed to acquire a refill for her scent, as the size of the atomiser had changed. I looked in on the Venetian Exhibition at Burlington House, which is somewhat lacking in kick. It stops before 18th century, but has good examples of less persuasive painters like, say, Moroni. I lunched with Evangeline Bruce at Albany. (When reviewing Macaulay's *Letters* not so long ago I noticed that he writes his address as Albany, The Albany, indiscriminately.) Other guests were Nicko Henderson, former Ambassador in Washington, Paris, etc; John Saumarez Smith, who now runs the Heywood Hill Bookshop in Curzon Street. He was amusing about current literary matters, describing A. N. Wilson's *Belloc* (which I shall no doubt in due course review) as excellent. He said Alan Bell (who has written on Sydney Smith) is writing a book about Evelyn Waugh and his friends. Splendid Lynch-Bages, I failed to get the year. Enjoyable party.

Thursday, 16 February

Richard Boston (who also interviewed me ages ago for *New York Times*) lunched here to talk about Osbert Lancaster, of whom he is writing a life. Osbert is not at all an easy person to analyse (as I found when saying a few words about him in my Memoirs) because he has so stylized his own behaviour, appearance, expression of views, etc, there remains little to say not already known. At least that is how it looks from outside. Intimate knowledge of Osbert when younger, details about his family, might perhaps modify this judgement, tho' I doubt that. Boston said he was anxious to emphasize Osbert's writing, and serious painting, as opposed to the cartoons, stage sets, etc. I am not sure that Boston, nice, well disposed, quite carries the guns to cope with the world in which Osbert has moved, there being Proustian subtleties. Boston may, however, have line of his own developed from living in cottage next door to the Lancasters' Newbury residence. Osbert's first wife, Karen (Harris), used to drop occasional remarks which suggested inherent complications within. There may be more to know. One hopes so. Osbert himself is pretty well *hors de combat* these days as to giving information or remembering things. When Boston was last at the Lancasters' cottage, Osbert said: 'Isn't there some fellow you're writing the life of?' Curiously enough Boston began talking of Richard Ingrams, as the luncheon party had done a day or two before at Evangeline's.

Saturday, 18 February

V and I and John dined at The Stables for Georgia's fifteenth birthday. She is very sweet, intelligent, still not at all grown-up in manner, a Pakenham characteristic that probably pays off in the long run, keeping them young. Archie remains formidably good-looking, and plays the guitar well, Tristram thinks Archie's future lies in some branch of 'entertainment', always Archie's chief interest. It is still a shade painful to me that Archie did not go to Eton, but his own choice (so far as one can possibly grasp implications at that age); while who can tell these days about advantages, disadvantages, of an Eton education? It is simply that I look back on my own Eton period as a perfectly tolerable manner of having got through that tricky stage of growing-up, and feel rather cut off from Archie's school life, which would not have been the case at Eton. My own feeling about a day school is that one at least unloaded one's home/school worries in transferring from former to the latter, but Archie's home no doubt more 'relaxed' (to use a horrible word) than my own was ever able to be. Nonetheless both Archie & Georgia have great charm, nice manners, general air of being bright.

Monday, 20 February

A play about T. S. Eliot & his first wife Vivienne is now running, the author of which, Michael Hastings, has been making a fuss because Valerie Eliot (no doubt rightly) offered him no help with letters. The play sounds ghastly beyond words. John happened to mention that Tristram had known Hastings in days of the Gunter Grove flat, so, when Tristram & Virginia looked in on the way back to London, I asked what he was like. It turned out they had seen the play and found the dialogue bad, like an essay transferred into conversation, but the acting sufficiently competent to pull the performance through, making it just bearable. One ludicrous point is to suppose that when (quoted in play) Edith Sitwell said: 'Tom went mad, and locked his wife up', she was speaking seriously. That was a typical Sitwell joke, would have been understood as such at the time by anyone in the least conversant with the Sitwells, Eliot, and all that sort of world. Archie & Georgia stayed on alone at The Stables, so that when Mary (Clive) with her granddaughter Philippa Lennox-Boyd arrived to have luncheon with us, Philippa lunched with them. She is an attractive fourteen-year-old.

Sunday, 4 March

Barbara Bethmann-Hollweg, daughter of the painter (formerly Vorticist) Edward Wadsworth, is writing the life of her father, and asked to come here to talk about him. I never knew Wadsworth at all well, visiting his house (Maresfield, Sussex) only once, I think for dinner on the way back from possibly, Hastings, where Pam, younger sister of Mary Herdman née Cooper, was at a school to which she had been banished. I took her to cinema in the guise of an uncle, held her hand, in memory of a decidedly drunken night when staying with Mary and her husband Pat in Northern Ireland.

Perhaps John & Evelyn Heygate were staying with the Wadsworths, also Greta Wyndham, and the 1920s beauty Enid Firminger. Not very clear in memory, except my car would not start when I tried to leave, and I had to remain the night. Edward and Fanny Wadsworth turned in together so that I could have a room, the subject of much ribald humour among the other guests later. I met the Wadsworths again in Berlin in 1930, when Heygate[1] was working at the German film company UFA. They were always very great on Germany, where possibly Wadsworth had studied as a young man. This Germanophile attitude resulted in Barbara Wadsworth (quite pretty) marrying a German, Mopsy ['Pug'] Bethmann-Hollweg, not a close relation, I think of the 'Scrap of Paper' Chancellor, but from a reasonably well-to-do branch of the family. He was interned here during second war; now, one imagines, a British subject. He was an expert ice-hockey player, has survived to own some sort of *schloss* in Germany having been in the antique business here with Barbara for twenty years, now retired. Mopsy seems to tick over all right, looking like any other upper-class German who had weathered the storm. Barbara, now about seventy, also holds up well. The Wadsworths were of well-off North Country manufacturer origins.

Edward Wadsworth had a taste for large fast cars, in one of which, returning from the pub one Sunday morning a year or two before the war, he unfortunately killed an old man who carried drinks across the road to pub habitués sitting at tables on the other side. The old man zigzagged with disastrous results when he saw the car speeding towards him. Wadsworth was tried for manslaughter, and acquitted, but, by then much broken down, died a few years later. Barbara said at a recent auction one of her father's pictures went for £120,000, which staggered her, me too. They had expected £3/4000. Edward & Fanny Wadsworth occur in unflattering terms in Wyndham Lewis's *Apes of God* (1930), Edward also in *Tarr*. Wyndham Lewis treated all

---

[1] John Heygate's friendship with Anthony Powell, his ambivalent attitude to Nazi Germany and his marriage to Evelyn Gardner who was, confusingly, married to Evelyn Waugh until they divorced, are described in Powell's second volume of Memoirs, *Messengers of Day*.

his friends savagely, Wadsworth, as fellow Vorticist, rich (and no doubt helped Lewis out once in a way financially), particularly open to rough usage. We went through Barbara's engagement books of the period, which dished up a lot of long forgotten names, an unexpected number of which I was able to offer some help about.

Sunday, 11 March

Jim & Alvilde Lees-Milne, with Tony & Marcelle Quinton, to luncheon. Tony Quinton had attended Harold Macmillan's Ninetieth Birthday Dinner at Balliol (to which I did not go, February being too severe a month at my age to stay in College), said nothing much of interest happened, beyond Hugh Trevor-Roper (now Lord Dacre of Glanton) making a speech in which he emphasized how boring everyone was at Cambridge. The Lees-Milnes are undergoing a new regime as poor-man at the gate of Badminton, the Beauforts now being their landlords. The old Duchess (now nearly ninety) has not been evicted from the house yet. She is, to say the least, difficult, by all accounts. The subject came up of David Pryce-Jones's book about Bobo (Unity) Mitford (the Hitler fan) regarding which David P-J twice approached V. She in fact never knew Bobo Mitford at all well, and looks at the whole project of writing a book about Bobo with utter abhorrence, in short would have nothing whatever to do with it. Jim Lees-Milne said David P-J told him he was going to be in the neighbourhood and asked if he could look in, so was invited to luncheon. Meanwhile Debo Devonshire (Mitford sister) wrote to Jim, begging that the book should be discouraged. Accordingly, when David P-J arrived in front of the house, Jim went out, said; 'I know what you have come for and do not propose to tell you anything I know about the subject, but, as I was an old friend of your father's come in and lunch if you like, but only on condition that nothing is discussed about Bobo Mitford.'

Wednesday, 14 March

V and I attended the funeral of Mrs Hallett in Chantry Church. Mrs Hallett was a few days off one hundred and two (within a month of the age my father would have been if still alive) and mother-in-law of Mr Warrington. Warrington is a former petty-officer in the Royal Navy, a churchwarden, pillar of the parish church. The Revd Bertram Hardy took the service, a retired clergyman who does odd jobs in neighbourhood, and claims to be a distant relation of Thomas Hardy, the writer, which may well be true. John Heygate's parents' gardener at their house at Salt Grass, also named Hardy, was second cousin of the novelist, who was of genuine working-class stock, which he always attempted to conceal by implying his family had come down in the world.

Thursday, 15 March

Derry Moore again came to photograph, this time chiefly house, grounds, for American *Vogue*, reprinting the piece that appeared in *Time Out*. Derry staying with the Lees-Milnes for this and other jobs to be undertaken in the neighbourhood. Caroline Somerset (Henry Bath's daughter), new Duchess of Beaufort, dined with Lees-Milnes the previous night, she reported servants at Badminton during late regime worked one day on, two days off. There are two huge deep-freezes into which she had not yet dared to look. When the former Duke ('Master') was alive meals would be served for the two of them on a little tray (plastic cups for tea) under the Grinling Gibbons overmantel. At the funeral the Dowager Duchess kept on apologizing to the Queen because her husband was not there. 'Master would so much like to have been here, Ma'am, but he was prevented.'

Apparently the late Duke of Beaufort, walking through the churchyard a few weeks before his death, saw three or four foxes sitting on the graves of his relations. He asked somebody if they thought a sinister meaning was portended. Foxes are supposed to appear when a Lord Gormanston dies but I have also been told that foxes are often to be seen round the Gormanston mansion, as indeed they are round this house, whether the head of the family is about to die or not. It is not at all uncommon to see a fox, sometimes two foxes, playing about here in the Park Field.

Derry Moore has just returned from Australia. He gave an amusing account of sheep-shearers having a gigantic meal every two hours when shearing, bringing their own cooks, and washers-up called Slushies. We went down to the big grotto, which delighted him. He took a lot of photographs. I sketched in the outline of *The Fisher King*, with view to getting general information about photographers' behaviour. Derry Moore spoke interestingly on the subject, making the important point that different successful photographers use utterly different methods, cameras, employment of assistants. There is really no rule. On consideration I think this would be only relatively true of other arts, with no doubt obvious exceptions. It seems a novel about a photographer would be feasible with such material as I have at hand. That is if one's energy still holds up.

Sunday, 18 March

Tony and Marcelle Quinton had been asked by me to produce a picture of an Oxford don's room for the Sillery illustration in the Giniger Picture Book. Marcelle very sensibly wrote back to say it would be much better to mock-up a corner of Sillery's sitting-room here. One could do all the aspects required, framed photographs etc. Accordingly, this was set about in the billiard-room by Tristram, Archie and myself, all taking our own photographs of corners arranged to resemble Sillery's habitual background.

The Revd Donald Pritchard, new Rector, came in for a drink after church. He looked rather apprehensively at the Powell family gathered together – V, self, John, Tristram, Virginia (last two coming up from The Stables). It was rather hard to get him going at first, but he cheered up a bit after a few glasses of sherry. He is an ex-schoolmaster. V, John & I went on to Ammerdown, having been invited to luncheon by Joanna Hylton, again because Quintin Hailsham (a cousin of Raymond Hylton) was staying there, and would like to see us. As happened last year, I was put next to Betty Miller-Jones, on the other side Anne Oxford, looking rather frail after incessant car accidents. She said that as a girl she had been to school in Rumania, where her father (Palairet) was *en-poste* in Bucharest. She had loved it. Trim Oxford also present. I had a word with Quintin Hailsham (Hogg at school) before lunch started. He said he always wanted to stay in bed longer in the morning than circumstances allowed, nowadays he had a housekeeper (his wife having died), who calls him, takes the dog out. The last office was previously undertaken by himself, the dog playing a great part in his life. Before that he had risen at 6.30 or whatever time dictated by the dog. He has grown fatter since last year, in fact did not look particularly well. He complained of having to sit up late in the House of Lords to vote, however seemed quite lively. He told me he had never read the whole of *King Lear*. I find this rather shocking in a Lord Chancellor, tho' at the the same time, in general, I am not at all in favour of Cabinet Ministers being intellectuals. It is not their job. If given that way, they are likely to be middlebrows of the worst kind, with at the same time immense intellectual self-satisfaction. However, *King Lear* is a little different. Also Hailsham was in College at Eton. I talked to Per Hylton about getting clocks mended. She said there was a man in Kilmersdon who loves doing that, refused to be paid for it (could that be my fan who appearing on the doorstep, presented me with a clock? He lives elsewhere if I remember right?). Joanna Hylton, who is really rather jolly, complained that they were having a rough time with the police fussing round to prevent Quintin Hailsham from being blown up by the IRA. Today's papers review a novel called *Small World*, by David Lodge, in which Arthurian symbolism includes mention of The Fisher King – don't think that matters so far as my own project is concerned.

Sunday, 25 March

Driven by John, we lunched with David Cecil at Red Lion House. David in good form (eighty-two next month). He talked, among other things, of staying as an undergraduate with the Asquiths at The Wharf, Abingdon, a house constructed (like Red Lion House itself) out of a pub, with the addition of various cottages knocked together. The Wharf was intensely uncomfortable for guests. David said Leslie Hartley was once staying there, came down the stairs with Arthur Asquith ('the only respectable member of the family', David added), saw through a hatch (presumably relic of building's pub days) Mr Asquith, former Prime Minister, in a clinch with his mistress Hilda Harrison to whom, in Duckworth days, I gave luncheon at The Savoy, with the unattained object of publishing her Asquith letters. Another publisher offered more money. She had reddish hair, and was every inch a Prime Minister's mistress. The scene at The Wharf was essentially an L. P. Hartley novel incident. Leslie afterwards complained that Arthur Asquith was quite incapable of coping with this contretemps. Instead of saying something like: 'My father seems occupied at the moment, we'll go into the garden for a minute or two', he simply turned round, went slowly up the stairs again, leaving Leslie to do as best he could in the circumstances.

Margot Asquith lived in a kind of barn more or less separate from the main house. From there she was in the habit of sending notes over to guests, before breakfast, giving instructions as to how she wished them to behave. For example, David himself, then just nineteen, received a missive saying: 'Dear, darling David, do tell Elizabeth to do her hair properly. It looks as if she had slept under her bed, rather than in it.' Elizabeth was the Asquith daughter, later a nympho figure, who attracted many men, including Bowra. She was then married to Prince Antoine Bibesco, Proust's friend. David said Margot once remarked to Venetia Stanley (later Montagu, another of Asquith's girlfriends): 'It's a great bore having you here all the time, darling, but don't tell anyone I said so.' Enjoyable luncheon.

Wednesday, 4 April

V & I lunched with Lees & Mary Mayall at Sturford, other guests Milo (Lord) Parmoor, son of the celebrated White's Club figure, Freddie Cripps, and nephew of the all but forgotten politician Sir Stafford Cripps. Milo Parmoor lives at Sutton Veny, few miles from Sturford, a somewhat low voltage character, in his fifties, formerly, so Lees says, a flamboyant figure. John (Powell) later confirmed the name of Milo Cripps as being well known in the City as a notable personage. The Cripps family take their title from a house called Parmoor, near Hambleden, Berkshire, which they bought shortly after 1800, having made a pile in the Law.

Parmoor formerly belonged for several centuries to the D'Oyly family the last owner John D'Oyly whose portrait by Lemuel Abbott we possess, as I am descended from his sister. Abbott also painted the best-known portrait of Nelson. (Oddly enough the Abbott portrait of Nelson was mentioned in an *Observer Colour Supplement* interview last week.) We talked of the TV film *The Jewel in the Crown*. Lees agreed that the sinister District Police Officer Merrick (brilliantly played by Tim Pigott-Smith), who had chip on his shoulder because not at Public school, actually possessed many marks of having been at a public school, probably an Old Etonian. We talked of the film's treatment of the Subcontinent's handover, would it have been better if delayed. Lees said he had been working on Indian stuff at the time. He himself believed there was no alternative, the pressures were too strong in so many directions, even if deferment might have alleviated some of the slaughter, which was indeed horrific.

Wednesday, 11 April

Consequent on incessant badgering about my bibliography, I talked the question over again with Anthony Hobson (always much in favour). On the principle of hiring one beggar to keep off the others, agreed to G. L. Lilley doing the bibliography of my work. Anthony kindly arranged this, inviting George Lilley and me to lunch at Brooks's. Lilley, middle to late forties (I imagine), rather plump, apparently sensible, now Librarian at St David's University College, Lampeter, Cardiganshire (Dyfed), an establishment, after separate Church-in-Wales existence of more than a century, now part of the Welsh University. The locality was formerly dominated by the Lloyds of Maesyfelin (one of whom a Powell of the Radnorshire house The Travely, married at the end of 17th century), an eminent if somewhat sinister family. Their mansion, like so many Welsh country houses, was now totally demolished. While having drinks at Brooks's bar before lunch I had a word with Alan Bell, whose reviews I always find amusing. Anthony produced a nice claret.

Thursday, 12 April

V to London to give Archie a birthday lunch. She met Giniger, American publisher, at The Lansdowne Club and spoke more of the *Dance* Picture Book. A photographer, Dmitri Kasterine, came here to take photograph for a collection of (mostly American) writers. Kasterine knew Tristram; big, reddish-bald, high forehead, Kalmuck cheekbones, characteristic Russian of one type; his father, a Russian Officer, got out 1922, mother English. He seemed reasonably bright in that quick Slav manner, adapted to talk about anything. I spoke of the Fisher King novel, implications of writing about a photographer. Kasterine made an interesting and significant point that, as in the other arts, a photographer will suddenly find he can take no more photographs, just like writer being written out. Such a visitation would suitably accommodate the 'barren lands' aspect of *The Fisher King*, to which I had already given some thought.

Sunday, 15 April

Driven by John, we lunched with Barbara & Mopsy Bethmann-Hollweg, who for several months of the year live on top floor of a pretty 18th century rectory at Great Cheverell, Wiltshire; in fact just behind the Open Prison there, which one has often passed. The rest of the house belongs to friends; the furniture, pictures, even perhaps to some extent Bethmann-Hollweg/Wadsworth. Luncheon did not appear until 2.15, before which a bottle of German champagne was consumed, later Pauillac '69, nice. A strange party, a shade tiring one way and another. In the evening we had drinks at The Stables, where the Stockwells were in residence.

Tuesday, 1 May

I was lying on the sofa reading, when the telephone went about 3.30 pm. An American, announcing his name as Frederick Morgan, and saying he was calling from New York, told me I had been awarded *The Hudson Review* Bennett Prize ($15,000). He sounded agreeable, over and above the difficulty of sounding otherwise in the circumstances. I attempted to express suitable appreciation of so substantial a recognition of talent. Mr Morgan is coming to luncheon here in the near future to discuss ways and means, as he plans a visit to this country. The *Oxford Companion to American Literature* reveals him as one of the founders of *The Hudson Review* in 1948. He appears to be an American man of letters of some eminence.

Sunday, 13 May

To London. Saw Sussman in morning, who said the previous Thursday a lady sat down in his chair at 4.30 from which she did not rise until 8.30 pm (awful thought). Meanwhile her husband had been sitting in the waiting-room all the time, leaving 11 Devonshire Place only twice in order to re-park his car. At the end of this marathon, Sussman congratulated the husband on patience during such a feat of endurance. The husband replied: 'Quite all right. I've been roaring with laughter all the time reading this.' He held a copy of *To Keep the Ball Rolling*. The husband, of course, had no idea Sussman was my dentist. Sussman was, indeed, apologetic about revealing that fact, in consequence of which the reader (name, Graham Gordon) asked if I would sign the paperback. My rule (after being sent literally crates of books by the same man under different names) to sign only for persons met in the flesh, but, through legal fiction that we might well have sat in the same waiting-room, exchanged a word about the weather, I felt an exception could be made in special circumstances for such a proved enthusiast.

In the evening I attended the Royal Academy Dinner at Burlington House. Arrived early (as habitually), found no one I knew about yet, so sat with drink on one of the large divans in the round Central Hall, watching guests come up the stairs. One of these, clad in knee-breeches, purple from head to foot, gazed round the room on reaching top step. While I was wondering who this could be, the purple figure made straight for me. He turned out to be Robert Runcie, now Archbishop of Canterbury (first met lecturing on an Hellenic Cruise, when Bishop of St Albans). So far as I was concerned, this seemed a good Max Beerbohm Old Self/Young Self situation. We had in fact met at a previous RA Dinner (when he expressed himself a fan of *Dance*), but only in a crowd. Now he sat down beside me, rose at once saying 'I must get a drink', returning with glass of champagne, he began to talk about his son in the BBC: 'Rather old-fashioned young man,' he said. His son apparently likes his job, but has a horror (with which one would deeply sympathize) of staying in BBC for forty years.

We discussed all this, also the Archbishop's recent travels. He remarked that in China 'the poor old Anglicans' were preferred to Roman Catholics, or more rigid Protestant Christians, the former regarded as too redoubtable a power-focus, while religious dissenting sects of all kinds were associated with the US, a country regarded as dangerous. Runcie was delighted that I remembered the story he told when on the cruise to the effect that he visited the Patriarch/Metropolitan (whatever a top ecclesiastic is called in Rumania), who pointed to the picture of the Virgin Mary, which hung side by side with that of the Communist Dictator (some peculiarly vile tyrant I think), both of which adorned wall behind patriarchal throne, uttering the single word: 'Byzantium'. I always like Runcie when we meet. He is amusing, charming, perfectly aware of jokes.

At dinner I sat between David Piper (now Head of the Ashmolean Museum, Oxford, a friend since he was Director of the National Portrait Gallery, I a Trustee), and Lawrence Gowing (also known as fellow NPG Trustee, good painter, last of Euston Road School). Gowing recently opened the Henry Lamb Centenary Exhibition in Manchester (where Henry was brought up), for which I had written an introductory note in Catalogue. Gowing, an enthusiast for Lamb's painting, said show was well hung, other aspects not ideal. I could not quite understand what went wrong. My sister-in-law Mary (Clive) had given a somewhat similar impression in a letter to V. I get on well with Gowing, a slightly tricky character, who never allows a truly appalling stutter to be smallest handicap in his dealings. On the contrary, at NPG meetings he would always get up, argue minuscule (if usually cogent) points, after all appeared to be settled on whatever subject in hand, saliva pouring from his lips on to the table.

David Piper is invariably nice, intelligent, somewhat withdrawn; many supposed improvements at the NPG attributed to Roy Strong were in fact Piper's, the Strong's taste for publicity attracting more attention than the congenial quietness of Piper. Piper is always a shade mysterious. One suspects profound depths of appalling melancholy dating from days as a Japanese PoW. Opposite me at the table, Frederick Gore RA (son of the Camden Town Group painter Spencer Gore), turned out to have known Bobbie Bevan (son of R. P. Bevan also Camden Town Group, who painted mauve horses). Bobbie was at times an adman, longtime acquaintance of mine through the Widow Lloyd world. Half-Polish, he could be both amusing and tiresome.

To my left-front, the other side of table, a luscious blonde kept up a barrage of most alluring oglings, which I could not understand, having reached a stage when vanity is scarcely permissible. The table list showed a man rather than woman in that seat. When dinner broke up she turned out to be Neiti Gowrie, second wife of Grey Gowrie (current Minister of Arts, school friend of Tristram), with whom I had a brief word before dinner was announced. Neiti (daughter of a German General executed after the anti-Hitler officers' plot) is indeed a stunner. I felt quite bowled over after talking with her (she having by then introduced herself), as she possesses the Continental characteristic of feeling respect for writers, anyway conveyed that, which is always acceptable.

The Prince & Princess of Wales constituted *pièce de resistance* of this particular RA Banquet, both of whom I was glad to see close, when they proceeded through the guests before dinner, having never set eyes on either. He is attractive in general demeanour, dignified, at ease, quiet in manner, perhaps a little sad, none of the artificial swagger almost impossible not to develop in his position, which in later life was so unpleasant a feature of the Duke of Windsor. The Princess was prettier than I expected, undoubtedly a 'beauty', hard look, slightly spoiled by a somewhat jutting chin (which no doubt got her where she is). She, too, was doing her stuff well. Empire dress, high-waisted, sleeves caught in, with sparkling sequins, or suchlike, running all over. At dinner the Princess of Wales had Laurie Lee on her left, writer whose whimsical autobiographical novels I have found utterly unreadable. On the few occasions when we have exchanged a word, he has always seemed pleasant and civil.

Presumably the Princess wanted to sit next to him, or he would not have been placed there. Anyway Laurie Lee made the final speech at the end of dinner which was an absolute fiasco, appalling meaningless ramblings which continued for twenty-five minutes at very least. Such stuff was it, that his listeners continually clapped from time to time to persuade him to sit down. This he refused to do, even saying that seemed to be the action he ought to take. What the unfortunate Princess felt about this embarrassing interlude cannot be imagined. Perhaps she was resigned to an awful evening anyway. In any case one can't guess what Hugh Casson was thinking about as President when he put Laurie Lee on to speak. Food awful, wine got by. Enjoyable evening.

Tuesday, 15 May

I returned home in morning feeling shade exhausted. Some weeks ago something called the Ingersoll Foundation, Rockwell, Illinois, wrote to say I was under consideration for the Foundation's T. S. Eliot Award for Creative Writing ($15,000), which, if bestowed, involved going to Chicago to receive the Award, and making a speech to members of the Foundation. It was added that, in special circumstances, this could be undertaken by a surrogate. Various points at once arose. In the first place I really cannot face the journey to Chicago these days. Formerly a few drinks would have got one through, nowadays I am too old for that, quite apart from fact that it would disrupt work with jet-lag for weeks on return. In addition, I am not clear what this evidently Right Wing organization stands for (defined in their explanatory pamphlets as 'Judaeo-Christian Standards' and the 'Ten Commandments'), which, even if broadly speaking sympathetic to a 'traditional Tory', I certainly should not be prepared to make a speech recommending, tho' perhaps implicit (rather than explicit) in my books. Also one certainly wants to avoid anything of fascist flavour. I outlined the above in letter of reply.

This evening John Howard of the Ingersoll rang. He seemed to think the Committee would not favour one not turning up in person, unless for health reasons. People (especially Americans) find difficulty in understanding that one can feel perfectly well, while at the same time one's powers of writing (as they inevitably decline with age) have to be safeguarded, especially in the light of long journeys and public jollifications. Admittedly a few writers do seem to tick over on just such conditions. I happen not to be one of them. At a conservative estimate a trip to Chicago would knock me out for at least a month's work. Explained all this. Howard will put it to the Committee. He seemed a sensible man, and perhaps saw the point. It occurred to me that Bob Conquest might be prepared to go over from Stanford, California, to read my speech, if Ingersoll decided to give me the Prize anyway, at present uncertain. If they do, American Prizes are certainly descending in a gracious shower from Heaven.

Thursday, 24 May

Frederick & Paula (Dietz) Morgan, both of *The Hudson Review*, came to luncheon. They are New Yorkers (an essentially recognizable type, I think, even to me), really keen on books, as opposed to a professional academic concern with them. He is big, she (second wife), small, lively, and appears to some extent to run the show. The Prize is to commemorate Joseph Bennett, co-founder with Frederick Morgan of *The Hudson Review*, which is more or less based on Princeton. Fred Morgan is interested in genealogy (how seriously, I did not discover), the Morgans emigrating from Swansea in 1815. They founded a soap factory, Sapolio, fascinating name I well remember bandied about the kitchen in my childhood, it being some sort of special solution. Morgan *père*, tho' still running the soap factory, had a passion for military matters, serving in both the first & second war, and eventually promoted Major General. The presentation of the Prize to be 15 October, with luncheon at the US Embassy. The Morgans were to see Otway's *Venice Preserv'd* in London the following night, which certainly showed intellectual dedication.

Sunday, 27 May

Driven by John, we lunched with Anthony & Tanya Hobson at The Glebe House. Elizabeth Jane Howard (late Amis, having abandoned Kingsley) was staying there, also Fram Dinshaw. Charlotte Hobson, nearly fourteen, at luncheon. Elizabeth Jane, an old friend of Anthony's I believe, was in goodish form. She said she had not read Kingsley's recently published novel (*Stanley and the Women*), to which I replied there were quite a lot of funny things, if not one of his best works. The widely held supposition that it would contain an unflattering picture of Jane herself (as she had been extremely disagreeable about Kingsley in several newspaper articles) was not substantiated. So far as I was able to judge, there were only faint reminders of her tone of voice in some of the dialogue. In any case it seemed better not to go into too close examination of the novel in the circumstances. Fram looked a bit wretched, I thought, perhaps no more than his normally unbuoyant exterior. It was not in the least reproduced in his manner, so he is probably perfectly all right. He said he is on the point of completing a book on George Herbert, the poet.

Thursday, 31 May

My longtime American fan John S. Monagan (always known by V and me as The Congressman, as formerly Democratic representative in an area of Connecticut) & his wife Rosemary turned up, determined to take us out to luncheon, as he had lunched here once or twice in the distant past. They were retracking their honeymoon in these parts after thirty-five years. The Monagans live in Washington, where (like most Americans) he is a lawyer. He has a slight touch of Bill Davis (old American friend, very hospitable, entertained Hemingway among others), tho' an RC, and (one imagines) fairly strait-laced. She is nice, and both are distinctly bright. At our suggestion we lunched at Haligan's in Frome (where we went with David Cheshire after the filming was over). It looks like private house outside, except for a canopy now saying *Restaurant*. Hard to know how it keeps going; food not at all bad, and an excellent bottle of claret.

Tuesday, 19 June

A somewhat inarticulate young man rang up, asking if he could photograph me. His name was eventually revealed as Andrew Peppard, who is studying photography at a sort of polytechnic by the Elephant & Castle, which, apparently, as a kind of exercise, instructed him to photograph 'some literary people'. He was in Somerset for only a couple of days to see his parents, who live at Taunton, so I agreed that he could come. He turned out to be about eighteen or nineteen, intensely tongue-tied. He had started as painter then switched to photography, doing a course on the subject, which included Art History. He said he had wanted to be a photographer since age of sixteen, but his parents were 'scientific' (some form of engineering, so far as I could gather) and quite unfamiliar with the arts in any guise. All this is of interest in the light of writing a novel about a photographer, tho' I would have preferred an exponent who had been dedicated to photography from his earliest years.

Saturday, 23 June

Evangeline Bruce, Nicko & Mary Henderson (originally encountered with the Suttons at Westwood) to luncheon. The Hendersons, whose house is near Newbury, met Evangeline's train there and brought her here with them. Mary is Greek, blonde, formerly married to a Frenchman killed by Germans (Gestapo) during the Resistance, in which she too was involved. She was, in fact, very jolly at lunch, saying she objected to Frank (Longford) making a speech at her wedding (why, one cannot imagine, except impossible to prevent him from making speeches) in which he had said he was surprised at a Greek being 'so light in colour', as if he expected her to be a Negress. Nicko Henderson's mother had Bloomsbury affiliations, and when speaking of her Nicko implied affair with Henry Lamb. Nicko is a lively, amusing figure, with a lot of charm. Evangeline was in good form. Enjoyable luncheon.

Friday, 29 June

V and I to London for the John Betjeman Memorial Service at Westminster Abbey. We had booked seats. I arrived about an hour before the (11.30) start, and was first occupant of the Choir Stalls. I was taken up aisle with great pomp by a verger, between already full rows in the nave of the Abbey. I felt that the resentment at this was almost audible (V said later, unprompted, she too had same sensation). The verger who examined my card remarked: 'One of us is called Powell. We told him all his family was coming here today.' (Tristram & Virginia also booked.) I replied: 'You can't throw a stone in the Wye valley without hitting someone called Powell.' 'Ah,' he said, 'The Wye. Makes me think of the Usk, and catching salmon. I was there not long ago.' On that note we parted company. Philip Larkin & Monica Jones appeared in the row behind us, later joined by Kingsley Amis. The block opposite included Peter Quennell (a faint smile on his skull-like features); a couple (said to be the architectural historian/journalist, Gavin Stamp & wife), who rather exhibitionistically brought small baby with them; Richard Ingrams (face agonisingly racked) with wife; Peter Fleetwood-Hesketh (an old friend of V's, Eton contemporary and colleague of mine in War Office, architectural buddy of Betjeman's); Grey Gowrie; no doubt others one knew.

Service a tremendous affair, the Archbishop of Canterbury in charge; Prince of Wales reading the Lesson (which he did well), perfectly right for the Poet

Laureate. The address by a cleric named Harry Williams, who emphasized how much Betjeman loathed the smoothness of business executives. (Williams himself gave an unrivalled example of ecclesiastical smoothness, and for ingratiating himself in other ways Betjeman too unequalled.) After a polite reference to Penelope Betjeman as wife, he spoke of 'thirty years help and support from another', tho' Elizabeth Cavendish was not mentioned by name. Finally, in obeisance to the Prince of Wales, adding how much Betjeman would have agreed with 'certain recent remarks about architecture'. One could not help indulging in rather banal reflections about the seedy unkempt (but never in the least unambitious) Betjeman of early days, snobbish objections to him at Oxford, Chetwodes' opposition to the marriage, crowned at the last by all this boasted pomp and show. It was a remarkable feat. Emerging from the Abbey I was accosted by a man (whose name appeared to be Greenall) asking for my signature in his autograph album. I complied.

V and I walked across the Park to lunch with Evangeline Bruce in Albany. Other guests: John Wells and wife Theresa (née Chancellor, formerly Gatacre), whose excellent legs I had noticed in the Abbey without knowing who she was. I sat next to her, perfectly pleasant to chat with . . . Pat Trevor-Roper (Hugh Dacre's utterly different oculist brother) . . . Evangeline as usual in good form. She seemed delighted with three magnums of Château Batailley Pauillac, '70, which I gave her in preference to champagne for other friends in *The Hudson Review* Bennett Prize celebration, some of which we drank at luncheon. I am struck by how much more effusively grateful rich friends were than poor ones, generally speaking, tho' of course exceptions among poor ones. We met John at Paddington, returning with him on 4.45 train.

Saturday, 30 June

Tristram drove V, John, Georgia and me to Bristol for the Henry Lamb Centenary Exhibition at the Art Gallery, the show having moved on from Manchester where it opened. It was well hung, Lamb's painting is best when not making too insistent a comment himself, tho' Henry's colour is always a shade depressant. There were several good portraits. An odd-looking man, carrying an old army haversack stuffed with newspapers over his shoulder, was wandering round. He paused at Henry Lamb's portrait of myself, looked at the label, stood back and grinned broadly. One wondered what were his reactions. We were just by him. The show included a few photographs taken by Henry, including one of Dorelia John (Augustus's wife, with whom he had an affair), naked on the wooden edge of an old-fashioned bath. The oncoming expression of her face gave an entirely different impression of Dodo to any known to me before. I saw at last her charm, sexual attraction, hitherto hidden from me, as a force people used to talk about. These pictorial qualities here, naked by the bath, were obvious enough. I always found Dodo difficult, which was exceptional, most people adoring her, and saying she was restful to be with.

Wednesday, 4 July

I received a fan letter from Lord Bancroft, late Head of the Civil Service (Balliol man), who enclosed a copy of *The Journal of the Royal Society for Encouragement of the Arts*, which reproduced a lecture given by him. This referred to the late Desmond Keeling (fellow *haut fonctionnaire*), author of *Management in Government*, which Keeling dedicated to 'Short, Blackhead & Widmerpool'. Bancroft's fan letter must rate with that of Admiral Sir Michael Le Fanu, then First Sea Lord. Le Fanu's letter was written in green ink (in the Army allowed only to the top soldier, presumably the same for the top sailor, so that any notes by the CGS should be immediately noticed among other minutes). At present I can't equate Army and RAF fans with RN & Civil Service ones, tho' I have had an Air Commodore, & Colonel S. C. Grant, Royal Engineers, an Instructor at the Staff College. The latter said, among other things, that he reads out my comments on the requirements of a Platoon Commander to all the officers under his, Colonel Grant's, command. He may well rise to senior rank. (His junior officers too after hearing my comments.)

Wednesday, 18 July

Diana Beaufort-Palmer, known by me in ancient days, briefly married to that intoxicated figure Bobby Roberts. She is now widow of George Beaufort-Palmer (brother of Francis whose wife Jessie – Sylvia – Beaufort-Palmer is often mentioned in the early *Waugh Diaries*). Diana sent for my inspection a letter written by Evelyn Waugh to Bobby Roberts, which she rightly judged would make me laugh. It is written on Evelyn's oatmeal-brown EW-embossed writing paper headed from The Abingdon Arms, Beckley, Oxon, undated. It must belong to the early months of 1929, when Evelyn was spending only weekends in London, working in the country on his book during the week. Nancy Mitford at that time lodger with the young Waughs, newly married, in their Canonbury Square flat, Islington.

> My dear Bobby,
>   Nancy Mitford tells me that you were grossly rude to her the other evening when you were drunk. Naturally she is disgusted and so is

Evelyn who was chaperoning her and who made the initial mistake of
introducing you to her.

I need hardly say it will be impossible for us or any of Nancy's friends
to welcome you in the future unless you write apologizing to her and to
Evelyn.

In any case surely it is time you began to learn to behave like a
gentleman when you are drunk particularly since so large a proportion of
your waking hours seem to be spent in that state.

Yours Evelyn Waugh

One would be interested to know what Bobby's misdemeanour had been.
He usually tended to an extreme obsequiousness when in liquor. Bobby
Roberts was an early friend of Evelyn Waugh's (see *Waugh Diaries*), had indeed
introduced Evelyn Waugh to Evelyn Gardner, who, in fact, always found
Bobby too much to bear, a continuing burden. Bobby was also a great friend of
John Heygate's, whom I rather think he introduced to Evelyn Gardner too. I
suggested a copy should be sent to Selina Hastings (now at work on a
biography of Nancy Mitford) as an early example of Evelyn's pomposity. One
might add that Evelyn himself used to get as tight as a tick to the end of his
days, insulting everybody. Diana Beaufort-Palmer also sent photographs of
Evelyn Gardner, taken at the house of Diana's sister in Majorca. Evelyn G. no
doubt staying with her own sister, Mary Hillgarth, whose second husband, a
former Naval officer, was consul there. There were also photographs of D. H.
Lawrence with his wife Frieda in a car.

Tuesday, 24 July

The German translator of *Dance*, Dr Heinz Feldmann, of Münster University,
accompanied by a bright, good-looking, 'assistant', Claudia Pilling (who, to be
just, did seem to know the book pretty well), lunched here to discuss various
points. Dr Feldmann is, I think, sound, if relentlessly Teutonic, a little
exhausting on that account. For example, he pointed out that Sir Gavin
Walpole-Wilson is represented as lecturing on 'Collective Security' *c.* 1928. (It
was, I remember, suggested to me by Malcom Muggeridge.) I replied that the
only conclusion one could come to was that 'Collective Security' had been
coined by Sir Gavin as a diplomat, a concept later taken on by the League; its
originator forgotten, as, so often with brilliant turns of expression. This was
accepted rather doubtfully.

Dr Feldmann went on to assure me that the facetious term 'Piccadilly
medals' would be unintelligible to Germans. I really can't believe that

Germans, for generations a byword for their Orders and Decorations, can have no manner of colloquially defining lightly proffered laurels, which must exist in Germany as elsewhere. He was also worried by 'playing fields', in German a different word being used for agricultural fields, tho' there must be some terms for the open space upon which Germans play soccer. 'House', as a collection of schoolboys, also irked him. Indeed we found no answer to that except putting a note. Finally, when Jenkins thought something, did he think this-that-or-the-other at the moment, or later? I accepted these demurs, suggesting that the meaning of certain sentences should be taken for granted without too much agonizing. Nonetheless Dr Feldmann is dedicated to the novel as translator, and firm on absolute refusal to abridge in any way, which Frank Auerbach, of the publisher Eherinwirth, is apparently still bleating about. I think I am lucky to have him as a translator.

Wednesday, 1 August

Kingsley Amis & Neil Hughes-Onslow came down by train to luncheon. Neil was on the Hellenic Cruise which included the Amises and the Fussells (of the family which built The Chantry, completed 1826), both marriages subsequently busting up. He is an Etonian, White's Club, appears to have done well in the City, and now runs with considerable success the advertising side of National Art Collections Fund, as he is interested in pictures. His wife Susan, also on cruise, not at all unattractive, was apparently christened Grey Owl by the late Esmond Warner (an old friend, also butt, of the Pakenhams), owing to the Red Indian proportions of her inscrutability.

Neil himself's interest in art, relatively smart life, travel, embodies so much that Kingsley turns his countenance away from, anyway sets up to ignore, that one is a little surprised at their becoming friends, especially to extent of persuading Kingsley to take a railway journey. Inevitably they struck on the one Westbury taxi-driver who did not know the way to Chantry, so arrived, via Nunney, rather late. However luncheon (melon, lamb chops, blackcurrants, '70 claret, brandy/calvados) was enjoyable. Kingsley's last novel (*Stanley and the Women*) has a scene where the hero's neurotic son tears off the cover of Saul Bellow's *Herzog* ('As you know', said Kingsley to me, 'a pretty pissy book'). It has now been pointed out that 'Herzog' means 'duke', which, in *Stanley and the Women* is the surname of neurotic boy's father and theme, Kingsley remarked, for future doctoral dissertations. Neil Hughes-Onslow and V went down to the lake (I remained with Kingsley, unattracted by walking). Neil told her that on the cruise Betty Fussell had advised Jane Amis to get out right away, as she herself was doing on return. This presumably Jane passed on to Kingsley,

Kingsley to Neil, unless this was revealed to Grey Owl, which seems most unlikely. On the whole Kingsley in excellent form. He looked better than lately. Good party.

Saturday, 4 August

Driven by John, we lunched with the Nicko Hendersons at The Old School House, Combe, Hungerford, a group of cottages bought about twenty years ago, gradually put in order. Very pleasant unusual country round about. We ate in the garden off large mosaic-topped table made by a daughter of Boris Anrep, White Russian ex-cavalry officer, whose own mosaics formerly affiliated him with Bloomsbury. Also Bloomsbury in his matrimonial complications, tho' not his politics which remained staunchly Right Wing, I believe. Nicko brought up in that world through his mother. Other guests: Geoffrey & Dame Mary Warnock, he a don and Vice-Chancellor of Oxford, she, much in papers lately, Queen of the Embryos, owing to her pronouncements on abortion, similar politico/physiological subjects. They were both perfectly agreeable to talk to. Arnold (Lord) Goodman, still full of go, outwardly resembling George Robey more than ever. Arnold Goodman brought Evangeline Bruce with him, who took a lot of photographs. Alexandra, the Hendersons' daughter, now (second) wife of Derry Moore, with sixteen-month-old son. Nicko barbecued good smokey cutlets, just right, excellent claret out of magnums. I did not see the label. Mary Henderson is agreeable, rather a dark horse one suspects. Enjoyable party, out of the ordinary circumstances owing to some extent to a feeling of seclusion about the place.

Tuesday, 7 August

Andrew Peppard, the young man who asked to photograph me a couple of months ago, turned up with very tolerable photograph he had taken as a present. Rare & pleasant instance of good manners among shoals of people who ask one to do something or other, and never dream of thanks.

Sunday, 19 August

Drinks at The Stables in morning. Staying there were David Cheshire and Vicky Feaver: Vicky is writing a book about Stevie Smith, critical rather than biographical. Gerry Bowden, very nice chap, MP for Dulwich (Con), old Oxford friend of Tristram, also friend of John's, came to luncheon with the

Stockwells, bringing two daughters and an unknown young man. Gerry has just lost his delightful wife and looked rather haggard, as might be expected, otherwise in good form. He is not only nice but also sensible, with a lot of intelligence, an MP one is glad to see in the House, unlike (one regrets to say) not a few Tories. He brought four vols of my Memoirs to sign. David Cheshire was fed up to a degree at being landed with an obituary programme on J. B. Priestley, as well he might, having to waste time on, so far as one knows, a totally uninteresting literary figure.

Monday, 20 August

To London to see Sussman, who removed a tooth. Patricia Lomer of Manor Farm has been one of his patients for years. And people grumble about coincidences in novels.

Wednesday, 22 August

John A. Howard, Secretary of the Ingersoll Foundation, rang at 4.30 pm to say that I am, after all to receive the T. S. Eliot Award for Creative Writing, notwithstanding the fact of not being prepared to travel to Chicago to collect it. I seem to have acted like someone who declares: 'I would not got to Chicago for Ten Thousand Pounds' (in fact somewhat more owing to the exchange). In palmier days I should have liked to see Chicago, a city which always sounds rather beautiful by its lake. Also Chicagoans encountered often seem agreeable. The trouble of such jaunts is the horrors of airports, combined with being these days unable to drink except in extreme moderation at parties, of which no doubt there would have been a spate.

Thursday, 23 August

Roland Gant & Tom Rosenthal (also of Heinemann's) to luncheon. Rosenthal was brought by Roland in order to have his complete set of *Dance* signed. In return Rosenthal kindly presented me with a facsimile of Orwell's MS of *1984*. The weather was appallingly oppressive, far from ideal for visit of this kind, indeed any other. One felt it would have been greatly preferable to have dealt with either singly. Roland, an old friend; Rosenthal, to explore what he is like. Although outwardly matey, I suspect both get on each other's nerves as business associates, operating on totally different literary levels, perhaps one should say publishing levels, setting about authors each in his own individual manner.

V took them round the grottoes. All went well, if a bit exhausting owing to heat. Château La Tour-de-Mons, Margaux, '75, a shade disappointing, I thought. In the evening we watched a TV programme on Cecil Beaton, on the whole rather down-getting, as professionally 'social' people are apt to be when examined in detail, if at same time well worth investigation. Among concourse of friends who spoke about Beaton, far the best was Clarissa Avon; everyone was fairly acerbic, no doubt deservedly so far as that went. Cecil was always pleasant to V (an old friend of his sisters) and me, neither of us playing any part in his serious ambitions.

Friday, 24 August

We lunched with Lees & Mary Mayall at Sturford. There was present ex-Eton master Peter Lawrence, not previously met, son-in-law of George Lyttelton (also Eton beak, co-partner of the *Lyttelton/Hart-Davis Letters*). Lawrence was a fairly typical representative of Eton beakdom. He was collecting from Lees various items for the newly instituted Eton Museum (to be in some sort of a crypt in the Cloisters, I think), which Lawrence is organizing more or less from its foundation. He said my efforts to get *The Eton Register* relaunched in a proper manner had resulted in the job being put to some extent in his hands. He did not seem particularly enthusiastic about this. One can only hope for the best. No doubt computers have revolutionized books of reference of this sort. Lawrence said the Lyttelton family had been much irritated by the impression given in the *Lyttelton/Hart-Davis Letters* that George Lyttelton was abysmally bored during the latter years of his life. An interesting question. I should have thought the existing evidence of that in the shape of the *Letters*, suggested his boredom was largely owed to his own determination to remain intensely prim & buttoned-up. Rupert must have let off bombshell towards the end by revelations about his mother, and the fact he was unlikely really to have been Hart-Davis's son, etc. This obviously shook George Lyttelton to the core, as well it might. An interesting study might be written on the extraordinary lack of experience of schoolmasters.

Sunday, 2 September

Driven by John, we lunched with Rachel & Kevin Billington at Poyntington, over in the Sherborne direction, where they have an ancient house up by back of a church. Staying with them was a female American friend, Eden Lipson, on the *New York Times Book Review*, apparently brought over to lunch by the Billingtons some years ago, tho' I could not remember the occasion. She seemed perfectly agreeable. John Gross is said to be leaving the *NYT Book Review*. Kevin is doing a TV film of *Hay Fever* (Noël Coward), which we talked about. I saw the play performed only once, then by ENSA actors during the War Intelligence Course at Matlock, hardly to be described as a star cast; all the same one suspects it remains the best of what have become with the years pretty thin gruel, Coward's wit having little or no stamina.

Juliet O'Rorke, a great *habituée de la maison* at Ruckman's, Michel Salaman's house, always said *Hay Fever* was exactly like staying with the Salamans, at their Lutyens house (Lutyens's first house?). It is near Leith Hill, in pretty unbuilt-over Surrey country. Salaman rich, good natured, friend of Augustus John. The play was in fact written before *The Vortex*, with US background, I believe. When I told Kevin about Ruckman's he said he had already decided *Hay Fever* house to be by Lutyens in the film. Rachel, recalling their courting days in New York, said she could not get taxi one night, and a passing lorry driver offered a lift, which Kevin thought an excellent idea, 'Leaving me to be raped and murdered', said Rachel. Nice claret.

Monday, 3 September

John St John (whose chief claim to fame is that he served in the Royal Marines with Evelyn Waugh, then wrote *At War with Waugh*, reminiscences of that experience) came to talk about Heinemann's, as he is writing a history of the firm, by which he has been employed for thirty years. I rather think John St John was an early pseudonym of John Galsworthy. Possibly I reviewed St John's Waugh book. St John, with a white beard, looked like Father Christmas after rather hectic Yuletide Season. This appearance was to some extent explained by his remark that he normally drank two bottles of wine a day (no spirits). He seemed astonished that one thought this slightly above average alcoholic intake. He said Evelyn had been great alleviation to life in the Marines, quite hopeless at day-to-day duties as an officer and hated by the men. I was surprised at this last characteristic emerging so early in Evelyn's Service career, supposing it developed in consequence of delusions of grandeur consequent on his smart Commando Service life. Evelyn became a Company Commander in the Royal Marines only because units were so much under establishment. Also people were impressed by this famous figure, so much older than everyone else, and invited to Downing Street. However he was demoted to Intelligence Officer at time of the Dakar raid. Evelyn was always flamboyant in the Mess. When a young man, St John said, he went to Paris, and was picked up by Brian Howard (school contemporary, Vice President of the Eton Society of Arts) at the Coupole (famous Café in Montparnasse), then taken to a queer night-club in the company of Cyril & Jean Connolly. Howard continued to write to him afterwards 'without the least encouragement'. One presumes his attractions as a young man may to some extent explain being taken up by Evelyn Waugh in the Marines, tho' I seem to remember from St John's book that he also was, or became, Roman Catholic. In general St John appears never to have developed this early foothold in literary bohemian life. All slightly interesting about EW.

Tuesday, 4 September

Andrew Mylett, known for long time as a journalist/publisher/literary agent (years ago produced curious little symposium about *Dance* in semi-trade paper called *Summary* he then edited) rang to congratulate me on the Ingersoll Prize (seen by him in an Associated Press handout). He asked for an interview in the *Exeter Express & Echo*, of which he is now Literary Editor. My first surmise was that he had taken this job after being unsuccessful in employments mentioned above; on the contrary he was pleased to have managed to arrange it, wanting to live in the country. This explanation seems quite convincing, certainly understandable with children. Mylett has an extensive knowledge of the journalist/literary world and good stories of those who inhabit it.

Wednesday, 5 September

Bob & Liddie Conquest, over for short time, to luncheon. Bob had seen the PM (Mrs Thatcher), whom he reported in good shape. We talked of the Ingersoll party for T. S. Eliot Award, at which Bob has, most kindly, agreed to represent me, deliver speech, which he said he preferred not to read until back in US. I see point of that. He & Liddie travelled up to Houghton Conquest, original nest of Conquests in Bedfordshire, to inspect Conquest tombs in church, also brasses, of which Liddie took rubbings. This art she previously studied *ad hoc* at a place where that is taught, hard by (one feels that phrase is required in the circumstances) St James's Piccadilly. This shows considerable devotion in an American, and fourth wife. She is charming, and Bob a lucky man.

Sunday, 9 September

About a week ago rather dotty fan letter arrived from Denmark, asking for an autograph, mentioning that the sender had seen a TV programme about me, which he greatly enjoyed. Mystified by this statement, I thought possible he

had been in England when Cheshire programme was shown. As it happens
Tristram is doing a TV film about Karen Blixen. To shoot it he goes to Kenya
this week. He rang up to say goodbye, and reported that when he was recently
taking Blixen sequences in Denmark, of her home, the Platypus programme
about me (not bought by BBC or other company in this country) was being
shown. How characteristic of everything to do with the film world in all its
manifestations that no one concerned should have bothered to inform me or
my agent that the film was being shown in Denmark. Also, one might add, that
the BBC and the rest did not want it.

Sunday, 16 September

Driven by John, we lunched with David Cecil at Red Lion House. Jonathan
Cecil & his wife (second) Anna were there. Jonathan, a school friend of
Tristram's, therefore known by us for years, is now a comparatively celebrated
actor (comic curates), little difference off stage or on, in general demeanour,
Anna in the same profession, jolly, hair rather less pink than formerly. David,
looking perhaps a bit more battered than on our last visit, was in good form
nevertheless. We talked of the K. Clark biography, which has aroused strong
feelings. (When I reviewed it a furious former secretary of Clark's wrote saying
he wasn't a 'pouncer' on women. He may well not have pounced on her; in any
case I pointed out – as so often to correspondents – it was not me but the author
to whom complaint should be made.)

David (himself no Brummell) remarked that he had never regarded Clark as
well dressed. Clark was always very neat, but I agree something also looked
radically wrong for some reason. Jonathan is doing an E. F. Benson novel on
radio, said Benson fits into medium well. Anna, who had absented herself
immediately after luncheon, suddenly made a dramatic entry with the
arresting lines: 'The new Prince is to be called Harry.'

Friday, 28 September

Adam Lee, director of Child's with whom we lunched twice at the Bank, rang
to ask if he & his wife could look in 'for coffee' today, as he was on his way to
open a new branch of Child's at Taunton. V invited them to luncheon here.
Lee explained they were committed for lunch already. They could just drop in
for a moment at 10.30. This was agreed. He then arrived alone at about 11
o'clock (his wife having to stay with sick children), remaining in the house
until midday.

Thursday, 4 October

The new tenant of Garden Cottage, down Stoney Lane below The Stables, came to call, a young man called Nick Wigzell, a journalist, tall, romantically good-looking, his work based on Wells, a chain of small local papers. His girlfriend Ingrid (Sofering?) could not accompany him on this second visit (which was to discuss digging out damp on our side of his house) because of some complication in their move-in, only just taken place. Wigzell seemed perfectly tolerable.

Monday, 8 October

Negotiations have been taking place with Harlech Television, via the Rector, about shooting a film in the Paddock Field, with Chantry Church in the background; in consideration of which a substantial contribution has been made to Church funds. I have agreed to this. The plot of story being filmed involved the digging of two graves in the field. A young man, John Parris, with a red beard, came to talk about ways & means. I told him in the first instance to report whatever HTV wanted to Kenny Norris, who has the 'keep' (ie. grass-feed), of Paddock Field, and has already been informed of the film. After Parris had set off on this errand to the village, Mrs Poulson (our four-times-a-weekly) announced that Leslie Norris (Kenny Norris's father) had just died. I pictured some macabre misunderstanding arising between Parris & Kenny, the former adumbrating at the digging of a grave in Paddock Field; the latter supposing this intended for his father's entombment. The film, *Jenny's War*, apparently centres on a German PoW Camp, from which someone escapes by posing as being dead.

Saturday, 13 October

John had Maggie & Guillaume de Rougemont staying at The Stables, where we dined, dinner cooked by all three, Guillaume doing steaks as good as any I have ever tasted. Maggie, as Literary Agent, operates business from their house in London, this must need lots of energy, as she has several quite successful authors in her list, and also looks after Henry aged three. Guillaume described how on one of his trips to India as a courier, a lady wanted to find a quiet spot to relieve herself. Accordingly, went off on her own through the jungle. Local monkeys interested in this, followed her, eventually hundreds of them. This caused the Indian peasants round about to wonder what was reason for this disturbance among the monkeys, so the villagers followed the monkeys. In the end an enormous crowd gathered round her in the jungle,

Indians, monkeys, watching the fun. The HTV people rather a plague, wanting things done at The Lodge, and using the telephone. They had to be called to order. I told them I should not have slightest hesitation in kicking them out unless this stopped forthwith.

Monday, 15 October

HTV have begun their shooting, handicapped by fact that their Leading Lady, Dyan Cannon, had an accident and retired to hospital. Nonetheless, an extraordinary scene is now taking place in the Paddock Field, lots of white crosses all over the ground, newly dug grave, German soldiers in grey greatcoats, steel (first war) helmets, and a German pastor in bands. We lunched with John Parris at the mobile eating-place, buses parked in back parts of the farm on the corner of Mells Lane opposite our house. These made the infinitely untidy former pig farm, dump for old cars, etc, look quite like a movie 'lot'. Moussaka, chips, peas, chocolate gâteaux, banana, orange juice; rather like food on cruise, not too bad for once in a way.

Monday, 22 October

A telephone interview for the best part of two hours in the afternoon by Larry Kart of the *Chicago Tribune*, in connexion with the Ingersoll Prize, as that is an Illinois affair. Kart made unusually intelligent comments for that type of occasion. It is the sort of thing Americans do well.

Wednesday, 24 October

Our land-agent, Mr Percy Quick, of Cooper & Tanner, Frome (also auctioneers) came to discuss changes in tenancies, rents, etc, consequent on the death of Leslie Norris. Mr Quick, tall, white-haired, bronzed, handsome, same age as myself, a great local character, knows about everybody, about everything, very spry still. These discussions about local people, local lands, always make me think of similar ones in the past recorded in documents one has studied for genealogical information, so that when Quick notes down that a tenant has children, or not, I feel how useful that item may turn out to some genealogical researcher several centuries from now.

Thursday, 25 October

V & I to London for *The Hudson Review* luncheon party at the US Embassy in

Grosvenor Square. Paula (Dietz) Morgan was to meet us at Paddington with a car. As it happened, we took a 'relief' train at Westbury, which came to the platform a minute or two before the ordinary one, yet inexplicably arrived at Paddington a few minutes after. Accordingly, Paula Morgan understandably was in rather a stew, supposing we had missed the train. All being well, we set out for the Embassy, where considerable 'security' precautions were exercised before our admittance. A smart Marine was on duty. Like most chanceries these days this is a hive of offices, without the least pretence to old-fashioned diplomatic dignity.

After introductions to various PR personnel upstairs, we were conducted to curious underground area, a room with a bar at one end, where pre-luncheon drinks were consumed. There was a cloakroom for *les deux sexes et autres* just off. In the room itself was an unfamiliar piece of plumbing set halfway up the wall, which V supposed to be a urinal; John later explaining it merely ran iced water.

Almost everyone invited had accepted; refusals were Hugh & Caroline Montgomery-Massingberd; Jilly & Leo Cooper (the latter couple prevented at last moment); John & Iris Bayley, Hugh & Mary Lloyd-Jones, did not answer, either away or in a donnish coma. Our party ascended to first floor. The dining-room itself of a strange order, very large, on one side a long high screen, covered with posters (the nature of which I failed to ascertain, looking like those at railway stations advertising holiday resorts), the screen blocking off a row of offices, where typewriters were tapping. On the two sides opposite & at right-angles to the screen were high windows looking out on to Grosvenor Square. We had separate tables, about eight persons to each.

I sat between William (Bill) Pritchard (Amherst don met there in '64, visited Chantry in '77) and Roger Rosenblatt, a *Time* magazine whizz-kid. William Pritchard, who had written a nice piece in *The Hudson Review* (of which he is a pillar), bright, much better grasp of Twenties/Thirties writers, their relative importance, than most critics, British or American. He is not bemused by Bloomsbury, Auden, etc, like so many. Pritchard has, however, a different cruising speed from Rosenblatt (he looks young, yet son at Harvard), whom I liked, also decidedly bright. With Rosenblatt I felt I was living through one of the early chapters of blockbusting Jewish novel in which the hero would end as President, in the 'chair' for some exotic murder, or with possibly long beard, shovel hat, corkscrew curls, of some fanatical Orthodox sect in Israel. I could have got on admirably with Bill Pritchard, or with Rosenblatt, tête-à-tête, bit of a strain turning from one to the other, changing the key. Just beyond Pritchard was Mrs Lyn Chase, wife of a New York tycoon, a great supporter of *The Hudson Review*. She is also a keen *Dance* fan. Mrs Chase invited us to stay with her for a week in NYC, at the same time outlining programme of social activities, hair-raising in demands on physical energy. This culminated in a performance of *Eugene Onegin* at the Met; very kind, but would certainly have finished me off.

There were, of course, speeches at the end of lunch. Fred Morgan warned me that the American Minister at the Embassy, Ray Seitz, in face of considerable discouragement, insisted on making one of these. He began by saying he had never read any of my books, perhaps they would be more popular in the US if I pronounced my name in a manner other than I did. This understandably caused a good deal of embarrassment among the Americans present, indeed a more boorish observation would be hard to conceive. In my experience members of the American Foreign Service know how to behave, indeed I should have said have better manners, on the whole, than our own Diplomatic Service; tho' one must remember one speaks as a non-American.

Before beginning my thank-you speech, I gave the routine answer to question of how Powell is pronounced, when this matter arises in the US, (subsequently reproduced in the Peterborough column of the *Daily Telegraph*), that Americans do not – anyway usen't to – rhyme the Lowell family's surname with bowel. Fred Morgan, William Pritchard, Roger Rosenblatt all spoke, short and to the point, tho' Tristram said Kingsley Amis's face was pure H. M. Bateman while their speeches were in progress. They were delivered from a podium, to which I had to walk to receive the 'citation', and a cheque for $15,000. This was the most trying moment of the jollification; at the same time, once there, perhaps preferable, giving a sense of power, rather than the always awkward operation of pushing back one's chair from the table, and hearing muttered comments of one's next-door neighbour.

The Spurlings said that while I was making my speech they saw through one of the windows a man in the square below beginning to unfurl a banner; presumably a demonstration, whether in favour of my receiving the Bennett Award, or protesting the Prize should have been given to another writer, not revealed, as nothing further materialized from that direction. The food might have been worse: smoked salmon; chicken; fruit salad. I could not place the white wine, drinkable without pretension (or later ill effects), I thought possibly Spanish. It turned out, of course, to be Californian, which I should have guessed, having drunk a fair amount when in Hollywood. Kingsley complained he did not get enough. It seemed to flow reasonably freely. Amusing & enjoyable occasion.

Tuesday, 30 October

A bearded photographer, Richard Dudley-Smith, came to take picture for Andrew Mylett's piece, which, expanded with details of what I have for breakfast, etc, he sold to *Sunday Times Colour Supplement* for their'Day in my Life' feature. Dudley-Smith was so entranced by the oil-engine in the basement that he took all photographs with that as background, posing V and me in different positions in front. Trelawney showed himself at first in an amenable mood to be photographed (which he usually objects to), then the boiler started up, which upset him, so he retired upstairs, refusing all further efforts to include him in pictures.

Thursday, 1 November

George Lilley, Librarian of St David's University College, Lampeter, came to see file copies of my books, pasted-up journalism, etc, for my bibliography. His family was originally called Lilienthal and came from Germany in 1930s. He seems to know his stuff, and is obviously industrious, tho' I find bibliography, even my own, hard to take much interest in. It is the sort of pursuit that might have engrossed my father, had he possessed just that additional touch of intellectuality which he lacked, which undermined his interest in books, pictures, etc.

While Lilley was here Tristram rang with the sad news that Julian Jebb had taken an overdose. This is a most tragic affair. Julian was a friend of all the family, used to stay at The Stables for Christmas, go abroad with the Stockwells, occasional rows with them of the kind old friends have, tho' V and I always saw his best behaviour. I thought Julian not quite so full of his usual exuberance at the *Hudson Review* luncheon, tho' I only spoke to him for a second or two as there so many people one had to have a word with. Tristram is naturally very upset, not only at loss of a friend, but he bore main brunt of finding what had happened, owing to Julian failing to turn up for some BBC assignment.

When the *Death in Venice* film was being shown, Julian said he wanted to direct another version called *Little Death in Little Venice* (at that time he lived in purlieus of the Maida Vale canal), tho' by the time he did himself in he had emigrated to the Ladbroke Grove colony of intellectuals. Julian was a person one was always glad to see, hear from, a kind of infinitely old, infinitely high-spirited, clever little boy, who eventually, like Tithonus, would become without much difficulty, or alteration of appearance, a grasshopper, or suchlike, leaping round the literary world for ever. Alas, that didn't happen.

Tuesday, 20 – Thursday, 22 November

George Lilley came all day to bibliographize. He is staying at Evercreech (where Mrs Gould, former cantankerous hostess of The White Horse, Chantry, announced she wanted to 'lay her bones'). It is really too much of a business to put people up these days, so Lilley found somewhere for himself. All the ironmongery of writing (with its internal politics as ventilated somewhere like *The Author*) bores me to death, especially recording ephemeral journalism, tho' I suppose that has to be done. Lilley thrives on such stuff and is anxious to pay further visits, get down more, which so far as possible I discouraged. He is a nice hardworking chap. He presented me with the first volume of the *History of St David's University College, Lampeter*. I remember going through the Parish Register at Disserth, Radnorshire (where my gt-gt-gt-grandfather lived in the 1760/70s, and begot one illegitimate, and several legitimate, children) where there was an anonymous entry in the Deaths: 'The Boy from Lampeter'. Was he a runaway student like the Scholar Gypsy?

Monday, 26 November

John Hayes, Director of the National Portrait Gallery, wrote to recall that I once suggested he might lunch here, if ever in the neighbourhood: could he do that now? As it is at least eight or nine years since I ceased to be an NPG Trustee, when I last set eyes on Hayes, I was surprised by this request. We issued an invitation to choose his own date for luncheon, which proved today, to enable him to drive here from some residence near Hungerford, then return to London. He appeared dressed in a dark blue blazer with metal buttons, sombre trousers, hat of antique shape (also like the Scholar Gypsy which covers an extensive field).

Throughout the visit Hayes's self-invitation remained completely obscure. We made conversation, talked of such NPG Trustees who remained on the Board from my own day, spoke of those who had retired, then Hayes departed. He showed absolutely no interest whatever in the house, its date, or the outlook, let alone the pictures; the last of which are, after all, part of his own profession. Almost everyone who comes here speaks of the view from the library windows, or asks about the quarry. No such enquiry crossed the mind of Hayes so far as one could guess.

The portrait alleged to be the Duke of Marlborough might at least have stirred him to ask name of the subject. The Richard Wilson in the dining-room could have caught his eye as he is supposed to be an expert on Gainsborough. As it happened *Art and Power*, by Roy Strong, was lying on a table, as I am reviewing it. Hayes picked up the book, made a few mildly satirical comments on Strong as his predecessor in directing the NPG, mentioned the projected extension of the Gallery (contemplated in my day on the Embankment by Vauxhall Bridge Road), now likely to be in Orange Street, behind the present building. Hayes left as enigmatically as he arrived, like a ghostly visitant – not boding any good.

Saturday, 1 December

Our Golden Wedding Anniversary. Tristram & Virginia very sweetly gave a celebration party at The Stables, where Ferdie, Julia, Mary Mount, Simon & Alice Boyd, were staying. V, John & I went down about 6.15, with a Jeroboam or Rehoboam (not sure which) of Champagne (Deutz & Geldermann non-vintage), acquired, with other wine, twenty or more years ago in recognition of a contribution to *The Complete Imbiber*, hard to tell how many bottles contained, may be measured later. It seemed to last quite well, not outstandingly dry, if thoroughly drinkable.

Guests (all arranged by Tristram, a great alleviation of one's responsibilities, tho' naturally including only persons known to him): Lees & Mary Mayall; Henry & Virginia Bath; Joff, Tessa & Lucinda Davies; Joanna Hylton; Jamie & Sarah Maclean; Geoffrey & Mary Waldegrave; Michael Briggs; Mary & George Clive, the last two, sportingly, came over from Whitfield, would drive back. (Tristram assured me nothing to what George will do in distance to parties); Grey & Neiti Gowrie (quite unexpected from London, also returning that night).

Georgia, Archie and Mary Mount, did a lot of handing things round. The Gowries & Clives stayed for supper, also brilliantly laid on by the Stockwells. I sat between Neiti Gowrie and Alice, Grey much improved by being a Cabinet Minister, evidently what he needed. They now live in Montgomeryshire, after nearly buying what they described as a beautiful Folly at Poston, near Vowchurch, Herefordshire, the Parry family seat in ancient days. Queen Elizabeth's Maid of Honour, Dame Blanche Parry belonged to the family, a celebrated contemporary figure. The Parrys even related to Dr Dee, so in Welsh terms might almost be called connexions of the Powells.

Grey asked if I held any views on the Laureateship, vacant since Betjeman's demise, adding it was not in his gift as Minister of Arts, tho' one imagines his backing would carry considerable weight. I said Philip Larkin should certainly have it in my opinion, notwithstanding certain objections like not being a particularly nice man, reclusiveness, occasional public indiscretions such as saying he did not want it, and living in Hull. In fact, I think it probable that Larkin would not accept the Laureateship, but he writes the sort of poetry that would not make the implications of the job out of the question. If Larkin refused, Roy Fuller, although perhaps a shade old, tho' that is no real objection as Roy still produces buoyantly. I deplored the suggestion that tenure should be temporary, for five years say, or any other such utilitarian approach to the office. The fact that the Poet Laureate has quite often been a mediocrity in past centuries adds to the fun, its continuity illustrating official or public taste. Besides, a lot of good poets were Laureate too.

One cannot help feeling it would have been better for Larkin to have kept his mouth shut on the subject, but Kingsley Amis & Bob Conquest say that is something Larkin finds hard to do. Roy Fuller, notwithstanding political views unsympathetic to me, might easily find a facility for writing *ad hoc* about public events. Grey, regarding himself as a poet, seemed to agree with all this, but then he is also a politician, whose profession is so to appear.

Alice Boyd, who had piled her hair up on top, looking most attractive, says she is sometimes mistaken for Princess Anne in shops, but not at parties. Henry Bath goes to London every Saturday to preside over the Football Pool Board. He was in good form, as indeed was everyone present. The Mayalls prudently equipped themselves with a taxi to convey them home afterwards. At first supposed the driver a foreigner, then he turned out to be a serving private soldier stationed at Warminster with a Glaswegian accent. Ferdie said Mrs Thatcher, after five minutes conversation, decides whether or not she likes someone, always violently one way or the other. Thus a row of potential ambassadors to Washington will be dismissed as wet, then in despair Nicko Henderson is sent as a capable retired professional. Excellent party.

Thursday, 6 December

About 7.30 pm the telephone rang, a character announcing himself as Edward Steen, speaking from France (Lyons), asked if I could (1) tell him how to spell Mrs Erdleigh's name, (2) just how Dr Trelawney's invocation went: 'The Essence of the All, etc.' It appeared Steen is a journalist on the feature page of the *Sunday Telegraph*, is reporting the Archbishop of Canterbury's visit to a curious French religious sect run by a hierophant of some sort with a name like Brother Taizé. Steen said this figure was exactly like Dr Trelawney, similar devotional formulae and bearing. Runcie was utterly stumped how to deal with him, whether to kneel down or not. Steen declared himself a great fan, wanted to bring the Trelawney scenes from *Dance* in when writing his piece, tho' I doubt whether he will get away with that. He said he found people either liked the novel enormously, or hadn't the faintest idea what it was all about. Many persons have expressed the same experience to me, both ways.

Sunday, 9 December

V and I attended Percy Somerset's Memorial Service at Maiden Bradley Church, densely crowded. We sat on a bench in front of a righthand side aisle, opposite an extremely elegant reclining figure of one of the Seymours (not, I think, a Duke of Somerset) by Rysbrack *c.* 1707. What a fine sculptor Rysbrack was, his superb equestrian of William III at Bristol for instance. Did Rysbrack particularly work in the West? The parson taking the service looked exactly like the actor playing Bolt (porter at the brothel) in *Pericles*, which we had watched the night before. The two Seymour sons read the Lessons. Afterwards we had a brief word with Jane Somerset, who said she recently drank at the Mayalls some of the *Hudson Review* champagne I distributed. She looked rather shattered, not surprisingly. Driving away barely caught a glimpse of Johnny & Caroline Walker (neighbours, Johnny was a Major in Green-jackets), Lees & Mary Mayall, otherwise saw no one we knew. The *Sunday Telegraph* contained Steen's piece about the Archbishop of Canterbury attending some strange French religious sect, but as expected the reference to Dr Trelawney was cut. One notes again and again what amounts to censorship (particularly in the US, no doubt generally in all journalism throughout the world) of any original idea in a piece.

Wednesday, 19 December

Bill Ott, of *Booklist* and *Openers* (American Library Association), rang from US for telephone interview. He seemed quite sensible. Being interested in American regional types, I am developing a slight sense of the Chicago manner, less aggressive perhaps than NYC, tho' one might have expected the contrary.

Tuesday, Christmas Day

V, John & I lunched at The Stables, where Ferdie, Julia, William, Harry, Mary, Mount were staying. I am always struck by Ferdie's ability to be agreeable, amusing, without revealing smallest detail of the life that surrounds him, whether, as recently, at 10 Downing Street, now at *The Spectator*, early days of childhood in his own home. Enjoyable party.

Wednesday, Boxing Day

In morning the Mayalls gave one of their all-embracing drink parties, which I did not attend, V & Stables group going. Nowadays I don't care for standing for comparatively lengthy periods, nor, for that matter, making conversation to other people's neighbours. V reported Alexandra Mayall as turning up with a remarkable new boyfriend in a wonderful check suit. Tristram, Virginia, John, Ferdie and Julia, dined here, the young people entertaining themselves at The Stables.

Friday, 28 December

The Mounts left for Venn, their cottage in Pembrokeshire. V & I had evening drinks at The Stables to meet Philip Jebb, Julian's brother, Abbot and Headmaster of Downside. In appearance one could see touches of their grandfather Hilaire Belloc, of which no physical mark was visible in Julian, peculiarly lacking in the bodily heaviness Belloc always seems to have possessed. Philip Jebb was agreeable, with that slightly uncomfortable undertow that headmasters, especially clerical ones, can scarcely avoid. Julian's death was not mentioned, tho' I believe the subject had been touched on with Tristram before we arrived. In this connexion I received letter from Fred Morgan some weeks ago saying he met Julian at the *Hudson Review* luncheon party at the US Embassy, who mentioned he would like to write for the magazine; could I give any information about him. Another indication that Julian's suicide was wholly on impulse. All very sad.

1985

Wednesday, 9 January

An Australian academic, called David McKinley, came to tea. I saw him on the strong recommendation of Dr Donat Gallagher (James Cook University, North Queensland), who edited Evelyn Waugh's *Collected Journalism*, which I reviewed. McKinley was about to embark on a dissertation, *Dance* as the subject (he has already done one on Maugham). He plans it about 150,000 words and will take five years. He is agreeable, reasonably intelligent, with heavy black eyebrows. He said he had been married twelve years, then divorced, was now married five years to a Filipino lady, met on a holiday taken in the Philippines: at moment of speaking she is in an hotel at Frome. I asked what Brisbane was like, he replied: 'Accent nearer convict than Sydney or Melbourne.'

Tuesday, 15 January

The day of the Duff Cooper Prize party, when I was to present the Prize to Hilary Spurling for her two volumes of I. Compton-Burnett biography. For the previous day or two snow was thick on ground, and it is still snowing hard this morning, and arctically cold. It seemed unwise to attempt London. We might have reached Westbury all right, then anything could have happened on the return train journey (assuming the train to London had run in the first instance). Even the intrepid Mr Hillman, who drives our taxi, was a bit doubtful. Accordingly, I rang John Julius Norwich soon after 8 am, explained the circumstances, regretted we could not attend, and dictated my speech, which he repeated word by word aloud to be taken down by his girlfriend Molly Philipps, now installed at Blomfield Road, Little Venice. John Julius this time was sole performer on the platform. For the first occasion ever, his mother, Diana Cooper, now ninety-two, also could not face the weather and failed to turn up. I greatly regretted not acclaiming Hilary in person, but Winter was too forbidding.

Sunday, 20 January

Lees & Mary Mayall, Jim & Alvilde Lees-Milne, to luncheon. Jim is writing a biography of 2nd Lord Esher, an interesting subject in the light of the life of his daughter 'Brett' (D. H. Lawrence's friend), by Sean Hignett, which I reviewed, and thought goodish. Esher was such an unpleasant man that four or five other people (Max Egremont, Michael Howard, Philip Magnus, *et al*) began on him, then gave up as too unpalatable. Jim said Esher's homosexual goings-on were sufficient for Eton house-masters to warn each other about him, as the office of Constable of Windsor Castle gave a strategic position for adventures with Etonians.

Living as they do at the gates of Badminton, the Lees-Milnes were naturally interested in recent attempts by fanatical anti-foxhunters to disinter the body of the lately deceased Duke of Beaufort. Apparently the Dowager Duchess is now sunk into chronic mental confusion. She remarked to Alvilde a month or two before this thwarted act of malevolence: 'I know Master was murdered, and his head cut off.' This last was apparently just what the anti-foxhunting band of body-snatchers hoped to do, sending the ducal head to Princess Anne. The Lees-Milnes spoke of Helen Dashwood and her behaviour at West Wycombe (HQ of Hell Fire Club in 18th century), where the National Trust was accommodated during the war. They said Helen Dashwood (husband descended from Francis Dashwood, founder of the original Hell Fire Club), speaking of Georgia Sitwell (née Doble, also Canadian), commented: 'The Dobles were no great shakes in Canada. As a matter of fact Georgia's father was my father's agent.' It fell out that sometime later Alvilde happened on Georgia Sitwell, and Helen Dashwood's name came up in conversation. Georgia Sitwell observed: 'Helen's family were not regarded as much in Canada. In fact her father was my father's agent.' Luncheon started with a dish invented by John and V, *fond d'artichaud* with ham and mayonnaise; pheasant; apple pudding; Rosenthal's Château Kirwan '71. Party a success.

Sunday, 27 January

The Sunday papers are brought by two little girls of about thirteen/fourteen called Charry (Sherry, Chérie?) & Jane, sisters, tho' they do not look alike. I could hardly be less addicted to minors, but these two are very sweet, both pretty, Jane, the younger one, particularly cute. Every three or four weeks they change a five pound note for me, otherwise I run out of small change, therefore I warn them I shall want change the following week. This Sunday, in weather of peculiar foulness, they forgot to bring change. I said, 'I'm rather short of pound notes, but can probably find the amount', which I did, whatever it is. Just before luncheon there was a knock on the door. Jane was standing there in pelting rain with five £1 notes as change for a fiver. She had come all the way down the drive in sleet, as the car (I presume driven by their father) remains at the gate. Icy sleety rain descending in sheets. As, from her point of view, business between us was over, I was rather touched.

Saturday, 9 February

Notwithstanding quite deep snow, John & Hilary Spurling with Anthony & Tanya Hobson came to luncheon; also Tristram & Virginia from The Stables. In the first instance, the Spurlings were going to be in the neighbourhood, and the Mayalls wanted to meet them. Then, as it turned out, the Mayalls had to attend the wedding of Mary's cousin Lady Rose Cecil (whom I thought rather ravishing at the wake after Rachel Cecil's funeral) held at Cranborne. V suggested Jilly & Leo Cooper as possibly an amusing mix. It transpired (term rightly disliked by Henry James) that Hilary had more than once been less than enthusiastic about Jilly's books in reviews. We agreed another occasion might be preferable, then asked the Hobsons, thinking they knew the Spurlings well. On the contrary, they had only met momentarily and wanted to meet again, so the party was *ben trovato*. As a matter of fact the Hobsons first refused, thinking they had to entertain Cressida Connolly, then she put them off, so Anthony rang to ask if they could come after all.

The Spurlings are doing research on John's ancestress Lady (Eleanor) Fettiplace, who bequeathed the beautifully bound manuscript cookery book, which descended to them, from which Hilary venturesomely experiments. (Perhaps one should say her guests venturesomely sample.) The recipe for tobacco, there recorded, is noted in Lady Fettiplace's hand, as 'from Sr W. Ralegh', whose sons were her first cousins. Her daughter married a Horner of the Mells family. A Fettiplace tomb is at Cloford (busts of himself & wife), which we haven't seen yet, and, as near here, we offered to photograph for the Spurlings. Hilary says Lady Fettiplace's bust looks exactly like a cook.

The Hobsons dined with Elizabeth Jane Howard recently, where they met her stepson Martin Amis, whom they liked and said he now has a beautiful wife. Anthony thought Martin Amis usually an excellent critic, but could not take his novels, a judgement which I heartily endorse. Anthony went on to speak of novels of Ian MacEwan, apparently son of a Sergeant Major at Pirbright. I thought Anthony was going to say he liked them better than Martin Amis's. On the contrary thought MacEwan even less to his liking. We drank Rosenthal's Château Boyd-Cantenac, '70, excellent, better than when first tried. There is no doubt our cellar is a good one for its effect on wine. We have noticed that before.

Wednesday, 13 February

Braving the snow, a Frenchman, Patrick (*sic*) Mauriès, Literary Editor of *Libération* came for an interview. *Libération* is a daily paper founded by J-P Sartre as of the extreme Left, but has now apparently undergone many changes. Mauriès said it came out in the evening, and was of the same importance as *Le Figaro*. That may be its own staff's estimate. Mauriès was quite bright. He said his mother was half-Lebanese, tho' he had never been to the Near East. He was interested in pictures, knew about Conder and Sickert. He spoke good English, and talked with that French assurance about any British/American writer mentioned. He said there was some reaction now in France against all the *Nouveau Roman* and anti-Balzac novels, and all such stuff, the French having incurable taste for new cults in literature. French papers do not employ outside reviewers. All is done in the office, *Libération* has a staff of five for the book pages. It will be amusing to see what he produces, if anything. Mauriès is also scout for my publisher Flammarion, to whom he sent *Wheel*.

Sunday, 17 March

V, Tristram, John, I (Virginia and Archie, did not come) lunched with Joff & Tessa Davies at Whatley House to celebrate V's & Tessa's birthdays, both taking place on 13 March. The Davies daughters, Lucinda & Mary Anne, were really giving party, Mary Anne doing most of cooking. They are nice, pretty, intelligent girls; Mary Anne is in the Foreign Office, Lucinda in a stockbroker's, both seeming to enjoy their jobs. I sat between them. Lucinda told me that as recently as four years ago a man caught on floor of Stock Exchange without being a member was debagged, members forming a group round him singing: 'Oi! Oi! Oi!' Excellent lunch; superb Château Coutet (I think) '70.

Sunday, 24 March

Jilly & Leo Cooper to luncheon, for which I cooked curry. We drank burgundy, Mercurey '73, which seemed to go quite well, tho' possibly a delicate claret might suffer. The superstition that good wine is unsuitable with curry was exploded when we gave Vidia & Pat Naipaul curry with Rhône wine, which Vidia particularly likes. I mentioned I had felt mildly surprised that neither Little, Brown or Holt's had written to congratulate me on *The Hudson Review* & Ingersoll Foundation Prizes in the US. Leo assured me that American publishers have given up writing letters at all on any subject.

Wednesday, 27 – Thursday, 28 March

To London, mainly for another Prime Minister's dinner party; also taking the opportunity of lunching with the Spurlings at their new house in Holloway, the latter a fairly formidable trek across North London. Their house in Penn Road, as John Spurling pointed out, is authentic Pooter country, one of those early 19th century houses in terrace, bearded helmeted classical head over front door, deity or hero, I am uncertain: nor why in certain circumstances he is often placed there. The house formerly belonged to a photographer, so comparatively well equipped in an up-to-date manner when taken over. Hilary's workroom is done up entirely in crimson including the ceiling, bookshelves all round, extremely effective.

I was introduced to a large black cat, Biggles (so called for his intrepidity), rescued on a holiday in Wales. During luncheon Biggles brought in a large dead bird through the cat-door and had to be expelled. We talked of various writers. I told John I could not share his (also Nobel Prize Committee's) enthusiasm for Gabriel Garcia Marquez, who seems to me essence of pretentious middlebrow verbiage of the worst kind, the sort of phoney bestseller popular at all periods in different forms. Later the same day Vidia Naipaul agreed on this point.

In the afternoon I went to The White House, Bond Street to buy handkerchiefs, a shamefully belated Christmas present for Virginia; and I also got some for V. I rested in my bedroom at The Travellers until time for dinner. This, as before, was to have been at Hugh Thomas's house in Ladbroke Grove, then changed to 10 Downing Street at the last moment, because the PM had to vote that evening. I thought I would stroll from the Club down the Duke of York's Steps, across to the Horse Guards Parade, entering Downing Street from the alley at the back. This lane turned out to be closed, presumably for security reasons. I was not sure that the gates of the Horse Guards might not be closed too by this hour, so with some fear of being late I went round by Parliament Square. When I got there I found that by no means all the guests had arrived yet. Going up the stairs I was met by one of the nice girls who had 'waited' at the previous dinner, whether Thomas's daughter or not I am uncertain. She seemed to know me.

In the anteroom before dinner we were given well-iced non-vintage champagne (International Exhibition Cooperative Wine Society's?), extremely drinkable. It appeared that, owing to last-minute changes, the food (cooked mostly by Vanessa Thomas), which we subsequently ate, was brought down by car from Ladbroke Grove. It was eatable, without being at all exciting; the claret was decidedly dim (possibly also Wine Society, though I rather doubt that). Survivors from the previous dinner party of two years ago: Tony Quinton; Vidia Naipaul; myself. The rest (of those already known to me): Hugh Trevor-Roper (Lord Dacre of Glanton); Iris Murdoch; Raymond Carr; Max Egremont; Noel Annan; David Pryce-Jones. I headed David Pryce-Jones into a corner where he could give me a breakdown of those guests not already met. These were: John Vincent (Bristol History don), described by David P-J as liking to put every accepted idea the other way up; Dr Zeldin (another Oxford don, French expert), described as having written an authoritative, but somewhat unreadable, book on France. Anthony Polansky (also some form of academic), who subsequently turned out third generation Pole in this country and seemed rather jolly.

At dinner, to my great surprise, I was put on Mrs Thatcher's right, with Vidia Naipaul on her left; on my other side was John Vincent. At one time or another I had read a lot of reviews by Vincent, some of them no great shakes, so far as remembered, others pretty good. He has a notably prognathous jaw, perfectly civil manner. We did not have much talk, as I was fully occupied keeping my end up with the Prime Minister, while Vincent probably thought he had to make some sort of showing with his fellow don, Tony Quinton, on his other side.

I continue to find Mrs Thatcher very attractive physically. Her overhanging eyelids, hooded eyes, are the only suggestion of mystery (a characteristic I like in women, while totally accepting Wilde's view of them as Sphinxes without a secret). Her general appearance seems to justify Mitterrand's alleged comment that she has the eyes of Caligula and the lips of Marilyn Monroe; the latter a film star I never, in fact, thought particularly attractive. Mrs Thatcher has a fair skin; hair-do of incredible perfection, rather dumpy figure, the last seeming to add a sense of down-to-earthness that is appropriate and not unattractive in its way. She was wearing a black dress, the collar rolled up behind her neck, some sort of gold pattern on it. On her right hand was a large Victorian ring, dark red, in an elaborate gold setting. She only likes talking of public affairs, which I never find easy to discuss in a serious manner. In fact I felt myself taken back to age of nineteen, sitting next to a beautiful girl, myself quite unable to think of anything to say. Mrs T. is reputed to have no humour. I suspect she recognizes a joke more than she is credited with, if probably jokes of a limited kind, and confined to those who know her well.

David Pryce-Jones told me Fitzroy Maclean reported himself being present when Mrs Thatcher was on an official visit to Jugoslavia as member of the Opposition. There had been a dinner before meeting Tito, at which a superlatively good-looking Jug of about thirty-five had rested his hand on her knee. Mrs T allowed this to remain throughout one course. At the next course the hand began to work up. She took it in both of her own hands, removed it, said: 'Perhaps one day. Not now.' When she met Tito on this same jaunt he was in a bad temper, having just got rid of his third or fourth wife. He told Mrs Thatcher that women should not meddle with politics. She replied: 'I *am* politics.'

The talk at this Downing Street dinner, as before, was introduced at a certain stage by Hugh Thomas. It ranged over East Germany, to the condition of Young People in this country, topics on which I am not outstandingly hot. Mrs T did, however, please me by saying that everything from which we are now suffering is *all* discussed in the plainest terms in Dostoevsky's *The Possessed* (as I prefer, *The Devils*); a fact I have been preaching for decades. I wonder when, how, she got round to this. Did she read the novel, see its contemporary relevance herself, or was that pointed out to her by someone? I fear probably the latter.

When the PM went off to vote, Robin Butler, Personal Secretary (whatever the job is called), an agreeable young man in the Treasury, asked if I would like to see the larger dining-room. Hugh Thomas and Butler were the only members of an official entourage present at dinner. Accordingly, with several other guests, I went with him into the room where V and I had dinner with Ted Heath, when in office some years ago, an official party of about seventy to meet Japanese Prime Minister (later, I think, the Japanese Prime Minister was imprisoned for corruption). There was a lot of fine silver arranged about the room. I went over to examine the ornate coat of arms engraved on one of the large silver trays propped up on main sideboard. Butler, seeing what I was doing, said, 'They're the Cust arms. Lord Brownlow put all the silver on loan from Belton – the Prime Minister's Lincolnshire connexion.'

This must be admitted to be rather a comic footnote to Alan Pryce-Jones's story, when I met him just before the previous Prime Minister's dinner party I attended (26 October, '83), as to Mrs Thatcher being in reality the well-known womanizer Harry Cust's daughter; notwithstanding that being for dozens of reasons quite ludicrous, even to dates being all wrong. Still, in fantasy, an enjoyable thought that she should be using the Belton silver. Butler then showed the Cabinet Room, where Harold Macmillan had instituted a coffin-shaped table, built out at a certain point, to facilitate cross-talk. At the start of the party I had not recognized Noel Annan, having forgotten he was so bald. I mentioned this to David Pryce-Jones, who said: 'He's no balder than he always was. When he used to stay with us, and come up to say goodnight to me as a child it was like being kissed by an egg.' At the end of the evening several departing guests were standing about in the hall. Max Egremont remarked to me: 'It's like one of your books. I've just met my former tutor, Dr Zeldin, not seen since I was an undergraduate.'

Mrs Thatcher came down to the front-door, and saw everyone off personally. I was struck by how much the whole evening resembled going out to dinner in most households these days, when the hostess has herself most probably done the cooking. In this case, true, a friend did the cooking, but the atmosphere was just the same. I tried to analyse Mrs Thatcher's points, the main one being not perhaps her beauty and the colossal vitality she gives off. Would she be different if well born? On the whole I think good birth would diminish her attack. She says things like: 'When I sent the Task Force [to the Falklands]', which would sound no less egotistical from an aristocrat, while, I suspect, somewhat less tolerable. It is an interesting point, which I am still not quite sure about. Then Mrs T's voice would jar in a duchess. As things are, the voice is part of her bag of tricks, not without its spell. Much food for thought. Very enjoyable evening.

The following morning I saw Sussman. There is the business of the reconstruction of the lower jaw now in prospect. Having already dumped my bag at Paddington, I set out on a trip arranged to take Adrian Daintrey to lunch from The Charterhouse. Being rather early, I went to explore the new premises of Society of Genealogists, now near the Barbican. The building, which looks outside like tool-factory or suchlike, in an odd cul-de-sac. Inside it is notably well organized on several floors. The place was fairly full of members. I thought of the Society's old days in a corner house in Bloomsbury Square (could it have been Isaac D'Israeli's?), the comparative muddle there in dreadfully cramped space.

Thence I went on to Charterhouse Square. The square retains a few decent Georgian houses, most of it large ugly buildings of much later date, worst of periods. In one corner lies a low grey, apparently medieval (in fact Elizabethan) block that seems almost to be sinking into the ground. I went under an arch, entering a complex of utterly deserted quadrangles. It was like moving into the Fourth Dimension, several centuries back in Time, everything round about completely still, like a dream. Eventually I reached a larger quadrangle, across which a young man in a leather apron (who fitted perfectly well into the 16th century picture) was carrying a tray with food on it under covers. I asked if he knew where I could find Mr Daintrey. He recognized the name at once, indicating a more modern wing, giving the number of Adrian's room (8).

Adrian had some sort of a Civil List pension by the end. Discussing his translation to The Charterhouse, some friends have been saying: 'Adrian is wonderfully fixed up. What an excellent piece of luck that he managed to get in there'; others: 'Poor Adrian, it is quite awful. How can he stand it after the sort of life he has led?' Both comments in a sense true. On the one hand, Adrian is splendidly looked after, four meals a day, his own room with every mod. con., where he can eat, or, if he prefers, have meals in Hall with the other Brothers. The place is of immense historical character. On the other hand, there is the inevitable air of an institution, depressingly close to the sanatorium, or nursing-home; piles of sheets in corridors, etc, through which melancholy figures totter, and brisk female staff scurry.

I found Adrian's room without difficulty. It was quite reasonably large, with bed set back in kind of alcove, by now looking exactly like every other room Adrian has inhabited during the years (nearer sixty than fifty) that I have known him; incredibly untidy; his own pictures lying simply against wall or stacked in piles; half consumed bottles of wine on tables, unwashed glasses etc. Adrian himself has no teeth, more than a bit deaf, in general rather a sorry state, but seemed, however, in fairish form. No worse than his ups and downs in the old days. When we went out he walked with a stick. He suggested lunching either at the pub or a nearby Italian restaurant and could not make up his mind which. We looked into pub, which I think he would have preferred, but it seemed densely crowded, so we went on to a restaurant called something like Vecchio Polario, just round corner from Charterhouse Square. Adrian can walk quite well, but does not make much sense talking, and looks fearfully tumbledown, without a tie. On the way out of The Charterhouse he took me through the panelled dining-hall, like that of a College, where some of the Brothers were eating. They can do that, have meals in rooms, according to taste. As it happens Adrian is the only Old Carthusian among twenty-eight of them. He nodded to one or two.

After lunch I saw him back to his room. He said he sleeps well. He recently sold quite a few of his pictures, various ladies taking an interest in him as ever. I returned through still empty quadrangles, disturbed only by huge flocks of pigeons descending, then floating back into the air above. The Charterhouse's founder, Thomas Sutton, is said to have been model for Ben Jonson's *Volpone*. Adrian seemed as satisfied at coming to rest in Sutton's foundation as any man could be in the circumstances, grumbling no more than he has always grumbled. One of his patrons is a female barrister called Hagerty, described by Adrian as 'very charming'. In certain respects he could hardly be better placed.

All the same, I felt a bit upset on the way to Paddington. Forty-eight hours spent in London seemed to have provided an allegorical vision of life: the young Spurlings (one feels in a sense 'deep in the earth, forever young', like Tannhäuser and the Queen of Love), their new house in a pioneering district for intellectuals, abstract pictures, latest literary talk; then Downing Street, the world of power, up to a point Learning and Letters (so far as a few writers, reinforced by academics and Life Peers could be held to represent those); The Charterhouse, memories of an artist's career, bohemian goings-on, the beau monde, love, lust, decay, death. One was reminded of that strange 18th century diptych that used to hang in Gerald Reitlinger's house, Woodgate (where Adrian so often stayed, tho' he always abused The Squire, up hill and down dale, particularly when they shared a house in Bramerton Street, Chelsea) which symbolized the Human Lot. This also amusingly illustrated by how the 18th century regarded the 17th century:

> My Father and my Mother that go stooping to your grave,
> Pray tell me in this world what good may I expect to have?
> My Son, the good you may expect is all forlorn,
> Men do not gather grapes from off a thorn.

All the same, I suppose Adrian had quite a lot of fun in his day, one way and another. Such reflections saw me home.

Sunday, 31 March

At his own suggestion, my agent, Bruce Hunter of Higham's, came over from Chichester for luncheon, where he is staying with Hilton Ambler, himself once in Higham's, where I had dealings with him. Ambler used to arrange films. He was responsible for brief, if strong, interest shown by Binkie Beaumont in *The Rest I'll Whistle* as a possible West End production. (Incidentally the *Two Plays* are being examined by Sam Wheeler, who runs the Orange Theatre, Richmond, of whom Tristram speaks well, having been up at Oxford with him when Wheeler produced, I think, *Hamlet*, in which Tristram sustained the role of Guildenstern).

Bruce Hunter was nephew (not blood relation) of David Higham; from being totally different physical type he has grown a moustache, and somehow begun to look slightly like his uncle, if that was relationship, perhaps simply from the work. I find Bruce an excellent agent, making far less heavy weather than David Higham (who Edith Sitwell said looked like a Boar's Head, and should have had a lemon in his mouth, and be brought in at literary banquets). Bruce seems to get things done just as well, if not better. We hadn't anything special to discuss, it is all the same useful to have these meetings occasionally. I admitted to no more than proceeding fairly well with new novel, *The Fisher King*, in fact approaching 77,000.

Bruce repeated somewhat bizarre suggestion that V should write the life of Leonard Woolf; alternatively, a history of the Du Maurier family; both propositions unsuitable to put it mildly. We talked of Mrs Bradley, who used to manage Higham's clients' French rights, a great character, if never particularly effective so far as my own works were concerned. In fact, I suppose she placed the first three vols of *Dance* with Julliard (who died, then taken on by Christian Bourgois, but subsequently dropped). I met Mrs Bradley once in Paris. She was apparently Belgian, married an American officer billeted in her house during first war, who never left it. She herself died at age of ninety-seven, and to end of days drank a lot of champagne and liqueurs. Every Christmas used to send round a card portraying her Aberdeen, who must have been about same age as herself.

Thursday, 4 April

V & I lunched with the Mayalls. Lady Cranborne was to have brought David Cecil over, but owing to some muddle, it is just us. Lees & Mary attended the Memorial Service (second one, as twice celebrated) of Mary's brother David Harlech, killed recently in a car smash. They had been at a first Service in Westminster Abbey, which they described as vulgar in its pop music aspects. I asked why a kind of after-birth of those present took place, after second one, all media people appearing in *The Times*, *Daily Telegraph*.

Apparently Harlech Television paid for it all in first instance then were cross because none of their own names were given in the first list of mourners. They made such a fuss about this that another service was held, in which they were all lumped together. Edward Kennedy (brother of the US President) had been at the earlier ceremony in the Welsh Marches. The Mayalls reporting him seeming as if made of some material other than flesh and blood, possibly an unusual make of tweed. I told Lees & Mary about my visit to Adrian Daintrey, whom they said they would go to see at The Charterhouse. We talked about the Belton silver at 10 Downing Street. Lees had stayed at Belton. I asked how he found Lord (Perry) Brownlow (friend of Edward VIII, Evelyn Waugh). Lees said considerable charm. Enjoyable lunch.

Thursday, 11 April

To London. Driven to Westbury by Mr Hillman Jr, whose father died suddenly a short time ago. Hillman *fils* (Gary) told me he had rebought house in Westbury built by his grandfather, a haulier, in 1933, when it cost £9000. Interesting case of continuity. Saw Sussman. Antonia (Pinter) lunched with me at The Travellers in the Morning Room, where by recent arrangement ladies can now be taken; indeed, a few ladies are now even members of the Club. Antonia was in excellent form. She is writing a book about Boadicea, as the experts would say, Boudicca, name meaning Victoria. Antonia had read her mother's Memoirs. Apparently Hugh Gaitskell actually proposed to Liz, but did not touch her or kiss her, apart from the fact that she was apparently sitting on his knee. Sitting on knees, I remember, perhaps more customary then than nowadays. One wonders. Smoked salmon; veal; Antonia, cheese; me, meringues; bottle Club hock. Antonia left 3.45. Enjoyable.

Sunday, 14 April

Roy & Jennifer Jenkins had been invited to luncheon at longish notice. V then found herself in bed with flu for ten days, not sure when she would get up. Vidia & Pat Naipaul had also been invited. The tradition for Naipauls is to have curry, Roy Jenkins to drink decent claret. As it looked as if I might cook lunch, curry my chef d'oeuvre, it was decided to ignore anti-wine-with-curry prejudice again, make mildish curry, drink Boyd-Cantenac '70. This seemed to work perfectly well. V, in the event, getting up, we dispatched three bottles without strain. I always like Roy Jenkins very much. I had imagined he would know the Naipauls well: on the contrary they had only vaguely encountered each other before. Jennifer Jenkins, whom I had barely met before, is nice. She sat between Vidia & myself, as did Mrs Thatcher recently, which we pointed out. Vidia was in excellent form. He dished up some of the Downing Street party, reminded me that he and I had agreed across Mrs T (perhaps not the best manners) that *A Hundred Years of Solitude* by Marquez was rot. Roy is writing a book about President Truman. Good party.

Friday, 19 April

The Revd Gerard Irvine invited himself to luncheon with his sister, Rosemary, former Headmistress of a high-powered girls' school. We met her, also Gerard's mother, on an Hellenic Cruise. Gerard & his sister were doing a West Country tour, ultimately aimed at consecrating a lectern to their mother's memory at Wotton-under-Edge church, where we first saw Gerard praying, when we came over to look at his father's house, then for sale. We stayed with the Evelyn Waughs at Stinchcombe. Virginia, doing gardening at The Stables, was also at luncheon. Gerard grew rather purple in the face, but seemed to enjoy himself, his sister too. Afterwards Georgia & Archie took the Irvines down to the grottoes.

Saturday, 20 – Monday, 22 April

Ferdie & Julia Mount staying at The Stables. We had drinks there Saturday evening; drinks with us on Sunday morning. Ferdie is giving up Literary Editorship of *The Spectator* for the political side. One would say much more his line.

Tuesday, 23 April

To London. I saw Sussman. Lunched with Osbert & Anne Lancaster at Cheyne Court. Anne produced as usual an excellent luncheon: asparagus; smoked salmon; chocolate cream; Pouilly. Osbert is in a dismally poor state. He is deaf, finds his deaf-aid impossible to regulate (he throws it on the table as used Augustus John to do), gets in a rage, begins to say he can't hear before one has actually spoken. Almost impossible to make contact with him. However he went to sleep quite peaceably after lunch, having put back a drink or two, which Anne tries to limit. We talked of Arabella Boxer's Cookery Book. Anne really does do a magnificent job looking after Osbert, who is absolutely impossible these days, poor old boy. She gets no thanks. It must all be immensely trying for her.

Saturday, 27 April

I am suffering from a fluey cold, but got up to receive for tea Adam Low & Nicholas Shakespeare, who are doing a BBC TV programme on Evelyn Waugh. I was not particularly anxious to take part in this, as TV programmes, camera crews, waste a whole day at least, while all the producer wants is to obtain agreement in what he himself thinks. Not in least interested in the experiences, or views, of whosoever is being questioned. Indeed positively opposed to these (suppressing them), if they do not conform to his own desired picture. Even if the producer is sympathetic to one's views, half-baked sub-editors later snip the essential points away. All this was illustrated by programmes on Orwell in which I took part. I appeared on screen for a split second, uttering some received banality about Orwell. This is the same whoever is in question.

For instance, Tony Palmer came here to do programme on Willy Walton. I tried to ride this off on grounds of knowing nothing of music, nor even knowing Willy at all well. Palmer said he wanted Constant Lambert's relationship with Walton. Accordingly, I talked of that subject, notably, that, although jealousy might have been expected – Walton being regarded as the more distinguished composer, Lambert as the new friend of Sitwells (who more or less supported Walton), as being to that extent in competition. There was in fact no sign whatever on either side, quite the contrary. Palmer expressed great delight in recording all this. In the event, everything about Lambert, naturally including myself, was cut out of programme, the film being too long.

In the case of Evelyn Waugh it seemed hard to refuse, as I am now probably the sole individual to know him both as an undergraduate at Oxford, and later be on sufficiently good terms to see him on and off within a few months of his death. When this couple arrived, Low rather charmless at first I thought, somewhat improved later. I questioned Shakespeare about his surname. He alleged he was descended from the Bard's grandfather or brother, not sure which; the College of Arms allowed all his family to use Shakespeare's coat, thereby recognizing the descent. His maternal grandfather was S. P. B. Mais, now a forgotten writer, but model for the 'inspiring' young master in Alec Waugh's novel about Sherborne *The Loom of Youth*. Met Mais once, when I was staying with John and Evelyn Heygate in one of their Sussex cottages. He was something of a bore, Georgian verse, beer type, but quite genial.

Monday, 29 April

Alice Boyd to luncheon, she & V were going off in afternoon to a sale of pottery in the neighbourhood, Alice being interested in pottery. Alice is fascinatingly different from her brother George, for that matter from her mother Mary. She has great liveliness, and charm. Any lack of intellectual interest is perhaps exaggerated on her own part.

Monday, 6 May

Sally Colville, daughter of V's first cousin, Joan Colville (née Villiers), who is now Lady Pigot, married to a Major General of Royal Marines, came in for a drink before lunch on way to stay with a fellow baronet, in traditional manner of barts clinging together. Tony (Robert) Pigot, is seventy, a widower, retired, considerably older therefore than Sally, a nice girl, who, like rest of her family, had good deal to put up with from their father, David Colville, a City figure. Her husband was all a trim Major General of Marines should be, slightly like

Brian Horrocks. He seemed a little disorientated on arrival, but was put right by couple of stiff vodkas. He mentioned he had served on the staff of Caspar John (Augustus's son), when First Sea Lord.

Tuesday, 14 May

To London. I saw Sussman, who mentioned that his mother-in-law had died some years ago of over eating, reminding one of General Stavrogin (*The Devils*), who succumbed from indigestion on the way to the Crimean War. Alan Ross lunched with me at The Travellers. He was suffering from several severe blows: the fact that he would have to have further operation in connexion with war wound; *The London Magazine*, which he edits, is confronted with the prospect of moving to new quarters, a mess having been made about not extending the lease, when this could easily have been done. The landlord, Martyn Beckett, had formerly been a friend; finally, the probable conse- quences of the death of Alan's girlfriend's father. She will probably now have to look after her mother . . . Alan reported his son Jonathan was all right, but these various tribulations combined to make Alan rather gloomy, in fact somewhat his usual state. I always like talking with him, as he is intelligent, has read a good deal, possesses a pleasant degree of malice about friends, combined with realistic approach to most things. No nonsense. One wonders whether his own early cricketing success also affected him a bit, expecting too much, afterwards never quite able to realize itself adequately (cf. Cyril Connolly). Alan said he had no objection to my inserting bodily his own RNVR wartime functions for one or other of my two ex-naval characters in *The Fisher King*. I ran into Hugh Massingberd in The Travellers, who said he wanted to interview me for *The Field* Christmas Number. I suggested lunching with us at The Chantry some time.

Sunday, 19 May

Antonia & Harold Pinter to luncheon. They are staying in Bath, Harold directing a Tennessee Williams play in which Lauren (Betty) Bacall is the star. The atmosphere was a little tense when they arrived, then warmed up a bit, turning into an enjoyable party after that, lasting till teatime. Harold is an excellent person to talk about books, plays, people, regarding all of which he expresses quite uninhibited opinions, unlike many individuals who have made some name for themselves in the arts. (Perhaps more true of my generation than his.) The Pinters may be going to Hollywood, where Harold would act again, after a long time away from the boards. If they do, it will be interesting to see if Antonia becomes Queen of Hollywood (which one suspects she contemplates), or simply hates the place, either or both easily taking shape.

They had recently dined with Michael Pakenham (Foreign Office), another guest being Roy Jenkins. Somewhat to Harold's disappointment, Roy adroitly bypassed weighty political matters. Perhaps all actors aspire to political leadership since one of the profession was elected President of the US. I seem to remember that for relatively long period an actor posed as Roman Emperor in some remote outpost of the Empire. Pinters brought a bottle of Château Cissac, '70. Lunch: prawn & egg; Welsh chicken pie; strawberries (for us); cheese (Taleggio, for them); Boyd–Cantenac '70.

Tuesday, 21 May

Miranda Wood to tea. Miranda (née Phyllis Hayward) in the course of her life had many adventures. I am perpetually inciting her to write an autobiography (she can write quite tolerably), but she will do no more than produce odds & ends from time to time, never able to get whole thing into order. This inability is in some manner connected with her attitude to herself. Briefly, she came from Birmingham (lower-middle-class family with which she did not get on), read Aldous Huxley, etc, arrived in London about 1936 to have intellectual life, experienced a hard time working as a typist in spare-parts business, etc, occasional jobs as artist's model; about to give up, go home, when she fell in with John Heygate (no affair), through whom I met her.

I got her a job at Duckworth's as secretary-typist, the secretary there having suddenly died over the weekend. After a year at Duckworth's, not nearly exciting enough for her, Miranda transferred to the Oxford Press in India. There she married a German, war broke out, husband was interned. Miranda went to Sumatra. The Japanese then invaded. As Japan & Germany were then allies, Miranda just continued her job there. After the war she divorced her German husband (having had a daughter, Julia, by him), had affair with a rich Armenian stamp-collector, married a Regimental Sergeant Major in the British Army (Jimmy Wood, very proficient cricketer, therefore allowed considerable licence by the authorities). The marriage finally bust up, Miranda becoming a high-powered secretary in the Eagle Insurance, where she worked for the head of firm.

When she retired Eagle fixed her up with a flat near Baker Street. Her German husband died not long ago in Hamburg; although retired, Miranda does occasionally do odd jobs, chiefly helping out Woodrow Wyatt. Miranda grumbles a lot about Woodrow (as he does about her), but obviously rather enjoys it all (he too), always full of stories about Woodrow's idiosyncrasies, in his own household, social, and political fields.

One of her earlier adventures, when she first left home, was to take a job as secretary with an author who advertised and turned out to be some obscure young man who had written an unpublished novel. He seduced her (something she was anxious to bring off), her account of which she wrote. This was not quite good enough to publish on its own, if at the same time distinctly lively. In this Miranda described herself as 'not riotously attractive', a reasonable estimate for the plump Birmingham girl she then was. The extraordinary thing is that after returning from about seven years in the Far East, she had thinned down, developed slanting eyes, in fact if one asserted she had no Asian blood people would certainly have said: 'All that sort of girl says they have no Asian blood in the East.' Only knowledge of her in an earlier incarnation made physical change certainty. Since then she has remained good-looking.

She was brought here by her daughter Julia, married to a potter in Aller, a village some distance away from us in Somerset. Julia wanted to visit a local garden centre. Miranda is quite unchanged at about seventy. Really only interested in herself, but dry manner that can be very funny. I asked her why Woodrow, having (according to himself) refused a Life Peerage three times, then accepted a knighthood. Miranda said he thought he ought to be given an hereditary peerage. This certainly justifies Woodrow calling his new book *Memoirs of an Optimist*.

Wednesday, 22 May

An American academic/journalist, Jay Parini (whose name cropped up at time of my getting the Ingersoll Prize) asked for interview in *USA Today*, apparently the only 'national' newspaper in US (all the rest being State-based). He was to come at 3 o'clock. He arrived an hour and a quarter late, with his wife (named Devon); she was a nordic type from Illinois, he still looking quite Italian. His grandfather was from north of Genoa. He gave me his poems *Anthracite Country*, which seem not too bad. They are about Pennsylvania, more or less scene of John O'Hara's *Appointment in Samara*. He was a friend of Fred Morgan of *The Hudson Review*, William Pritchard, also Robert Penn Warren. After a slowish start Parini seemed reasonably bright.

In the evening we watched Ian Hamilton's TV Book Programme, usually well done. In this case Shiva Naipaul was talking to Mario Vargas Llosa, whom I met at the first Mrs Thatcher party I attended at Hugh Thomas's, Hugh somewhat given to Latin-American writers. Vargas Llosa seemed a nice chap when encountered momentarily, also in the interview, though I find those interminable South American novels (invariably hailed on appearance as

Nobel material) fairly unreadable and often intellectually empty. I still want to get hold of Vargas Llosa's first novel about a military school in Lima.

He was followed on Ian Hamilton's programme by the poetry of Keith Douglas, of which on the whole I am in favour. I was forcibly struck by the resemblance of Keith Douglas to George Orwell, both the physical appearance and style: for instance in his letters and girlfriends, so far as the latter were to be judged after forty-five years or so have passed in the case of Douglas, more than that with Orwell. Keith Douglas seems to have been difficult, unpopular, belonging to the Right politically at a period when it was fashionable to be Left. One wonders whether all that, too, was in the Orwell manner, George being more or less on the Right, even if rebellious, at school and early days of the Burma Police, although always a *mauvais sujet* where authority was concerned. Then he consciously turned Left. A most interesting pattern the two of them make. How poor old George would have loved to be a poet killed in action.

Thursday, 23 May

Alison Lurie to luncheon. She was in Bath for the Tennessee Williams play, and expected the Pinters to be there, but they had by then moved on. The play turned out a success, and further arrangements to be made. Alison (having hired a car) lost her way. She arrived about 2.20. We seem to be suffering a bout of late arrivals. She was quite jolly after getting here. I ran through with her most of Professor Kopf's dialogue in *The Fisher King*, the sort of thing at which Alison is adept, removing inversions and other mannerisms Americans do not use. She said she didn't feel any high regard for Hart Crane, whom I have been reading, having by chance acquired a paperback of Crane's poems, for some of which I have a weakness (Brooklyn Bridge).

Alison's novel *Foreign Affairs* is being considered for TV by Granada, it might be funny dramatized if well done. There is always the danger the best bits will be removed, or misinterpreted. V and I were very much amused by Alison saying she had been at what she regarded as grandish dinner party given by Diana Phipps, about sixteen people, where at the end of dinner Diana Phipps's cat jumped on the table, walked up and down as if owning the place, sampling remains of food, and being talked to by the guests. Alison said that in the US everyone would have had forty fits at such an incident. She could hardly believe – indeed refused to believe – we were speaking the truth in assuring her that no one here would think anything of it, indeed some people might say what an amusing, intelligent thing for the cat to do. They must persuade their cat to greet guests in that manner.

Tuesday, 28 May

Roland Gant of Heinemann's sent an Australian journalist, Richard Wallace of the *Canberra Times*, described by Roland as an Indian Christian (RC), who emigrated to Australia. One did not quite know what to expect. In the event, Wallace, blue eyes, showed no sign whatever of being Indian, beyond having been born in Calcutta. He is twenty-three, quite lively, wants to live here for year or two, possibly get a university grant. He keeps himself by working over weekends. He said Mrs Gorbachev, the Soviet headman's wife, has done a lot of shopping in London, using an American Express card. As Wallace seemed tolerable, I suggested he might try Kingsley Amis for an interview.

Wednesday, 29 May

An American journalist from Arkansas, Eugene Lyons, came in the afternoon for an interview for *Newsweek*, bringing his wife. He is tall, rather good-looking, reasonably bright. He had been taught by Paul Fussell at Rutgers. Like all Americans, he eventually wanted to talk about politics. Said he attended a meeting of Anthony Wedgwood Benn in North London, where everyone put a case for queers, black lesbians, etc. An obvious proletarian got up, complained his garbage was never collected where he lived, other domestic hardships suffered by him, suggested something might be done about these before getting on to homosexuality in various forms (he used some comic working-class phrase to define such things, which Lyons had forgotten). He was at once fiercely hissed, booed. Diane Lyons, small, dark, does something in hospital administration, went round lake during interview. Lyons said it went against all he stood for, at same time he had to admit up to date that Reagan hadn't done too bad a job. He remarked that he was staggered by the partisan attitude of reviewers in this country. Quite right for him to be staggered.

Friday, 31 May

About fourteen years ago Maggie Lewis, then a student at Berkeley, California, wrote me a fan letter saying her English teacher told her you could not write a novel unless you felt confused (interesting example of the brilliance of Eng. Lit. teachers); she, Maggie, considered my works confuted this view. We corresponded, Maggie came to England with a widowed mother and sisters. They took Osbert Sitwell's former house, 2 Carlyle Square, and invited me there. For some reason I couldn't go in first instance, so we asked her down here to luncheon, everyone prophesying she would turn out hideous monster. In the event she was very pretty, quite bright; later V & I were entertained by

Maggie's family in London, all agreeable. Later Maggie worked on the *Christian Science Monitor*, Boston, and continued to send letters from time to time. She came here about six years ago, for some reason never married until in her thirties. She is now making a visit to this country with a newly acquired husband, Owen Thomas. They asked if they could come to lunch. He, Welsh origins, going to see relations in Brecon and Montgomeryshire. Maggie still pretty, looked a bit harassed, I thought; her husband one would guess somewhat younger, obviously not used to conversational styles over here. Like several Americans lately, they did not manage to reach the house until 2.15, after we had given them up. This may somewhat have discomposed him. Neither of them drank anything, which did not make things easier. V and I survived by splitting between us a bottle of (goodish) Valpolicella. [However, Maggie wrote very nice letter afterwards, saying how much they enjoyed themselves, both with us, and on their trip generally, so perhaps everything went all right after all.]

Monday, 3 June

Mary (Clive) for tea. She had been attending the funeral of her brother-in-law, Johnny Walker (married Meysey Clive's sister Caroline), at Sutton Veny about eight miles from here. She said she heard her brother Frank tell Harold Pinter (now Frank's son-in-law, something hard to remember): 'All right, I'll get Gubby [G. O. Allen, England cricketer, at Frank's house at Eton, where Allen was a few years older] on Tuesday.'

Monday, 10 June

A photographer, Homer Sykes, from *Newsweek*, came for the Eugene Lyons piece. He seems quite agreeable. He said family came from Yorkshire (cf. Sykes of Sledmere), where they had been clockmakers (cf. Kipling's Yorkshire clockmaker forebears), also Quakers (cf. my own connexion Thomas Howell, Quaker, clockmaking ancestry, who sold blankets to George Washington, gt-grandfather of William Dean Howells, US novelist, & father-in-law of Thomas Joseph Powell who emigrated to America 1819, clockmaking and Quakerism apparently going together, Kipling's antecedents also being dissenters). Homer Sykes said his grandfather keen on the Classics, and gave his father that name, then passed on to himself; he remarked he found it chiefly shared with dogs in England. It turned out that, as a boy, he had worked on Tristram's photographic publication *Album*, which ran for a year. Another coincidence that Sykes had taken some of the stills for *Jenny's War*, film partly shot in Paddock Field not long ago. Like all concerned in that film, he agreed that Dyan Cannon was not easy to deal with. She is also to be judged an indifferent actress, we thought, watching *Jenny's War* on TV last night.

Sunday, 16 June

Bob & Liddie Conquest to luncheon, bringing Liddie's daughter Helen by an earlier husband (Robinson?, Helen calling herself by her mother's maiden name Wingate). Bob in good form, Liddie a shade plumper than she used to be, which rather suits her, like little round bird. Helen pretty, all but speechless, in the manner of certain American female adolescents in company of older persons. Liddie's mother heard a woman talking about herself (that is, Liddie's mother) when both were in the hairdresser's (in the US), saying her daughter was married to a man who had written a lot of books about Russia, one of them called *War and Peace*. Bob & Liddie seem to have had quite an enjoyable time in Chicago, when Bob delivered my speech at the Ingersoll Foundation Dinner for the Prize Presentation. Bob, finding himself in that part of the world, went on to Detroit, and saw ex-Presidents Ford and Carter. The latter told Bob that he 'identified' with hero (named Carter) in the space-fiction of Edgar Rice Burroughs.

Wednesday, 19 June

Innes Lloyd, put forward as potential producer in latest BBC negotiations about TV *Dance*, came to luncheon. About sixty-five, big, slightly like pictures of P. G. Wodehouse, he served in the Royal Navy during the war. Lloyd made a good impression. The proposal is fifteen episodes of fifty minutes, possibly more. I am objecting to clause which says, if thought best, this amount may be reduced, but not less than twelve. So far as I am concerned the latter is not on. Innes Lloyd seemed surprised this clause had been put in and saw no difficulty in altering it. After Innes Lloyd left, I rang Rachel Billington, with whom he has done various TV plays and asked her opinion. Rachel gave a favourable account of him: quiet, intelligent, wants to do the best he can by the author. He is apparently 'on contract' with BBC at moment, ie., retired more or less. One will just have to see how things work out. The other (more powerful) executive producer involved is Jonathan Powell. He is about thirty-eight, has done several successful things.

Thursday, 20 June

V and I to London to lunch with Evangeline Bruce at (A3) Albany. Evangeline is habitually over from Washington at this time of year. Guests: Miriam Gross; travel writer Patrick Leigh Fermor, 'Paddy'; Nicko Henderson; Peter Quennell. The drink was the final magnum of claret I gave Evangeline at the time of the *Hudson Review* Award, which she very sweetly kept for our next appearance at her table. Quennell and Nicko had a great argument about David Herbert, son of Lord Pembroke, now living in Tangier. I don't think I ever met him. Nicko remarked that 'David never made anything of his life'. This roused Peter, who poured contempt on such an ambitious concept. What did it mean? He glanced round the table: 'Of course, a retired Ambassador . . . a famous novelist . . .' His eyes reached Paddy. Definition understandably eluded him, Paddy being in any case rather quieter than usual.

When this difference of opinion as to the Meaning of Life subsided, Paddy and Peter deplored to each other the sort of people becoming members of White's Club these days. I was glad to have lived to hear this conversation, wonderful Max Beerbohm Young Self & Old Self, Quennell Cartoon, which would certainly have included the ghosts of former White's members Evelyn Waugh and Cyril Connolly in the background as deceased bohemians who had also made the White's Club grade. Incidentally, on the subject of White's, Christopher Holland-Martin (MIL War Office with me, later John's god-father), an essence of City Upper Class life, who would have become member of White's as a matter of family routine, used to say he took no interest in who became a fellow member of White's; on the other hand, he very much kept an eye on Brooks's election list, to which he also belonged. Interesting social opinion from an agreeable chap with whom there had been no question of having to take thought as to whether or not he would be elected to either Club; feeling desire to retain at Brooks's what always seems to me fairly stuffy 'Establishment' atmosphere.

When we got home Bob Conquest rang to say Philip Larkin was very ill in hospital, but gave no details.

Thursday, 27 June

To London. Saw Sussman, who had watched the production of *Richard III*, in which Richard anachronistically used elbow-crutches, which outraged Sussman: 'After all the trouble you took about getting the crutches right in the book you are working on.' Regarding *The Fisher King* Sussman on this aspect had been most helpful, supplying catalogues of medical appliances. Kingsley

Amis lunched with me at The Travellers, he said Philip Larkin was better, but various domestic complications were taking place in connexion with his girlfriends, a former one of these having turned up to look after him in Hull, causing mixed (perhaps unmixed) feelings. Presumably this is the friend, who replied to my recent letter congratulating Larkin on CH conferred in the Birthday Honours, reporting 'Dr Larkin' was unable to answer my letter. Kingsley mentioned his next novel to be about 'senile delinquency in South Wales'.

In that connexion he said the late Aneurin Bevan at political meeting in Wales asked: 'Any Welsh speakers present?' Several hands were raised affirmatively. 'Well, get to London as soon as you can, and join the BBC. You're losing votes here.' I enquired about what Richard Hoggart is like, having agreed in a weak moment to talk about books with him on ITV, can't imagine why. Kingsley said 'Lefty, all the same not at all bad', in fact he gave Hoggart quite a good chit (as my father would have said). Charles Moore, the new young Editor of *Spectator* invited Kingsley to lunch at 'the restaurant of his choice', which was The Connaught. When Moore handed Kingsley Wine List he said: 'Don't mess about with clarets in the middle of the List, have what you'd like best.' Kingsley needed no further pressing. The most expensive one being £106 or thereabouts, he plumped for it. 'That's all right,' said Moore. 'You'll have to drink most of the bottle yourself.' Kingsley said that was all right too. He reported the bottle (had forgotten Château) as good, by no means best claret he had ever drunk in his life. He has been asked by the *Sunday Times* to do an interview for my eightieth birthday in December. I had a word in the Club with both Anthony Hartley, and Denys Sutton. (Separately.)

Monday, 8 July

V and I attended Johnny Walker's Memorial Service at Sutton Veny. The church very full, it was a somewhat extraordinary occasion. Johnny Walker's own musical compositions were played; his more or less devotional poems read aloud; finally his voice on a cassette, recording Tennyson's *Crossing the Bar* in slightly adapted wording, presumably Johnny Walker's. The address given by General Sir Frank Kitson (C-in-C UK Troops), whose Company Commander was Johnny on Kitson's joining The Rifle Brigade. Kitson himself was much in the news about fifteen years ago when he wrote a book called *Low Intensity Operations*, dealing with street-fighting (the Army taking with immense relish to contemporary taste for euphemistic phrases). The book was much attacked by the Left as being inimical to terrorists, revolutionaries, *et al*. Kitson, from the pulpit, said that when their battalion was in the Middle East, the rule was made that anyone who criticized the food in the Mess would automatically be put in charge of Messing. It had been suggested that a form of desert rock-limpet (something of the sort) might be edible, specimens of which were collected and served for dinner. Johnny Walker exclaimed loudly about the incredible nastiness of this dish, then suddenly remembering the fearful threat hanging over all critics of the menu, added: 'But beautifully cooked, of course.'

At one moment in the Service, towards the middle, Henry Bath was inserted to say a personal word about Johnny. Henry does this sort of thing with extreme skill, all the deep conviction of tone that belongs perhaps most of all to the profoundly cynical. Perhaps I do Henry a wrong. He may not be profoundly cynical. It is really impossible to say. Our nephew George Clive turned up rather late at the church. A Greenjacket bugler in full rig sounded the Last Post. Interesting to see who stood to attention. I am never sure whether or not one stands easy when the call changes to Reveille. I must consult a soldier. I suspect one remains at attention throughout. In the army did one stand to attention at Reveille as one does at Last Post? I suppose one merely got out of bed.

Thursday, 11 July

I finished *The Fisher King*. We had a bottle of fizz at dinner.

Sunday, 14 July

Driven by John, we lunched with Roy & Jennifer (recently created DBE) Jenkins at St Amand's House, East Hendred, near Wantage. It is a large rather suburban village. The Jenkins' house is black & white, with a nice garden. Lord & Lady Anglesey were staying. We met them a long time ago with the Mark Longmans when they lived in Wiltshire before Mark died. I failed to recognize them. Henry Anglesey and I had in fact corresponded fairly recently about attempting to preserve the Old Castle at Dynevor. (A former stronghold of Rhys the Hoarse, forebear of the Powells, as well as V's connexion, much more recently.) As it happened, I had also given one of the vols of Anglesey's *History of British Cavalry* a good notice. I had taken it because there was nothing much about in way of books to review, and I found it admirably written. He sent most appreciative letter. Shirley Anglesey was daughter of the novelist Charles Morgan. Both of them very agreeable. Other guests: Mark & Leslie Bonham-Carter, she is American, daughter of Condé Nast, glossy paper publisher. I forgot that when sitting next to her, and asked if she knew the US. Jennifer Jenkins, on my other side, is easy to talk to, a little sad, cheered evidently by her DBE. Mark Bonham-Carter looked decidedly battered. Diana Phipps arrived with the Bonham-Carters, going back on her own. I had no opportunity to talk with her.

After luncheon there was a discussion about traitors, among others, whether or not Roger Hollis could be included, a former Head of MI5, alleged to be in Russian pay. Fred Warner was also discussed. I was dining at one of Antonia's (then Fraser) large parties at Campden Hill Square, V for some reason was not with me, possibly flu. When I started to say goodbye at end of the evening, Antonia said: 'No, you are not going home, you are coming on to a party with me.' There was never any lack of drink at the Frasers (Hugh absent by then, probably as MP, gone to vote), so I was not outstandingly sober. I agreed to accompany Antonia. She took me to what was normally a subterranean night-club in Duke Street, St James's Square, where Prince Azamat (Persian, I think, said to be directly descended from Genghis Khan) was giving a birthday party. We were handed jorums of champagne. I found myself talking to Fred Warner, who was even drunker than myself. We got on to Proust, for whose writings I expressed wholehearted admiration. Warner at once asked how I could admire such decadent rubbish, producing a diatribe against wealth, aristocracy and social life.

Good claret, name like Château Riverne, '78. Enjoyable party.

Tuesday, 16 July

Adam Low and Nicholas Shakespeare came to shoot the Evelyn Waugh BBC TV programme. They arrived about 3.15, having said they would be here at 2 o.c. Apart from that, things went all right, Low was greatly improved in demeanour, perhaps earlier due to mere awkwardness, or shyness. Shakespeare did questions well. I had sudden doubt whether Evelyn actually wore his grey bowler when lunching here, so omitted that in question of his outfit. I am now certain a grey bowler was on his head once when I opened the door . . . Low and Shakespeare had interviewed Pansy (Lamb) in Rome with success (Pansy had shared flat with Evelyn Gardner when the Waugh marriage took place). They reported Pansy's apartment in Rome as pleasant.

Thursday, 18 – Monday, 22 July

Tristram & Virginia came to dinner on Thursday night. Tristram is just back from Naples, and filming a programme *Norman Lewis Naples '44*. Andrew Murray-Threipland is staying at The Stables with two children, Madoc (gnome of nine, who has already acted in a film of *Frankie & Johnnie*),

Charlotte, age three (Andrew's wife Tammy is away doing Law exams); also a couple met in Greece, Norman & Paola Hewitt, she Italian, both teaching at Lugano University. Hewitt comes from Wigan, walrus moustache, rather like the comedian Billy Bennett; she dark, pretty, from Genoa; a sympathetic couple. They too had a child with them. Edward, age three. With Georgia & Archie, it is hard to know how they all pack in at The Stables, fortunately not one's own problem.

Wednesday, 24 July

Two females from TV South came to arrange a talk about Books with Richard Hoggart. After they refused to listen when one of them rang up and I offered to give instructions how to find the house, they arrived at 3.30 instead of 2.30. I was irritated at this, as quite unnecessary. However they turned out to be not too bad in the end, so stayed for tea: Pat Phillips (Australian), and Jean Orba. The former asked V if she, too, were of Australian origin.

Thursday, 25 July

The BBC now suggest that *Dance* should be televised in two halves of ten episodes, the whole thing being too complicated to break down in one go, also difficulties of tying-up actors, etc. This seems reasonable, indeed an excellent idea. It was put up by the adapter Ken Taylor, recommended also by Innes Lloyd. Taylor's first six vols roughly sketched in arrived today, I think well done. I shall try to see Taylor & Lloyd as soon as possible to discuss further steps. The chief adjustment seems to be that Jean Duport's unfaithfulness to her husband is pinned on Widmerpool, perhaps not too bad an idea, as characters will no doubt have to be reduced in number, though this change would of course have thrown the novel itself out of balance. One must remember that Jean's lover Brent is exceedingly awful too.

Incidentally, the Automobile Association has large ads (in such places as the Sunday paper colour magazines) to obtain staff for training at Widmerpool Hall, Nottinghamshire (apparently described by those who have been there as 'Colditz'), a picture of The Hall appended. I had not known such a house existed, tho' adumbrated on in *Dance* as a fantastic possibility. This must have ben formerly the seat of the Widmerpool mentioned as a Cromwellian Captain of Horse in Hutchinson's *Memoirs of the Civil War*, where I found the name in the first instance, and noted it years ago. I have quite a lot of Nottinghamshire ancestors through the Waterhouse family. It would be amusing if Widmerpool connexion ever cropped up, but at present no trace.

Thursday, 8 August

Innes Lloyd & Ken Taylor, arriving at 10.30 am, stayed to luncheon to discuss the new project of doing first six vols of *Dance* in ten, possibly more, episodes. Ken Taylor, who is to adapt, did *The Jewel in the Crown* by Paul Scott, generally regarded as great success. I was rather apprehensive as to who might appear (somewhat like an arranged marriage without meeting, wondering what one's vis-à-vis would be like in bed). In fact I took to Taylor immediately. Small, sprite-like, slight touch of Malcolm Muggeridge, sympathetic, intelligent, on occasion saying: 'Oh, we can't possibly do without that' when I should myself if necessary have been prepared to make a cut. I had been mistaken in supposing he wanted to involve Widmerpool with Jean Duport. Far from it. A sentence had just been awkwardly expressed. That is a considerable relief, as such an alteration might easily have unforeseeable effects.

Taylor hopes to have thirteen episodes if all goes well. I don't feel at all certain he will get away with that. I have always set my face against single vols of *Dance* being done separately on TV, but, as the sequence falls naturally into two parts owing to the war, I see no objection to this division. It would clearly be a mammoth job to do twelve vols in one showing, while, if the first half is successful, it might be a positive advantage in whetting viewers' appetite for a further round. All the same, I have suffered so many disasters in TV projects falling through that nothing is to be expected until *Dance* is actually projected on the screen. Innes Lloyd is a thoroughly agreeable chap, as well as Ken Taylor. A lot of work was got through.

Tuesday, 13 August

We are suddenly plagued with implementation of the Reservoir Act 1975, which decrees that pieces of water over a certain capacity must be inspected every year, with innumerable circumstances of trouble, expense. Accordingly, Michael Joyce & Martin Hemmett, the former understudying Mr Quick of Cooper & Tanner, the latter his assistant, came to measure the lake. A great relief if this turns out comfortably outside the terms of reference of the Act. They seemed sensible couple of young men to deal with. A black swan on the lake which V alleges to be different from the Lomers' black swans, which habitually trespass there. I can hardly believe it is not one of their exotic birds.

Thursday, 15 August

To London. I saw Sussman, where Tristram preceded me, so we met and had a word. I lunched with the Lancasters at Cheyne Court. Anne had been away for couple of days, and things were rather better than sometimes, Osbert is hearing more, in general slightly improved form, if only slightly. He talked about Walter Goetz. Archie knows Goetz's son, and is going to stay with them and fish. Goetz's drawings in *Punch* were always good, and funny, he himself I have never met. Osbert said he gave up drawing to become an art dealer in Paris. Tristram reported Mrs Goetz as rather fierce on telephone. Anne said Elizabeth Cavendish had refused to see Bevis Hillier at all in connexion with his officially commissioned biography of John Betjeman. It now must be near completion. Understandable. Osbert has removed his moustache (recommended in the first instance by his former mother-in-law Lady Harris. It was on the whole wise advice, one would say), tho' the change makes less difference than might be expected, in fact it was some time before I noticed.

Sunday, 1 September

Driven by John, we lunched with Anthony & Tanya Hobson. Their children Charlotte & William were there, also Elizabeth Jane Howard (late Amis) staying. Anthony a bit *piano*, recently come out of hospital for 'tests', in manner of so many of one's friends at age one has reached. Tanya was in excellent form. Jane told me Martin Amis was the first to suggest the Amis/Kilmarnock ménage, which recently moved house; where, we have not yet been informed. The Hobson children are nice. William is in third year at Lady Margaret Hall (which I still find strange for a boy), looks decidedly Russian from Vinogradoff blood.

I recommended *The Burra Letters* to Anthony which I have been rereading. Claret as usual excellent.

Friday, 6 September

Miriam Gross from the *Observer* came for an Eightieth Birthday interview. She turned up at 1.30 for luncheon, having missed the train at Paddington, in spite of arriving specially early at station. At first a trifle discomposed by this, she later recovered and conducted an intelligent interview. John Gross gives the same address in *Who's Who* (St Petersburgh Place, W2), in fact seems to live in New York. He apparently still works on *New York Times Book Review*.

Miriam Gross is a great friend of Sonia Orwell, at one of whose dinner parties at Gloucester Road (Sonia's happiest period before she emigrated to Paris) I first met her. Miriam said just before taking her present flat she met Vidia Naipaul in her local supermarket and discussed her change of address. Vidia walked to another part of the shop, suddenly turned back, shouted across rows of people: 'Let's hope the Blacks don't move in.' *Newsweek, USA Today, Libération* (Paris) arrived, all containing interviews, the last of which (Patrick Mauriès), described the family portraits hanging in the library as 'gauches, sepulcreux', which hits them off rather well; he referred to Widmerpool as Wilberforce.

Tuesday, 10 September

I finished a reread of *Anna Karenina*; and I am now well into *War and Peace*. John Bayley, Russian expert, comments that one speaks of a Dickensian character, a Proustian character, a Surtees character, etc, but not a Tolstoyan character. Bayley (I may be wrong) appears to applaud this lack of authorial flavour, in Tolstoy's case certainly true. My own feeling (expressed before) is the reason lies in Tolstoy never truly grappling with individual character, as (say) the above novelists do in their different ways. In fact Tolstoy seems to me to write *magazine stories of genius* for that very reason. His novels have the outward appearance of life, and contradictions of human character that convince the reader owing to an extreme skill in handling narrative. They are really stylized types placed against each other, dodging the difficulties of portraying flesh & blood people. They are never in the least grotesque, which human beings in life are, indeed, most of the time. True, Tolstoyan characters sometimes behave inconsistently, but their inconsistencies are equally machine-made when compared with (say) Proust's, or Dostoevsky's.

Dostoevsky is always thought of as specifically Russian, but I was struck how extremely *Russian* everyone's behaviour is in Tolstoy's novels; this is perhaps not surprising, but seems often overlooked in praise of his 'ordinariness'. Alick Dru used to say what a great relief he found getting back to Balzac, the Western Mind, after reading Russian novelists. In *War and Peace* this Russianness begins with the convincing character of Pierre, then tails off into stock characters (Pierre's wife, Prince Bolkonsky, etc) set against each other in such a way as to 'contrive' the 'plot', while the (certainly brilliantly depicted) 'large canvas' of the Napoleonic Wars is really a gigantic movie 'treatment'. One notes that Rostov's simple-hearted squadron-commander, Denisovich, has the same name as Solzhenitsyn's *One Day in the Life of Ivan Denisovich*, another thoroughly 'normal' (Russian) man.

Simultaneously I am reading Painter's two vol Proust biography, which holds up extremely well. It is possible to underrate Proust's social success as a young man (passed off by some critics by just complaining he was a snob). Even allowing for French smart life of the period being extremely different from British smart life, it is hard to think of anyone with even roughly Proust's background, without qualifications beyond wit and intelligence, and – it should cerainly be added – money, being friendly with so many young grandees. One glances at the case of Wilde to see the huge contrast. Perhaps Disraeli would be a better parallel, Disraeli & Wilde were earlier than Proust, Disraeli with advantage (in Great Britain) of being political, even if wholly (rather than half) Jewish.

I once sat next to the painter Ethel Sands, then eighty or more, at dinner party (*c*. middle 1950s) of the Glenconners. Miss Sands (said to have been model for Maisie in *What Maisie Knew*) (in fact, I think, Nanda in *The Awkward Age*) remarked that when people talk about snobbery nowadays they have no conception whatever what snobbery was like in Victorian times. She instances the novelist W. H. Mallock (by no means without talent as a writer), a snob of unbelievable obsequiousness. Also Augustus Hare. Mallock a member of an old West Country family, but notably ugly and unattractive; Hare's condition was not dissimilar.

How would these compare with Proust, son of a professionally distinguished doctor, but up against French (more savage) anti-semitism? The answer is neither of them got off the ground, anyway when young, compared to Proust. I finished Chaucer's *Troilus and Cressida*, Nevill Coghill's version, which certainly makes things easier, notwithstanding moments of vulgarity in Coghill's phraseology (to be fair, some of Coghill's apparent modernisms turn out to be Chaucer's own words when one looks at both texts, but by no means all of them). Glad to get back to Shakespeare (*Richard II*). I am as far as Browning in John Hayward's *Faber Book of English Verse*, in which the 16th/17th centuries are far the best selections.

Thursday, 12 September

V and I went to Cloford, intending to photograph Horner memorials in the church for the Spurlings. Unfortunately flashes in my camera failed to work, so we will have to pay another visit. The Memorial is splendid, busts of Sir George Horner and wife Anne. He d. 1676 aet. 72. The busts suggest portraits from life, clothes perhaps ten or more years earlier than their individual deaths, as they are reminiscent of our Hurt/Brudenell/Harpur portraits (if the young woman *is* Nicholas Hurt's wife, rather than his sister, the latter possible as she so much resembles him). However people in that part of the world, Derbyshire/Nottinghamshire, are strong type, as I noticed when staying with the Sitwells. The persons in these three portraits all seem in mourning, which would fit in with Nicholas Hurt's father having died in 1667 (see Heraldic *Visitations*), Nicholas's drop of lace at throat (Aubrey says that came into fashion in 1667) has been painted over a former simpler (possibly Roundhead) neckband. Was there a proletarian implication in this? The Horner clothes suggest this earlier period, tho' no doubt people went on wearing their old clothes, especially in the country. Anne Horner, of the Cloford memorial, daughter of Sir Henry Pool, of Sapperton, Gloucestershire, younger brother of Eleanor, Lady Fettiplace, the owner of Hilary's famous Cookery Book. As Hilary says, Anne Horner looks like a cook, square, redfaced, forceful.

Saturday, 14 September

Tristram & Virginia to dinner. They had been staying with George Clive at Whitfield. Tristram's programme, *Naples '44* due in November.

Sunday, 15 September

Driven by John, we lunched with David Cecil at Red Lion House, Cranborne. David, in spite of having suffered a rather bad time some months ago, was in goodish form, better in fact than when we last saw him. He talked of Selina Hastings's life of Nancy Mitford, of which Tristram gave us a proof copy. Only V read this, as I shall certainly review it, and prefer to write a notice after immediate reading. David said he always had good relations with Nancy, at the same time thought there was something harsh about her as a person, that was not very nice. I would agree. Nancy could be funny, very hospitable, at the same time she was hard, immature, ununderstanding, making one think of an unkind, unhappy schoolgirl, perhaps what Nancy remained all her life. There was certainly a strong strain of naivety.

When V & I were in Paris on one occasion we took her out to dinner in a restaurant (something that rarely happened to Nancy). Before, or afterwards, we sat in a café, where one of those itinerant artists not uncommon in Paris was doing drawings. He asked if he might draw Nancy. She refused. He made a movement with his hands close round her face, to express the beauty of its contours. That greatly upset her, and she shrieked almost hysterically: 'Send him away, send him away!' This utterly characteristic Parisian incident discomposed her dreadfully.

David Cecil said he always detested her brother Tom Mitford (a professional bad-mannered man), whom I think I only met once. He left no impression. David said early in his own married life he & Rachel dined with Alice Astor (then von Hofmannsthal). Tom Mitford had been put between Rachel & Eve Curie (the unusually pretty daughter of the Radium Curies), then living with Henry Bernstein, the dramatist. Tom Mitford spent literally the whole of dinner talking to Eve Curie, not addressing one single word to Rachel Cecil throughout the meal. David was so furious at this that after dinner he made a point of monopolizing Eve Curie for the rest of the evening, making sure that Tom Mitford could not get near her, much less talk with her. This sheds interesting light on David's tougher side, not always appreciated.

Talking of Max Beerbohm (of whom he wrote a biography) David said he thought Max probably went to bed at least once when young with Constance Collier, a determined woman (still going in my young days, when I saw her in Maugham's *Our Betters*), but had not liked the experience, henceforth avoided it. Beerbohm's doctor told David he thought Max never had physical relations with his wife Florence, herself unkeen on sex. David did not feel this sufficiently positive to state in his biography. He said there was never the smallest suggestion that Max Beerbohm was homosexual, tho' no doubt men (eg. Reggie Turner, a member of the Wilde circle) had been in love with him when young. Max himself was, David thought, purely narcissistic, liking sex in neither form. I remember a letter from Max to Turner in printed selection where Max mentions occupying Turner's former room in some hotel, which 'must have witnessed scenes of which I could not approve'.

One of Malcolm Muggeridge's most idiotic outbursts was to write that Max lived in Italy because he was queer. Malcolm had not the smallest reason for saying that, beyond envy of success in a man who had always been friendly to him. According to David, also no reason to suppose the Beerbohms were Jewish, another of Malcolm's insistences. They were German Balts, David said, granted lands by Catherine the Great. Isaiah Berlin believing the same, tho', true, Harry Goldsmid supposed otherwise, remarking, 'You've only got to think of Beerbohm/Bierbaum as names.' If it comes to that many non-Jewish names are also Jewish. The Beerbohms used coat of arms with a tree (possibly reason for Beerbohm Tree's stage name). The 18th century landowning elements in the Baltic States seem to contradict accuracy of Max appearing in *Jewish Encyclopaedia*.

Wednesday, 18 September

Southern TV (based on Southampton) shot the programme with Richard Hoggart for *Writers on Writing*. I had not met Hoggart, who lunched with us. He was small, dark, professionally 'working class', in fact not in the least outwardly different from anyone else in the TV 'personality' line of business. I liked him. He has some idea of a joke. At luncheon he somewhat defiantly tucked his napkin into his waistcoat, which suggested old-fashioned French bourgeois life, more than the modes of today's lower income brackets. When doing the talk (recorded before lunch) Hoggart was a bit taken aback by my views on Tolstoy, anything less than unqualified Tolstoy worship often coming as a surprise. He was also troubled by my lack of enthusiasm for E. M. Forster. Hoggart said he was son of a Sergeant Major in a regiment of the Line, but not able to say which, he knew no more than one of the Yorkshire regiments, he thought. His father died, like his mother, when Hoggart was a child, and Hoggart was brought up by his grandmother. There were eccentric aunts (not uncommon literary background at all social levels).

Hoggart went to Leeds University, where Bonamy Dobrée (soldier/don mentioned in my Memoirs) was Hoggart's tutor and patron. [Hoggart later sent me an amusing account of Dobrée he had published in some periodical.] The camera crew of nine was quite tolerable. My new electric typewriter (Smith Corona EL2000 bought in mail order lot) suddenly seized up this morning. Consulted crew's electrician Charles, delightful chap, not particularly young, real 'working-class' member of that most interesting branch of the electrical vocation. The typewriter, plainly not working properly when Charles examined it. On switching everything off, and switching it on again, it miraculously recovered, which it had refused to do when I had gone through the same motions.

I received a letter from Dean of Westminster, Dr Edward Carpenter, asking if I thought the late J. B. Priestley should be allowed a memorial in the Abbey. I can't imagine, to put it mildly, anything I think less. I wrote a recommendation in the negative, adding a few unctuous comments on difficulties of advising on such points for a fellow writer. [The Dean later thanked me with equal unction, and, I suspect, satisfaction.]

Thursday, 19 September

John Bowle obit. I always (so far as possible) avoided John Edward (as John Betjeman always called him) when we were undergraduates at Balliol, feeling sure that Matthew Ponsonby, Arden Hilliard, *et al*, 'taking Bowle up' as a freshman would lead to trouble. It did indeed, resulting in all of them 'dropping' him after a bit on account of his bad temper, general goings-on, in short condition of being *insortable*. In consequence of this caution on my own part, John Edward and I were able to meet on good terms after we went down, relations uncomplicated by earlier awkward incidents.

His Marlborough contemporary, John Betjeman (fellow competitor at one moment for job as Sir Horace Plunkett's secretary, hence Members/Quiggin rivalry with St John Clarke in *Dance*) said with truth Bowle looked as if his nose had been permanently stung by a bee. Bowle was brilliant teacher of History to boys, all history scholarships, which in the senior history master Henry Marten's day had gone to Eton, were diverted to Westminster while Bowle was history master there. (By that time Marten was no longer teaching History.) This scholarship winning ought to have transferred when Bowle became history master at Eton (after inevitably quarrelling with Headmaster of Westminster), Eton being a school for which Bowle had great romantic admiration. Unwisely, he imported his mother, but perhaps in any case he was not quite right for Eton.

What was John Edward right for? While at Westminster he arranged (through Betjeman) for Lord Alfred Douglas to lecture to the boys; then (according to legend) got so drunk himself that Lord Alfred and Angus Wilson (then a boy at Westminster) had to put Bowle to bed. Bowle had various bureaucratic employments during the war in which he consistently drove all his superiors (notably Sir Archibald Sinclair, Air Minister) mad. After the war he settled down to be a don, and obtained a Fellowship at Wadham (largely through Maurice Bowra). He failed again to dig himself in securely. His Fellowship was not renewed (something fairly rare) when the moment came for re-voting it. He then became an itinerant academic, teaching in Europe and America, with fair prosperity, producing a stream of unreadable books on Thomas Hobbes, etc.

The fact is, John Edward Bowle ought to have lived at Hobbes's period. He was not fitted to this century. His direct ancestor, Colonel Bowle, had been 'out with Penruddock' in Penruddock's Cavalier rebellion against Cromwell (whether or not executed I am uncertain), but the Colonel's descendant should have belonged to same epoch, uncontrolled tempers the rule rather than the exception. John Edward was one of those monsters I could put up with in small doses (Betjeman once commented to Tristram he could not imagine how I did it), others were often less tolerant. In that connexion V reflected that Betjeman, so recently deceased, having undoubtedly fixed himself up as comfortably in the Next World as he had in this one, would have a nasty shock when his old Marlborough crony, successfully jettisoned on Earth, suddenly turns up almost immediately to join him in Heaven/Hell.

With reference to proposed *Dance* Picture Book, Giniger, having failed to place it with either British or American publishers, also lost his wife, talks of retiring from publishing, causing project to be abandoned. However, by chance sorting business letters, I came across one from Thames & Hudson, written about three years ago, which adumbrated a similar scheme of illustrating pictures mentioned in *Dance*. That was turned down at the time on account of Giniger. The letter's writer, Jamie Camplin (it transpired given that diminutive as first name at birth), lunched here today to discuss the new situation. He is in his late thirties, slight in build, long upper lip, married, three children, mixture of being rather shy and rather formidable. He is evidently a committed publisher, who knows everyone in that, or any art line. Camplin still seems keen on idea of a Picture Book, with the great advantage of Thames & Hudson being a firm that would market the book themselves (rather than a middleman like Giniger) a firm professionally concerned with art books as such. Incidentally, Thames & Hudson also have close connexions with Norton's in the US, where Tom Wallace, late of Holt's, now works, which might be advantageous. Jamie Camplin took away material collected by V (about 100 pictures, list of other potential ones, general notes on the subject) and will report on matters after examination.

V (now involved with her E. M. Delafield book) does not want to do more on Picture Book. My idea is she should remain in the background, but name on title page as General Editor, and someone appropriate found to write Introduction. It is not easy to decide off the cuff who this should be, I am anxious the Picture Book should not have the air of being composed by myself, tho' I am prepared to write a brief Foreword, the point being that Picture Book illustrates the effect on the reader, rather than being an addition on my part to what I have written. Though familiarity with *Dance* would be *sine qua non*, also readable style and a good grasp of art matters. Camplin, whose publishing work must be largely devoted to such problems (ie. finding competent editors, introducers and some pictures) agreed about difficulties. He seems extremely sensible discussing such subjects. I shall have a further word about it all with Bruce Hunter. Incidentally, Jamie Camplin's wife occasionally 'reads' for Higham's.

Saturday, 21 September

I was amused to receive a press-cutting from the *Western Morning News* containing an interview with Ken Taylor, in which Ken's projected TV script for *Dance* spoken of as already arranged, tho' in fact I have no confirmation of this from BBC, or contract. Ken Taylor is photographed reading the paperback of my Memoirs, the name easily visible on the cover. I received a letter from Norman Mailer, President of the American PEN, inviting me to be Honoured Guest at PEN Congress in NYC. Daunting thought. Declined with appropriate thanks.

Wednesday, 25 September

For some inexplicable reason (no doubt editorial heavy weather) Miriam

Gross wanted to come down today for further questions in her interview for *Observer*. I cooked curry for luncheon. She herself is quite agreeable, her questions were unexciting, such as 'What does it feel like to be eighty?' I cannot conceive why it is thought necessary to send her toiling down here again. The triviality of the questions of even better-type journalists is fathomless in interviews, probably due to editorial instructions. They are, for example, duller than the general run of fan-letter writers.

Since her previous visit, Miriam Gross interviewed Joan Collins in Hollywood (voted the most famous woman in the World after the Queen, or something of the sort). Joan Collins & her sister Jackie (who writes immensely successful pornographic novels) used to be children of about eleven/twelve, in Park Square, when we lived in Chester Gate, Regent's Park, and frequented the Square a good deal. I remember Joan Collins suddenly appearing through the bushes, certainly looking strikingly pretty. At the time V had commented: 'That little girl will get off with man, woman, or child.'

Thursday, 26 September

I signed a BBC contract for first six vols of *Dance* on TV, subject to various options. V & I went to Cloford in afternoon where I took more photographs of the Horner tomb, the flashes working this time. We had to get key of church from Mrs George of New House Farm some little way away, as Mrs Snowling, in the cottage next door, was not at home; New House Farm was rather a pretty place.

I am reading for review Selina Hastings's life of Nancy Mitford. My first meeting with Nancy was finding myself sitting next to her at a deb dinner party at the Ralph Yorkes about 1927, in the Radnor Place part of the world. Brigadier-General Yorke (11th Hussars, I think), uncle of Henry Yorke (Green), two daughters.

Nancy Mitford must have been 'out' at least two years by then, wearing a dress of rather unhappy blue (Saxe?) sequins. She was tall, good-looking, neat figure, without being at all a 'beauty'. She opened conversation (no doubt in reference to some dish we were eating) with the words: 'Don't you *adore* mushrooms?' Nancy could be funny in conversation, but never at all at ease, always desperately self-conscious, a condition that continued through her life. Selina does the Mitford background well, interesting on her father's side, long line of Northumberland gentry going back as landowners and Knights of the Shire to the 14th century (something rarer in traceable pedigree than might be thought); her mother's father was illegitimate issue of a Liberal MP called Bowles & a housemaid. Bowles founded various periodicals, *Vanity Fair, The*

Lady, etc. Strikingly comic photograph of him shows distinct resemblance to Frank Harris in appearance. There was possibly also similarity in behaviour.

This heredity, mixture of stocks, explains almost too appositely Nancy's complexities, and the antics of her generation of Mitfords: social unease masked under aristocratic arrogance; love of violence in politics, individuals; journalistic abilities; flair for publicity. Selina is rather less successful in sorting out Nancy's early personal life, having obviously swallowed a good many legends promulgated by the Mitford family. It was no doubt difficult to do otherwise for Selina. Even Debo Devonshire, by far the best of the Mitford bunch, probably not very reliable when describing Nancy's passion for Hamish Erskine (who gets unjustly rough treatment), perhaps other aspects of Nancy's life too. Nancy's love affair with Palewski so far as I have read seems satisfactorily handled.

Wednesday, 9 October

Rosamund Dashwood came to see us. She is the daughter of E. M. Delafield (née De la Pasture, French *noblesse*, emigrated to this country at the time of the Revolution). She married a member of the Dashwood family, baronets, whose house was near North Aston Hall, Oxon, where the Pakenhams lived most of the time as children. Rosamund Dashwood is the widow of a doctor named Truelove, who practised in New Zealand and Canada. She has now gone back to her maiden name. She is in her early sixties, bright without being at all literary in the manner of her mother. She said various writers used to come to the house when she was a child including Virginia Woolf, who 'to a rather bouncy little girl', seemed ugly, disagreeable, boring. Rosamund Dashwood warmed up after a couple of beakers of wine, and some of the Chambery liqueur Archie brought back for me from his trip abroad.

Wednesday, 16 October

V to London. Hilary Spurling rang in evening to say she, and various other friends, thought it good idea to present me with my portrait as an eightieth birthday present. Very sweet of her (and them), but certain difficulties come to mind. Who would paint the picture, could enough money be collected to pay for it? What would be involved in presumably going to London for sittings? So far as possible I prefer to keep out of London these days and am certainly not anxious to have an extended series of journeys there.

Hilary, with characteristic force, brushed aside any such pretexts, hesitations about organization. She wants the painter to be Rodrigo Moynihan (oddly enough never met, I think, tho' we know lots of people in common); alternatively some (unspecified) young man Hilary has up her sleeve, said by her to be good but untried. The National Portrait Gallery seems in some manner involved, that also undefined. I thanked Hilary for so kind a thought, said I would like twenty-four hours to ponder the project's various aspects.

Thursday, 17 October

I told Hilary I would very much like the portrait to be painted, if she really felt she could manage administration that struck someone like myself as daunting to a degree, in fact a prospect the arranging of which filled me with horror. Hilary cared nothing for all that, and said she would go ahead, Rodrigo Moynihan as the painter to be aimed at. She talked in terms of two sittings in London, then perhaps Moynihan, driven by Hilary, coming down here for one or two more. This strikes me as fewer sittings than the average painter would put up with. We shall see.

Saturday, 19 October

The Stockwells at The Stables with Christina (Noble) Singh, her two children, also staying. Georgia talked to me about possibility of her going up to Oxford. She wants to stick to her Classics, at the same time is not too keen on Greats (accordingly suggested) because that would mean four years residence. Tristram, Virginia, Christina, to dinner. We (John does not drink) polished off three bottles of Cot Touraine, nice light table wine.

Tuesday, 22 October

Interviewed for my Eightieth Birthday by Tony Gould, Literary Editor of *New Society*, at his suggestion. I know little or nothing of this weekly, associated with anthropological, scientific, matters. Gould said he lived in Devon (Bovey Tracey, where Wyndham Lloyd ended his days) and came past this house on weekly trip to London for Tuesday-to-Thursday work, so we asked him to lunch. Big, late forties, on two sticks from polio contracted in Hong Kong during military service (7th Gurkhas) in Malaya. He was brighter than average journalist interviewer, and interested in genealogy (related to the Horners of Mells), also military matters. He had been at Bruton School with our nephew Val Lamb. Field Marshal Sir Gerald Templer (then GOC Malaya) had taken an interest in him owing to his polio (as in all similar sick cases under Templer's Command).

After leaving the army Gould had been in the BBC (Bush House), married twice, children by both unions, and written a biography of Colin MacInnes. From what Gould said MacInnes (met by me only once for a moment) was more like Maclaren Ross than I was aware. If with different sexual tastes, he had the same need to be paid in cash immediately for everything he wrote, always on his beam ends with colossal chip on his shoulder (which Maclaren Ross did not suffer from). I told Gould about *The Fisher King* (seeing perhaps slight parallel in his lameness, tho' not at all sexual abilities).

Thursday, 24 October

Hugh Montgomery-Massingberd came for an Eightieth Birthday interview for *The Field*, of which Hugh is now a contracted contributor. He brought with him Martin Goddard, a bearded photographer in leather. Goddard is said to be good, certainly brighter than usual run of photographers. Goddard is doing the pictures for an Arthurian book by Geoffrey Ashe (who writes about Glastonbury). Hugh seemed in excellent form, and expressed a wish to return to live in John's Kennington house, where he formerly occupied the basement. Both V & I noticed that living in this proximity had caused both Hugh & John to develop a certain similarity of manner, hard to say who influenced whom. Martin Goddard took a lot of photographs by the lake, where the Lomers' black swan (now established as theirs) was determined to get in on the act. Bright autumn sun on the water. It all looked marvellous after morning of thick blue/grey mist up to and round the house. Hugh & Goddard did not leave until 7 o'clock.

Wednesday, 30 October

Allan Massie & Philip French came for a BBC radio programme for my Eightieth Birthday, celebrations to include radio production of *Agents and Patients* (1937), adapted by Freddie Bradnum, produced by Graham Gauld. Neither Massie nor French would drink anything at luncheon. I like Allan Massie, notwithstanding a somewhat forbidding Scotch buttoned-upness, which meeting him more than once scarcely lessens. He is one of the best contemporary critics, having some grasp of what writing is about, an insight frequently wanting among general run of novel-reviewers.

Philip French I met some fifteen years ago at a radio interview with John Spurling about *Books Do Furnish a Room*. I remembered French as utterly different from what he looks like now, just showing how memory goes adrift regarding appearance. It turned out that French did his military service with

The Parachute Regiment, something one might not have guessed, and indicates him as rather a dark horse. He evidently knows what he is talking about when speaking of the Cinema, on which he is a media authority, so I asked for information about *The Loves of Jeanne Ney*, which I always vaguely class as my third favourite film, Stroheim's *Foolish Wives*, Rene Claire's *The Italian Straw Hat* first two.

Jeanne Ney utterly vague in my memory, was seen centuries ago; begins with Bolshevik troops marching down a more or less dried up watercourse, various scenes in low restaurants, nothing left of story in my mind. French said it was Pabst, *c*. 1926/7, which would have been when I was first working in London. [Philip French wrote later saying *Jeanne Ney* 1928, enclosing piece about the film by Paul Rotha.] We talked of my forthcoming novel *The Fisher King*. French told me the Fisher King myth has been used as framework for plot of *3.10 to Yuma* (1957, producer Delmar David); and was also employed by Bernard Malamud for his first novel about a basketball team. All this familiarity of the myth seems on the whole advantageous, rather than the reverse. For once quite an interesting interview.

Thursday, 31 October

To London for luncheon to meet Jonathan Powell, head (possibly assistant head) of BBC drama, in either case principal producer of TV *Dance*. I saw Sussman, and begged release by 12.30, when BBC would send a car to pick me up. The car turned out to be taxi, which announced itself while Sussman was still tinkering about. When at last I escaped, the driver enquired where to go. I told him I had no idea, so he had to ring BBC on his telephone. While doing this he closed glass shutter between us. When he opened it again I asked where we were going, supposing that to be the Television Centre. Taxi-driver replied: 'It's a secret.'

It turned out that we were 'to' (as they say in the West Country) a destination about three minutes from where we started, in fact we just circled the block, fetching up at a restaurant called Langan's Bistro in Devonshire Street, round the corner from Sussman's in Devonshire Place. Innes Lloyd and Ken Taylor were already sitting at a table. Jonathan Powell (who rhymes his name with towel) arrived short time later. Tall, thin, dark, fashionably frizzed-out hairdo, not bad looking, he had the odd outward characteristic that he could equally well be American, French, German, even Russian, in fact wholly international in appearance . . . He showed more interest than I expected in the possibility of our being distant relations (reasons for which I gave). His father dead, he said his mother or an uncle might have information. He would enquire. Believed family came from 'the West', which could, I suppose, be taken to mean Pembrokeshire, whence link in common would have almost certainly derived.

On return to Westbury, taxi (Hillman) driven by high-powered lady called Judy – 'like Punch & Judy', she said – who also does a milk-round, getting up every day at 3 am. She likes job in open air, which she said difficult for a woman to find. She grilled me about being a writer (a fact known to most of Westbury taxi-drivers, owing to Americans and others coming to house for interviews). She asked, among other things whether my books had been adapted for films. I admitted my reason for being in London was connected with that particular subject. She asked if the books were 'domestic drama'. I was interested in this definition, really not too bad a one, so replied yes. It happened I had just finished reading *Tess of the D'Urbervilles*, and struck me Judy much what Tess might have been had she lived today, not been hanged, which, in any case, would not have happened nowadays. She'd have been out in eight years at most, back at her job, dairy to milk-round and driving a taxi.

In spite of many absurdities there are splendid passages in *Tess*, which I used not to be able to appreciate (some still remain a struggle), chiefly accounts of agricultural work and the climate of countryside. If Hardy had taken a little more trouble with the mechanics of a plot, the story would be just believable. Kilvert's *Diary* often speaks of 'old Hannah Whitney', also remnant of ancient Norman family (the Whitneys occasionally intermarried with my Powells) on Radnor/ Hereford border. She too to some extent aware of having fallen into poverty from formerly distinguished stock when Kilvert talked to her. In *Tess*, has it ever been pointed out that, when Angel Clare and Tess's sister watch black flag run up over the gaol after Tess's execution, Clare obviously married the Durberville sister later on, whole story repeating itself again with her?

Friday, 1 November

Richard Ingrams, Editor of *Private Eye*, wrote saying he was working on biography of Malcolm Muggeridge to appear posthumously, could he come to talk about Malcolm. The signature of his letter was wholly illegible. Ingrams's identity seeming likely, I wrote to Malcolm, asking how he felt about this proposal. It seemed hard to refuse, as I did not wish to impede the biography, if Malcolm wanted it to be written. Malcolm replied enthusiastically that he would like everything about himself to be revealed, speaking at the same time of Ingrams with unqualified admiration.

Accordingly, Ingrams was invited to luncheon. He and I had met before, only once I think, when Ingrams & his wife (Irish, RC) lunched with the

Osbert Lancasters at their Aldworth cottage, near Newbury, Ingrams living in same village. Ingrams announced at once that his doctor did not allow him to drink alcohol . . . he said he was much upset by bad language when he did his military service (Sergeant, Royal Army Education Corps). He told me (this was expected) he had asked Malcolm why he (Malcolm) and I ceased to be friends, Malcolm replying all that was obscure to him.

I stated categorically that nothing could be less obscure, showed Ingrams (on request) Malcolm's review of *The Valley of Bones* in the *Evening Standard*. This review (like a Cabinet Minister's speech on an otherwise non-political occasion, such as the Royal Academy Banquet) seemed to me (still does) a declaration of policy on Malcolm's part: ie. that he did not wish to be friends any longer. He and I (with everyone else accustomed to write reviews) are perfectly familiar with problem of confrontation by a friend's book which the reviewer happens not to like. Any veteran reviewer (nobody could say Malcolm was not that) knows a dozen ways of making damn clear without causing unnecessary offence to any but the most touchy.

Towards the close of the Ingrams session, Trevor Powell (potential cousin, genealogist, putatively stemming from common late 17th century ancestor) rang to say he was at Castle Cary with his (second) wife, Elizabeth, not yet met, could they look in? This had to be delayed to 4.30, as threatened juxtaposition with Ingrams presented too many complications to be faced. When Trevor Powell (who does not look wholly unlike miniature of Philip Lewis Powell, *c.* 1820) arrived Ingrams had been disposed of. Elizabeth Powell seemed a nice girl. She was first encountered as fellow Officer in RAEC. V said afterwards she was Daphne or Sarah (we could not remember which) in *The Jewel in the Crown*; adding with great truth a rare occurrence to have three personnel of the Education Corps in the house on the same day. Reading *Henry IV*, Part II in bed I came across a construction I sometimes use that makes reviewers grumble:

> Our business valued, some twelve days hence
> Our general forces at Bridgnorth shall be met.

It is a matter on which I prefer to take Shakespeare's opinion.

Saturday, 2 November

Tom Rosenthal (late of Heinemann, now Deutsch) wanted an Introduction to the new edition of Cyril Connolly's *Enemies of Promise*, which Deutsch is reprinting. I agreed. Tom was pleased with it. All this some little time ago. The Introduction paid for. Distraught letter arrived this morning from Tom saying

Cyril's widow, Deirdre (now married to Peter Levi, ex-Jesuit priest, poet, miscellaneous writer) refused to have my name associated with any book of Connolly's 'after my Memoirs'. Tom Rosenthal in deep distress. Apart from anything else, I am one of the few Etonians left of Cyril's period capable of doing the job. I am at a loss to understand Deirdre's objection as I wrote nothing in my Memoirs not very generally known about Cyril.

As the Introduction was paid for, it does not matter in least to me whether published or not, though it, or anyway the items the Introduction covered, well might be thought advantageous for reprint. I bought *Enemies of Promise* (1938) on publication, Cyril Connolly then living in Chelsea flat (312A King's Road) with first (American) wife Jeanie (Bakewell). Later – I think many years later – when he, with second wife Barbara (née Skelton), were staying at The Chantry – he inscribed it:

> Tony, from Cyril
> who, like me,
>> was
>>> an
> ### AFTERNOON BOY

This last designation (referring to title of my first novel *Afternoon Men*) not wholly justified, because Cyril infiltrated only to a small degree level of bohemian life, its parties, and girls, there depicted, tho' he might be regarded as fitting into the category in a fairly general sense. More than thirty years after first publication of *Enemies of Promise*, returning from weekend with Goldsmids at Somerhill, near Tonbridge, V and I lunched with Cyril & Deirdre (by then his wife) at 48 St John's Road, Eastbourne, where Cyril had come to rest; Deirdre now third wife, tho' Lys Lubbock before her had been longtime 'living-in' mistress. Cyril then presented me with *Enemies of Promise*, Revised Edition 1949, which contains many adjustments (some slightly droll in their cranking up of the Connolly family background), to what had been said in original publication. He inscribed it:

> Tony from Cyril
>> with love
> – survivor from survivor
> 'What is hell but happiness when it
> comes too late?' F. H. Bradley
> 'And when it comes too
> early?' Father Connolly K. S.
> July 1971

The philosopher F. H. Bradley wrote, among other works, *Appearance and Reality*, concepts which I take to have been in Cyril's mind with relation to the two quotations, on which hung, if not all Connolly's Law and Prophets, certainly his Personal Myth, the message he taught regarding himself. He defined the house at Eastbourne, in Le Corbusier's phrase, as a 'machine for living'. Its exterior was, in fact, most un-Corbusierlike, a yellow-and-red brick villa, in a long charmless street running north from the front, nowhere near the sea, which might be thought one of the attractions of Eastbourne.

The house was, however, within walking distance of where Cyril's prep school St Cyprian's (vividly described in the section of *Enemies of Promise* subtitled *A Georgian Boyhood*) once stood, before destruction by fire (sent from Heaven?). After reading what Cyril has to say about the school (no more disagreeable than my own, undoubtedly better teaching) one might think its neighbourhood the last place on earth where he would wish (in the phrase of a fellow Eton KS, the poet Gray) to smuggle a few years, even tho' Cyril had by then made his peace with the Headmaster's formidable wife (both by now dcd). In fact one would have expected him to shun Eastbourne, and all memories of St Cyprian's, let alone make the place refuge of old age. Not at all. The Connolly Myth was paramount. Good or bad aspects had equally to be faced. Above all else the Myth must be forever set before its maker. For that Eastbourne was ideal spot.

One thinks, of course, of the possibility of Eton itself as final harbour, but at Eton (apart from difficulty of finding accommodation) Time's fell hand would probably have swept away too much in way of memories. The struggle would in a sense have to be renewed in less favourable circumstances.

[It was later suggested that Deirdre's demur at my writing Introduction might have been because of inclusion in my Memoirs of Osbert Lancaster's cartoon showing Evelyn Waugh presenting Cyril Connolly as a penitent before the Pope. Objection seems to be that I did mention in Memoirs hesitation at showing Cyril the picture, therefore should not have published it after his decease. This is scarcely sound reasoning. I showed the cartoon to Evelyn Waugh, who was far from delighted with it. When Cyril was last in the house there never seemed the right moment. In any case many caricatures, like much writing about individuals, might most suitably be published posthumously. Incidentally, Cyril before the Pope is by no means the only portrait of him by Osbert that I possess, several of which remain unpublished. Fram Dinshaw put forward the amusing and subtle suggestion that all *jokes* about the Roman Catholic Church outraged Deirdre's North of Ireland blood from her grandfather Not-an-inch-Jimmy.]

Sunday, 3 November

Driven by John, we lunched with Kevin & Rachel Billington at Poyntington. Other guests Richard & Vivian King (known to Tristram & John) and Richard King, a successful tycoon, also (says John) interested in such projects as raising wrecked galleons. Big, bespectacled, RC. Had been at Downside with Julian Jebb, for whom he & Tristram are planning some sort of memorial in way of a literary prize. I said my usual piece about it being more important to help old writers than young ones. Some such benefaction (had he not ended as he did) might well have alleviated Julian's own declining years in the light of his temperament. Richard King was tutored at Cambridge by Hugh Lloyd-Jones, now Regius Professor of Greek at Oxford. He said the legend was that during the war Hugh learnt Japanese in the army, and was employed in the Intelligence Corps to interrogate Japanese prisoners during the Burma Campaign. At one moment Hugh was left by an odd chance senior officer on the spot in some sector when immediate orders had to be given in relation to troop movement. Hugh, supposedly interrogating a Japanese general in a tent, in actual fact was discussing French Impressionist painting with him. The dispatch rider suddenly arrived with a message that 2000 troops required immediate orders. Hugh told the rider to leave tent while he prepared a movement order. He consulted the Japanese general as to textbook solution for particular circumstances with which such a body of men was confronted. The Japanese general gave his considered opinion. Hugh recalled the rider, and Hugh ordered advance, retirement, consolidation, whatever needed.

Tuesday, 5 November

Kingsley Amis is doing a *Sunday Times* interview for my eightieth birthday, and rang saying he could no longer travel by train alone these days, could he bring Hilly (his first wife, now Lady Kilmarnock) with him. This was excellent, as we have not seen Hilly for some twenty-five years, and always regretted the bust-up of the marriage. The last occasion, in fact, when Amises stayed here weekend, was when *Take a Girl Like You* just published. We had arranged for weekend not to clash with publication, then book for some reason put forward, received uniformly unfavourable notices in *all* Sunday papers. Then we lunched with Leslie Hartley, at Avondale, on the outskirts of Bath, and it turned out that Kingsley had given Leslie's last book a pasting . . . Kingsley did Questions/Answers interview, which he said he hoped, when edited, would turn out less boring than interviews usually are. Inevitably the taxi which drove them here lost the way from Westbury, as on previous Amis/Hughes-Onslow occasion; clearly subjective misfortune brought on by some chemistry in Kingsley, as nearly every Westbury taxi-driver knows The Chantry from previous visitors. Egg hors d'oeuvres; shepherds pie; mince pie; Château Latour de Mons, Margaux '75. Enjoyable.

Wednesday, 6 November

Day of the first Rodrigo Moynihan sitting, as arranged by Hilary Spurling for my eightieth birthday presentation by friends. Set out for London. Not having stayed the night for some time, I forgot to put my bag in the car, accordingly missed my usual train. The next one reasonably fast, rang Moynihan, lunched at Paddington, and not too much time was lost. Moynihan's spacious studio is in a block consisting entirely of studios in Sydney Close, small cul-de-sac off Fulham Road not far from the Onslow Square turning: two lofty rooms, first floor actual studio as such, ground floor with a gallery on one side, where Moynihan sleeps when in London, uses rest of room as studio. Rodrigo Moynihan is a characteristic painter type physically, half-Spanish (born in the Canaries), brought up to some extent in the US, archetypal painter's face, somewhat on lines of Goya. He is doing the portrait in the ground-floor room. I found him sympathetic. I cannot imagine why we have never met before, as we know lots of people in common; possibly were both at the same party given by the Glenconners for Cyril Connolly's birthday, such occasions apt to be celebrated in their house, as Elizabeth Glenconner is one of the people Cyril long enthralled. In any case Moynihans live much of the year in France, which would to some extent explain not running across each other. The sitting appeared to go all right.

When I went to The Travellers (where I was spending night) Hilary had very sweetly sent a welcoming postcard there. I decided to dine at Pratt's, where I had not been for years (not, I think, since being made life-member by Andrew Devonshire, present proprietor). When I became a member in 1929, the club belonged to Willy Walsh, legendary figure (late captain Brigade of Guards, who called the Life Guards 'The Plungers', and used other Victorian phrases). Willy Walsh became Lord Ormathwaite not long before he died, and the club might well have died with him had not Andrew rescued it. In those days the two subterranean rooms were all but empty except for the occasional guardee dropping in for dinner somewhere where it was not necessary to change. Since the second war it is packed with members, Brigade of Guards, MPs, City, even sprinkling of journalists.

On arrival the impression was that the City had taken over completely. While waiting in the outer room for my dinner to be cooked, a couple of young men behind me (whom I judged to be City types) were discussing some comic incident '. . . came up, said (splutter, splutter) "That man's asleep – and he's a corporal. (splutter, splutter)" . . .' There were roars of laughter. I realized that officers of the Guards these days wear striped shirts, non-Brigade ties, are cleanshaven, in short no way different from young merchant bankers. The Club began to fill up. Andrew Devonshire came in. As I was having brief word with him, George (traditional name for all Pratt's waiters now, I think, recruited from guardsmen on night off, adding to income) announced my soup was on table.

In the dining-room next door three rather unforthcoming characters on my right at the table were talking rather ponderously about shooting. Then a big grey-haired man came in to sit on my left. He leant across me to join in shooting conversations: '. . . Arab tipped my headkeeper eighty pounds . . . well, I mean . . . for instance, what do you give your beaters? . . . my view is, etc . . .' At that moment Andrew arrived, sat on big man's left, at once introduced me as 'far the best and funniest novelist'. The big man had clearly never read a book in his life, probably did not know what a novel was. Andrew proceeded to follow this up by expressing surprise that some lady known to both of them (more of the big man later) had never read *From a View to a Death*.

All this recognition from the Club's proprietor rather cowed the assembled company, my righthand neighbour now showing himself more amenable to conversation. He turned out to be called Salisbury-Jones, son of late General Sir Guy Salisbury-Jones, sometime Marshal of the Diplomatic Corps, one of the first, most succcessful, then new race of British vignerons. Salisbury-Jones *fils* was a musician. We talked of the pleasures of bad wine. Later, in next room having coffee Andrew sat down with me. I asked identity of big man. Andrew said: 'It's quite awful. I'm sweating. I was laying down the law on financial matters, explaining just what was happening in the City at this moment, and he turns out to be a tremendous tycoon whom I was telling just what was what in the workings of the market.'

Thursday, 7 November

Moynihan sitting in the morning. I mentioned I liked pictures by his first wife Eleanor Bellingham-Smith, with whom it seems he is still on good terms, four years older than he, therefore eighty. His second wife, Anne Dunn, youngest daughter of the Canadian millionaire Sir James Dunn (by the former Lady Queensberry) must be at least twenty years younger, and exceedingly comfortably off. They have a house about twelve miles from Aix-en-Provence. At one time the Moynihans had certain amount of Cyril Connolly life, Cyril having rather fancied Anne Dunn himself when younger, probably toying with

idea of marrying her, getting set up for life. I enquired if Rodrigo knew how
Barbara Skelton/Connolly/Weidenfeld/Jackson was getting on. Rodrigo said
Barbara dined with him only about a year ago. She now lives at Neuilly, moves
more or less in the Françoise Sagan set. When Barbara married Derek Jackson
(fourth or fifth wife, her third husband) they came to stay with the Moynihans
in Provence. Barbara's first words on arrival were that she and Derek must
have separate bedrooms. This was achieved after some difficulty, all bedrooms
running along the verandah, limited in number . . . This was only two or three
days after the wedding.

Rodrigo described painting Mrs Thatcher. He said the squint he was
alleged to have given her in the portrait was due to trouble with retina of her
eye during sittings. I remarked on the strange hooded eyes. Rodrigo said he
was almost more impressed by the lips than the eyes. He thought the former
very sensual, perhaps a trifle cruel, a powerful sensuality relegated to power
responses. Terrific sex-appeal, in his opinion. Rodrigo described Mrs T's sex
as 'one degree off', like an actor giving a superb performance of sexual emotion
in which the beholder, although not directly involved, is deeply moved. He
had the impression that she enjoyed playing the part allotted to her by the
press but the imputed whole-hearted philistinism (imputed, one might add, by
forms of all philistinism, press and media) not at all his estimate of her
sensibilities.

My own views, with fewer opportunities than Rodrigo to observe Mrs T
closely (and tête-à-tête) are very much the same. She was apparently a 'good'
sitter, except finding it difficult to relax. Rodrigo also spoke of painting the
conservative political philosopher Friedrich Hayek (*The Road to Serfdom*), who
now lives in Germany (Freiburg, I think Rodrigo said). Hayek's house was full
of heavy German furniture, family portraits. The sitting-room was neatly
divided into what belongs to him and what belongs to his wife. Hayek,
formerly in favour of Mrs Thatcher, is now dissatisfied with her restraint in
government. 'She should *at once* have abolished Social Security. But . . . there
would have been trouble for a week.'

Friday, 8 November

The bearded photographer from the *Sunday Times* came to take photographs
for the Kingsley Amis piece. He had been working in Tigrè, the insurgent
Ethiopian province. His name escapes me. He seemed agreeable, and had
experienced considerable adventures all over the place.

Monday, 11 November

To London for Moynihan sitting. I asked Rodrigo if he did not look rather like Goya. Rodrigo replied that he himself had always thought so . . . Rodrigo & I lunched at Italian restaurant just round the corner in Fulham Road, Al Ben Accolto, a good place.

That evening in The Travellers I came upon Alan Pryce-Jones over from the US for ten days, looking perhaps not quite so young as once, all the same pretty good for seventy-six or seven, which he must have reached by now. We agreed to dine together at Pratt's. There we found Oliver van Oss, former Lower Master at Eton (briefly acting-Head Master), until appointed Master of The Charterhouse, where, he said, his last act to install Adrian Daintrey. Van Oss was lecturer on one of our Hellenic cruises, and seemed agreeable. He mentioned that Harold Caccia was not regarded as good Provost of Eton during his tenure. I had Alan on one side at dinner, on the other Tory MP for Devizes, Charles Morrison, son of a Morrison (whom I did not know) who was more or less my school contemporary, later created Lord Margadale. The latter lives at Fonthill, in Wiltshire, with what remains of Beckford's house in the grounds.

Having read in the papers there was trouble at Fonthill owing to implementation of Reservoir Act, which is plaguing us (of course on infinitely smaller scale), I spoke about that. Morrison said he thought William Waldegrave (whom I do not know personally) the Minister responsible [in fact turned out to be John Patten, MP for Oxford].

Alan said in 1947 or thereabouts Cyril Connolly, dining with Lady Cunard, met Andrew Devonshire. After dinner Andrew said: 'Come to a little club I belong to', took Cyril to Pratt's. Later said: 'You're just the sort of member we want, would you care to join?' Cyril replied he would, so Andrew approached old-so-and-so (who was sitting on the other side of the room): 'Do you know Mr Connolly?' 'No.' 'Would you all the same mind seconding him for this club?' 'Not at all.' Nothing happened for two years. Cyril again dining with Lady Cunard, found old-so-and-so also present. Cyril and old-so-and-so left the house together. Old-so-and-so said: 'You're just the kind of member we like, do you know the Duke of Devonshire?' 'Yes.' Old-so-and-so said: 'Oh, Andrew. Do you know Cyril Connolly?' 'No.' 'Well, all the same, would you be prepared to second him for this club?' 'Of course.' Cyril did eventually become a member, my impression is that was not for long. Alan to some extent involved in last days of Robin McDouall, for many years Secretary of The Travellers. Robin's final scenes were apparently truly awful, Robin more or less up the wall most of the time. Glad to recall I had sent some Hudson Prize champagne to his nursing-home (which he rang up to thank for) not long before he died. Mayalls visited Robin there, found him extremely difficult and bad tempered, hard to know how to alleviate his state. Alan described him as getting up in a dressing-gown, trying to leave the place to see (in Alan's words) 'characters called Charley and the like'. Derek Hill, the painter, apparently behaved very well, more or less keeping Robin McDouall during last few weeks alive. If Robin had not died he would have been completely penniless.

At breakfast following morning, Alan said that many people, including himself, possessed letters from the late Ann Fleming they considered too deliberately spiteful, generally unpleasant, to hand over to Mark Amory for publication. Evangeline Bruce had already told me she was not releasing her own Ann Fleming letters on that account . . . Alan is writing an autobiography provisionally entitled *A General Thanksgiving*.

I returned home to find letter from Eric Anderson, Head Master of Eton, saying definite start made on *The Eton Register*, regarding which I totally failed to evoke any response from Harold Caccia (born on same day and year as myself, therefore should be amenable to another cusp of Sagittarius/ Capricorn, tho' possibly Harold first saw light in some distant clime), when Provost; nor from his successor Martin Charteris, neither of whom seemed capable of grasping that matter not merely question of Old School sentiment, publication of such documents of untold use to historians and biographers in their work. I am pleased that my years of campaigning at last showing some effect.

Tuesday, 12 November

Moynihan sitting in morning. The portrait seems to be coming on all right. He forgot to add that when, last time, Anne Moynihan rang from NYC she said: 'Tell Mr Powell that Hughie Wyndham is like Widmerpool.' Rodrigo took me up to studio on first floor, where a portrait of the Queen was on an easel, very like her. Also he showed me some excellent photographs, quite different from any I had seen before. Royal sittings for painters always take place in the Chinese Room at Buckingham Palace. HM talks all the time about her various trips abroad. Rodrigo's picture is for themselves, most of the portraits of both going to regiments, or institutions of one kind or another. They want a *pendant* of Duke of Edinburgh. Rodrigo is having trouble with his health, something to do with his circulation. A decision has to be made whether not have an operation, all rather worrying. We lunched again Al Ben Accolto, particularly good pasta.

Thursday, 14 November

The photographer Jane Bown, a little round body of sixty or so, came to take both of us for Miriam Gross's *Observer* piece. She said photographed me before, neither of us could recall when. I think she must have confused me with someone else. Kept up brisk patter of talk all the time rather like a fortune-teller. [She turned out correct about a previous sitting.]

Friday, 15 November

A little American photographer, Jerry Bauer was sent by Heinemann's for no particular reason, when a moment's thought would have told them I must be up to my eyes in photographers and interviewers, while Eightieth Birthday pieces were being produced, while dozens of pictures already taken are available. Bauer photographed me twenty or more years ago. He is the sort of photographer who makes you sit at the telephone, then removes the telephone itself. He said he lived in Rome, his mother in New York. She is not well. His own kidneys giving trouble.

Sunday, 17 November

The Stockwells at The Stables. Tristram, Virginia, Georgia came to luncheon. I reported meeting Jonathan Powell. Tristram was amused by account, and spoke of knowing him in days before his eminence. I made enquiries from Tristram as to whether he had any idea who should be thanked for the Moynihan portrait. He thought the National Portrait Gallery represented a considerable contribution. Enjoyable party. Roland Gant (who had been feeling too rotten the previous day to come down) brought proofs of *The Fisher King* in the afternoon. Extremely kind of him, as he is in poorish shape at the moment. What's wrong appears undiagnosable, he breaks out in fearful sweats at night, then feels cold, like malaria, but no reason to suppose malaria was ever contracted. He went on to his Dorset hide-out at Plush.

Sunday, 24 November

Tristram rang to say the whole family had been to see a performance of *The Garden God* put on by an amateur company called Q2 (as celebration of my Eightieth Birthday) at the Methodist Hall, Kew Road, Richmond, an enjoyable setting for the play in question. My agent John Rush says Q2 is one of the best of the amateur companies. Apparently it was an uproarious evening, greatly enjoyed by Georgia, Archie, and Andrew Murray-Threipland, a farmer and journalist, for some reason included in the party. Andrew took rather a fancy to the Leading Lady. I look forward to a full acount when Stockwells are next down here.

Monday, 25 November

To London for Moynihan sitting. The train was so crowded that John & I had to stand all the way over the link between two cars, packed like the rush hour on the tube. Anne Moynihan had flown from NYC this morning and joined us for lunch at Al Ben Accolto. Not surprisingly she looked a bit battered after the flight, otherwise in goodish form. They seemed on friendly, if somewhat formal, terms. With soup over I reminded her that we had not met since the Violet Wyndham party when, on introduction to Anne, Mark Culme-Seymour (professional seducer) took step backward, exclaiming: 'Seventeen! How wonderful to be seventeen!', an incident she too remembered. She spoke of having seen Alan Pryce-Jones in New York. On that occasion Alan said a woman had asked him if it was all right to consult Sachie Sitwell, now eighty-eight, about something; Alan said, 'Yes, but Sachie would certainly propose.' I dined at Pratt's, nearly as crowded as the train. An unexciting evening, during which I sat next to a member (educated at Downside) who had been pricked for next High Sheriff of Oxfordshire. He said Sheriffs are circulated with a Black List of awful judges, as (in theory, I'm not sure nowadays in practice), they have to house, and entertain judges during the Assizes. Andrew Devonshire came in when I had all but finished dinner, and I had no more than a word with him. While drinking coffee in outer room, just behind me a bespectacled, rather scholarly-looking middle-aged man, slightly resembling our local GP (Dr Rawlins) sat. Somebody asked him a question, to which he replied: 'No – I only commanded The Blues for three years.' I am now resigned to accepting that I no longer know what soldiers look like, least of all Household Troops. I returned early to The Travellers.

Tuesday, 26 November

Moynihan sitting in morning. Rodrigo is about to have three days running painting the Queen. My portrait is now finished, I think it is all right, tho' no great exercise in bravura. Curiously enough, my experience is that sitters usually like their own pictures, contrary to what one might expect. Rodrigo is anxious for V to see it, no doubt with memories of wives making difficulties. I said: 'She is quite used to looking at pictures.' He replied: 'You say that as one might say "She is quite used to being knocked about".' I answered that I thought the parallel an apt one.

Apparently Buckingham Palace made some demur at the price Rodrigo was asking for the Queen's portrait. The Secretary said he would have to enquire about it. The reply came back that it was acceptable, owing to the 'takings' for showing visitors round Sandringham. Rodrigo talked about Cyril Connolly. He said: 'It is all right being a complete monster all the time, people positively like you for that. They discuss you among themselves, pleasurable, spiteful gossip, even if they have suffered. What they don't like is a personality that only occasionally behaves in monstrous manner.' Very true . . . Rodrigo has decided not to have the operation.

Wednesday, 27 November

I had to do the *Telegraph* review (*Selected Night and Day* volume) in a rush as Jamie Camplin, with assistant, Mrs Alla Weaver, came to luncheon to discuss further arrangements for the *Dance* Picture Book. Mrs Weaver, who can't be very young, yet exceedingly spry, originated in Russia, emigrated after Revolution, a refugee in Berlin and Paris, eventually fetching up in this country. She was trained at the Courtauld. Mrs Weaver is the essence of her type in demeanour, excellent English, distinctly intelligent. She knew *Dance* extremely well. They brought some material and preliminary mock-ups. I think headway was made. It is still a bit hard to know who should write the Introduction, captions, etc, and precisely what form the latter should take. I am inclined to make an approach to John Bayley, though only after agreement on part of Bruce Hunter & Jamie Camplin.

Sunday, 1 December

Geoffrey Grigson obit. I met him (we did not talk) at Cyril Connolly's before the war, when Grigson was devilling for some publisher. He telephoned some time later, asking for his firm to see my new novel (*Waring*), by then, I think, fixed up. Anyway I didn't much take to Grigson's extremely aggressive manner. We had no subsequent contacts. Grigson was familiar only from rows with the Sitwells and others. Some few years ago he did a piece in *Country Life* about the remains of the motte-and-bailey Crûgeryr Castle in Radnorshire, from which my direct ancestor Llywelyn Crûgeryr took his cognomen. I wrote to Grigson, who lived near Andover (therefore within reasonable distance), suggesting he might like to lunch here sometime, see the grottoes (the Romantic Revival long one of his subjects, if I remember right). Grigson did not answer the letter.

The obituary notices dwelt a good deal on his incorruptibility and forthrightness. My own conviction is that Grigson's studied unpleasantness was solely due to a taste for being unpleasant, a kind of paranoia generated by his own gigantic conceit, flavoured with disappointment at the modesty of his accompanying creative gifts. He tried to ape (Ape of God?) Wyndham Lewis, without a particle of Lewis's dual talent (writing and drawing), his sense of style (even if at moments bad style). Grigson was a first-class compiler of anthologies, both verse, and pictures. He was a very minor poet (if no doubt a genuine one), but had an uncontrollable vanity, combined with a lack of humour.

All these factors inhibited his keen critical faculties by boiling them down to handing out good and bad (mostly bad) marks to other writers. In this (not seldom) envy, hatred & malice played at least as prominent a part as considered opinion. Grigson also possessed a vein of dishonesty as well as spite. For example, in his last book *Recollections*, he repeated his invention that Dylan Thomas upset fellow-guests at a Connolly dinner party by telling dirty stories, shown to be untrue more than once at least twenty years ago (eg. Constantine FitzGibbon's book on Dylan Thomas etc). I was present at the dinner in question and therefore know. That was what Grigson would have liked to happen, but did not. In a similar manner he records hearsay (from Evelyn Waugh, I think) about Connolly scolding his mistress Lys Lubbock, Grigson adding that Connolly slapped her, which was never said by Evelyn. No doubt similar instances of disregard for truth could be found. I had not wished to review *Recollections*, feeling that knocking Grigson about at this stage was waste of time. But circumstances at the *Daily Telegraph* (exactly what I can't remember) forced the book on me. Grigson began with one of his own poems, expressing his view that none of his contemporaries was any good at all, listing their present occupations, including 'writing lead reviews', which obviously included myself. I therefore took the opportunity of giving him a pasting, for which I am not at all sorry, most other reviewers lacking the guts to do so. I should add that Grigson once described me as 'an able novelist', so my feelings about him owe nothing to personal bias for being rude to me.

Today is the Anniversary of our wedding so we had a bottle of fizz, then watched *The Jewel in the Crown*, followed by *Fawlty Towers*, the latter extremely funny. The former from time to time irritated me by improbable military situations, such as Merrick (Tim Pigott-Smith, always good) being promoted Lieutenant Colonel with another posting, forcing the Intelligence Corps Sergeant (whose name I can't remember, played by Charles Dance) to serve under him in his new appointment. It would surely depend on what establishment Merrick was given and from what establishment the Sergeant had come. It would be extremely unlikely the Sergeant himself would have no say in the matter, especially as he was doing some semi-secret work. I suppose the situation is not impossible, probably better explained in the book.

Monday, 2 December

Roland Gant rang with the news that Philip Larkin had died, and ITV had asked if they could send a camera crew for my comments. Roland sensibly replied he did not think me likely to have anything to say, he would however enquire. That was correct on Roland's part. I never knew Larkin sufficiently well to speak on such an occasion, should have been committed to clichés about his poetry and 'image', better avoided I always feel. Such meetings as Philip Larkin and I had were pleasant, and we also exchanged quite a few letters. Larkin with his girlfriend Monica Jones (said to be the model for Margaret in *Lucky Jim*), lunched here when they were on a Dorset holiday ('doing' the Thomas Hardy country, I think). They ate more onion sauce at luncheon than any previous guests had ever approached. V always makes a lot, and all was completely polished off, very complimentary. Larkin took one of his interval-shutter photographs, in which he himself returns to be included in group. Some kind of power or narcissistic element perhaps coming into play, as he always does this.

Larkin undoubtedly imposed himself on his own Oxford generation, Kingsley Amis *et al.* One can see why, without actually feeling any 'magic' oneself. Larkin was obviously extremely intelligent, a good poet, if essentially not on a very extensive scale, tho' output is on the whole beside the point, lots of good poets writing reams of rubbish, some writing little, always good stuff. I had not realized Death was quite so near, although I knew he was ill. I hear *The Times* gave a grudging obit, several of these likely, as Larkin was a Tory (the popular press would say 'Young Fogey', anyone on the Right under eighty, in an effort of disparagement), the real 'Establishment' being on the Left, a kind of half-baked semi-Marxism, with which journalism and media are soaked. There was something of a dyed-in-the-wool provincialism about Larkin that always suggested a kind of resentment of the modern world. He was perhaps not really a very nice chap is one's final conclusion, but a good if limited poet.

Wednesday, 4 December

Hilary Spurling rang, partly to thank for my godson Gilbert's birthday present

(Max Hastings's *Military Anthology*), more to announce her own dissatisfaction with Rodrigo Moynihan's portrait. V is going to see it tomorrow, so I was able to temporize. It seems all right to me, if somewhat lacking in dash. Hilary wants something like Sargent's Henry James, which is not on, I fear, neither painter nor subject having the equipment required for that sort of brio performance. I rather doubt further fiddling with the canvas will have good effect. A classical situation with presentation portraits, to some extent any commissioned ones.

Thursday, 5 December

I finished a reread of Cyril Connolly's *Letters to Noel Blakiston*. I enjoyed these as giving the best available picture of Cyril himself at that age: in fact over three years an extraordinarily full, and convincing account of a romantic passion on Connolly's side. Blakiston was flattered, interested in having aroused such feelings, never, I think, at all deeply involved, which in a sense makes Cyril's relatively prolonged love more remarkable. That is not to say Cyril's love was a crystal stream of innocence. I had forgotten how often he invoked Noel's brother Jack (whom I never met) with obvious bitchy intention of arousing jealousy. I am inclined to think nothing physical ever took place, if so, minimal. Noel Blakiston's religious beliefs, general integrity (both qualities alien to Connolly's temperament) were in part factors which retained Cyril's love so strongly for so relatively protracted a period in a way he never probably achieved with a woman; anyway in the same manner. Noel Blakiston was a nice, not an unintelligent chap.

Perhaps a wife somewhat on the same lines might have been the answer for Cyril; religious, virtuous, reasonably intelligent. Such wives are not particularly easy to find, then fall in love with. In these *Letters* Cyril's vulgarity emerges in speaking of his first (American) wife Jeanie Bakewell's money, the life they were going to lead making use of it. By the time Cyril wrote about these things, the 'lyrical' quality of the letters (1924/1927) had in any case already passed. All the same there is interesting stuff.

Immediately following the death of Philip Larkin and Geoffrey Grigson came that of Robert Graves, age ninety. After rereading *Goodbye to All That* fifteen or more years ago I wrote Graves a fan letter, to some extent because he had been attached in the front line to the 2nd Battalion, The Welch Regiment (my father's unit), before joining one of the regular Battalions of The Royal Welch Fusiliers. Graves speaks of several of my father's contemporaries in The Welch, including Bill Hewitt, who was Commanding Officer when I was in the 1/5th (Territorial) Battalion of the Regiment at the beginning of the war in

1939. Graves replied most agreeably. He was a good poet, one would say, tho' not one very sympathetic to myself, while being decidedly uncertain as a critic. I share several of his poet-dislikes, although of course not Eliot. Graves wrote competent historical novels. His totally dogmatic approach to Myth spoils otherwise often amusing conjectures in that field. Graves was one of those writers one feels would have been a better artist had he been rather less of an egotist as a man. Is that always true? I'm not sure. One likes to think of Graves, Larkin and Grigson being ferried over the Styx together.

Wednesday, 11 December

Lees & Mary Mayall to luncheon. I made curry. The party was originally given to hear the Mayalls' adventures on the trip to Tashkent and Samarkand now some months past as things prevented their coming here. There were the usual Iron Curtain discomforts, but places interesting; Tamerlane's tomb has been restored, they said, in the manner of Betjeman-ware.

Sunday, 15 December

V is suffering from fluey cold. Dr Rawlins looked in to see her. David Rawlins in appearance rather like Woodrow Wyatt. Today, Sunday, glass of sherry relaxed him a bit before he left. He had been lecturing in Australia, and said he would emigrate there if twenty years younger. He spoke of a house they, the Rawlinses, inhabited in Maida Vale, on edge of low life in that district, the tart in the house opposite had 'photographic sessions'. He did not enlarge on what forms these took, and we did not like to press him on such a subject, but made me think of Henchman's early days in *The Fisher King*.

Valerie Rawlins, his wife, is one of the nicest of people, in fact only to be described as a saintly figure, always good humoured, always prepared to take on any tedious duty in the neighbourhood, in fact quite often going out of her way to do so. Dr Rawlins was at Christ's Hospital, as is his son, the latter now waiting for results of the Cambridge entrance exam. The son wants to go up to Caius, so I supposed intending medicine as a career. On the contrary, languages are his thing. He hopes to become an air pilot for twenty years, then go into teaching, an unusual project I found rather interesting. Rawlins remarked that doctors he knew who had emigrated to the US told him you could own a cheap car for a year, then if you kept it people thought you were not a success and would not employ you. It was considered improper in America to say: 'You have a sore toe', all diagnoses must be expressed in convoluted pseudo-scientific jargon. This all very much recalled Hollywood.

Wednesday, 18 December

I wrote to John Bayley a week or two ago asking if he would do an Introduction to the *Dance* Picture Book, I received no reply, so today I rang him. He seemed surprised that I did not know he would willingly take it on, which I am pleased about. John seems to combine all the qualities required when one considers them. Thames & Hudson sent printed copy of annual lecture they produce to celebrate their firm's founder, this year an essay on Thomas Jones, 18th century Radnorshire painter, by Lawrence Gowing. Through Radnorshire interests I already knew a certain amount about Jones, his family owning a house called Pencerrig, formerly belonging to some Powells (not mine). I was aware Jones was a painter worthy of more attention than hitherto received, but did not grasp quite how original he was in later output, which Gowing, in an excellent piece, emphasizes. Some of Jones's pictures at this period (for instance, of Naples) are altogether different from Jones the disciple of Romanticism, even of Jones a pupil of Richard Wilson; white houses almost like Utrillo. Gowing is an acute critic as well as good painter. His painful stutter, habit of dribbling profusely when he speaks, made him embarrassing at times when on National Portrait Gallery board, but his views as always worth hearing. Long intervals of spluttering, saliva dripping on table, the only person not in the least embarrassed was Lawrence himself. In fact he is always prepared to hold forth at length on the least provocation, never attempting to be brief about what he wants to say.

Saturday, 21 December

My eightieth birthday. Slight intimations of flu. Tristram & Virginia very sweetly gave party at The Stables, where Ferdie, Julia, William, Harry, and Mary Mount are staying for Christmas. All arrangements were in Tristram's hands, including guests invited, thereby relieving one of responsibility as to individuals invited. This naturally cut out persons not known to Tristram. It emphasized Tristram's own friends, but all worked out pretty equably. It began at 6.30, almost everyone invited turning up, in spite of a filthy night, rain, wind, like the Witches of Traquair fighting for the Justified Sinner's soul. Guests: Roy & Jennifer Jenkins; Grey & Neiti Gowrie, bringing Evangeline Bruce; Anthony, Tanya, and Charlotte Hobson, bringing Clarissa Avon; Tony & Marcelle Quinton; Jilly & Leo Cooper; Hilary & John Spurling; Denys & Cynthia Sutton; Roland & Nadia Gant; Pat Naipaul (Vidia, suffering from delayed shock from death of his brother Shiva, feeling he must go abroad); Rachel & Kevin Billington; Lees & Mary Mayall; John & Victoria Jolliffe; Andrew & Tammy Murray-Threipland; making with John,

Georgia, Archie, ourselves, about forty in all. In the course of party Denys Sutton remarked to Tristram: 'My second wife [Cynthia is his third] was a Dane. While married to her I lived through every Ibsen play with her, *every single scene in one form or another*.'

Relations were rather delicate between Coopers and Spurlings, because Hilary has (on more than one occasion, I think) been rather rough in print about Jilly's novels, designed for extensive sales rather than highbrow reading; nonetheless Leo seemed to find no difficulty in recognizing Hilary's attractions, at least sitting extremely close to her. Clarissa Avon, dressed in velvet breeches & bows like a Principal Boy in Pantomime, made rather a fuss about wanting to drink white wine instead of champagne (Tristram at once produced the former). Then Clarissa said: 'I thought we were going to have dinner', when smoked salmon snacks first handed round, commenting 'This is like Ethiopia', when queuing for risotto, later available. However she seemed to enjoy herself, tho' Evangeline was generally regarded as, in appearance, star of the party.

The Gants were going to France the following day. I cannot imagine where they stayed for the night, nor indeed where several of the other guests did. The Spurlings remained until at least midnight, John Spurling explaining to Andrew Murray-Threipland his theories about how to write a play, Andrew lapping it all down, and unstoppably talking (this seemed to bear out Andrew's distinct resemblance to Bobby Roberts). In short, party could be judged unqualified success. Tristram later reported thirty bottles of champagne were drunk. As that did not include John, nor young people, and Clarissa, they did not do too badly. V and I retired about 10.30, I must admit pretty tired. Memorable occasion.

Sunday, 22 December

Owing to the immediate pressures of the party, I had not fully examined all presents, various items later coming to light with their hilarious side. The Mayalls brought (together with a pot of foie gras), a square parcel in brown paper looking rather like a picture. V suggesting an engraving. When opened this turned out to be a folding-up, all but life-size, effigy of Mrs Thatcher. It was received, when opened, with great applause. The Roy Jenkinses presented a bottle, which, rather characteristically for a politician, Roy said he would put in a special place of his own in the kitchen. In fact several guests brought bottles, collected together with names attached, among which it would perhaps have been wiser to place the Jenkins offering. Tristram told me today that in the course of supper Grey Gowrie remarked once or twice to him how outstandingly good the Latour was which he was drinking at the sitdown meal, Tristram not knowing what Grey was talking about as we were drinking St Emilion (whatever it was), thinking Grey's mind was wandering. It now turns out that Grey (on his part perhaps also characteristic of a politician) had somehow got hold of Jenkins Latour '77 (hidden in Roy's secret place), only about a third remaining. This, however, V and I drank at luncheon with pheasant she had provided for my birthday, which we decided to eat day following; just about amount of wine one wanted, as still feeling rather exhausted.

Tuesday, Christmas Eve

Flu, hanging about for some days, finally struck. I spent Christmas, and the ensuing nine or ten days, in bed, feeling like hell for first two of them, when Ken Taylor's Second Episode of *Dance* TV script arrived. I just managed to cope with it and write to him.

1986

Wednesday, New Year's Day

Jonathan Cecil rang to say his father had died. David had been ill only a short time. I had known David Cecil for sixty-seven years, since Goodhart's House at Eton, where for one term I was his fag. Later, as an undergraduate, I met him at least once at Lady Ottoline Morrell's in her Garsington days. David by then had gone down, but not yet a don, I think. We can't be said to have become friends until after V and I married, David himself was married by then to Rachel MacCarthy (met occasionally in London, but I scarcely knew her). At that period David's literary criticism seemed to be old-fashioned and stuffy. Now one sees much to be said for the stand he took about Scott, George Eliot, Hardy, in fact the Victorians in general. David was always well disposed to my own writing so far as fan letters were concerned, even if he never allowed his praise to appear in print until quite late on. He did a nice piece for my eightieth birthday in *The Spectator*, probably last article he wrote.

I was very sorry not to get to his funeral at Cranborne, but had only just risen from a peculiarly noxious flu, and was not up to it. David remained astonishingly the same from a boy of sixteen or seventeen when I first remember him to last time we saw him a few months ago lunching at Red Lion House. Breathless, rapid, amusing, characteristic phraseology of his own, he was always worth hearing on writers he liked. He usually remained on the safe side in controversy, eg. not specially keen on Conrad, at the same time unwilling to defend an anti-Conrad position. David Cecil's Oxford generation was last to sustain a small set of well-behaved, relatively smart, relatively intellectual, undergraduates with social life of its own (Virginia's father Archie Lucas, was one of that category). These (slightly overlapping) fitted in between undergraduates who had been in the war, and the somewhat disreputable younger Hypocrites crowd, which made the going during (and

just before) my own time. David Cecil, always known as Slingsby by the
Pakenhams (from some children's story), was famed for cutting invitations,
and not returning lent books, but in spite of this and a preference for soft
options in general, he was kind, and essentially good natured. He played an
active part in rescuing his old friend, Leslie Hartley, from an intensely sinister
man-servant not long before Leslie's death.

Leslie always had a taste for shady butler-valets, indeed employing them
was a kind of hobby, perhaps his chief amusement in life. They constituted an
extraordinary dynasty during the years we knew Leslie as neighbour. To
mention only a few; the retired major; there was also an ex-JP, who had gone
bankrupt – every time one took a sip from one's glass, he filled it up, resulting
in drinking about twice as much as usual; then there was the ex-naval
Lieutenant Commander, tall, good-looking, who stole Leslie's duty-free
cigarettes, then, overcome by guilt, bought him another box from ordinary
shop at three times the price; the ex-policeman another example, used to
nudge one during dinner when handing round dishes with the words, 'Have
some of the potatoes, they're rather special.' The boy called Roger arranged
that his whole family should move into Leslie's house. Once when we dined
there Leslie, on greeting us, added: 'I don't know whether we'll get any dinner,
as Roger's crying on the stairs.' Roger was last heard of some years ago
running an establishment in Copenhagen.

I did not set eyes on the penultimate factotum. Those who saw him were
unable to express in words the patent villainy of his countenance. By that
time Leslie himself was physically going downhill. Friends (David Cecil and
others) somehow managed to install another man (this final one, was said to
be of good character, tho' in the last resort driven to drink by Leslie's own
eccentric behaviour). Leslie's house, Avondale (now a guest-house),
Bathampton, was on outskirts of Bath. While the scoundrel remained in
Leslie's flat in London the good valet was in Avondale with Leslie (possibly
vice versa). The scoundrel turned up at Avondale, resulting in fight between,
as it were, Leslie's Good Angel and Leslie's Bad Angel (the police when
summoned by telephone replied they could not be bothered with such minor
matters). However, the Bad Angel was at last overcome, locked in a room,
somehow later disposed of. Leslie was delivered from all this by David Cecil,
one or two other friends lending a hand, possibly Alick and Gabriel Dru
among these. V thinks all this happened in Leslie's London flat, rather than
Bath, which may be true. Anyway I feel with David Cecil dcd another friend
has gone, sympathetic, intelligent, style entirely his own, who had shared
with one some of the more exotic aspects of life, as well as much literary
happenings.

Saturday, 11 January

John's fortieth birthday. We all lunched at The Stables, where Virginia cooked excellent veal, Birthday Cake, etc. I took photographs with the Minolta camera V gave me for Christmas, the automatic flash a great improvement. Christopher Isherwood dcd in California. We met for a moment once in London not long after war (probably at John Lehmann's). By then Isherwood was completely Americanized. I invited him to Chester Gate, which tho' civil, he did not accept. The typescript of *The Memorial* passed through my hands at Duckworth's, but I remember no more about it than recommending it for consideration.

The MS made no such impression as did *Mr Norris* (1933), with which I was immensely taken, and must have sold several copies by insisting how good it was. Isherwood's failing, I suppose, was his unplumbable narcissism, from which he drew most of his material, but in the last resort sunk him. He ought to have been able to bring off the planned long novel about Berlin to be called *The Lost*, instead dispersing its elements – no doubt much else, which would have been generated by sustained action, in the way of useful narrative writing – in short bursts, some of these not particularly accomplished. Arguably the most gifted of that group (tho' Auden scooped the pool where publicity was concerned), Egotism, Communism, Homosexuality, Wisdom of the East, all taking their toll in reducing Isherwood as an artist. Finally perhaps some lack of sensibility laying him open to these debilitating handicaps, bringing him down from such promising beginnings. Perhaps also Isherwood (like to a lesser extent Aldous Huxley) fitted a bit too easily into Hollywood life, a streak of secondrateness, vulgarity, which – unlike Auden – he never managed to harness to good effect.

Tuesday, 14 January

Bruce Hunter, of Higham's, Dorothy Olding, of Ober's, my American agent ('It was down by the dark tarn of Ober' obviously what Poe meant, rather than Auber), both advise, as not under contract for my next book, that *The Fisher King* would be better sent to Norton's where Tom Wallace (late of Holt's) is now employed. Holt was recently taken over by the German firm Holtzbrinck Publishing Group (Goethe's publisher, I believe, also did one German translation of mine), making Holt's future uncertain. Tom Wallace published my Memoirs when at Holt's and lately sent an enthusiastic letter about *The Fisher King*, so change seems sensible.

In general I have always had scruples about abandoning a publisher unless something specifically unsatisfactory has taken place. Holt's certainly showed no great interest after Tom Wallace left, for instance not a word from them (nor for that matter from Little, Brown) about either the *Hudson Review* or Ingersoll Prizes. Up to date, people appear to like *The Fisher King* (including useful marketing medium John Saumarez Smith, of Heywood Hill Bookshop), all to some extent 'committed'. As usual I find it impossible to predict the reactions any given book of mine will arouse.

Wednesday, 22 January

V and I lunched with the Mayalls. I had two copies of Wilde's *Additional Letters*, edited by Rupert Hart-Davis, so brought one along; also a copy of *Iron Aspidistra* (at V's suggestion). The latter I think Mary & Lees found a bit obscure. Their son Robert has left Rota's bookshop in Long Acre, and is now set up with a partner in Cecil Court, between St Martin's Lane & Charing Cross Road. (Was Cecil Court where they bought the Golden Bowl? No, that was somewhere near British Museum, perhaps Cecil Court comes in another James novel, or elsewhere.) Mayalls seem somewhat worried at this new venture of Robert's.

Mary reported Gabriel (Mrs Alick) Dru in a bad way, not making sense, incapable of taking in prices affected by inflation. V borrowed a biography of Rex Whistler written by his brother Lawrence Whistler, poet and glass-engraver.

I've just finished a reread of *Kim*. I am struck by Kipling's extreme originality as a writer, making his work all but impossible for reviewers to deal with, reviewers on the whole having no idea of criticism beyond comparing one author with another, and incapable of picking out unfamiliar characteristics. Even Henry James thought Kipling would be an English Balzac, than whom it is hard to imagine a more inept comparison. By coincidence also had for review Kipling's hitherto unpublished pieces in *The Lahore Civil & Military Gazette*, written during couple of years after arrival in India at age of sixteen. They are astonishingly mature. Among other things one notes him speaking of Peshawar as an exceptionally vicious town, mentioning 'bejewelled boys dressed as girls with their admirers', a subject rigorously kept out of later writings. Homosexual emotions would be extremely difficult to negotiate side by side with the Afghan horsedealer Mahbub Ali's early interest in Kim, perhaps the reason why Mahbub Ali's womanizing is so much emphasized in the novel. Incidentally, a letter included in *Uncollected Sketches* expresses Kipling's view that it is necessary to 'have a woman' from time to time. Would this have been an Indian lady, one wonders or an Army brothel?

Monday, 27 January

I am now reading the Rex Whistler biography. It is written in rather a soggy style, so far as narrative goes, except Rex Whistler on active service, his death, which is well done. Lot of information is new to me and interesting. Rex Whistler (b. 1905, Haileybury, The Slade), was son of apparently a somewhat unpresentable builder. His talent for drawing got him to The Slade, where good looks, obviously considerable address even at an early age, did the rest. He enthralled Stephen Tennant, also studying art there. From that moment Whistler never looked back so far as smart life was concerned.

I met him once or twice in 1927/28 at a dinner party of Tom Balston, publisher at Duckworth, possibly also Osbert Sitwell's. My impression at that time that Whistler was probably quite nice chap, but his overwhelming smoothness was more than I could bear at that age. I also thought his painting, in spite of its facility, arch and awful (an opinion I still hold), tho' a capable stage designer, eg. *The Rake's Progress* ballet. In those days it never occurred to me that Whistler not homosexual, but apparently quite mistakenly. Indeed he might have been more at home sexually had he been queer, as he never seems to have felt at all keen on the physical side with women. All the same he was involved with a lot of pretty girls, even if rather uncomfortably; and actually got to bed with Tallulah Bankhead, regarded as key figure, sexually speaking, of that period.

V says we met Rex Whistler at a dinner party of Alice Astor (Obolensky/Hofmannsthal/Harding/Pleydell-Bouverie), of which I have no recollection, only an impression of him in the Twenties remaining. When war came Whistler went into The Welsh Guards, remaining a subaltern in the Guards Armoured Division until killed 1944 aged thirty-nine. He must have been regarded as a reasonably good soldier to have been allowed to carry on in that rank on active service when so old. He also did much painting when overseas.

I am always staggered by the amount of spare time certain individuals seem to have achieved while serving in the Army. From the moment I joined 1/5th Battalion The Welch Regiment, to the time I was demobilized from War Office, I had to work like a horse, ending the day absolutely exhausted. Whistler seems to have been extremely popular in The Welsh Guards, behaving with bravery, tho' apparently making wrong decision in leaving his tank, which led to death. Women of all ages were mad about him, nonetheless he regarded himself as failure in love owing to an unhappy affair with Lady Caroline Paget.

Photographs in the book show an immaculately neat studio in Fitzroy Street, where he clearly never associated with other artists of the quarter. Moving both by personal taste, and social agility, in the beau monde, using that term in its 'smart' comparatively exclusive sense (I certainly don't mean Balston's dinner parties), one has impression of an intense narcissism, perfect knowledge of which side his bread was buttered, superhuman free-loading, all brought to his highest pitch, almost more than a touch of male bitchery, yet on the whole a nice nature. I can now see why, at that particular moment of my life, I found him utterly intolerable. I don't think I exactly got him wrong, and later would myself probably have been less censorious. All this caused reflections on other contemporaries who, from unpromising background, took the beau monde by storm; similarities, differences, parallel with Rex Whistler.

Of course everyone has their own personal criteria as to definitions of social success or failure, for that matter what constitutes being 'smart'; beau monde wide term, which to some small extent one might be said to live in, or have lived in, oneself, at least relatively smart occasions from time to time. What I mean in these special instances examined here, is perhaps those who saw regularly, over a given period of some length, persons of a smart world, relatively speaking, with whom they had no particular tastes in common; just saw each other *because* they were 'smart', anyway smartish. To underline fallibility of such judgements, it should be added that someone staying with Gerry Wellington (7th Duke) was unwise enough to refer to a woman they both knew as 'smart'. Gerry drew in his breath slightly. 'A nice woman, certainly. But smart? I don't recollect ever having seen her at the Sutherlands, or the Ancasters.'

One just notes this to underline that there are no more than a few outstanding examples of individuals known to myself, holding cards comparable with Whistler's, ending by passing fair amount of their time with people who may not have been smart in Gerry Wellington's eyes (in which presumably high birth had to be one concomitant), but might have been held so by less exacting standards. Nothing absolute is intended.

My specimens are: Evelyn Waugh; Cecil Beaton; John Betjeman; Peter Quennell; Adrian Daintrey; all of whom moved in smartish circles for at least part of their lives, with varying credentials, very definite intent. I omit, for example, Cyril Connolly (b. 1903, Eton KS, Balliol, Oxon), devoted to *mystique* of smartness, at same time never achieved it himself, in spite of bringing off fantastic benefactions of various sorts (financial, etc), stretching from, say Maurice Bowra to Harry Goldsmid. That (getting money out of people) is something rather different, an art of its own. Connolly's inability to put up with sustained smart life largely owing to his own cantankerousness, even his intelligence, was to some extent a fact (on the whole doing him credit) that he could not mask such characteristics in himself, notwithstanding fantastic powers of ingratiation, if he desired to exercise them.

Evelyn Waugh (b. 1903, Lancing, Hertford, Oxon), most straightforward case, as he never made any bones about wanting to advance himself socially (until, in a sense, he felt he had arrived, assumed for daily use what he imagined to be persona of a Duke). Waugh also cantankerous, eccentric to a degree, gifted, one would say, rather than exceptionally intelligent, usually happy to be among those with whom intelligence played little or no part, provided they satisfied his notion of smartness (all the same driven all but mad by being cooped up in Jugoslavia with two dyed-in-the-wool middlebrows like Freddy Birkenhead & Randolph Churchill). Here it should be noted that Waugh never clarified in his own mind (if you're going to make a study of such things) concepts like 'smart', 'grand', 'middle-class', 'common', etc, eg. a smart jockey, middle-class duke, common member of White's. He was undoubtedly set on social aims from the moment of his first marriage, Osbert Sitwell's boyfriend David Horner asserting he knew someone familiar with Waugh when both were growing up, who reported social ambitions as an adolescent, if not as a schoolboy, even if a publicly declared goal only after first marriage bust-up.

Waugh started with great talent, no money, little or no idea what upper-class life was like, at the same time literary, theatrical, bohemian, entrées through his brother Alec. A good deal of shaking off of detrimental links took place on Evelyn's earlier upward ascent (Bobby Roberts, et al) while consciously getting to know nobs who suited his targets. Some of this Evelyn did by giving large luncheon parties at the Ritz, one would guess (from contemporary stories) making not a few blunders. This was, of course, after money was coming in from Evelyn's books. Connolly managed to turn his own ugliness into almost an advantage, Waugh's appearance (even if regarded as 'faunlike' by Harold Acton in early Oxford days) was no great help in the sort of circles to which he aspired. Always prepared to have blood rows with others on the social escalator (eg. Beaton), thereby complete contrast with the good-looking, good-natured Whistler, for whom males and females equally fell.

An almost essential weapon in British upper-class climbing is a facility for buffoonery. In the case of Whistler this took the form of comic drawings, even his 'serious' works possessing near-facetious side. Waugh was a practised buffoon and, in his early days, he could be very funny. When getting on in life, usually drunken, his buffoonery was boring, continuing much too long. Waugh's buffoonery narrowed down to what might be popular in a White's Club milieu, this eventual social objective developing to some extent during war-service with such types and all revealed without least concealment in the Diaries. In fact not long before his own death Waugh notes that he does not want to be amused by his friends, but to amuse them, which he was now failing to do in his later efforts.

The discovery that the Haileses (Buchan-Hepburn, youngish Tory MP, created a Life Peer) thought him a bore when staying with them (kindly revealed to Waugh by his friend Ann Fleming), a subject to which he returns more than once in the *Diaries* and the *Letters*, could almost be held contributory to Waugh's early demise. In later stages of this ascent Waugh could be egregiously rude, even to the sort of people he courted (perhaps to be put forward in his favour). For example, by the period when he had taken to using ear-trumpet, he found himself in Pratt's extremely drunk, sitting next to Lord de Lisle (Guardsman, VC, son-in-law of Lord Gort, also Guardsman, VC). Presumably they were alone in the dining-room, Bill de Lisle himself was the source of the story. Waugh apparently remarked that the tradition of the Foot Guards was one of cowardice. (Waugh having served latterly in the Royal Horse Guards.) De Lisle, in his description of what happened, not knowing Waugh (nor, rather surprisingly, *vice versa*), spoke of 'Little old man with an ear-trumpet'. Asked how he had answered this reflection on the Foot Guards, replied: 'I just said fuck off, and walked out of the room.'

Another comic scene in Pratt's involving Waugh took place when Osbert Lancaster was there at the dining-table, Sir Edmund Bacon, a Norfolk landowner, was also present. They were chatting about county matters, Osbert himself having Norfolk property. The Bishop of Norwich was then Percy Herbert, younger son of Lord Powys, relic of bygone days of aristocratic prelates. The Bishop was always referred to by fellow East Anglians as 'Percy Norvic', Latin rendering of his episcopal see, and what he signed on documents. Osbert made some remark to which Sir Edmund Bacon replied: 'Well, we'll have to refer that to Percy Norvic, I think.'

Waugh, also at the table, probably irritated at two people discussing county matters of which he himself was totally ignorant, suddenly broke in: 'Percy Norfolk? Percy Norfolk? I know Bernard Norfolk [the Duke of Norfolk]. I've never heard of Percy Norfolk.' It had to be gently explained to him that the Duke had not been invoked, but an aristocratic Anglican Bishop (by implication known to everyone except Waugh). Waugh was then forced to listen to the whole story, the C of E being well rubbed in by Osbert, something Waugh never cared for.

The Waugh parents played no part in Evelyn's social life, neither helpful nor embarrassing, tho' naturally they had to see their grandchildren from time to time, otherwise simply left out. Here one notes that Rex Whistler, doing quite well for a single man in the 1930s (ie. earning £1200 or more) transported his parents to a more eligible neighbourhood and seems to have paid for his brother to go up to Oxford. Waugh, like Whistler, recognized the Services as almost an essential choice to forward his ambitions when war came. Waugh

certainly would have taken that step anyway, even if the social aspect was not
to be disregarded, like learning to ride, then going foxhunting.

Between Evelyn Waugh & Cecil Beaton (b. 1903, Harrow, St John's,
Cantab) existed fathomless mutual hatred, dating from Waugh bullying
Beaton at the Hampstead day-school they both attended. Beaton represents a
different area of social ambition, abutting more on the world of Rex Whistler,
Whistler showing distinct signs of jealousy of Beaton, laughing at latter's fitful
heterosexual forays from predominantly homosexual ambiance. Beaton,
unintellectual, starting off with relatively small talent, completely unabashed
purpose to get on, managed to turn modest abilities to draw into extremely
effective stage-designer; his photography, entirely self-taught from scratch,
becoming world famous; in fact all done by sheer will-power. Beaton *père*
moderately well-to-do in the timber business, apparently a somewhat
precarious trade, parents' house in Bayswater, perfectly presentable as
residence (butler called Manley), supplying Beaton's early basis for studio,
cocktail parties, journalist-photographic-stage-designing activities, with
closely inter-knit bits of social life. Basic homosexuality (Beaton thought good-
looking at Cambridge, where he already achieved publicity beyond
University), later tinged with small degree of heterosexuality, culminating in
an affair with Greta Garbo, certainly to be regarded as the pinnacle of a
social-sexual career of one particular kind.

The beau monde, in its aristocratic implications, might be said to have
been taken by Beaton in his stride, through astute use of photographer's
professional opportunities, from an angle that did not include (except by the
way) what might be called the White's Club area. Beaton had quite other
social peaks in view, eg., considerable success with Royalty, something again
rather on its own. Beaton, if a performer in his own manner, could not be
regarded as a buffoon. Latterly, one imagined him more concerned with high
theatrical/movie connexions, rather than aristocratic ones, tho' always
maintaining contacts with smart Wiltshire neighbours (Pembrokes, etc)
where he lived. Beaton's two sisters, Baba & Nancy, of whom he was genuinely
fond, played some part in his early advancement as 'beauties' (both
reasonably pretty) then left behind. Baba made rather a mess of her life;
Nancy's husband, Hugh Smiley, baronet, Grenadier, a school contemporary of mine (perfectly agreeable, as a boy) wrote to Cecil saying he
'preferred Nancy to be thought of as the wife of a plain English gentleman,
rather than one of the notorious Beaton sisters'.

Cecil got his own back for this after Hugh retired from The Brigade and took
up cooking. When people asked after his brother-in-law, Cecil (who spoke the
curious sub-cockney shared with Cyril Connolly, George Orwell, all from

same prep school, St Cyprian's, Eastbourne), would reply: 'Well, Hugh loves his cooking, but he *does* feel his feet all the same.' Hugh Smiley might be said to have had last word, because he read the lesson at Cecil Beaton's funeral ('Let us now praise famous men'), remarking to me after the Service (a much attended affair in the country): 'I left out the verse about their seed shall continually remain a good inheritance, and their children are within the covenant.' Cecil was always pleasant when V and I had anything to do with him, which wasn't often, luncheons occasionally exchanged. We abutted in no way on his career, except that Duckworth (through the Sitwells) published his original *Book of Beauty* (1928, I think, not produced very well). After I left he had a row with the firm (as with a good many of those involved with him professionally), and took his work elsewhere.

John Betjeman (b. 1906, Marlborough, Magdalen, Oxon) probably most interesting case of those examined here, in a sense the most socially successful, particularly because at the same time avoiding almost all opprobrium for being snobbish, anyway to the extent of such cases as Waugh, Beaton, and other fellow-climbers. Betjeman, as with Waugh, had exceptional talent allied to practical ability in journalism and advertising, and untiring social energy, making his relatively unpromising personal appearance (green face, rotting teeth) acceptable. The Betjeman parents were said to be shade embarrassing, but few of his friends were ever allowed to meet them, even at an early stage. At the same time his father played a role in Betjeman poems, anecdotes, legend (eg. allegedly turning his son out of the house because he refused to sweep the crazy pavement).

Betjeman was the supreme buffoon in company of any kind, ill-at-ease unless allowed to put on some sort of performance. Wherever he was he had to be the centre of the room's attention. His social ambition was by no means limited to aristocratic circles, unlike Waugh, who was intensely jealous of Betjeman's social success. Waugh also nagged Betjeman about not being RC, to the point of persecution. In religious matters Betjeman was eclectic, Waugh was exclusive. This was especially bad after Betjeman's wife Penelope (Chetwode) became an RC. Betjeman was still less like Beaton and Whistler in social ambition, much wider in scope, all embracing, everyone had to fall. He presented Ted Heath, former Conservative Prime Minister, with a picture of Heath's home town, Broadstairs, and promoted the poems of Mary Wilson, wife of the Labour Prime Minister, Harold Wilson.

In this general campaign, the smart world, anyway certain sections of it, was simply included by the way. Although admiring Betjeman as a poet, I always felt I was regarded by him as not sufficiently captive to the Betjeman cult. People could be suspect for not accepting more than vocally that he was a Great Man, which in the end became *sine qua non* wherever he went about.

Peter Quennell (b. 1905, Berkhamstead, Balliol, Oxon), another interesting case. Quennell started life as a schoolboy-poet (quite a good one) with immense conceit of himself, from which he really never wholly recovered. This early personal vanity not surprising, as Edmund Gosse (others too) expressed the view that Keats and Shelley were nothing to Quennell. This was taken up by the Sitwells. In early stages one would guess Quennell had little or no social ambitions of the Waugh/Beaton variety, more to be a 'genius', with beautiful women at his feet. When he first appeared on the scene he held Liberal-Leftist views, rather opposed in theory to 'snobbishness', romantic looks an asset, even in early life his malice to some extent obstructed progress in literary world (eg. almost immediately with the Sitwells).

Accordingly this characteristic was in due course kept in rather better order (at least outwardly), though certainly still existent. Quennell soon embarked on series of assorted wives, certainly none of whom could be said to have brought social advantages (with the exception of the one he himself called *La chère cinquième*). In fact most of them were positively handicaps, after Quennell settled down to pursuit of the beau monde, which seems to date from the war, when, like Connolly, he was usually available as a spare man, being more or less sacked from various unglamorous jobs in the Ministry of Information, and later the Fire Service.

Quennell's parents modest highbrow types, father upwardly mobile architect, giving him good intellectual start. He met Eddie Marsh, editor of *Georgian Poets*, early on. His parents always (like his brother & sister) kept in the background. All perhaps comparable with Evelyn at a lower level with less distinguished forebears. The two of them knew each other when young, later at Oxford where they were friends. Waugh finally loathed Quennell with savage hatred. In fact Waugh almost immediately went down after Quennell arrived, but he hung about Oxford a good deal. Quennell was terrified of Evelyn when they met at Ann Fleming's or elsewhere. During Quennell's period as an adman at which he seems to have been efficient and certainly well equipped to do required share of drinking in the profession, he was more concerned with women, business, working at his Byron books, than with social advancement.

The Duff Coopers (as with Connolly) played a considerable part in this during the post-war years, Duff Cooper getting Quennell into White's Club, largely to annoy Waugh. As such things go in the literary world, Connolly (also White's member through Duff Cooper) was well disposed to Quennell, *vice versa*. Quennell was not a buffoon in the sense that Betjeman, and Waugh, to some extent Rex Whistler, were, tho' always well stocked with spiteful gossip (often very amusing) for patrons. He wasted no time with women (for

that matter anyone else) he thought neither smart, nor useful, or hoped to
seduce. Quennell's later period of womanizing was possibly to some extent a
path for advancement.

Quennell for years sustained the role of useful spare man, his outward
demeanour these days accordingly became somewhat chastened. A strange
career, distinctly Balzacian, not least in Quennell's legendary meanness
(favourite characteristic in Balzac's depictions), an undoubted ability to write
elegantly, without anything of great interest to say. Even Quennell's Byron
stuff is strangely lifeless, compared with most other Byron authorities,
although he clearly 'identified' with Byron to some extent in his own eyes.

In contrast with all those mentioned above, at the same time a man who has
spent a good deal of his life among the beau monde, Adrian Daintrey (b. 1902,
Charterhouse, The Slade), by now probably my oldest living friend, coming
up for eighty-six in June. Daintrey, another frenetic womanizer of quite
different kind from Quennell (far more universal in his tastes, not at all
committed to 'pretty' women). Like his fellow-painter Rex Whistler, from the
start Daintrey always had a natural instinct for smart life. When I first knew
Adrian (c. 1927), although chronically hard up (which he remained
throughout life), he always had a few smart invitations (possibly dating from
his affair with Dorothy Warren, whose Warren Gallery gave him his first
show).

Daintrey *père* a solicitor, apparently made rather hash of his own life, a
subject sometimes touched on by Adrian. It was never quite clear what
happened. Anyway, he was no help to his son financially, tho' Adrian was fond
of his father. Adrian always maintained bohemian behaviour and clothes in
whatever world he moved. Admittedly painters are in a privileged position as
regards seduction (studio, situation *à deux*, slightly hypnotic element in being
painted). Even allowing for all that, Daintrey's exterior seems always to have
been attractive to women of all classes. His own preferences in that field was an
odd mixture of the general (typical painters' types, plump, massive), the
eclectic (what he once described to me as 'young countesses in berets & gym
shoes'), together with straight tarts (Edna, who worked Dean Street, Soho),
and black bus-conductresses.

Some of these mistresses were no doubt advantageous in the way of social
advancement; equally, he once remarked to me that no invitation he was on his
way to was, could ever be, sufficiently alluring that it would prevent him from
abandoning it to follow a woman who had caught his fancy. This characteristic
in him was no doubt plainly marked on his exterior to be read by every woman
with whom he came in contact. Adrian, when younger, had a line of his own in
being a buffoon (imitation of a mad convict) for undiscriminating audiences.

He could be funny in conversation, at same time took himself extremely seriously at moments; in certain respects, a simple soul. Success in the beau monde meant more to him than I ever grasped in the old days (never able to rid myself of romantic views about dedication to art), and could have been hindrance to his painting, at which he probably never worked hard enough.

Whether Adrian's talent was sufficient for that to have made a difference is an open question. V thinks not, that he would not, by an effort, have become appreciably more proficient than he was, and might as well have the fun, which he certainly experienced. There is much to be said for this view. In a curious manner Adrian always lacked creative fantasy, inner intelligence, sensibility of some indefinable sort, required as much in painting as writing, or any other art. At the same time he could make penetrating, individual comments on art, and much else. It may have been best (as for Wilde, albeit in very different manner) to create a work of art of his life, which to some extent Daintrey might be said to have done.

When I visited Adrian at The Charterhouse, he said: 'Was there a moment in your life when you were always in the Ritz?' That question revealed a lot. The answer in my own case was decidedly not. Connolly, too, had a mystique about the Ritz (possibly borrowed from Proust, tho' Connolly was less of a Proustian than might be expected. Proust was perhaps too dedicated a writer, producing *Angst* in Connolly). Alan Ross told me he once left a party given in a private suite at the top of the Ritz with Cyril. Cyril at once began to hold forth on his own lifelong familiarity with the hotel as they proceeded together down the stairs. Somehow they took the wrong turning, became hopelessly lost, the two of them ending up in a kind of broom-cupboard.

With Adrian, whatever social heights he might be scaling, there were always odd (sometimes very odd) mistresses in the background at one social level or another. Only a few aspects of Barnby in *Dance* are at all like Daintrey, many quite unlike, for instance Adrian was not at all interested in what terms he possessed a woman, tho' he would often grumble at women's behaviour. I once remarked to him that many, perhaps most women, were surprisingly unsensual, didn't he agree? Adrian (immeasurably more experienced in that line than myself) replied: 'I don't think I've ever thought about it.' He seemed surprised at the question. I told this to Malcolm Muggeridge, who commented: 'Rather as if you asked Lloyd George if he didn't think politics very corrupt. Lloyd George might well have given same answer, that he'd never thought about it.'

Daintrey barely knew Evelyn Waugh, so far as I know, though they must have met at parties. Waugh records in his *Diaries* that he & Daintrey dined together in some South Italian town towards the end of hostilities, but without comment. Much the same, I should imagine, regarding Betjeman (who late on praised Daintrey's painting as insufficiently recognized), Beaton and Quennell, tho' I remember Adrian designating Beaton a 'dancing-master'. In not frequenting the worlds of those mentioned above, at the same time knowing a lot of smart people, Adrian resembled Rex Whistler, whom he must have met. Adrian would certainly have found Whistler's painting unsympathetic, probably *vice versa*.

Osbert Lancaster (b. 1908, Charterhouse, Lincoln, Oxon, The Slade) at first sight suggests himself for inclusion among the above names under examination, yet seems to me (like Connolly) somewhat different, not to be categorized with them. Osbert, always reasonably well off as young man, loved parties (he was quite a lot in the beau monde, tho' happy at all sorts of others). Osbert stayed, for instance, with the Rupert Nevills when the Queen was a fellow guest (something not likely to happen with, say, Waugh), at same time never made the least attempt to be 'smart' as such. In his role of cartoonist Lancaster had to be *au fait* with political, social, domestic matters, public events, of the moment when he did his drawings. He possessed a personal preoccupation with architecture and art generally. In fact Osbert's interests took him all over the place. He might like smart invitations, but they never became his sole aim. He had slightly spiky relations with fellow-Carthusian of an earlier vintage Adrian Daintrey. One of Daintrey's best portrait drawings was, however, of Lancaster, altho' never greatly appreciated by the subject.

Evelyn Waugh always behaved rather *de haut en bas* to Osbert Lancaster, while making use of him when convenient (Osbert was good natured in that sort of way), at least once having Osbert to stay as a lion for a garden fête. Evelyn, proficient at drawing, may have regarded himself as in rivalry with Osbert. In this field V made a good point that Charles Ryder (with whom Waugh 'identified' himself in *Brideshead*, even if Waugh said in his *Letters* that he looked on Ryder as a 'bad artist') would in real life have been very like Rex Whistler, at ease with the beau monde, but not a highbrow. All rather interesting.

Reading the book about Whistler brought on these not particularly lucid reflections. They make some sort of a pattern in my own mind, whether or not conveyable to others. The point is did, or did not, these writers and painters, who became professionally bound to smart life as something more than a relaxation, show that to have detrimental effect on their art? I should hesitate to pass judgement. Clearly Proust is just as good with M de Charlus as with Françoise, but Waugh is much better with seedy schoolmasters (whom he had really got the hang of) than aristocrats.

Examples could easily be found of artists who picked a contrasted way of life. Constant Lambert (b. 1905, Christ's Hospital, Royal College of Music), whose musical activities (for instance via the Sitwells) could easily have given entrée to the beau monde (a path taken by Willy Walton and Freddie Ashton) disliked nothing more than 'high society'. Ed Burra (b. 1905, Royal College of Art), well-to-do upper-class background, destined for Eton (did not go for health reasons), family approved art-school training at early age. Ed, an artist not in the least attracted by smart life in practice, tho' Burra's *Letters* show him as intensely interested by the vagaries of fashionable life of the period (in what might be called a Firbankian manner). That was also true to some extent of Constant Lambert, a specially notable example of the way the beau monde likes musicians best, then painters, writers scarcely at all. I would say being a writer is almost a handicap.

Tuesday, 28 January

Rodrigo Moynihan rang to ask for another sitting, wanting to 'do more work on the coat', so to London, nobly driven by V to Westbury, through unpleasantly snowy roads. When I saw the picture, already improved by Rodrigo in my absence, I fully grasped why additional modelling of the face demanded more detailed treatment of the clothes. One never knows what one looks like, but the general impression of likeness seemed reasonable. I remarked that the portrait suggested rather a worried man. Rodrigo replied he always gave sitters the characteristics he was himself experiencing at the moment, in this case anxiety about his operation (which he decided not to have). I asked if he knew Rex Whistler. They turned out to have been at The Slade together during Whistler's 'second coming' there. Rodrigo said Whistler was 'pretty', and habitually silent. He admired Whistler's facility, while agreeing the figures in his painting are dreadfully whimsical. This admiration for Whistler's *facility* is almost universal among painters, possibly even Daintrey felt that. Rodrigo said Tonks, then head of The Slade, always had great crushes on certain students, both male and female, Rex Whistler one of these Tonks crushes. Incidentally, Daintrey told me that Tonks, bearing out V's theory that no one ever thinks their own surname funny, asserted that Cézanne owed his fame solely to having such an unusual name.

Attribution of paternity through facial resemblance is exceedingly tricky. Malcolm Muggeridge once showed me picture in book about G. B. Shaw, saying: 'Can you believe this music-critic was not father of Shaw, rather than the drunken idiot Mr Shaw?' The bearded music-critic, lover (I think subsequently husband) of Shaw's mother, certainly looked like Shaw. I asked if there was also picture of Mr Shaw. There was. This too looked exactly like Bernard Shaw, similarly bearded it should be added, which gave a resemblance anyway in both cases.

In this connexion Wyndham Ketton-Cremer (Oxford contemporary, friend and historical biographer) & his younger brother Dick (killed in the war) could not conceivably have looked and been less alike; physically, intellectually, temperamentally. No one who ever met their mother could have imagined for a moment that Mrs Ketton-Cremer had slipped up, otherwise it would have been difficult not to have suspected that Wyndham and Dick had different fathers. There was, however, amusing evidence of that not being so. Felbrigg (their family seat near Cromer) was full of ancestral portraits. Among these of the middle-to-late 17th century, one picture looked the image of Wyndham, another (of the same period) closely resembling Dick.

Rodrigo & I lunched as usual at the Ben Accolto. He is going to reduce slightly the size of my portrait, cutting a strip from across the top. He said: 'It was all right when I started at that point with the Queen. For some reason now you look too low on the canvas.' I wholly agreed. Rodrigo, as I thought he would, has now been buffaloed into painting the Duke of Edinburgh. The Secretary, equerry, whatever he was, said: 'Will you be at Windsor at 12 noon for six sittings [however many it was to be]', suggesting nothing about luncheon. Rodrigo made some demur about disruption of painter's days, at which was at once mentioned car to convey him both ways. Rodrigo said he was rather glad not to be involved in a formal luncheon with the Royal Family. He habitually takes several photographs of his sitters from close range while in course of painting them. Those of the Queen were quite excellent, different from any photographs I have seen of her. Much more convincing in the way her character was suggested. Rodrigo also took some good ones of me. In the evening V and I watched Tristram's TV programme on Norman Lewis, travel writer, chiefly Lewis's book *Naples '44*, the campaign in which Lewis served as an Intelligence Officer.

Wednesday, 29 January

A photographer, Ken Sharpe was supposed to come for *Fiction Magazine*, but decided snow too thick. Probably wise on his part. I had casually asked Rodrigo Moynihan if he proposed to send my portrait to The Academy. He replied, equally casually, he might or might not. Thinking this over, it occurred to me that picture ought to go to the RA, as a method of giving contributors an easy opportunity to see it. I was about to ring Hilary Spurling on this subject when Roland Gant rang to say Hilary's *Handbook to Dance* had

At The Stables. Francesca George, John Powell, and Maggie de Rougemont with Henry.

Tom Rosenthal and Roland Gant from Heinemann. 'I suspect both got on each other's nerves as business associates.'

Virginia Powell, Archie and Georgia
with the aesthete Sir Harold Acton at
La Pietra, Florence, in 1984.

Jennifer and Roy Jenkins. At AP's
8oth birthday party Roy Jenkins tried
unsuccessfully to hide the present, a
Latour '77, he had brought. It was
discovered and enjoyed by Grey
Gowrie.

Ken Taylor and Innes Lloyd, key figures in the BBC's *A Dance to the Music of Time* project, at The Chantry.

Cyril Connolly, who 'managed to turn even his own ugliness into almost an advantage'.

AP with Trelawney, a Cornish Rex of
aristocratic origins.

Malcolm Muggeridge 'did not wish to be
friends any longer'.

Hilary Spurling
presents the
Moynihan portrait to
AP. She organised
this tribute for his
80th birthday.

Evelyn Waugh, 'never made
any bones about wanting to
advance himself socially'.

Cecil Beaton, a man of 'relatively small talent', who yet 'became world famous by sheer will-power'.

John Betjeman, the 'supreme buffoon'.

Peter Quennell, off on honeymoon with Joyce. His 'assorted wives' were mostly 'positive handicaps'.

Adrian Daintrey, photographed about 1935. AP's 'oldest living friend', who created 'a work of art out of his life'.

At *The Fisher King* party, 8 April 1986, at Claridges. Above, V with Kingsley Amis and Selina Hastings. Below, Anthony Hobson and VS Naipaul.

been accepted for paperback publication. This is excellent news, so I was able to congratulate her on that, and also say I thought an Academy display of Moynihan portrait was desirable, as a form of recognition to subscribers. Hilary agreed. She is going to speak to Rodrigo about this. Roland had telephoned from the box nearest to his Dorset cottage, at that moment deep in snow. This is the type of weather in which Roland appears to flourish most when in the country.

Friday, 14 February

V and I acquired tickets for the Philip Larkin Memorial Service at Westminster Abbey, but the weather then became so foul, without prospect of change, that we decided to run out. I offered the tickets to Roland Gant, who welcomed them, having rather vaguely thought of going anyway, with Nadia. The Gants appeared later to have enjoyed the occasion greatly, Roland as a Jazz expert is qualified to appreciate the recitation of jazz played as tribute to Larkin's involvement with that end of music.

Nadia, three-quarters-French, quarter-Russian, was staggered at jazz being allowed in The Abbey, also at a reference to Larkin's agnosticism. She said neither could conceivably have taken place in Notre Dame. She herself was rather impressed. I was reminded of when I received my Hon. Doc. at Oxford, after which we proceeded in robes through streets. I was beside a distinguished French female academic also being honoured. She remarked how wonderful to live in a country where ceremonies like this one could take place out of doors in public. In France, she said, people would throw things. I was astonished at this. Shades of old-fashioned Francophilia. [Undeservedly, V and I appeared in list of those present at the Larkin Memorial Service.]

Monday, 17 February

With some relief I finished reread of *Jude the Obscure*. Hardy's determination never to let up on a hard-luck story is as undesirable in a novel, as to impose an artificially happy ending. Besides, not all Jude's hard luck is believable. Sue, on the other hand, is convincing; Arabella is also at moments not at all bad. In fact Hardy has a quality rare in male novelists of being better at women than men. Incidentally, after making all the fuss about going to bed with Jude in the first instance, nothing at all is said later of how that problem was resolved when Jude and Sue had offspring. Little Father Time (one feels he was a close relation to Little Father Tiny Tim) is figure of sheer fantasy, comparable with the most grotesque characters in Firbank, whom I have always held to derive a lot from Hardy. I also finished reread of *The Greek Anthology* (Allen Lane, 1973), most enjoyable, eg. Nikarchos (before 90 BC) tr. Peter Porter:

> Take note who stoop
> I am the goat-foot, Pan the Great,
> Reticulator of all falling water,
> Heed my warning!
>
> You may drink as much
> As you please and fill your pitcher here
> But never dare defile
> The crystal issue of the nymphs by washing
> Your filthy feet in it!
>
> If you do,
> Fear my ithyphallic armour,
> You shall not speak a word
> But submit upon the instant to be buggered –
> That is my rigid law!
>
> And if by any chance
> You're pathetic and like such punishment
> I have another weapon:
> My club is harder than my prick and with it
> I'll break your head open.

Rereading *Henry VI* (I) I was struck by the competence, yet complete unShakespearianness of most of it, although I believe contemporary doctrine is that Shakespeare did write the play. Mortimer dying convinces as Shakespeare, yet is it conceivable Shakespeare would have introduced Falstaff so tamely, unless recognizing that name represented another individual than later Falstaff? I suppose he may have thought up the classical Falstaff pondering relations with Prince Hal.

Wednesday, 19 February

An advance copy of *The Fisher King* arrived. It doesn't look too bad. Georgia, whose seventeenth birthday was yesterday, has two friends staying with her at The Stables, Kate Bigelow and Francesca Machiavelli, the latter said to descend from – certainly the same family as – the political philosopher who added such useful concepts to the subject.

Friday, 21 February

I read Stephen Spender's *Diary 1939–1983*. This received on the whole rather indifferent notices. I found it more interesting than I expected. I cannot take Spender at all seriously as a poet (pondering on the Truly Great, etc), but he is a very amusing talker, who all but fits into category of the upwardly mobile listed earlier (Evelyn Waugh and so on). Spender's ambitions have never been purely beau monde, even if appearing there when convenient. Auden always seems to me overrated as a poet, at the same time an extraordinary, perhaps even rather sinister, figure (especially as shown in this *Diary*), which Spender is not. Acres of the *Diary* are taken up with conferences about The Writer's Relationship to Society and the like, stupefying boredom, while at same time Spender's capacity for getting on is not at all uninteresting. He shows himself particularly at ease coping with rich Left Wing circles, at the same time perfectly capable of adapting himself to the Right, if hospitality from that quarter is on offer.

This two-pronged social and sexual attack is combined with willingness, even passionate desire, to speak publicly on Causes, sign protests, answer questions on Reasons for Writing. This makes the speaker a very acceptable guest.

Usually the *Diary* gives little or no description of the individuals whom Spender meets, many of whom may well have been too tedious easily to describe. Once in a way, however, he can be distinctly acute about certain people, eg. Sonia Orwell, whom he hits off exceedingly well. I had not grasped the full extent to which Spender himself was under Connolly's domination. One sometimes imagines tricky customers like Cyril are different in company of different people (in this case someone I have heard Connolly speak of as his closest friend). That is, always, of course, a fallacy. Cyril was just as tiresome – apparently even more tiresome – with Spender, as with, say, oneself and others with whom he did not feel the necessity to be obsequious.

Spender gives a hair-raising account of Auden's egotism, ruthless selfishness (not precisely the same thing), squalor, sheer boorishness. Auden himself is recorded as making the distinction (a very true one), between being boring and being a bore. One would wholly agree. I feel increasingly that this group's undoubtedly strong influence on intellectual life was almost wholly for the bad, and contributed a good deal to the country's general *dégringolade* of standards. The Auden gang lacked clarity of thought among other things. They were woolly-minded in what might be called a Public School manner, without the supposed Public School virtues, such as they are, few enough no doubt, but existent in some degree. This can be seen by the latter careers of those concerned. At the same time one must admit poets like Roy Fuller, and

Alan Ross, for instance (in the latter's phrase), had their eyes opened to 'poetry without pomposity', although I should have thought that could be found long before Auden & Co. Indeed for centuries, if you looked in the right places.

In one of the synopses at the beginning of Spender *Diary* sections he says his adaption of *Mary Queen of Scots* (Schiller) opened at Edinburgh in 1961. In fact, Spender was staying with the Glenconners at Glen, when V and John were also there (Henry Yorke and his wife 'Dig' too) in 1958. This suggests low standard of accuracy. Incidentally, not recorded in *Diary*, an episode took place some few years ago at a dinner party of Hamish Hamilton's, which V and I attended. It was the only occasion when I met Auden. After the men had been left 'over the port' at end of dinner, feeling myself in mutually unsympathetic company, and wanting not to appear grumpy on that score, I remarked to Spender that, in his recently published autobiography, I had enjoyed the story of his father visiting him at school, reading the Lesson in school chapel. When Spender *père* came to the words: 'This is my beloved son in whom I am well pleased', he removed his spectacles, and looked down the aisle to the seat where Stephen was sitting. As soon as the words were out of my mouth I became aware that this attempt to be agreeable had gone wrong. There was a short pause, during which Spender made no acknowledgement of my commendation. Then, from the other end of the table, Auden remarked in a rasping voice: 'Yes, Stephen, that happened to your brother, didn't it?' Spender sheepishly agreed that was so. Collapse of middle-aged party, in this case I suppose myself.

This morning the programme with Richard Hoggart about books was shown. It had been competently cut and went reasonably well, I thought. Hoggart looked less as if he were about to expire with anguish on the spot, than when talking to Edna O'Brien in the same series. TV appearances are largely matter of practice. I have ceased to bother whether I have said it all before. No one else ever dreams of showing scruples about repeating themselves.

Sunday, 23 February

The Stockwells are down, Archie with two school friends, Daniel Barraclough and Richard Evans. Virginia, still suffering from flu, stayed in bed. Tristram to dinner on Saturday, drinks Sunday morning with the three boys. Archie's friends are all well conducted, nice boys. Barraclough's mother produces TV programmes about the Queen, Mrs Thatcher, etc; her husband, formerly a doctor, has now taken to architecture, and more or less built their house opposite Royal Naval College, Greenwich, with his own hands. Evans, fair, good-looking, rather dominates the other two, according to Tristram. Tristram himself just returned from Hollywood, where it rained all the time. There he interviewed James Stewart and Cary Grant for his Hitchcock film. He said the two ancient stars looked utterly broken down when they entered the studio, then, like old warhorses, they snapped into their routines when shooting started. Fifty years ago, thereabouts, James Stewart was wandering about the MGM commissary when we were given lunch there to meet Scott Fitzgerald. Fitzgerald followed Stewart with his eyes: 'A Princeton man, I believe,' he murmured.

Thursday, 27 February

Robert McNamara (not, as it turned out, ex-head of the World Bank) came to luncheon with his wife. He is a retired publisher, somewhat older than the egregious US Secretary of Defence. Seventy-eight, rather vague, shaky on his pins, devoted fan, anxious to promote *Dance*, especially at Princeton (see previous entry), where he was educated and appears to have some pull. McNamara regards himself as a Chicagoan. He is an old-fashioned type of American, saying 'Pardon me', etc. Mrs McNamara (Frances) has a faint suggestion of a Continental accent, possibly Russian origins, not (her husband explained early on) mother of his children. They were married 1969. V thought her mink-lined mackintosh suggested considerable affluence. McNamara said in the US of today a book had 'shelf life' between milk and yoghurt. A publisher he knew recently referred to a 'good brand book'. All rather strange. The sort of Americans one does not come much in contact with these days. [The McNamaras subsequently sent a large box of literally the best chocolates either V or I had ever tasted, provenance Belgian.]

    I finished a reread of *The Unquiet Grave*, a work of which I never held very high opinion, certainly less than its general reputation. I always preferred *Enemies of Promise* or the *Connolly/Blakiston Letters*. This time, I found first half, perhaps first three-quarters, of *The Unquiet Grave* not at all bad, anyway a painful record of Cyril's melancholia, the logical carry-on of *Enemies of Promise*. It is the latter part which tails off so lamentably. The explanations of what is happening in the world are all badly dated, indeed mostly shown to be entirely wrong. There are also long tedious quotations from Dryden's translation of Homer in connexion with Palinurus, whose myth is never at all clearly assimilated with Cyril himself. It is full of characteristic Connolly inconsistencies, such as *The Grave* putting Montaigne in the 'essential' class, tho' Montaigne is condemned as a bore in *Enemies of Promise*; Stendhal, another 'essential', is denigrated in *Previous Convictions*.

Of course one feels differently about certain writers at different periods of one's life, it would readily be agreed. In connexion with Stendhal, I remember Cyril asking if I knew a tolerable current publication he could review for his next *Sunday Times* piece. As it happened I was doing myself (for the *DT*) a translation of Stendhal's *La Vie de Henri Brulard*, which I recommended. It is rather a favourite book of mine. Cyril asked the *Sunday Times* for *Brulard*, then complained that Stendhal was 'too masculine' for him. The Connolly attitude towards writers has something in common with the Connolly mystique of the life of pleasure, which he was always extolling. In fact (as he himself repeatedly emphasizes in *The Unquiet Grave*) he is chronically existing in state of deep depression, irritation and guilt. When one reflects on examples of 'men of pleasure' one has met (amongst whom, in his own particular manner, Malcolm Muggeridge would come high) Cyril possesses few if any claims.

In his writings, his own feelings are always attributed to everyone else. Novelists cannot do this, that, or the other, because Cyril himself cannot write novels, an inability which, equally characteristically, he also fully recognizes by saying: 'If we have no appetite for the idiosyncrasies of minor personalities, then we must fight shy of the novel.' An excellent definition of what the novelist has to ponder, even perhaps most of the time. All the same, Connolly could never quite persuade himself of the basic truth of this precept. What he was most proficient at is usually to be found in short pieces, criticism, introductions, or parodies. In fact he is a brilliant literary journalist, while always telling himself (sometimes convincing others) that only sloth prevented him from becoming a great novelist.

Quite late on he announced that he was going to write 'some plays' in the manner of Beaumarchais. One suspects Cyril possessed elements of a poet, at least a streak of frustrated poetry seems to have been in him, certainly not a novelist. Both Cyril and Henry Yorke/Green, were probably thwarted poets, by temperament unable to express themselves in poetry. Both were also immensely vain. Henry was not all that intelligent, or at all well read, both of which Cyril was. *The Unquiet Grave* is not so much a 'Commonplace Book' as a deliberate self-analysis. *Enemies of Promise*, so to speak, explains why *The Unquiet Grave* is flawed. All the same, the latter is enjoyable, acute, but comments in *The Unquiet Grave* are often weakened by inept conclusions.

Sunday, 2 March

Driven by John, we lunched with Vidia and Pat Naipaul at The Dairy Cottage, Salterton, near Salisbury, not far from their former residence on the Wilsford estate (which more or less faced the 'big house'), a bungalow most unusual in character. Jenny, widow of Vidia's brother Shiva, was staying, with her son Tarun, aged about nine. Jenny is a high-powered secretary at *The Spectator*, tho' apparently herself of somewhat Leftish orientation. She said Mark Amory adored his job of Literary Editor, and although only three days or so of work needed, always first in office every morning. *The Spectator* has instituted a Literary Prize in memory of Shiva Naipaul for 'his' type of journalism.

I do not wholly approve of such Literary Prizes, thinking them apt to travel far from persons they are meant to memorialize, in fact sometimes exactly what they would least approve. In any case, my opinion is that writers need money in old age rather than youth; the Orwell Prize, for instance, is bound to be presented to the embodiment of what George most disliked. This one will probably go to a Rastafarian, something equally unsympathetic to Shiv. Would it not have been far more sensible to present Jenny with some sort of nest-egg? Accordingly I took the opportunity of telling her this, suggesting I hand over what I should have given to fund had I been in favour. She replied she would at once pass it on to the Prize, so there matter rested.

Vidia is in good form, on point of producing book (about 130,000 words) on the subject of life and feelings, after coming to live in Wiltshire. He said much as he likes this present cottage, he still regrets Wilsford. The extraordinary out-of-the-world Through-the-Looking-Glass atmosphere there was certainly unlike anything else I myself ever encountered. If we can claim several witches amongst our friends (Alison Lurie, Hilary Spurling, Nadia Gant), Vidia Naipaul certainly grades as a warlock. He possesses, for example, a strange gift for interpreting handwriting (astonishingly good, for instance, with that of John (The Widow) Lloyd – 'this *terribly* mutilated person, yet with gifts that somehow come through a tiny aperture of his personality', a most subtle grasp of The Widow's wit, unique qualities, emerging from a painful buttoned-upness of the Wykehamistical sort). Pat does not like Vidia to exercise this semi-psychic power. Why should this be, one wonders? Is it like those severely rationalistic persons who become upset by playing planchette, putting cards out, anything of that kind? (For example Wyndham Lloyd.)

In rather the same genre Vidia began talking of faces of individuals, how they almost embarrassingly display characteristics of their owners after certain age, revealing everything inscribed on them by the years. One would agree. This arose from discussing the hooded eyes of Mrs Thatcher, which Vidia says indicate ambition; this characteristic even more emphasized in eyelids of Harold Macmillan. I would have liked to have talked about this matter further, the point at which faces can be examined over and above obvious examples of individuals being debauched, or conceited, but that was not feasible in circumstances. Tarun, nice little boy, had been to an Adventure Camp, which he greatly enjoyed. He said the boys let down girls' tents; girls in return released wasps in tents of boys. One feels this a very healthy relationship between the sexes. Pat seemed a bit tired, we thought, no doubt she has an exhausting time dealing with the Vidia dynamo. We had a really splendid Pomerol '70 (missed the Château) at luncheon, before which a bottle of 'my' champagne was opened and burst. Another bottle proved all right. The IEC Wine Society subsequently replaced the faulty bottle without least demur. Good party.

Rereading a selection from A. C. Benson's *Diaries*. This is entertaining. ACB's House at Eton (ie. boys taken over, rather than building) was that from which A. M. Goodhart's, my own Tutor's derived. Goodhart himself somewhat resembled the photograph of Benson; possibly modelling himself on Benson. On the other hand, equally possibly that was merely what all Eton beaks of that period looked like. A photograph of Swinburne's friend Watts-Dunton is also similar. Conceivably that was one of W-D's attractions for Swinburne looking like an Eton beak. Benson, who visited The Pines, thought Watts-Dunton 'not a gentleman'. The sort of thing one likes about Benson (an infinitely more intelligent man than Goodhart incidentally) is that he inveighs against people who, in his day, were sweeping such things as Georgian woodwork from churches, because the 18th century was out of fashion. Benson did not live to see M. R. James's vandalism as Provost in removing the Early Victorian gothic stalls from College Chapel at Eton, thereby utterly wrecking the interior to reveal medieval frescoes. The latter could have been made available by a system of stalls opening on hinges, as suggested by the Prince Consort.

Benson wrote (August 1901) that such persons 'can't see that continuity is the essence of beauty. There is no such thing as *absolute* beauty, *absolute* taste, and if there is, no one generation can see it.' One ponders these things. Even in South Italy, where an aesthetically puritan Vatican has cleared away all the junk of baroque images, one felt the loss a bit, if only on account of the temperament of locals. That is notwithstanding my own taste for the severity of a mosque-like interior. No doubt there was much rubbish and Norman interiors can now be seen, all the same the theatrical emotions of the South Italians were there recorded, which is one of the important things in these cases.

Tuesday, 4 March

Georgia rang to say she was going up to Oxford for the day tomorrow to interview two Balliol dons, Hinchliff and Murray, something arranged by her school, as she wants to continue Ancient History. I looked up dons in the *Balliol Register*, Hinchliff, a South African, is Tutor for Admissions; O. Murray, Marlborough, Hertford, a Classicist, married twice. This visit, done on Georgia's own initiative, I think admirable.

After something of a struggle, I finished *The Woman in White*, never previously read. Although full of improbabilities and inconsistencies, there are also goodish moments in its own particular genre. The hero, a young painter who had fallen in love with girl of higher social position, went to Central America (Honduras) to join an expedition, as did Charles Ryder, hero of *Brideshead* in comparable circumstances. Was this pure chance, or did *The Woman in White* prompt the situation? I have a memory of talking to Evelyn Waugh about Wilkie Collins's novel apropos of my missing the last bus and walking back to Shepherd Market from the Waughs' house in North End Road, Golders Green after dining there. It was a journey which took me exactly past the place where the Woman in White herself first appeared, escaping from the bogus lunatic asylum where she had been incarcerated, all of which Evelyn may have mentioned when we discussed missing the bus at our next meeting.

Thursday, 6 March

In course of reading *Henry VI* Part II (unlike Part I, obviously by Shakespeare), I referred to H. T. Evans's *Wales and the Wars of the Roses* (1915) for information about the Welsh captain, Matthew Gough, mentioned in the play, and other points about the period. Among those rewarded by Parliament in 1467, presumably as Yorkists, Evans names John ap Ieuan ap Llywelyn, a direct (Powell) ancestor, again listed in 1486, so he was possibly at Bosworth. The book itself formerly belonged to David Lloyd-George, whose bookplate it contains (name, feeble drawing of Big Ben framed in Art Nouveau daffodils), heavy pencil markings clearly made by Lloyd-George himself in margins. I am always struck by the comparative lack of interest shown by collectors in 'association copies'. This book, for instance, bought for about fifteen shillings, the normal price at time for a scholarly work of that sort. There was no increase for Lloyd-George's ownership, tho' not without interest, especially in light of these pencillings.

To return to A. C. Benson. When Benson went to Stratford he borrowed a ladder from the verger in the church to examine Shakespeare's bust. Benson thought the face 'intelligent' close up, almost certainly from death mask, indicated by lips and eyes. This is a convincing theory. One of Bernard Shaw's many idiotic remarks was to the effect that the bust could not be like Shakespeare because it resembled a prosperous tallow-chandler. What a ludicrous supposition that poets always look 'poetic' (Dryden, Browning, Hardy, to mention a few who seem to have looked far from that); for that matter Shakespeare was by no means without his prosperous tallow-chandler side. One thinks of poets one has known: Eliot, Dylan Thomas, Betjeman, Roy Fuller, Larkin, and sees no particular pattern.

Saturday, 8 March

Virginia (at The Stables to garden), to dinner. She brought the photographs taken by her sister, Julia Mount, at my eightieth birthday party, some of them very funny. Jilly Cooper, saying goodbye, appears to be holding my head in her hands, like Salome kissing the severed head of John the Baptist; Evangeline Bruce, Marcelle Quinton, Rachel Billington, and self, on a sofa seem to be a brothel group by Toulouse-Lautrec.

Friday, 14 March

Tony Gould (Literary Editor of *New Society* for which he interviewed some months ago) reviewed in two or three lines *The Fisher King*, which he did not like, but sent a copy of a book come into his office astonishingly titled *Basically Bach* (by H. Kupferberg), surprising coincidence, because the character in *The Fisher King* wearing T-shirt inscribed BASICALLY BACH was a complete invention (modelled on two middle-aged Americans on an Hellenic cruise round Great Britain, who had MOSTLY MOZART on their shirts). I had toyed with several other composers whose names began with B.

Sunday, 16 March

Joff & Tessa Davies for drinks before luncheon, partly in celebration of Tessa's birthday, 13 March, shared with V; partly for V and Joff to discuss local government matters. Always struck by how pretty and elegant Tessa is. We both like Joff, at same time feel something a shade mysterious about him, perhaps because one knows nothing whatever about his first wife; perhaps anyone who works in oil automatically attaches to themselves a touch of Secret Service aroma.

Saturday, 22 March

Billy Chappell & Anne (Lady) Ritchie (Ed Burra's sister) to luncheon. Billy, must now be seventy-seven, in good form, tho' he has rather lost the elfin look retained till quite late on. He says he is about halfway through an autobiography, never went to bed with anyone before he was twenty-three. Lady Ritchie cannot be much younger than Billy, if at all. She looks, dresses, and behaves like a quiet country gentlewoman of sixty or seventy years ago, who has lived all her life in some remote backwater. In point of fact one cannot guess what, at one time or another, she must not have seen and heard, via her brother and his friends (also twice married herself); nor what they can think at The Francis Hotel, Bath, when this strange couple arrive together, notwithstanding that the hotel caters for showbiz.

When Anne Ritchie removes her specs one can see a resemblance to her brother Ed. She told me she had been 'rather frightened of the American poet Conrad Aiken', one of Ed's friends, who 'drank rather a lot'. Billy described how when he was in the army, Captain, The Wiltshire Regiment (Duke of Edinburgh's), the Commanding Officer, when the battalion served in North Africa, announced he was going to Biskra, and asked Billy if he would like to come too. This Billy did. Billy said Biskra was a charming little resort, French boulevards, and Edwardian hotel. He & the Colonel watched belly dancing together, an infinitely comic scene to contemplate.

Tuesday, 25 March

Nicholas Shakespeare, young man working on an Evelyn Waugh TV programme (not yet completed) in which I took part some months age, came to interview me for *The Times*, where he is Deputy Literary Editor. Quite agreeable, reasonably intelligent. I had previously warned him that he must get his pedigree straight before coming here again. It appears his family descend from The Bard's *grandfather* (Richard Shakespeare of Snitterfield), if I remember right, obviously Shakespeare's grandfather, tho' not absolutely proved by documentation.

The Heralds have confirmed the arms to this Nicholas Shakespeare's family, father a Wykehamist, Ambassador to Peru. He was Counsellor at Lisbon when we put in there on the Amis/Fussell cruise. Nicholas had come aboard and seen us. He is writing a book on Londoners. He visited a lunatic asylum, where a prostitute was confined, who persuaded men into a suicide pact, then did not herself jump out of the window as previously arranged. She had disposed of two men in this manner. Nicholas Shakespeare said he had been reading *O, How the Wheel Becomes It!* with enjoyment in train coming here.

When I told him both *Wheel* and *The Fisher King* were, rather to my surprise, being translated into French, said French publishers nowadays are keen on English books, utterly different from fifty years ago. We talked of Jeffrey Meyers's biography of Hemingway. He said he had interviewed Martha Gellhorn (Hemingway's third wife), who had an affair with H. G. Wells.

Tuesday, 1 April

On recommendation of Higham's, I saw a young American journalist, Anthony Weller for an 'in flight' magazine produced by North West Orient Air Lines, which go all over the place, Japan, Ireland and Canada, used chiefly by businessmen. One knows by experience boredom compels reading every scrap of print put beside bag to be sick into, so these magazines represent quite good publicity. Weller (also fell into category of 'agreeable, reasonably intelligent') said this publication often includes quite highbrow pieces. He recently left New York for Amsterdam as good place from which to operate. He said he had just read *Venusberg* (1932) with enjoyment, which greatly pleased me, as showing an ancient number holding up. The Stockwells down, Virginia, Georgia, to tea.

Thursday, 3 April

The Fisher King published. Kaleidoscope (radio) on the whole satisfactory last night, tho' the Chairman (whose name I did not retain) was evidently unable to understand a word of it. A. S. Byatt produced elaborate comments on the symbolic significance of all sorts of things, among them Henchman's name. I was pleased to hear but quite unthought of by me, also the point of *Alecto*'s name. I await the grasping of the Lebyatkin vodka reference. I fear John Bayley will be the only sufficiently Dostoevksyan to get it. Good quote from *Henry VI*, Part III, if Mrs Thatcher does not get in next Election: 'Where's Captain Margaret, to fence you now?'

Friday, 4 April

My agent John Rush rang in the afternoon to say the BBC (ie. Jonathan Powell) have decided not to do *Dance* on TV. Rush says he is going to try Granada with the Ken Taylor/Innes Lloyd script as a package. After the last eight or nine years of BBC ineptitudes about *Dance* nothing surprises me, I feel one of the commercial companies certainly would be no worse to deal with, probably better. Why *Dance* should now appear unsuitable after 'passing' three scripted episodes is beyond comprehension. For that matter, after reading the sequence itself, a quiet beginning leading up to deeper matters is an essential aspect of the construction. Rush rather distraught. He has taken a lot of trouble about *Dance* over the years, and is understandably disappointed at this.

Monday, 7 April

Main reviews of *The Fisher King* are now in; a generally satisfactory press, important thing is to let people know book is out, what it is about. Reviewers mostly approving, tho' one is always struck by the ingrained philistinism, illiteracy, humourlessness, their fear and hatred of literary references. American reviewers can be careless (eg. when I wrote Constant Lambert had dreamt I said to Virginia Woolf: 'How now, bluestocking, what about the booze?', an American reviewer remarking that it was a strange way to address a distinguished literary lady), but they maintain a certain respect for writing.

British reviewers tend to hate writing as such. This also applies to most interviewers. I always say the same thing to interviewers, because they always ask the same banal questions. They subsequently write facetiously, desperately anxious to show they are not in the least impressed by anyone or anything. American interviewers, on the other hand, seem grateful and surprised at being received politely. Of course this is probably less true when American journalists deal with fellow Americans. Connolly commented with truth that all novels which prove any good in the long run have delayed action, so one has no objection to a certain degree of demur in the first instance. In fact too much immediate acceptance could easily produce a sense of fear that one had begun to write drivel. Few post-war novels enthusiastically received hold up on later reading, one exception being Lampedusa's *The Leopard*. Sometimes looking up press-cuttings of fifty years ago (indeed much less) one comes upon astonishing forgotten novels (reviewed with one's own) hailed as works of genius. The Stockwells at The Stables for the weekend, Georgia's friend Emma Bowden (Dulwich MP Gerry Bowden's daughter) is staying, also Andrew Murray-Threipland, with daughter age two, Charlotte (tho' Archie says her christian name is 'negotiable').

Tuesday, 8 April

To London for the Heinemann luncheon party at Claridge's for a combined Eightieth Birthday/*Fisher King* publication (Roland Gant's suggestion, thereby avoiding crowded moment before last Christmas). I arrived at Claridge's (where I had not been for ages) about 12.30, and sat in the entrance hall watching comings & goings. This I always enjoy, today mostly South Koreans, whose Foreign Minister is over here. The place has been rather cleaned up since my last visit (which was probably a year or two ago, to Antony & Lily Hornby's flat – he a stockbroker and art-collector, she a dancer – on one of the higher floors). Luncheon was in the drawing-room straight ahead of front entrance, a big room, plenty of space for drinks before, large sofas, and a long table for twenty-four set in window. Heinemann's rather jolly PR girl, Susan Boyd (wife of novelist William Boyd, not previously met), scarlet frock, black pancake shaped hat, did an excellent job arranging everybody, and everything. I had not met Heinemann's new chairman. Nicolas Thompson, an Etonian (rather a sad character, one feels, tho' people speak well of him), is said to be staunch supporter of my books. One of his claims to fame is having joined Weidenfeld's on same day as Antonia (Pakenham then). Brian Perman, newish director appointed to keep an eye on the pennies, had developed more dashing hairstyle since party given for *O, How the Wheel Becomes It!*

Joanna Lumley was invited on the strength of her fan letters and reading my works from the pulpit of St Mary Woolnoth, a message arrived at 12.55 that she had flu. On the other hand Lord (Ian) Bancroft, late head of Civil Service, also invited on strength of fan letters, turned up. He sat next to V, appeared greatly to enjoy himself. I warned Ian Bancroft earlier, on learning he was keen photographer, that an *haut fonctionnaire* photographer was already a character in *The Fisher King*, then in process of being written. Hilary Spurling was on my left, where Joanna Lumley was to have sat had she turned up. Tanya Hobson, with Anthony, the book's dedicatees, on my right. Regrouping did not make too much of a mess, apart from several men sitting together (keeping sexes level at this sort of party is always difficult). These, as it happened, were all keen talkers of publishing shop. Tom Wallace, of Norton's (my new American publisher), turned up in London, so he was included, also Alan Ross, with his pretty girlfriend, Liz Claridge, both just back from Kenya. There they missed John's friend Jim de Vere Allen, director of the Lamu museum, which would have been an amusing meeting.

The table, running right from me: was AP, Tanya Hobson, Vidia Naipaul, Rachel Billington, John Spurling, Jane Turnbull, Thomas C. Wallace, Elizabeth Claridge, Roy Fuller, Nicholas Thompson, V, Ian Bancroft, Selina Hastings, Alan Ross, Susan Boyd, David Holloway, Brian Perman, Bruce Hunter, Anthony Hobson, Roland Gant, Miriam Gross, Kingsley Amis, Hilary Spurling, AP. Tanya Hobson said when she first knew her, Liz Claridge was called Glazebrook, but uncertain whether she was *née* that. Food not too bad (délice de saumon, selle d'agneau, poire pochée; Sancerre, Clos Paradis '83, Ch Lanessan '80, all good). Really splendid party of its kind where everyone seemed to enjoy themselves. The last confirmed by subsequent letters. Joanna Lumley, after reading *The Fisher King*, wrote saying she was heartbroken not to have been able to come, enclosing invitation for me to sign. Feeling even a celebrated actress might have sent her refusal a shade earlier than 12.55 inscribed card: 'Alas, Miss Otis regretted . . .'

Saturday, *12 April*

This afternoon I went down to the lake to meet by appointment two members of Fishing Syndicate, Stephen Hale (Bathwick Grange Lodge, Bathwick), Roger McCortney, to discuss making good the east bank of lake, especially in light of the Reservoir Act. Hale, a builder, suggests he buy material at cost price, then they would do work themselves, prevent fish escaping, etc. This about £430. In principle, I agreed.

I received a letter from Ken Taylor and Innes Lloyd about the BBC running out on *Dance*. Both of them sound upset, as well they might. Innes Lloyd enclosed a copy of Jonathan Powell's letter announcing the deal was off, complaining there wasn't sufficient 'muscle' in the script. As soon as I set eyes on Jonathan Powell, I felt him unsympathetic. No objection made now could not have been foreseen from the start. Obviously the narrative is going to open without great drama, then build up. Precise opening (and closing) shots always agreed with Taylor & Lloyd to be a matter for later discussion. I myself would have favoured an opening with Widmerpool in the mist, as in book, then cutting back; I am still sure the book's sequence is in any case better than a chronological beginning with Stonehurst, which might well have been preferred to start off the second six vols . . . Ken Taylor & Innes Lloyd deplore the decision genuinely enough, I think. One can only hope for better luck elsewhere. It is chiefly annoying because the project offered an 'ongoing' interest for one's declining years, also these days TV puts an almost essential imprimatur for the sales on a 'serious' book. I have no doubt *Dance* will be televised in due course. It would have been nice to have kept an eye on the making.

This irritation was somewhat offset by satisfaction in fact that Chatto's (that part of firm called The Hogarth Press) is doing a paperback of *John Aubrey and His Friends*. I am immensely pleased about this. It is the only book which deals fully with Aubrey's life, product of first-hand research (Joan Sumner's Will, Westminster Rate Books regarding Mary Wiseman, etc). I am as little given to jealousy of other writers as could well be, but did find a certain exasperation

ANTHONY POWELL'S SPEECH AT HEINEMANN LUNCH, CLARIDGE'S, TUESDAY 8 April

I am overwhelmed by the kind things that have been said. It is nice to be congratulated on becoming an octogenarian, but the advantages, I can assure you, are in themselves rather dubious, I find.

Such as they are, they are greatly enhanced by getting a book out, and by having that celebrated by a luncheon party like this one.

In expressing my thanks to the Chairman, Directors, and Staff of Messrs Heinemann, I cannot help being struck by one thing.

That is to say the number of new pupils who have arrived at the school this term.

Most of these are among our hosts, but even if some of them are among the guests, several of the latter must feel that the proceedings ought to have begun by singing that hymm which opens with the words:

Lord, behold us with thy blessing,
Once again assembled here.

I wonder whether these new pupils know what they are in for at the school.

As you may remember, the hymn goes on to beg for strength to withstand Temptation's fatal power:

Safe in every careless hour,
Safe from Sloth and Sensual Snare.

I am afraid that, so far as the writers present are concerned, they will by now have made up their minds just how far it is safe to go with these fatal obstructions, and still produce a manuscript on the deadline.

It is not the writers themselves who will pray to be preserved from Sloth and Sensual Snare, but their publishers who will pray that the writers may be preserved from those.

I worked in a publisher's office myself in my early days, and I know just what authors can be when it comes to Sloth and Sensual Snares.

Of course, I admit that publishers are not absolutely immune either, but my wife always says that I am like that picture in *The New Yorker*, where the woman complains to her husband:

'You are always on the car's side.'

My wife says I am always like that with publishers, having once been one myself.

From publishers' failings, however, I would certainly except he to whom Shakespeare refers in the opening line of Richard II:

Old Roland Gant, time-honoured Editor

Certainly there is nothing Roland does not know about the ways of Heinemann authors, and their bad habits, not least my own.

With every book I write I feel it would never have appeared without Roland, and I should like to take this opportunity of thanking him personally again, and thanking all those who have had a hand in producing *The Fisher King*, and laying on this delightful luncheon for the book's launching.

Thank you all.

that Evelyn Waugh's *Campion*, and Graham Greene's *Rochester* (both put together from printed sources, and 'romantically' elaborating from existing material) should be in print when *Aubrey* was unobtainable. Owing to Scribner's having omitted some formality about copyright in the US an edition has been pirated in Chicago, just as in Victorian times. The Americans really ought to be ashamed of themselves that such things can happen in a civilized country, not the Soviet Union, or some People's Republic. Apparently The Hogarth Press taking Aubrey on is due to Carmen Callil, now Queen of Chatto's.

Sunday, 13 April

Tom Wallace, of my American publisher Norton's, staying with Gerald and Gillian Seymour, who live near Radstock, came to tea, bringing the Seymours. Gerald Seymour writes successful thrillers, which Norton's publish. He was formerly a 'newscaster' for ITV. Tall, bespectacled, hair receding a bit, possibly approaching fifty; she, a plump blonde, good legs, silent, perhaps feeling others should do the talking. Seymour was just back from Indian North-West Frontier (now Pakistan), making film there about the Falklands campaign. He said lorries loaded with stuff go through Khyber just as usual to Afghanistan, in spite of Soviet war. These are half-million Afghan refugees in Pakistan, most of them in or about Peshawar, which he described as a town of great villainy. I was interested in that designation, precise words Kipling used about Peshawar, in his *Early Journalism* (nearly a century ago), which I recently reviewed.

It appears that Gerald Seymour's father (minor poet, worked in bank, seems to have been much involved in literary politics of the period) first married Beatrice Keen Seymour, prototypical female successful middlebrow novels of the 1920s. Gerald Seymour said he knew nothing of why they parted, about which there is no information in *Who's Who*. His mother, Rosalind Wade, is also prolific novelist and prominent figure in literary organizations. He volunteered all this himself, remarking on the pecularity of his own ignorance of his father's first marriage, his parents' life generally. Window was opened on middlebrow writing of fifty or sixty years ago, slightly fascinating. V spoke afterwards of Margaret Kennedy's (*The Constant Nymph*) dislike for Beatrice Keen Seymour and vice versa. Tom Wallace wanted to arrange a 3000 word piece somewhere in the US, when *The Fisher King* appears there in October. He asked who I thought should do it. I suggested Gene Lyons, who wrote a piece in *Newsweek* for my Eightieth. Tom knew Lyons, thought it a good idea. Tom is an intelligent publisher. I am impressed by his having noted down Allan Massie as a capable critic.

Tuesday, 15 April

In the afternoon an American girl journalist, Katherine Stephen (née Field, married to an Englishman) interviewed me for the *International Herald Tribune*. She was from Chicago, living in Islington, nice, pretty, lived in Alaska when young, said description of Orkney in *The Fisher King* brought Alaska back. I finished *Henry VI*, Part III, good, especially Henry talking to the Lieutenant of the Tower, none of the essentially non-Shakespearian character of Part I. I am rereading Michael Levey's *Pater*, and Peter Ackroyd's *T. S. Eliot*.

Wednesday, 16 April

Dr Rawlins arranged for me to see Mr W. F. Southwood about slight rectal bleeding, which Rawlins thinks piles. I doubt this as I had an operation for their removal some years ago. Southwood, who performed hernia operation seven or eight years ago, quite sympathetic, tho' walking image of Widmerpool. Found a polyp, which has to be removed. This will be done in the Bath Clinic, Claverton Down, and take a day or two. The Clinic is more accessible as on this side of Bath than Southwood's former surgery in the west suburbs, or Lansdowne Nursing Home in the north, nevertheless a bore.

Friday, 18 April

V drove me to the Bath Clinic, where I was given an X-ray by Dr Roberts, young, jolly, bearded, and a strapping blonde, Pauline. Although not my favourite process, a great improvement on what happened in similar circumstances eighteen or more years ago.

Friday, 25 April

Finished Michael Levey's *Pater*. Interesting that this repressed homosexual don, looking like a 'retired major of the Rifle Brigade', living with two spinster sisters, should have had an overpowering influence on Wilde, the Nineties, and much else. Pater's books are now unreadable in bulk, which I confirmed by looking at *Marius the Epicurean*, an Eton Prize, in the Medici Society's Riccardi Press edition, cardboard covers, labels, a format which seemed of indescribable beauty when I chose it, tho' even then never managed to read.

Tuesday, 29 April

I finished Ackroyd's *T. S. Eliot*. This is well done within its limits, which included not being allowed to quote, possibly in long run an advantage. Ackroyd has not much humour, perhaps also no great loss for what was required here as more or less first biography, humour sometimes blurring an issue when one merely wants facts. I now grasp far better what Tom Eliot's first wife, Vivien Haigh-Wood, was like; that is to say one of those slightly (only very slightly) 'liberated' girls, mildly highbrow, of immediately pre-first war period. As a small boy I can actually remember some of them, a great to-do made about their drinking and smoking. The fact that, even as a child, one was aware of the slight difference they represented. One can easily imagine a girl of that sort holding a fascination for Eliot, coming from his particular American puritan background, which was of course 'grander', in American terms, than the Haigh-Woods (his wife's name) in British. The opposite has been absurdly suggested, ie., that Eliot was attracted for 'snobbish' reasons. I came across Vivien Eliot's brother, a regular army captain in The Manchester Regiment, when both of us were on the politico-military course at Cambridge during second war. I did not take to him, tho' contacts were minimal. So far as I remember he snapped at me for making some derogatory remark about Mussolini and Italian Fascism, I suppose assuming me to be aggressively Left Wing; not usually regarded as an orientation of mine.

Eliot's period of sharing a flat with John Hayward is rather insufficiently emphasized in Ackroyd's book, being no doubt hard to reconstruct by someone who had never seen them together. I have no doubt at all the juxtaposition had considerable influence on both, certainly Hayward gave a lot of advice (accepted) about Eliot's poems. Osbert & Karen Lancaster were once watching a circus or some show of that sort, processing through Battersea Park. After the last vehicle, a cage on a float, had passed, there followed Tom Eliot pushing John Hayward in his wheelchair. Osbert said they looked exactly as if they were the final promenading spectacle of the show.

Ackroyd makes the acute point that no one becomes public figure of the kind Eliot was without a wish for that sort of publicity. Not everyone is intelligent enough to grasp that fact about Eliot; one of the reasons why a similarly publicity-obsessed person, Malcolm Muggeridge, hated him so much, overcome with envy by the efficiency of Eliot self-advertising machine (based, of course, on true brilliance). Foundations of such publicity had been laid early in life by Eliot, a deliberate policy of withdrawnness, planned methods of impressing people as a hermit-like highbrow (cf. Graham Greene, Henry Yorke). Another side of Eliot, that equally liked pottering about eating iced cakes, making the smallest of small talk, with such as the Mirrlees family, is more difficult to convey on paper, though no less an Eliotesque aspect.

These Eliot reflections caused a rereading of *The Confidential Clerk*, a kind of country house charade, something I suspect true of all Eliot plays except perhaps *Murder in the Cathedral*, its ecclesiastical setting making it a sort of miracle play. (As it happens, I am pro-Henry II rather than Becket.) *Prufrock*, *The Waste Land* (particularly the first bit, with certain later sections), still hold a peculiar magic for me, also I like some of the comic earlier poems such as *Cooking an Egg*. Impressive in some respects as the *Quartets* are, they remain a bit self-conscious, a Great Man speaking while retaining his humility. One notes that when Eliot joined Faber's he was taken on by the firm as much for his financial knowledge, acquired by the banking years, as for prestige as 'literary adviser'. In fact, Eliot seems not to have specially disliked the bank, as such, taking a keen interest in the money market, which included a certain degree of canniness in his own spending. The true story of his sojourn in the bank is at complete variance with the legend current when I was young, ie. that some rich people (usually identified as the Stoops), provided him with the wherewithal to be independent, accordingly were annoyed at his becoming a publisher, one of those total inventions that get round from time to time.

Wednesday, 30 April

I am reading *Excellent Women* by Barbara Pym. Someone in the novel comments, with reference Matthew Arnold: '*Thyrsis*, *The Scholar Gypsy*, tramps over the green Cumnor hills, how one longs for that world.' I certainly have had moments when that world does seem greatly alluring. As it happens I am also reading Katherine Chorley's life of Arthur Hugh Clough (reviewed by me perhaps twenty-five years ago), which effectively cures any such nostalgia for the Arnold/Clough period; impossible to get an academic job unless you subscribed to Thirty-Nine Articles, which your own high- mindedness prevented you from doing. There seems to have been a general atmosphere of appalling tedium and philistinism, combined with all forms of liberal optimism, from the ills of which we still remain heirs.

The Clough biography itself is quite well done, if dreadfully heavy going. Barbara Pym has her own brand of originality, always at her best dealing with a self-imposed background of clergymen and jumble-sales, which in fact she never sufficiently develops. V said with truth that although B. Pym herself was not soft-centred, she appeals to a certain kind of soft-centredness in some intellectuals, tho' she was well worth resurrecting – possibly more than say, Jean Rhys – even if I would not go all the way with David Cecil and Philip Larkin about her.

Friday, 2 May

I arrived at the Bath Clinic soon after 4 o'clock with V and John, who drove us. The Clinic is built on what was once a country house apparently Victorian. It is less depressing than some institutions of that kind, my room (bath) looking on to oldish buildings, giving slight air of being abroad, perhaps Germany. I brought another Barbara Pym, *A Glass of Blessings* (1958) as I am near the end of *Excellent Women* and did not want to run out of books. The clerical life she depicts is often funny, but, V agrees, wholly imaginary, almost as much as the Wodehouse world, material not in least naturalistic.

During last thirty years or more we have seen plenty of ecclesiastical comings & goings at Chantry, much of which would be well worth writing about, if such were your vein. None of them bore any resemblance whatever to Pym life, even if she could no doubt point to her own instances. In fact one feels she misses a lot of tricks. Probably she has a certain type of novel in mind which much of Chantry scenes from clerical life during the last few decades would not have fitted into, too grotesque, painful (drunk in charge for example). I also brought Jeffrey Meyers's *Wyndham Lewis*, and Aldous Huxley's *Texts & Pretexts*. Huxley's anthology is rather a mixed bag, with welcome excerpts marred by Huxley's truly dreadful vulgarity in his introduction, which has the intellectual cocksureness of the period. It gives a good idea of what sort of a highbrow Aldous Huxley was, that is not precisely Bloomsbury. The differences are of interest. At the Clinic nothing happend for the rest of the day. I just sat, read, had temperature and blood pressure taken, latter not as low as formerly, then dinner: tomato soup, lemon sole, peas, potatoes baked in skins, fruit salad, three biscuits, Danish blue cheese, 'carafino' of white (Jugoslav Lutomer) in canister shaped like bomb; unexciting, eatable.

Saturday, 3 May

The anaesthetist, Dr Stephen Hill, came about 9.30, youngish, tall, thin, good-looking, I imagine all nurses are in love with him (one nurse asked if I did not think him nice). He put various questions, including if I took a lot of exercise? 'None.' 'Then you are a disgrace. Here are hundreds of people killing themselves with jogging, while you take no exercise at all, look extremely well.' He said he thought I should have a heart test, so a young woman in a green spangled cocktail dress, who had taken my blood pressure the previous day, reappeared, bound my wrists and ankles with rubber bands (something no doubt addicts like Adrian Daintrey would pay highly for). She put contraption with lot of red bobbles (like a Calder mobile) on my chest, attached to an object like a primitive typewriter.

She asked my christian name. As she was wearing a gold chain round her neck attached to a gold cross with the letter E, I enquired if hers was Elizabeth. She replied no, she had rather strange name, Elfie. At 10.30, after being given a small blue pre-anaesthetic pill, also a large yellow one, I was wheeled down to the operating theatre. When first experiencing an operation twenty or thirty years ago, I was given an actual injection. Never since have I experienced such a sense of acute bliss as on that occasion. Nowadays they must do something different, perhaps deliberately use a less pleasurable drug. This time I took longer to come round than on previous occasions, remaining still muzzy when V very sweetly came to see me in afternoon, not expected, really wasn't demanded in the circumstances. I was quite hungry in evening, a sandwich welcome (as Wodehouse, or Joyce, might have put it: the eponymous nourishment of the Montagu earldom).

Sunday, 4 May

Southwood looked in about 9.45 am. I greatly prefer him to previous Bath surgeon, tho' the likeness to Widmerpool never ceases to fascinate me. He said nothing to worry about, heart all right too, but would like to see me in a year's time. When Southwood left, he took my two feet, which were sticking up under the bedclothes, shook them in goodbye, an authentically Widmerpoolian gesture. John drove me home, heartily glad to be back. I inherit all my mother's horror of doctors, hospitals, the medical world, what she used to call the 'smell of iodoform' a now obsolete anaesthetic, all of which V finds rather enthralling. On this occasion all went as easily as might well be.

Tuesday, 6 May

I received a letter from D. F. Harris from Lincoln, asking if I could provide various details of my maternal gt-grandfather, Dymoke Welles (formerly Wells), of Grebby Hall, Lincs, with references to his lawsuit, 1814/1820, with Lewis Dymoke, of Scrivelsby Court, in same county, regarding their respective claims to the Barony of Marmion. Harris is researching that case as twenty-five per cent of his History A-levels.

This enquiry is of considerable note to me: first, on account of those reviewers who complained no one could be in the least interested by genealogical sections of my Memoirs, merely bored to death; secondly, contemplating the manner in which developments in education necessitates constant searching round for additional material suitable for historical investigation by students, thereby totally refuting those who regard genealogy as anti-egalitarian waste of time (such persons missing, among other points, its topographical importance). In fact genealogy demonstrates, among many other things, the extreme fluidity of class in this country, doing that in a manner no other type of research can achieve in quite the same manner. I gave all the information I could to Harris, telling him to write again if any problem arose with which I might be in position to help.

Wednesday, 8 May

Colin Hughes, formerly Secretary of the Frome Rural District Council, also its Registrar (a powerful local position) came in for drink to discuss raising funds for repair of St John's Church, Frome. I at once contributed a modest cheque to avoid further pressure. A quarter of million needed. Mr Hughes (a great figure in V's *histoires* of local life), is also former Secretary of Chantry/Whatley Parish Council, a job taken on for more or less benevolent motives, if not without its small-scale power angle. Mr Hughes is a substantial figure in Frome civic life, better-to-do than the average holder of his handful of jobs, with a cottage at Llanstephan on the Radnorshire/Brecon border and a villa in Crete. The last he said he was selling, describing it as small (three bathrooms installed by himself), facing the sea opposite an island, until 1954 a leper colony. He plans to move to a farm, preferably renovated by himself, in South/South-West France.

Mr Hughes, who likes high-life gossip, went on for some little time on this theme, the subject mostly neighbours of his in Wales, notably Hugo Philipps at Llanstephan House. Hugo Philipps (whom we've met once or twice) has pulled down his residence (Victorian, I think), in favour of something more comfortable, 'very modern, hideous', says Mr Hughes, twitching with horror. Hugo Philipps is heir to the only professedly Communist peer, Wogan, 2nd Lord Milford, by Rosamond Lehmann (*Dusty Answer*, etc). Wogan Philipps had an explosive love life in the 1920s, after Rosamond Lehmann, marrying Christina Casati, finally *en troisième noces* Tamara, the widow of the Communist Editor of the *Daily Worker*, called Rust.

Wogan Philipps had a stormy affair with, among others, Barbara Ker-Seymer, who ran him round a bit, I believe. Rust always remains in my mind as one of those examples of unctuous cant to which the British, particularly British journalists, are so devoted. Just after the war Malcolm Muggeridge and several other members, including me, used to sit through the National Union of Journalists meetings, deliberately prolonged by Communist members to (literally) four or five hours, in order to get rid of non-Communist members, so that all voting could go as the Communists wished. In due course, by this determined holding on, the Anti-Communists managed to vote the Communist majority off the board.

Rust, having committed some dereliction of journalistic etiquette, was summoned to appear before NUJ committee and members. On hearing of this summons he fell into so great a rage that he died in a fit of choler (like some medieval character such as King John) just before the meeting took place, possibly even on his way to it. I was present when Rust's demise was announced by the NUJ Secretary, who executed one of those wonderful demonstrations of sanctimoniousness referred to above: 'We may have differed politically from Bill Rust, but he was a man, etc.'

Hugo Philipps, Wogan's son, focus of Mr Hughes's gossip, like his father has suffered matrimonial stresses, deserted by two wives: the beautiful Margaret, then Molly Makins, so Mr Hughes had good deal of ground to cover. Wogan's younger brother, Hanning, functions at Picton Castle, Pembrokeshire, doing local duties, owing to his eldest brother's Communism. Hanning was in War Office with me, staff-officer to a Lt. Gen called Grasett, whose only function was to give the Allies a direct representative on the Army Council. (My father disliked him, alleging Grasett stole other people's ideas at the Staff College.) In the circumstances Hanning Philipps naturally had little to do, used to talk a good deal to me about modern painting ('Rouault is a man who's seen God, etc'). Accordingly, when V and I did a tour of Pembrokeshire, I thought Hanning might be asked to stand us luncheon at Picton. Hanning, in this case, would only rise to tea.

The present Philippses, tho' in direct male line as owners of Picton, bought the Castle back (after a long period of alienation) from Sheila Dunsany, whose family owned it through heiresses for several generations, changing their name to Philipps more than once. Sheila's family seemed originally to have been called Grant, which apparently can be a Welsh surname, whether indigenous or not one would like to know, Oliver Cromwell's paternal Williams family also descended from Grants (see the *Lyvr Baglan*).

Saturday, 10 May

Alice Boyd, with her youngest daughter Philippa Lennox-Boyd, seventeen, close friend of Georgia's, came at short notice to luncheon, after staying with Alice's Aunt Caroline (née Clive), widow of Johnny Walker, Caroline having moved from Sutton Veny to Longbridge Deverell after Johnny's death. Johnny is buried at Sutton Veny, his grave inscribed: *Major, The Rifle Brigade; Poet and Musician*, one of his own poems is incised on back of the tombstone. Philippa will be pretty when older, tho' now dressed in the awful garments affected by the young, that is to say jeans beneath a shapeless blue sack.

The 'little girls' (as they continue to be called, although rapidly advancing in years), who bring the Sunday papers, wear much the same, but they are out in all weathers, contrive to bring a touch of style to such unbecoming rags, anyway manage to look better. Alice, always attractive, was also dressed on this occasion rather like a fugitive lady of the Old South from *Gone With the Wind*. Nice to see them both.

Sunday, 11 May

Driven by John, we lunched with Anthony & Tanya Hobson at Whitsbury. As it happened John Julius Norwich & Molly Philipps (wife of Hugo Philipps referred to above) were staying there, also a couple called Mr & Mrs Adrian House, publisher (Collins), old friends of Anthony's. Both seemed agreeable. I sat between Charlotte Hobson, a nice girl, & Molly Philipps (met some few years ago), daughter of Roger Makins (now Lord Sherfield), former Ambassador at Washington, her mother American. Molly Philipps, tall, attractive, went grey early on, is easy to talk to. Although not in the least like Diana Cooper physically, association with John Julius (one presumes, tho' possibly what attracted him to her) has caused her to adopt some of his mother's mannerisms. At least once or twice when talking she recalled Diana. I supposed her to be married to John Julius by now, but apparently not. They are looking for a house in this part of the world. Both Anthony & Tanya spoke well of Nicolas Thompson, the new Chairman of Heinemann's. He used to be with the firm publishing the *Encyclopaedia Britannica*.

The Naipauls recently lunched with the Hobsons, and Tanya had been much impressed with Vidia's forcible personality when she sat next to him at my Heinemann's Claridge's luncheon; for instance, when he sent for the claret bottle to see the label. Pat Naipaul is apparently not allowed by Vidia to garden (quite why is not clear), if she does so clandestinely while he is resting in afternoon he will suddenly pull aside the curtains and denounce her from the window. Nice food, excellent burgundy (I think Mâcon).

I have been exchanging letters with Sir Thomas Armstrong, former head of Royal Academy of Music, understandably much upset by things critics have written about Constant Lambert, when reviewing Andrew Motion's book *The Lamberts*. I could only reply that more often than not reviewers are stupid, incompetent, often envious, rarely grasp the point of any given book, if subtlety is required, that I wholly agree with him, and had reviewed *The Lamberts* myself in a manner I hope he approved. I would not deny that

Constant had his failings, also that his particular brand of good nature, wit, quite unusual intelligence, is not easy to put over, perhaps Andrew Motion's account falling rather short on that score, as they never met. Sir Thomas Armstrong (b. 1898) wrote charmingly of his own memories of Constant, at the College (as it then was) 'so nice, so funny'. Few reviewers took in these qualities at all.

Sir Thomas himself writes with that curiously rapid flow of words and phrases characteristic of musicians, if they can express themselves on paper at all. When I read Alick Dru's translation of Kierkegaard's *Diary* I felt sure K was musical from the manner (even in translation) that the sentences pattered out. This proved correct. Constant Lambert is the supreme example (*Music Ho!*) of that sort of style. Cecil Gray, who always said he himself wrote with greatest difficulty (tho' quite well) is the sole exception in my experience.

Thursday, 15 May

Lees & Mary Mayall to a curry luncheon. Both in good form. They spoke of discords among Longleat entourage, Alexander Weymouth having stated unequivocally that, when his father dies (which Henry Bath at present shows no sign whatever of doing), he will insist on his brother Christopher Thynne leaving the house at Horningsham. Alexander dislikes Antonia Thynne (née Palmer, a sister of Sir Mark Palmer, whose visit to The Chantry in his hippy days is suggested in the opening part of *Hearing Secret Harmonies*). I enquired why Alexander disliked Antonia so much. Lees said that, among other things, she went on TV and was unfriendly about Alexander. Lees spoke with some annoyance of having talked with Philip Ziegler about Diana Cooper (when Ziegler was in process of writing a biography of her), then Ziegler put in a lot of stuff Lees had not meant for publication. This is a hazard only long experience can circumvent with interviewers, formal or informal, even then things slip out accidentally, not to mention what interviewers and journalists themselves invent (of which I could provide striking examples). The Mayalls wanted to get Daphne Fielding, formerly Bath, over for luncheon. Daphne has apparently become pious these days in old age, refusing to talk of former goings-on, a classic development in such cases.

Friday, 16 May

Mr J. D. Humphries, of Mander, Rakes & Marshall, engineers, Bristol, came about 10 am to report on the lake in light of the Reservoir Act 1975 requirements, with which we are persecuted. On the telephone I imagined him a relatively young man, but he turned out probably late fifties, biggish, grey-haired, rather sad. Humphries & I went round lake together, through the Lost World of marsh, undergrowth (now more or less an official Somerset Nature Reserve), as far as end of the property at Dead Woman's Bottom. Then we crossed road between end of lake & Quarry Land to examine the culvert through which the stream flows on the Quarry side. V went down to explain various points on which she is expert, such as the deep hollow on east side, which we call the Water Garden. When Humphries returned to house to make his report we gave him a glass of sherry. He said he did not think lake sufficient size to fall within terms of the Act, a judgement I heard with deep relief. It would be most desirable if we could avoid the whole thing, previously made difficult by inexact drafting of the Act, eg., 'holding so much water or designed to hold so much water', etc, original eight & half acres of lake now reduced by more than half, creating what we call the Lost World. This is clearly not the slightest danger to life from potential overflow (water area always on the decrease), Humphries's opinion simply confirms one's own. Humphries is going to speak to Michael Joyce of Cooper & Tanner, whom I have alerted.

Monday, 19 May

V & I went down to the lake in the afternoon to look at two large trees, roots of which Humphries said needed attention: one actually hanging over lake itself; the other on slope of the Water Garden, on steep descent more or less above old Wheel House, from which water supplies formerly pumped up to The Chantry. Humphries had suggested first tree probably required a block of concrete to prevent water from running from the side into the waterfall (rather than over the sluice), thereby erosion. Roots of second tree, he said, ought to be filled with sand or suchlike, through which water can penetrate slowly, harmlessly.

Both these look extremely difficult jobs, the latter because sand would never stay there owing to steepness of the slope. Similar difficulty in the other case. In the evening we both attended a Conservative Meeting at The Stables, where V also registered her retirement as Chairman of the Conservatives, an office she held for thirty years. She gives place to Mrs Angela Durston, a comparatively new arrival in Chantry. The Durstons live in a recently built, somewhat architecturally stark, house in Chantry, which will no doubt weather in due course. Mrs Durston made an excellent impression. The minutes were taken by Joff Davies, nobody else turning up, general agreement having been given earlier as to what went forward.

Wednesday, 21 May

I saw Southwood at the Bath Clinic, who wanted to check after the operation. All was well, and he recommended eating bran. I asked if he knew a good place to lunch on way back. He suggested The Red Lion, Wolverton, a short way the Bath side of Beckington. Was indeed good, largish room, hot food at the bar. Potatoes baked in skins, with cheese, ham, onions within; pint of draught stout. Various baked potato dishes with different elements. The barmaid looked like a Tudor princess. Hilary Spurling sent some postcards of the Moynihan portrait, which she reports as hanging in Room 1 of Burlington House, RA Exhibition not yet open. I asked what I should do to thank contributors. This Hilary will look into.

Tuesday, 27 May

Hilary rang last night to say she is sending contributors' names in due course, about a hundred or more, including institutions. This is held up by David Holloway, Literary Editor of the *Daily Telegraph* (who undertook a great deal of administration in getting contributions going) suffering an accident to his back when on holiday abroad. He is now in hospital, likely to be *hors de combat* for two months.

I finished Meyers's *Wyndham Lewis*, also Lewis's novel *Self-Condemned*, never before properly read. I find difficulty in defining just how I feel about Lewis, obviously an important figure in the Arts at beginning of the century, yet full of unsatisfactory characteristics. I was devoted to *Tarr* when young. *The Apes of God* did not really come off, in spite of brilliant passages. All the same *The Apes* is still disciplined writing, which *Self-Condemned* wholly fails to be. The fact is Lewis, notwithstanding immense powers over language, did not know how to put a book together, in addition to a taste for dreadful triviality in much of the material he deals with, his subjects often taken from the popular press. He is utterly unable to grasp what is, essentially, ephemera.

This triviality is never quite so apparent in his painting, tho' similar faults and virtues can be traced there too. Many of the pictures are without either particular interest nor charged with feeling. The two war canvases (*Battery Shelled, Canadian Gun-pit*) Lewis himself called 'dull', nonetheless a sense of violence, puppets operating automatically, seem appropriate to representing war. *Siege of Barcelona*, for instance, has real originality in design, and colour, for that matter subject, comparable with some of the early Vorticist paintings. Paradoxically, so far as portraits concerned, Lewis is always at his best with Edith Sitwell, notwithstanding Edith's and her brothers' bitter hatred, in spite of Lewis being the only man on record to make a pass at her. The Sitwells unhappily shared Lewis's inability to disregard journalists' trivia. All the same, when Osbert Sitwell remarked that Lewis's later portrait-drawings showed the influence of Olive Snell (a popular portraitist of the period depicting Stage, Society, and personalities) he spoke with touch of awful truth, even if some were goodish likenesses. The Lewis drawing of Constant Lambert, in conductor's uniform of morning coat and winged collar, which some ass described as 'foppish', bears little or no resemblance to Constant, tho' Lewis was well disposed to him, even inscribing a book 'with admiration'.

Both in writing and painting, Lewis lacked empathy, he did not know what other individuals were like. He speaks nothing but truth when he says he represents only what is external. This approach results in a certain monotony, lack of development, even poverty of creative fantasy. Considering the gifts with which Lewis was endowed, it is worth noting that during his life, early or late, Lewis never experienced any period of humdrum normality (except to some extent, I suppose, in the army), which can be of inestimable use to a novelist, probably in the other arts too. Lewis sneered at Joyce's lower-middle-class manners and demeanour (as he did equally at upper-class behaviour when it suited him), but Joyce's Dublin lower-middle-classness, dyed-in-the-wool, was one of his immense strengths. This specialized knowledge Lewis patently lacked at all levels, including, in a sense, day-to-day doings of fellow bohemian painters and writers, through his own intense narcissistic egotism and separateness.

If the cases of other novelists are examined, usefulness of run-of-the-mill family, social, or professional life, cannot be overestimated – Jane Austen, Proust, Flaubert, all the Russians (largely in the light of the simple nature of 19th century Russian life and social conventions). This ought to be true of the American novel, somehow it isn't (Edith Wharton, perhaps; William Dean Howells had not quite enough ability). One of the paradoxes about the US is that novelists like examining themselves in some ways, but not in others. Perhaps all this is less true of American writers than formerly. Dickens, who lived a rootless early life, never really possessed any clear idea of how anyone earned a living. Maugham, another rootless figure, can be convincing dealing with Malayan expatriates, even if his sensibilities are not up to Conrad's in relation to the Far East. Conrad is a writer with a deeply understood profession (the sea) behind him. He also knew about political matters. Maugham is a rare instance of a writer who spoiled material by cheap satire. He is not convincing, for instance, when he attempts upper-class characters.

The last is also true of Wyndham Lewis, always harping on being himself an 'artist', while latterly lacking the discipline so essential to an artist, especially in spending time, energy, in futile vendettas instead of being industriously creative. *Self-Condemned* is mostly straight autobiographical material about Lewis's own tribulations in Canada during second war, certainly awful enough, but quite shapeless, not at all convincing in the transmogrification made in representing himself as a professor rather than painter/writer. The books ends in something not much less than a virulent attack on the author's wife, who had, in fact, devoted her life to him (I believe took jobs at Woolworth's, after his death, while always active to keep his memory going). All this is without offering any real intellectual nourishment to excuse Lewis's own unpleasant behaviour. I think undoubtedly Lewis's paranoia, anyway latterly, amounted to madness, even if that had not always been so. I found him most unappealing the only time we met, but there were people who said he could be charming, intelligent, a brilliant talker. They also tended to be those against whom he turned most savagely, especially if they had also helped him with money. Constant Lambert always maintained an amused sardonic attitude, never speaking of Lewis as he spoke of his close friends, even when he laughed about their behaviour.

Thursday, 29 May

A photographer Nick Powell asked to take a picture for his folio of writers. I answered that he could on strength of his surname. He turned out to be a rather good-looking young man, twenty-two, very inarticulate, not easy to understand, reminding me strongly of the young miners in the 1/5th Welch. Asked if his family had always lived in Gwent (formerly Monmouthshire). He said no, his mother came from Merthyr, father from Mountain Ash. 1/5th Bn The Welch Regiment (Territorials), recruited one Company from Merthyr, one from Mountain Ash, one from Pontypridd, small mining towns in Glamorgan. I was pleased to have marked him down as from The Valleys. Apparently he went to Newport (Gwent) College, where they have a good photographic department. This seemed his chief reason for being a photographer, just as he might have chosen accountancy, or surveying. All the same, Nick Powell spoke intelligently about photography. He mentioned Kingsley Amis as one of his subjects. I asked how he found Kingsley. 'Well, at first he was rather like a schoolmaster, then at the end he loosened up a bit.' I was interested in this definition, as something similar had been said occasionally by interviewers about myself, perhaps the impression writers give. Nick Powell said he got his living from 'industrial' photographs and portraits. I was uncertain what the former were, John later explaining that a considerable market exists for illustrating company reports and brochures. Nick Powell asked if I had not known Orwell. On my replying yes, he spoke of the 'backlash about Orwell in the Labour Party'. I enquired what exactly he meant by that. He explained: 'You know, the cloth cap and suet pudding image.' Undeniably that was poor old George's view of the Working Classes, now apparently giving offence.

While we were talking of Nick Powell's family having come from The Valleys, he said he thought he was related to Dick something-or-other, name I could not catch, even after he repeated it. Later research revealed this was evidently Dick Penderyn (actual name Richard Lewis, 'penderyn' meaning, I think, 'resolute'), who was hanged, apparently unjustly, after the so-called 'Merthyr Rising' of 1831, when a soldier was killed quelling riots. Evidently Nick Powell is something of a repository of such traditions. He also asked what I thought about 'modern art', Picasso, etc. He spoke of Snowdon's photograph of me 'with the cat' (Trelawney then quite young, in the air, more or less a blur, jumping from my shoulder), which he admired. He had tried to read *O, How the Wheel Becomes It!*, evidently quite unintelligible to him. Rather fascinating encounter. [Nick Powell later sent half-a-dozen or more copies of good photographs taken which was nice mannered of him.] Bridget Hardman-Mountford (Secretary, Literary Editor *Daily Telegraph*) forwarded a list of names (about 108 including several individuals never heard of by me) of contributors to the Moynihan portrait.

Sunday, 1 June

Diana Beaufort-Palmer (in ancient days briefly wife of Bobby Roberts) wrote that friends of hers, Peter and June Luke, have taken Railford Cottage (now apparently Railford Mill) in the woods at the bottom of the hill ten minutes away from us: would we call on them. Accordingly, the Lukes came for drink before luncheon today. Peter Luke wrote various plays, notably dramatisation of Corvo's novel *Hadrian VII*, a notable success some years ago, other jobs in that line, including a spell at the Gate Theatre, Dublin (formerly associated with V's brother Edward Longford), also for some years in the wine business in Spain. Etonian, Rifleman during war, MC, late sixties. She, third wife (one dcd, one div.), is perhaps ten years younger, gives impression of not being wholly English, from something said, possibly South African, possibly just showbiz manner. He is tall, grey-haired, a little like the actor Michael Hordern, style of one long habituated to BBC sort of world. He has female twins, aged about seventeen, by this wife, five other children, some by previous unions. He seemed agreeable. He is elder brother of Mickie Luke (now apparently reissued as Michael Luke). Their father was a proconsular figure who turned up on one Hellenic cruise, an egotistical old bore always holding forth; the family is of Hungarian origin, took name of Luke in 1919.

Tuesday, 3 June

To London to see Sussman. He had copy of *The Fisher King* to inscribe. This I did, forgetting to add Sussman himself had supplied all medical material used in novel. I can do that on the next occasion, as he is contemplating one of his extensive reconstructions. He had looked up the Fisher King legend, the complex nature of which we discussed. Sussman (who wanted to be a composer rather than a dentist, and write opera about King Arthur) said he had never previously grasped that Parsifal was same as Percival.

I went on to the Academy to see the Moynihan portrait hanging in Room 1. The picture, as I remember I commented earlier, could not be called notable exercise in bravura, tho' certainly there was no other painter in the show by whom I would prefer to have been painted. Nowadays pictures in the RA consist for most part of what might be termed immensely feeble Spencer Gores, together with a few even feebler abstracts in style of half century or more ago. One regrets the Academies of yesteryear, problem pictures, pirates, and society beauties. I decided to lunch in the restaurant downstairs. I'm sorry to say they have removed Orpen's *The Chef*, formerly most appropriately hung at the top of the stairs leading down to lower regions where you eat.

The place turned out to be inordinately crowded. True, *The Chef* would have heralded a rather different sort of meal to what was on offer at a long table laden with bowls of Continental messes being spooned out. I use term messes in no pejorative sense, indeed think that quite good combinations could have been concocted with time to choose, or if already familiar with what on offer; as it was, fighting in the queue, I had an odd mixture of salads, and a glass of wine. It all might have been worse. On the walls were frescoes of startling hideosity, perhaps by Gilbert Spencer (brother of Stanley Spencer), a painter met once or twice at Garsington, where, as an undergraduate, I found him embarrassing to sit next to, as, for patrons like Lady Ottoline, he was inclined to put on a performance of wild artist-man. Perhaps always did. Henry Lamb had one or two of his pictures.

Wednesday, 4 June

Dealt with thanking letters to Moynihan portrait contributors. It now appears that, although various individual members of *Daily Telegraph* staff subscribed privately, David Holloway did much of the secretarial donkey-work organizing things. The paper itself (ie. Michael Berry, Lord Hartwell) said it was too poor to contribute, a typical piece of *DT* stinginess, even if the Berrys *are* selling it. One way and another I have worked on the book-page over a period of just about fifty years. Latterly, for several decades, I have accepted payment quite incommensurate with my name as a writer, simply because regular reviewing supplied me with a permanent stream of current books to read.

When one considers how the *Sunday Times* used to treat (and pay) Cyril Connolly one can get some idea of the depth of Berry niggardliness. As against that it might be argued that the *DT* was indeed in dire distress, resulting in having to be sold; that I like reviewing, without which I should go bankrupt buying books, or mad from having nothing to read; finally, that few people on earth possessed Cyril's mesmeric powers of extracting money. Nevertheless, considering how various publishers with whom I have been fragmentarily concerned came across with a contribution, I should have thought a token sum might have been ante-ed up. After all, there was nothing to prevent Michael Berry himself sending a five-pound note as an individual, in the interest of someone who had often been a guest at his house (albeit at invitation of his wife, Pam, who was herself always openhanded). If Michael Berry's far from royally paid staff thought it incumbent on themselves to give something, which several did, some of whom I did not know personally, so could he. These unamiable reflections are characteristic of sentiments often aroused by benevolent actions.

Tuesday, 10 June

I reread Ted Morgan's *Maugham* (the author's name is apparently an anagram of the French noble family de Gramont to which he belongs). It is extremely interesting, tho' Morgan often shows an odd ignorance of the social life and conventions in this country, and British institutions generally. On the whole it is a devastating picture of Somerset Maugham himself, probably not unjust. Maugham was always asserting that he was merely a shy writer, his only desire to entertain. In fact he was immensely ambitious in just those areas in which he complains of other people's ambitions, snobbery and literary pretensions.

He was racked with envy, especially in relation to not being taken as seriously as he would have liked by the intellectuals he purported to despise. He possessed exceptional powers in constructing a dramatic story, more often than not at the price of misrepresenting, or covertly changing the pace of, human behaviour in a given situation. This is often easily detectable, taking the form of altering the standards of moral judgement of the matter in dealing with the individuals involved in the same story. One wonders to what extent

Maugham himself was aware of this, deliberately going for what the public liked, rather than what was true, or whether he was genuinely taken in by the vulgarity of his own standards.

His ghastly last years suggest that he was to some extent tortured by consciousness of certain inner dishonesties in dealing with other people, that perversion of the truth inevitably reflected in his own books. This is not to suggest that he always failed to entertain, merely to indicate where he falls short of earning the sort of praise he himself so much coveted. Maugham wanted to have his cake and eat it.

Incidentally, the publishers sent me a proof of the American edition, which I eventually reviewed in the British edition. In the latter a passage is omitted emphasizing Maugham's canniness in limiting domestic expenditure in housekeeping at the Villa Mauresque. His unfortunate secretary, Alan Searle, was hauled over the coals if routine items, such as lavatory paper, were exceeded. Alan Searle was in trouble when too many towels – certainly a surprising number – were used when Ian and Ann Fleming came to stay. It then appeared that the towels so prodigally sent to the laundry were used to alleviate the smart when Ian Fleming whipped his wife during the sexual encounters taking place during their visit.

The Reservoir Act is probably not being concerned with the lake in the light of Humphries's opinion. Joyce and Hammond came again to do measurements. They had a foul day for undertaking that, rain descending in sheets. They ultimately retired to sort out figures noted. One sincerely hopes an annual inspection will not be necessary.

V and I were talking about someone (possibly Rimbaud) remarking that he saw letters of the Alphabet in different colours. I said I did; V uncertain herself, suggested I ought to write down what these colours seem to me, so I do so: A, very dark red, almost black; B, very dark brown, almost black; C, light blue, almost grey; D, very dark blue; E, lightish brown; F, slightly lighter brown than E; G, about same sort of brown as F; H, black; I, black; J, lightish brown; K, fairly light grey; L, darker grey; M, purplish red; N, brownish red; O, white; P, light green; Q, pale yellow; R, dark grey, almost black; S, darkish green; T, dark red; U, very light pale yellow; V, palish brown; W, darker brown; X, black; Y, lightish brownish yellow; Z, black.

Sunday, 15 June

We had 6 o'clock drinks with the Lukes. I had not seen Railford Cottage for some time, and forgotten what an attractive place it is. Reached by a track of two or three hundred yards through deep woods, the cottage itself has been much improved by various tenants. It is entirely enclosed by trees, with a small stretch of lawn in front, wistaria growing across the façade. The inside is now thoroughly reorganized. The Luke pictures included framed Hungarian coats-of-arms, not I gathered of actual Lukacz family (don't know whether or not related to the Marxist apologist, and thought better not to enquire). Mickie, alias Michael, Luke was staying. It appears he and I first met with Adrian Daintrey, whom he recently saw in The Charterhouse, Adrian having forgotten about arranging the visit. I told M. Luke, who is writing a history of the Gargoyle Club (somewhat unpromising subject it might be thought), that his wartime remark 'Awfully smart to be killed' had gone into *Dance*. Drinks, canapés, in the garden. Peter Luke indicated extensive piles of boxes in the garage. They were his father's papers, unsorted, contents unknown. Enjoyable evening.

Monday, 16 June

About 6.10 am the telephone rang. V came in to say a call from US, Cambridge, Mass. The character who said his name was (I think) Keith Green, speaking English rather than American, rang to say he heard another book of mine was coming out. He thought that this would be memoirs, but it seemed it was novel. He continued to waffle in this sort of way, and no particular direction, saying how much he liked my books, brilliant he thought them, until I told him in the plainest terms I was extremely fed up at being rung at this hour. He said the US telephone people had misinformed him about time of day it would be over here. I hung up.

Incredible as it may seem he rang again about 9 o'clock, and apologized for making earlier call, continued to talk for literally half an hour. Indeed he would not have rung off then had I not said I had work to do, all this was devoted to saying how much he and his friends loved my books, I was greatest writer of 20th century etc. He was somewhat incoherent tho' he did not appear tight. He said he taught German in an American school, had been sitting up waiting to receive a tennis team in small hours, that it was about 2 am when first rang, presumably about five on the second occasion. At long last I got rid of him, but not without threat of ringing again. He said he felt like a bobbysoxer with Sinatra. He had known Isherwood and seen him not long before he died.

Tuesday, 17 June

To London. Saw Sussman, who said his brother, if asked to look left or right, always dithered. I enquired what his brother did. The answer was that he sold wallpaper. Sussman agreed knowing your left from your right was not specially vital in that profession. I lunched at The Travellers with Hugh Montgomery-Massingberd (infinitely remote connexion of my mother's Waterhouse grandmother who had a sister married to a Massingberd, enjoyable for genealogists like Hugh & myself, and our meeting would have delighted my mother). Gunby, in Lincolnshire, the Massingberd house (Tennyson's 'haunt of ancient peace') is quite near Grebby Hall, where the Wellses lived. Gunby is now National Trusted. I mentioned I was a shade late owing to a dentist's appointment. Hugh said his (second) wife was also having a dental morning, with (appropriately) the only dental peer, the 3rd Lord Colwyn.

Hugh is to take over the *Daily Telegraph* obituaries, hitherto meagre in form. He complained all the plums like the Duchess of Windsor and Lady Diana Cooper were dropping from tree before he could get to work. He spoke of the present Garter King of Arms, Sir Colin Cole, who once interviewed Hugh as potential Herald. . . . Hugh also said that Carmen Callil, now Chairman of Chatto's/Hogarth Press/Virago, when she first arrived in this country from Australia, was a waitress in a trendy night-club called The Establishment.

On returning home, by odd coincidence, was a letter from Anthony Wagner (late Garter, probably greatest since William Camden four hundred years ago), now, alas, blind, tho' says he manages to do some work, and gets a lot of social life too. I had passed on to Anthony a pedigree sent by a female descendant of the Waterhouse family (see Massingberd above), forebears of whom, in one direction, were four generations of Hull ship-owners and sea-captains. Anthony himself is descended from whalers from Hull, therefore interested.

Friday, 20 June

Quite by chance I have been rereading *Ulysses*, almost reached end, when *The Corrected Ulysses* (putting right some 5000 misprints) arrived for review. I had been following certain things up by also rereading Richard Ellmann's excellent biography of James Joyce. In the 1920s, even when a schoolboy, one was conscious of feeling this was an exciting intellectual epoch in which to grow up. Reading about Joyce I am struck by how correct was that sense of stimulation in the air. It was indeed as extraordinary era, as different from now as the Nineties, everyone seeking messiahs in the Arts, quite a few of whom made themselves available. The atmosphere characterized by Miss Weaver (was she related to the husband of Mrs Weaver of Thames & Hudson?)

shelling out money for Joyce, Larbaud lending him a Paris flat, Sylvia Beach printing his books. I remember Constant Lambert remarking on the odd similarity of character and aggressive egos of people born in the 1880s. Constant was speaking apropos of the painter Edward Wadsworth's resemblance to Wyndham Lewis (of course those may have been acquired from seeing a certain amount of each other as fellow Vorticists). They all considered themselves geniuses, D. H. Lawrence, Wyndham Lewis, Edith Sitwell, Virginia Woolf. In a sense I would almost include my father in his attitude towards himself, conviction of his own absolute rightness in everything. Given same sort of talent existent – genius of some sort if you prefer – in these and other cases, it is impossible to imagine anything like the same public reaction to writers and painters today.

Joyce at his best is extremely good, yet he never seems able to keep up his own naturalistic technique, far his strongest line. Sooner or later he falls back on pastiche, grotesqueries and puns, perhaps to conceal an inherent sentimentality clear enough in his verse. He is always dodging the innate difficulties in writing a novel by using extraneous means to avoid narrative. Joyce had of course exceptional command of language, indeed languages, speaking four or five fluently; also, as mentioned above, he possessed the inestimable advantage of knowing lower-middle-class Dublin, from every angle a provincialism all its own. Even for an Irishman his egotism was fathomless, also his personal vanity. At the same time Joyce can be extremely funny. Someone in *Ulysses* mentions seeing a poster in France advertising *Hamlet; ou le distrait*, at which Joyce comments 'The Absent-minded Beggar'.

One of Joyce's most valuable bequests to writers is that none of them ever need write a novel like *Ulysses* again; a benefaction unhappily sometimes disregarded, especially in the US. One feels that Joyce, even if pretty able, is not quite in the Proust, Dostoevsky, even Balzac, class; useful to be learnt from, but not to be imitated. I am inclined to think that Joyce was always a bit mad, in the medical sense. Having himself inherited mental troubles, he passed them on to his children. This is something quite over and above writing in an unconventional manner. His obsession with himself, paying a good dividend in certain respects, was a handicap in others, narrowing the sphere of vision. As regards the novel itself, one wishes the Brothel scene was done in the same manner as the Martello Tower. I feel certain Joyce simply found himself unable to bring that off, falling back *faute de mieux* on 'experimental' methods, not because those really gave a better picture. Perhaps it might be argued this stuck closer to the Ulysses myth.

It is interesting that H. G. Wells was one of Joyce's early supporters. I have never been able to get on with Wells, tho' George Orwell, an admirer, made me read (indeed gave me) *Love and Mr Lewisham* and several others. The other day, coming across *The World of William Clissold* (three vols, inherited from my father) I decided to have another try. This was not a success. Tedious ramblings about history, politics, economics, totally unconvincing characters. Wells had no idea whatever of the nature of human beings (a not uncommon failing in novelists), his conclusions on other subjects in *Clissold* have been invariably proved wrong by the passing of time. Wells, in fact, is all but unreadable, something certainly not to be said of Joyce, however limited his purview. I once told George Lyttelton at the Lit. Soc. that I had not been brought up on Wells and in fact could not read him, which George reported to Rupert Hart-Davis, who brushed it aside as obviously untrue.

Tuesday, 24 June

Virginia, down for the night to keep an eye on The Stables garden, to dinner. Spaghetti Carbonara (Arabella Boxer's recipe, always known simply as Arabella), Rubesco '79, nice Umbrian wine. Tristram she reported rather tired, back home from New York, where he has been for the Hitchcock film.

Friday, 27 June

Alison Lurie came to luncheon on the way to stay with Diana Melly in Wales. Diana Melly lives in a fortified tower between Abergavenny and Newport (Gwent), the fishing of which she sometimes lets. Alison was in good form. The next novel is to be about a famous writer (female, I think), now dead, complications of finding out facts about her life, cf. the case of Robert Lowell, whose only true love at least three ladies claimed to be; and the same Lowell poem found to have been sent to several different girls. Alison said the last play Harold Pinter produced by some young American was terrible stuff. It made her ashamed to be a member of the Democratic Party. Alison is now beginning to regret that she left Heinemann's as her friend (female) at Michael Joseph's has now moved on to another publisher, an endemic ailment of writers. Alison was very disparaging about the Moynihan portrait (certainly not at its best in reproduction).

Tuesday, 1 July

To London. Saw Sussman and added an inscription to his copy of *The Fisher King*, to the effect he had provided all the medical material there. On enquiry it turned out Sussman knew Hugh Montgomery-Massingberd's dental peer,

Lord Colwyn, who, if the only hereditary dental member of the House of Lords, is supported in that profession by Baroness Gardiner of Somewhere, a dentist, married to dentist, so urgent toothache in House of Lords is usually treatable on the spot in emergency. I bought postcards at the Medici Society in South Kensington, forgetting one of their shops off Bond Street, also some portraits at the Victoria & Albert nearby.

Wednesday, 2 July

The Thames & Hudson team, Jamie Camplin, Mrs Alla Weaver and Ian Sutton, to luncheon with a view to 'finalizing' what seems likely to be called *The Album of Anthony Powell's Dance to the Music of Time*. This rather a mouthful of a title, can in practice be abbreviated to *The Album*, in any case best to say exactly what the volume is. Ian Sutton, tall, fiftyish, rather inscrutable, was described by Jamie Camplin as 'the best writer of captions I know'. At first sight that designation may not sound a very dazzling qualification, but one saw immediately that in this particular case caption-writing would be a valuable, if not essential, ability.

I had taken the precaution of buying a brace of pork pies at Fortnum's, which we ate with salad, new potatoes, strawberries & cream, litre magnum of Trentino. I am keen for the French postcard *(The Acceptance World)* headed *Sex Appeal*, to be reproduced in *The Album*. I thought it had been mislaid, then found it stuck in end-papers of the book itself. This postcard is now being despatched to Thames & Hudson. Headway was made, I think, even if hard to judge what the final product will look like from individual mock-ups. Among other experiences, Mrs Weaver was taught English (which she speaks excellently) by Vladimir Nabokov, both of them refugees in Berlin after first war. [By a most regrettable oversight we forgot to include *The Omnipresent* in *The Album*, a framed copy of which was presented to me by picture-dealing fan. It hangs on the stairs to the top floor, therefore only seen occasionally.]

Sunday, 6 July

The Lukes to pre-luncheon drinks to meet the Stockwells. Peter Luke said his brother Mickie's association with Jennifer Fry/Heber-Percy/Ross has gone on about fifteen years, anyway to the extent that Mickie Luke, now separated from his wife (Alvilde Lees-Milne's Chaplin daughter) dines with Jennifer every Saturday. Striking example of tenacity. June Luke is playing Bella Cohen (Madame of the brothel) in a radio adaption of *Ulysses*, which comes on soon. I finished Ellmann's biography. One remains astonished at the amount of fuss Joyce managed to have made of himself, even allowing for being a remarkable personality, above all an accomplished performer (eg., when he stood on the table and sang the *Marseillaise* to several hundred French troops he found himself among in 1939/40; to be looked on as his chief, indeed sole, contribution to the war effort in two wars). Peter Luke, speaking of his own Dublin period with the Gate Theatre, remarked how dim they found Gogarty (Buck Mulligan in *Ulysses*) when they met; that was much my own impression in Dublin in 1934 (during the week after staying at Pakenham). He was undistinguished to a degree, grumpy, two foot high, tho' admittedly I only saw him for about ten minutes.

On the recommendation of Hugh Massingberd (I felt Hugh would be reliable on that question) I bought paperback of *Money* by Martin Amis, out a year or two ago. I greatly dislike the earlier novels of Martin's I have already read. Hugh was right. *Money* is not at all bad in its genre; true, not my favourite one, showing remarkable powers of keeping up a style for 400pp or so. Apart from his taste for Nabokov's novels (I thought *Lolita* appallingly third-rate tinsel stuff) Martin is on the whole a goodish critic. I sent him a mildly pornographic fan-postcard (Maclean Gallery's Erotic Show), a naked lady playing with herself, in keeping with *Money*'s subject matter. When Alison Lurie was here she saw *Money* lying on the table and said: 'That's really rather good. I hated Martin Amis's previous novels.' Just what I feel.

Wednesday, 9 July

V to London to see a character called Jeffrey Spence (writes books about railways), and said to be working on a biography of E. M. Delafield. V's object was to find out exactly the existing situation in that field. Roland Gant rang in afternoon. He talked for long time about his own plans and publishers' gossip. He & Nadia have sold the house in Napier Road, Earls Court (news of the completion of sale came through this morning), and bought a house in the neighbourhood of Draguignon, South of France, thirty miles in from Saint Maxime, 2000 feet up. It was built about fifteen years ago by retired Captain RN, small, with a studio, not in the village, the country somewhat Alpine, with a brook and poplars. The Gants are leaving London almost immediately. I heard all this with a distinct pang. Roland has done so much for my professional life during the last few years, it is difficult to contemplate publishing without him. He works with complete disregard for trouble to himself, a publisher in a million.

Pondering on recent Joyce rereadings, three potential Joycean items seem to have been unused by him (1) Norah Joyce, née Barnacle, Joyce's friend

Italo Svevo (author of *Confessions of Zeno*, possibly to some extent model for Bloom), in everyday life Trieste businessman called Schmitz, whose firm produced solution to keep barnacles off ships' hulls; (2) Norah Joyce, like The Owl invoked by Ophelia in *Hamlet*, a baker's daughter – discuss; (3) Joyce had a row with a former Irish friend named Judge Michael Lennon. Joyce, contemplating a visit to Ireland, wrote of certain area that it was to be avoided as marked on map *Hic sunt Lennones* – 'Here are Lennons'.

Monday, *14 July*

Mr Millard, builder, came to discuss repairing the wall leading down to the basement back-entrance, details as where to place skip, etc. He was followed by Mr Joyce, of Cooper & Tanner, with report on capacity of the lake. I am relieved to hear this has now worked out as something below the amount required for annual inspection. The previous estimate had been on the safe side for size specified, but now modified by Humphries's opinion. In any case, area of lake lessens every year on account of natural processes. I informed Mr Greenfield of the Somerset County Council that the lake was below the capacity defined for a piece of water specified under the Reservoir Act, writing a letter to confirm what I said on telephone. I hope this will settle matters.

Tuesday, *15 July*

To London. Lunched at The Travellers. I spoke with Martin Kenyon who when quite young used to sit on one of Club's committees with me years ago. He said he was now a neighbour of Tristram and Virginia, sending his daughter to the same school as Georgia, because he & his wife so much approved of her. He is, or was, on the Baltic Exchange, which always sounds romantic, but I think merely deals with marine insurance. Stewingly hot in London. Returned feeling extremely tired. I was driven from Westbury by Judy, the lady of the milk-round. I had not seen her in daylight. She slightly resembles the late Beatrice 'Bumble' Dawson, stage designer and friend of my youth; perhaps a female career type.

Wednesday, *16 July*

The telephone rang at 7.30 am. V said it was Peter (not, as previously supposed Keith) Green, ringing from Cambridge, England, not Cambridge, Massachusetts, the imbecile who rang about month ago supposedly from the US. I asked what the hell he meant by ringing at this hour, at which he seemed surprised, said he would call later, I hung up. Lees Mayall rang in the evening asking if we could lunch with them, Arthur & Mary Duckworth being the other guests. We have not met the Duckworths for ages, visions of being asked to Orchardleigh and returning invitation with other commitments caused us to excuse ourselves. Lees is always good about that sort of thing, both asking the Duckworths, and not minding nor surprised when one opts out.

He told a fantastic story about their son Robert. Robert recently set up on his own in a bookshop in Cecil Court. Going through a parcel of newly bought secondhand books, a postcard fell out of one of them. The postcard was addressed to Robin McDouall (dcd), formerly Secretary of The Travellers Club, dated 1980 or 1981, signed 'Tony', at once recognized as from me by Robert Mayall. After a message or greeting, it added: 'Don't you think the couple overleaf look like Lees & Mary?' The picture on the postcard was by Picasso (which I don't remember, nor whether posted here or abroad). This was about the year we went on an Hellenic cruise to France/Portugal/Spain, and visited the Picasso Museum at Barcelona, where a lot of cards were acquired. The points of coincidence are almost too many to enumerate. If despatched from The Chantry, a bright bookseller might have recognized the signature, plus address. Mention of Lees & Mary confronting their own son was a little startling. I am somewhat perturbed at what the picture may be like, tho' Lees assures me it is very flattering. Not for the first time the incident confutes those who claim the coincidences in *Dance* are overdone, and unlike real life. Archie has four school friends staying for couple of nights at The Stables.

Thursday, 17 July

A photographer, Granville Davies, with young assistant, Jim McCue, came in afternoon, Davies, bearded, fiftyish, said the National Portrait Gallery kept copies of his portraits in its archive. Both were reasonably agreeable, brought copies of books for me to sign, also *Iron Aspidistra*. They would not reveal how they obtained the last. Davies told me Philip Larkin replied to a request to photograph him by saying his charge for a sitting was £50. Davies called Larkin's bluff by sending a cheque for that amount, Larkin, recognizing his leg was being pulled, returned the cheque, but still refused to be photographed. That was bad, I think. He ought to have sent it back and allowed him to photograph him. It was perhaps two years before Larkin died, so he may have been feeling rotten. As it happens, there is a piece in the paper this morning saying Larkin left instructions for all his MSS to be destroyed, Will worth about £280,000. This seems rather a lot, but no doubt includes his flat, accommodation always having to be taken into consideration for largish sums these days. I think Monica got something, then RSPCA, Authors' Society.

A curious footnote to the Robert Mayall postcard story above, additionally coincidental, that the young photographic assistant McCue normally works in Bertram Rota's bookshop, indeed took Robert Mayall's place there. He knows Robert, and said his bookshop in Cecil Court deals only in extremely expensive books. Robert sells one for several thousand pounds, then no business for three weeks.

After tea Archie and his four guests came up to the house: Daniel Barraclough, Tom Nicholls, Richard Evans (all of whom have been here before), and Justin Abbott. They seemed nice boys, they wanted to look up in Collins' Dictionary the definition of 'working class', also asked about Dadaism, a subject upon which we have several works.

Wednesday, 23 July

V and I watched on TV the wedding of Prince Andrew & Miss Sarah Ferguson, now Duke & Duchess of York. Unusually good show. The bride's father, Major Ronald Ferguson, late The Life Guards, had braid piping on his tailcoat. As he is not old enough for this to have been a normal fashion for tailcoats (Goodhart, for instance, had it on his) one presumes him still wearing coat he had at Eton when in Pop, braid being a Pop privilege. It would be interesting to check this.

Thursday, 24 July

I had treatment for creaking joints by Mrs Gould this morning. Later in the day a *Daily Telegraph* secretary rang to say that Max Hastings (recently appointed Editor) had sent something by express method called Red Star (ie. by train) to reach me as soon as possible. Max Hastings the son of Anne Lancaster by one of her earlier husbands, Macdonald Hastings, prototypical journalist in his day, who did a lot of eagle-watching. I could not imagine what this urgent communication might be, which V very sweetly went into Frome to collect from the afternoon train. It turned out that a paragraph in *Private Eye* said I was to be asked to stand down from being chief reviewer for the *DT*, as Bron Waugh himself was to take that over. Max Hastings wanted to make it abundantly clear, with the least possible delay, that nothing of the sort was in the air. On the contrary, he said, he hoped I should review for *DT* until the age of at least a hundred. He added, no doubt with truth, this was all part of the *Private Eye* campaign against himself, going on since The Falklands War, in which Max Hastings, a notable war-correspondent, thereby provoking professional jealousy, especially among the seedy crew who write for *Private Eye*.

Friday, 25 July

I telephoned Max Hastings at the *DT* to thank him for taking so much trouble to deny the *Private Eye* smear. He said he had immediately got into touch with Bron Waugh on reading paragraph, who alleged Richard Ingrams (recently retired from editing *Private Eye*) put it in. Max Hastings then rang Ingrams ('Who worships the ground you walk on, as we all do,' this somewhat hyperbolic phrase covering Ingrams having apparently gone so far as to say he thought me among the better reviewers) . . .

   In the afternoon arrived a girl looking for a location for a TV film of *Northanger Abbey*. Summoned V as the Jane Austen expert, who grilled the girl, then decided she was all right so we allowed her to look round. She afterwards said her Director (Giles Foster) might be interested. On consideration, with camera crew activities in August, I don't want another disruption on the premises for the moment.

Saturday, 26 July

Driven by John, we lunched with Roy and Jennifer Jenkins at St Amand's House, East Hendred, about two hours run, rather more than usual for our luncheon range these days. About halfway there I began to wonder whether acceptance had been wise. In the end, however, the party was enjoyable. Guests: Michael Howard, now Regius Professor of Modern History at Oxford; Ludovic Kennedy & wife (neither met before), she the dancer Moira Shearer; Laura Grimond, unaccompanied by Jo (at the moment recovering from illness); Sarah Morrison (also unmet), née Long, daughter of Laura Charteris/Marlborough, wife of Tory MP, whom as it happens I sat next to in Pratt's towards end of last year, and we talked of Reservoir Act. V believes them now separated. I was first put next to Mrs Morrison, who was then moved by our hostess almost immediately to the other side of the table, so I did not talk to her at all.

   Her replacement, Moira Shearer, is pretty and reasonably bright. Curiously at that moment I did not know about her former dancing and stage career, being informed later by V. She must have danced somewhat after our chief Ballet period, tho' no doubt one has seen her on the stage at one time or another. The Kennedys have a son, now Gurkha officer (which he greatly likes), and three daughters. Ludovic Kennedy, a tremendous BBC type, was once never off the screen. He is quite agreeable as such types go, if full of every known 'liberal' cliché.

Michael Howard (a *Dance* fan, didn't like *Infants*) we have often met; rather an odd fish in whom traces of the Bowra manner remain. He complained that, having been made Regius Professor, the implication being he was quite good at History, he is now so overwhelmed by administrative duties that he has no time to write a book. He spends his days handing out money for various forms of scholarship, which has its amusing side, but keeps him away from real work. He talked about the return of the Anti-Soviet Russians and Anti-Tito Jugoslavs. I could not feel more strongly about deploring the horror of these negotiations, at same time it is impossible not to appreciate the difficulties at the moment of it all happening; not least because Russian units fighting on the side of the Germans seem to have been (in the manner of our Russian allies) among the worst disciplined, most badly behaved, of our opponents. In any case, what was to be done with them?

Michael Howard, who had been in the midst of all this, said there were two quite separate problems; first, personnel in German uniforms travelling round with womenfolk, and carts of belongings, who talked Russian, regarding whom, in the general muddle of everything going on, it seemed best for the Russian authorities to deal with as we had plenty of problems of our own: secondly, Cossacks, in which case an officer with huge moustaches, high fur cap, would say: 'I wish to be taken before your Colonel.' That being done, would announce: 'I wish to put my unit at your disposal to continue the fight against Communism.' Reactions of an overworked Colonel (in Michael Howard's case Coldstream Guards), probably at that moment shaving, to reply: 'Fuck off.'

Laura Grimond suggested such Russians might have been handled in same way as other 'displaced persons', a recognized category of the period. Anyone who has experienced even non-operational muddle of army in the field can understand what appalling problems a million of such Russians raised, not to mention the Jugs. Also now forgotten is all the pro-Soviet, pro-Stalin, propaganda to which Great Britain had been subjected since the Germans invaded Russia, most of all the Army, to whom ABCA (which contained many card-holding Communists among those who produced it) issued supposedly 'educational' pamphlets of this kind. Besides, these Russians were, after all, fighting for Hitler, all he stood for, wanted our defeat. In short there was a decidedly different 'climate' from what prevails now, everyone knowing about the Gulag, etc.

Michael Howard remarked with truth that one must realize that in Eastern

Europe the second war (as, in fact, the first) was looked on purely in terms of settling local political arrangements. This is never understood by people who waffle about war being avoidable in 1914. They cannot understand that in Eastern Europe most of the Austro-Hungarian minorities *wanted* war in order that they should become independent. One cannot blame Mihailovitch, for instance, for trying to keep troops in reserve for later combating Communism, even if, for us, defeating Germany came first. Unless you are a Communist, there are good enough reasons for fighting it; active doubts remaining whether backing Tito was wise. Michael Howard said he thought there might have been a brief moment when Montgomery had a chance to push forward to Berlin, even if that was uncertain, possibly never feasible.

There is much here of the first war, people in this country saying it was 'unnecessary', when nothing any government had done would have kept us out in the light of what was desired in Eastern Europe. For that matter people go on saying the same thing even more about the Crimean War, but that probably kept Russia from annexing Constantinople, which would have been most undesirable in the light of later history. Roy Jenkins (who recently emerged from hospital which probably explained why Jennifer looked rather worried) seemed in excellent form. Both Jenkinses take a real interest in books, something rare in political circles of either side. In fact Roy, holding open the door of our car when we were leaving, seemed unwilling ever to stop discussing his reread of Painter's *Proust*, no doubt starved of such talk. At luncheon were really excellent magnums of Château Haut-Bages-Libéral '76, which Roy said he hoped I should be able to drink in spite of it being Liberal. Enjoyable party.

Sunday, 27 July

The imbecile who rings from time to time saying what a fan he is, did so again about 8.30 am. I told him if he had anything to get off his chest about my books to write a letter. Now I realize the call at 6 am saying he was in the US was pure fantasy on his part. The Stockwells, at The Stables, came to pre-luncheon drinks. Georgia & Archie were immensely amused by the impending visit for luncheon of Miss Nancy Cutbirth, who runs The Anthony Powell Society of Kalamazoo, Michigan. I don't think I have ever seen them laugh so much. [Mad fan who rings up at strange hours wrote a letter, to which I replied. He rang again once or twice, when fortunately someone else answered, and told him I was not available, except on one occasion. Then I asked why he did not consult a psychiatrist. He said he had. Told him to do so again. He has now faded away, I hope for good.]

Tuesday, 29 July

Osbert Lancaster's death was announced on the news. This was not altogether unexpected, as Michael Howard, who, like the Lancasters, has a cottage in the Newbury area, said at the Roy Jenkins party that Osbert had suffered another stroke about three weeks before. When we came home V had rung Anne Lancaster, who reported Osbert unable to speak. The past few years must have been peculiarly awful for someone who existed entirely within his own work and as an extension of that going about meeting people, for which Osbert possessed a boundless appetite. I don't think I have ever known anyone with quite such a universal passion for parties. Before Karen died we were dining on one occasion *à quatre* with the Lancasters, Osbert restless whole evening because he had received invitation to the Italian Institute for evening reception, than which one can think of few entertainments less likely to be socially intoxicating.

Karen rarely wanted to go anywhere (Anne, curiously enough, to some extent shares her predecessor's lack of enthusiasm for unabated social life). Osbert (for whom I wrote an obituary memoir in the *Daily Telegraph*) had so formalized his appearance, public – indeed private – personality, manner of speech, that it is difficult to know what lay behind the stylized façade. Perhaps there was not a great deal more than what was revealed. He possessed strong feelings about the Arts and Architecture (in all of which he performed), his taste, one would say, good, if not impeccable; sometimes a bit odd about books. He boomed away in the Bowra manner (often literally, Maurice having been great influence). Osbert was not a very good listener, nor in learning from others, possessing his own irrevocably established views on every subject. These worked on the whole pretty well, if not in a specially subtle manner.

Many of Osbert's jokes were first-rate, altogether original, but he became a shade repetitive as he grew older. He was kindly, tolerant on the whole of different sorts of people (he greatly detested Cyril Connolly, I never quite knew why so violently), liked smart invitations while never making fetish of them, preferring a High Bohemian world, the routines of Fleet Street always in background of his mind. He would have loved his two children – anyway in early life – to have lived conventional upper-class young persons' 'lives'; Cara as a deb, William, a young man about town. This turned out the last thing on earth either wanted, nor were in the least cut out for.

Osbert's first wife, Karen, was a daughter of Sir Austin Harris. His wife Cara was a startlingly odd mother-in-law to have. Sir Austin in his own way was pretty odd too. Karen was devoted to Osbert, but had poor health, used to grumble a lot and bawl him out. Anne, strangely enough, did that too. Oxford, his life as a young man (which ended quickly owing to an unusually early marriage) meant everything to Osbert. I remember, at a dance given by the Evelyn Waughs with two other hosts for their respective daughters in 1950s, Osbert, then only in his middle forties, exclaiming: 'Oh! Oh! Oh! to be young again!', sentiments I far from shared (or indeed share to this day). Osbert felt passionately about lost youth.

From time to time he moved in quite a smart world, remaining totally untouched by anything resembling Evelyn Waugh's illusion of being a nobleman of the Old School. Osbert's mind was too satirical, too practical, for such self-deception, also too politically oriented (less to the Right than might be supposed). He was said (by Pam Berry, not the most reliable of sources) to have a lot of affairs with secretaries, of which I never came across any traces. Anne profoundly shared Osbert's Fleet Street interests, holding that curious belief all professional journalists seem finally to develop that Fleet Street life, its convictions and pronouncements, are of universal interest, application, and truth, in spite of overwhelming evidence to the contrary. Anne's distaste for meeting extraneous people was illustrated by making a great fuss when staying here because she was put next to perfectly amiable retired General at dinner with the Duckworths at Orchardleigh. Nonetheless Anne was marvellously good during Osbert's last unhappy years, when he was deaf, not making much sense, chronically bad-tempered. Indeed she was absolutely saintly, never leaving the flat, looking after him twenty-four hours a day, with – so far as one could see – little or no thanks, only perpetual grousing.

As with certain other individuals who have come one's way, I always felt there was something about Osbert's background which remained unrevealed. His appearance (for instance those deep facial pock-marks) suggested exotic blood of some kind, such as Near Eastern, Turkish perhaps. I shall miss him greatly, tho' he began to move out of my life inevitably when he fell into decline, brought on apparently by two minor operations going wrong; all perhaps exacerbated by some lack of inner life, everything important seeming somehow on the surface. This may be a wholly inept judgement. Although expected, his death upset me. I was very attached to him.

About midday Nancy Cutbirth, organizer of Kalamazoo Anthony Powell Society, arrived for luncheon. She had been on a botanical tour of England, which seems to have been only a moderate success. She was more 'Western' (as Bill Davis used to typify some of his countrymen) than I expected, middle forties, big, hair centrally parted, then brought round to nape of the neck. This gave a somewhat 'Red Indian' touch, rather increased by huge earrings of geometric design. I was at once reminded of Lady Archer-Shee, probably the first individual of American birth (rather grand, I think, in American terms) I ever set eyes on, wife of Sir Martin Archer-Shee, commanding one of the battalions of the brigade stationed round Codford in Wiltshire, to which my father was Brigade Major in 1916.

We lived then for the moment in Boynton Cottage, Dower House of Boynton Manor, where the large family of Archer-Shees were quartered. V and I often pass the house now on way to the Hobsons. At another house of the Archer-Shees (possibly Virginia Water) I first saw the four volumes of *Battles and Leaders of the Civil War*, which, for some reason, at once fascinated me, interest in the War between the States having never entirely departed from me. Nancy Cutbirth, although at South Michigan University (20,000 or more undergraduates), comes from Texas on both sides of her family, tracing back to the 18th century, which (she said) usually means an ancestor transported. (Her name, of course, is merely a form of Cuthbert.) Her special subject in the English Department is the poet Spenser. She is jolly, keen on cats, of which she has a least half-a-dozen, Trelawney for once made himself reasonably agreeable. We went down to The Stables in afternoon. I was amused to see how easily Nancy Cutbirth got on terms with Georgia & Archie. V and I both rather exhausted at end of the day, if a pleasant one.

Wednesday, 30 July

Treatment by Mrs Gould. I was put under machine until buzzer sounds, rather like boiling an egg. Bruce Hunter reports that *The Fisher King* is one of books included in the 'annual presentation' to HM at Balmoral for her holiday reading. Its opening sentence perhaps a bit dispiriting for royalty ['Exile is the wound of kingship']. Tristram and Virginia to dinner. We drank a magnum of Gruaud Larose '76 (from Grey Gowrie for my Eightieth), very good, if not quite so lively as the Haut-Bages-Libéral magnum of the same year produced at the Roy Jenkins luncheon. V thought just the reverse. She sat at the other end of the table with a different Jenkins magnum. There is always tremendous variation in individual bottles.

Tuesday, 5 August

Mr Mosley did not turn up with new car as arranged. About 6.30 pm Larry Kart, of the *Chicago Tribune*, (interviewed me intelligently by telephone some months ago for my Eightieth) rang to say he is doing *The Fisher King*, and wanted to read aloud what he had written. It sounded admirable, which was cheering, as the US trade paper was rather fatuous in advance notice. The telephone rang in middle of night, which V at once marked down as maniac of previous calls, so when voice asked: 'Is that Deutschland?' she replied 'Wrong number', hung up, disregarding possibility of Gerard Manley Hopkins's ghost.

Wednesday, 6 August

Treatment by Mrs Gould. She told me her husband conducted when the BBC did *Songs of Praise* (TV Sunday programme of various different church services) at St John's, Frome, all her children were in the band; Mr Manley (formerly at The Lodge here, now lives in Nunney) was also in the programme.

Thursday, 7 August

After several false starts during the last two or three days, Mr Mosley finally arrived with the new car, which we took over. I am glad to say it seems almost identical with last Maestro. Roland Gant rang in evening. He is now installed in their new French house. This seems satisfactory apart from routine initiatory troubles with all new houses.

Saturday, 9 August

About 6.30 pm a bearded Austrian with his girlfriend in shorts, knocked on the front door. He said a friend of his was writing a thesis on my work, could he take photograph of the house, which friend had asked him to do. Permission granted. Reread Rupert Hart-Davis's *Hugh Walpole*, which remains as amusing as ever. I rather regret never having met Walpole, tho' no doubt in earlier, more austere, days would have regarded him as a ludicrous literary figure. To some extent Walpole certainly was absurd, pouring out a flow of rubbish, as he himself was in part prepared to recognize. At same time his *Diary* shows a real ability for self-analysis, his mind infinitely more interesting than, say, his friend and contemporary bestseller, J. B. Priestley, whose mind was of stupefying banality. *Mr Perrin and Mr Traill* no doubt Walpole's best book, which I reread some years ago. It did not hold up well. Walpole belongs somewhat to the Dennis Wheatley category (represented by Beals in *The Fisher King*), of relatively intelligent men who write more or less conscious drivel.

Tuesday, 12 August

Saw Sussman, who wants another visit in October. He said then he will have no more territorial claims. I lunched with Evangeline Bruce in Albany.

Guests: John Wells, Janet Stone, much cheered, and smartened up, since last seen at the Lees-Milnes', probably due to getting K. Clark out of her hair, going to live at Salisbury, which she likes; Ludovic Kennedy (recently met at the Roy Jenkinses). Kennedy said he spent six years in Royal Navy without ever having heard it called The Andrew (characteristic ignorance of a publicist of his particular kind); Harriet Crawley, daughter of Aidan and Virginia (née Cowles), jolly girl in her middle-thirties, going to stand against Ken Livingstone (publicity-seeking Left Wing local government boss in South London) as parliamentary candidate in next election.

She was impressed by my pointing out that Fascism had begun, in essentials remained, a party of the Left, altogether opposed to traditions of British Toryism. She asked me to come and help her in the election. Evangeline was in good form. She manages to be unique in striking a balance of demeanour, neither wholly American nor wholly British, a subtle mixture of two, outwardly more American, with much that is instinctively English (rather than British). Excellent Gewürztraminer (failed to get year), and stunning Lynch-Bages '66, both given Evangeline by Nicko Henderson. Her Albany dining-room was the Melbournes' bedroom. They had twin beds. Afterwards I looked into Hatchard's and bought the paperback of Mario Vargas Llosa's novel about a military school in Peru.

Saturday, 16 August

I reread Anthony Burgess's *Malayan Trilogy*, three loosely linked novels enjoyed sufficiently on first round to write Burgess a fan letter. This time they made less impression. Burgess is undoubtedly talented, has great energy, a genuine feeling for words, in which he is keenly interested. Occasionally he uses an obscure term that has to be looked up in the dictionary, a practice I approve, if employed aptly. The trilogy gives a convincing picture of what Malaya was like at the period of handing over from British rule. There are amusing scenes; at same time no particular thread holding the narrative together, except for Crabbe, its anti-hero. The characterization is on the whole thin, except for Crabbe's second wife, Fenella (who leaves him). Fenella comes across. One feels a shade suspicious (technically speaking) of events seen through the eyes of Asian characters (of whom there are many). These are represented as having processes of thought in no way different from the British, or, rather, thinking as British suppose Asians to think. I have a similar objection to male/female writers describing thoughts of the opposite sex. Both techniques may sometimes seem to work all right, but always risk being utterly wrong.

Nonetheless I am inclined to rate *Malayan Trilogy* as best of the Burgess novels. *Earthly Powers* contains undoubted *tours de force* (the clerical brother, for instance), but never quite comes off, in fact on balance more often than not the book is boring. Burgess is almost always an entertaining reviewer, according to himself he should be regarded principally as a composer of music. Something – possibly this musical side, possibly the RC Church (cf. Waugh, Greene, etc) – seems to inhibit free play of character, perhaps just inability to control the writer's own ego; one of the novelist's most essential needs.

Monday, 18 August

I reviewed the late William Empson's *Shakespearian Essays*. These are enjoyable. Empson's earliest claim to fame as young (Wykehamist) don at Magdalene, Cambridge, was being reported by his gyp for having a french letter in a drawer to the Master of the College, then A. B. Ramsay (The Ram), former Lower Master at Eton. The Ram was a somewhat ludicrous figure of great pomposity, who made no secret of enjoying birching Lower Boys which was one of his functions. The gyp's behaviour seems extraordinary, even at that period, and, in manner of all farcical situations, at once began to build up. The Ram, having never seen or heard of a french letter, commented later that 'it seemed to be a machine for aiding self-abuse', masturbation no doubt only sexual relief The Ram himself had ever practised. The upshot was that Empson accordingly lost his job at Cambridge (the other Magdalene dons being presumably as naive as Ramsay), subsequently spending most of his academic career in China.

Empson greatly pleased me once by referring in an article to some character (Templer, I think) in *Dance*, without mentioning the book, as if every literate person would be familiar with the passage. Not so many years ago, meeting Empson at a party, I was able to express my satisfaction, also to confirm the french-letter story as perfectly true in essential. In *Shakespearian Essays*, as an amusing if perverse critic, he puts forward the convincing view that Polonius and his son Laertes were intriguing for Ophelia to marry Hamlet, therefore did not want her to sleep with the Prince, as that could easily prevent bringing off the marriage. Also it is Empson's view that Macbeth was already planning the murder of Duncan when witches were first encountered (which would make no more than effective mind-reading necessary).

Finished Mario Vargas Llosa's *The Time of the Hero* (in Spanish *The City and the Dogs*, first-year cadets at Lima Military School being called Dogs, a much better title, typical piece of US publishers' ineptitude). The translation is intensely North American in tone, perhaps not altogether unsuitable for subject; indeed one would like to know from a Spaniard or Portuguese to what extent Latin American speech and behaviour compares with North American vis-à-vis British. The plot, as such, more substantial than usual in novels of this genre, eventually falls a shade flat after its earlier tensions, the general atmosphere always remaining lively. One would suspect this is likely to remain Vargas Llosa's best book; one of those novels stemming from intensely felt personal experience in early life, tho' it must be admitted that Musil brought off *The Man Without Qualities* after writing *Young Torless*, the latter book very comparable with the Peruvian novel, if more delicately handled.

The scene of *Torless* is also a Military School in Austria, but unlike most novels of this kind it is seen from the point of view of the bullies rather than the bullied. At the Bulgarian Literary Conference, which I attended in 1977, Peter Elstob, Secretary of PEN, made me promise to read Mario Vargas Llosa, whom Elstob thought exceptionally good. I failed to do that at first owing to the London Library cataloguing name under Vargas rather than Llosa (correctly, owing to Continental double-barrel taking different form to ours, in that what might be called tacked-on name is put last, rather than first, eg., Saumarez-Smith rather than 'Smith, Saumarez-' (tho', in fact, John does not hyphenate his name). In due course I got hold of a Vargas Llosa novel about establishing a military brothel up the Amazon, which I did not care for, not a patch on the Military School. I wish I had read the latter when I met Vargas Llosa at Hugh Thomas's dinner party for Mrs Thatcher. I should like to have discussed the book with him. In the novel a General, giving pep talk to cadets, says: 'I hope you will all behave like Peruvians.' This makes one laugh, but I suppose is perfectly reasonable in Peru.

Wednesday, 20 August

The Foreign Office (David Dain, head of the Eastern Department) rang, saying our Ambassador in Luxembourg (Oliver Miles) had asked if I would consider delivering The Churchill Lecture in Luxembourg. Previous lecturers were Quintin Hailsham, and Michael Howard. I gave a polite refusal, tho' I would have rather liked to see Luxembourg after dealing with its military affairs during the war. The writing of the lecture and general upheaval would have been too onerous.

Friday, 22 August

Some time ago an American film producer called Gary Conklin asked for a TV interview on 'British Writers Between the Wars', to which I agreed, as Paul

Fussell was to do interviewing. Conklin, who came today, so it appears, was given a large grant to make this series, over which he had already taken several years. He turned up about 12.30, with his daughter Alexis, Paul Fussell and Paul Fussell's girlfriend. So I sent them straight off to Mells to lunch at The Talbot, where they also wanted to photograph Raymond Asquith/Edward Horner memorials and Siegfried Sassoon's grave in churchyard, about all of which I had written in my Memoirs; also on account of Paul Fussell's interest in the first war. Conklin seemed reasonably agreeable, rather filmstar-like himself. He said he was married to a Latin American, his daughter was pretty, young, operating Sound for film, Conklin himself handling the movie camera, doing so in manner suggesting he had never seen one before. In earlier negotiations Conklin only spoke of 'Mr Fussell's friend', so V and I had one of our increasingly frequent discussions as to what sex the friend would turn out to be, V was correct in guessing female, I mildly plumping for male on grounds of a more likely adjunct to filming, in which the girlfriend played, in fact, no part.

She was called Harriet Berringer, a plump, jolly blonde of mature age, of whom V (who saw most of her during visit) gave a favourable account. She had four children by a previous husband unspecified, and had run a children's magazine. In this a picture of a leopard was accidentally captioned as a tiger which evoked two-hundred-and-fifty letters of complaint. Fussell himself I met a long time ago with Kingsley Amis at a Bertorelli luncheon, where I used occasionally to appear. Then again, with his wife Betty, on the France/Portugal/Spain Hellenic cruise. After this cruise both the Amises & Fussells parted company with their respective spouses.

Paul is now at University of Philadelphia which he likes. He is an odd chap, especially in his concern for military matters, unusual in most Americans one meets, tho' one now recalls Fred Morgan of *The Hudson Review* saying his father was keen on the army; Bill Robinson also liking to talk of his experiences during the war. Paul Fussell was an infantry officer (badly wounded), and regards American lack of 'sense of regiment' as national deficiency (Bob Conquest says this does not apply in the US to what with us would be Territorials). These are well observed in Paul's book *The Great War in Modern Memory* (though it is not put together with much facility). Paul notes manner that, until this day in England, names, and units, appear in the *In Memoriam* column of newspapers.

The filming party did not get back from Mells until 3 pm. Having someone I knew asking the inevitably banal questions makes that more tolerable (in fact I should probably have refused an interview had not a friend been in question), tho' it becomes increasingly hard, in fact really impossible, to describe one's past life – especially young married life – in relation to other persons of one's generation who have survived. Clichés by this time encumber the ground so much when, in fact, generalization often nowhere near the truth. Paul Fussell & Harriet Berringer were afterwards catching a train at Bristol to stay for couple of nights at an hotel in Swansea to see Kingsley Amis, now checking up on material for his new novel. Kingsley has an affection for the town anyway.

Thinking over this question of generalizations to which one is reduced trying to recall earlier days, struck me, as I happen to be rereading Robert Gittings's biography (well done) of Keats, that what is said there of Keats himself, his friends, their daily life, would no doubt sound as grotesque to the Poet, or any of his mileu, as does the picture people now have of the 1920s/1930s. Gittings referring to Keats's friends, draws apt parallel with middle-to-lower-middle-class young men described in the novels of Dickens, probably as true a record of those times as exists at that particular social level. It is one to some extent touched on by Surtees, tho' Surtees usually deals with slightly older, richer, individuals, such as Mr Sponge and Facey Romford.

Sunday, 24 August

The Stockwells at The Stables. They had enjoyable time in Tuscany, where Georgia remains for day or two. Archie came to tea. He said: 'I've just started *The Fisher King*.' I surprised myself by feeling an odd kind of thrill at his mentioning that.

Sunday, 31 August

Driven by John, we lunched with Anthony & Tanya Hobson at The Glebe House, Whitsbury. William & Charlotte Hobson were there, the former has just got a First in Greats. Staying in house was Anne Chisholm, now married (second wife) to Michael Davie, columnist, who edited the Waugh *Diaries*. Anne Chisholm (one of group who lived in Gunter Grove during Tristram's early London days) is a successful journalist like her husband. She wrote a book about Nancy Cunard (not yet come my way), now 'reads' for Jonathan Cape, a job she says she likes. She is easy to talk to. Michael Davie explained how quite by chance he edited the Waugh *Diaries*. The *Diaries* came into the *Observer* office handwritten, generally in a frightful mess, with the possibility of serialisation. Davie was told to look through them. Having spent a certain amount of time in deciphering them (rather like Shadbold in *O, How the Wheel Becomes It!*) it seemed easiest that he should now do the editing. He had no special interest in Evelyn Waugh at the time, tho' I believe he later developed rather an obsession about him and his life. Considering all that, the Waugh *Diaries* might have been edited worse, apart from the lamentably inadequate index: a good index is absolutely essential for that sort of document. After talking about all this with Michael Davie, I thought I might have another look at the *Diaries* myself.

The Hobsons recently went on an Hellenic cruise, which included Lebanon, with Selina Hastings and Elizabeth Jane Howard (late Amis). Doing a trip to Petra, when you have horses led by Arabs to go through mountain pass, Selina, Jane, another woman, were in front of this cavalcade. Anthony, who speaks a little Arabic, was talking to the Arab leading his horse. As they approached the 'rose-red city', the Arab said: 'Two of your wives have gone on ahead.'

Tanya Hobson attended Hermione Baddeley's funeral at Wilsford Church, where Hermione was interred beside her first husband, David Tennant (other spouses having occurred later in both cases). Nobody particularly notable turned up from the theatrical world, as might have been expected. After all, Hermione was quite a figure there in her day. It was mostly producers and dressers, rather surprisingly. One of the hymns, *All Things Bright and Beautiful*, included the verse the 'Rich man in his castle/Poor man at his gate/ God made them high and lowly/And ordered their estate', at the insistence of Pauline Rumbold, Hermione's daughter. Superb Château Gruaud Larose '71. Anthony lent me his translation of an Italian novel he liked *The Tartar Steppe*, which sounds rather like unusual TV film V and I enjoyed not so long ago.

Tuesday, 2 September

V went to London to lunch with her sister Pansy, do research on E. M. Delafield, tea with Anne Lancaster. Peter Mumford, of Oliver & Lang Brown came to inspect the cutleaf beech on the corner of the drive in Paddock Field. This I thought looked rather dead, but Mumford reported all right for another year or two, good news. Mumford went down to lake, where he says several trees must come down. He agreed sand or gravel would never remain in the hollow place under a tree on the steep slope down to the Water Garden as recommended by the engineer Humphries. Anyway he thinks a tree ought to be felled as dangerous (whatever Humphries's advice that it should remain), which can be done (to some extent implementing that advice) by felling in such a way that it sprouts again.

Wednesday, 3 September

V and I lunched with the Lukes at short notice instead of drinks there in the evening. The latter disturbs V's writing time, anyway I no longer much care for it myself, as only drinking my quarter bottle glass of wine at dinner. A friend of Peter Luke's, Fitzroy Fletcher, his Eton contemporary, came over from Castle Cary. Fletcher spent war as PoW, being captured early on. He described himself as retired from Ministry of Defence, and appears to have been attached to various embassies at one time or another, so that I presumed that (like almost everyone else one knows) he was formerly in MI6. He brought a book of mine to sign. It now appears that June Luke is half Irish, half Brazilian. Manzanilla; followed by white wine from Whatley vineyard a mile away run by Witts (not too bad): a rather special red Rioja. Drinking at a luncheon does not suit me these days (nor for that matter more than at most half bottle at night). I slept abominably in consequence.

Friday, 5 September

A fan letter about *The Fisher King* from Jennifer Plowman, Headmistress of a girls' school in Bromley. She said she herself was author (in collaboration) of a biography of W. E. Johns, the creator of the Biggles books, and asked if I would like a copy. I replied yes. [Turned out by no means without interest. At one moment Johns was Recruiting Officer for the RAF (Quarters at 4 Henrietta Street, next to Duckworth's former office in Covent Garden), where he first saw, and turned down, T. E. Lawrence for RAF, when trying to join. An amusing disparity between what actually happened on that occasion and Lawrence's account of it. Lawrence was, of course a fantastic liar.] In middle 1960s the Biggles books were 29th most translated literary works in the world, the top juvenile. The only country where they did not sell was the US. Interesting. The same true of the very widely translated Dennis Wheatley, on whom Valentine Beals in *The Fisher King* is slightly modelled, in so far as Beals is an intelligent man who writes absurd historical romances, not of course in any other respect.

Tuesday, 9 September

I reread *Lucky Jim*, not done for some time. The opening ninety pages remain immensely funny, the depiction of Professor Welsh (modelled, Kingsley told me, on his first father-in-law) making one laugh uncontrollably. Dixon's lecture holds up well too, also the journey in the bus at end of book. The weakness of the novel is Dixon's relationship with the physically unattractive, in all other respects maddening, Margaret. One cannot see why Dixon felt in duty bound to stick by Margaret, even after telling her in the plainest terms (about halfway through the narrative) that there is no emotional bond between them. Dixon later contradicts this to the extent of explaining to the pretty girl Christine (for whom he has more or less fallen) that he cannot pursue matters further because of his involvement with Margaret.

One suspects some actual personal relationship in the mind of the author, possibly one of his own which Kingsley found impossible to rationalize to himself, anyway impossible to handle as a thread in novel. It constitutes a warning against certain insuperable difficulties in narrating a novel in the first person (which, of course, *Lucky Jim* is not), where the Narrator is represented as not being the author; or, in this case, chiefly the author, but in certain respects distinctly someone else. The technical complications of such a method are extreme.

A definite failure is Bertrand, Professor Welsh's painter son, who is having some sort of an affair (what sort?) with Christine. Bertrand does not come off chiefly because author is obviously unfamiliar with the professional life and habits of painters, adequately nasty examples of whom would not have been too difficult to find and make credible. The reader is never told whether Bertrand makes a living out of painting, and has shows, or is complete farceur supported by his father. One suspects the latter, if so, it should be made clear. Would Professor Welsh have been able to afford that, even if willing? The old novelist's trouble (from which Evelyn Waugh suffers) of allowing the characters the author dislikes no marks at all is a self-defeating practice, if one only too easy to fall into. Nonetheless *Lucky Jim* remains a novel of very considerable skill and originality, streets better than any of the stuff being produced at the same time with which it was fatuously compared.

I also finished the Italian novel Anthony Hobson lent me *The Tartar Steppe* (first published in Italy 1945), by Dino Buzzati, one of those Italian fantasy novels (an Italian genre Duckworth's did some translations of). This time it is about a sinister fort which blights the army career of any officer posted there. Names of officers Italian, circumstances implying Austria-Hungary or Russia in 19th century. When Anthony mentioned the book I suspected it was the basis of goodish TV film seen about four years ago, *The Valley of the Tartars*. This proves to be so, the film really a more suitable medium for the theme than a novel for handling that particular sort of fantasy.

Thursday, 11 September

To London to see Sussman for, in principle, final reconstruction. Operations began about 11.45, working on to about 3.45. Halfway through, Jean, Sussman's assistant (whom he takes great delight in jollying up), was sent out to buy sandwiches from a place called Dion (?) Giovanni in Thayer Street, run by family of Sicilians. Sussman says that really first-rate item there is hot salt beef sandwiches, eaten on spot, too sticky for transport. I ordered beef with rye bread, Sussman liver with white bread. He insisted on splitting a smoked salmon sandwich between us as hors d'oeuvres, also standing lunch. All this we ate at a long desk which runs from the door to the telephone, sitting facing each other, Jean eating her sandwiches, and making tea at the far end was cut off from us by three plaster casts of complete sets of teeth. (At first I supposed them to be elaborate Viennese pâtisserie to make the final course.) I suppose this visit will bring to a close an association made pleasant by Howard Sussman's niceness, intelligence and able dentistry.

Sunday, 14 September

Bob and Liddie Conquest to luncheon (ferried both ways from station by John). They brought with them, at his own request, Kingsley Amis, all in excellent form. Bob is now on the committee of the Ingersoll Foundation T. S. Eliot Prize, and Political Book Award, in consequence of having deputized for me on being given the former at the Chicago Presentation Dinner. The next T. S. Eliot choice (not yet announced) is to be Vidia Naipaul. The only objection to Bob's presence on board seems to be the fact of his own eminent suitability to be awarded the Political Book Prize (notably for *The Great Terror*), something that can no doubt be in due course sorted out. Bob's latest work, *Harvest of Sorrow* (sent by him earlier, and describing Stalin's politically engineered famine in Ukraine) is well reviewed in today's papers.

Good press also for Kingsley's newly published novel *The Old Devils*. I have not yet read much of latter, owing to *DT* review book (life of *Enid Bagnold*) arriving late, so must be dealt with under pressure. *The Old Devils* is enjoyable so far.

Kingsley and Andrew Motion (writing the Larkin biography) travelled to Hull for Larkin's funeral. This was not attended by Monica Jones on the grounds that she was too upset: for the same reason she would not have Andrew and Kingsley in the house, which they had never seen, and naturally wanted to cast an eye over.

In honour of *The Old Devils* V cooked from a Welsh recipe, chicken-&-leek pie, which dish later we found actually to occur in the novel. Three bottles of a drinkable light Burgundy, not at all outstanding. Bob now has some thing about keeping off heavy red, indeed is supposed to drink white. The Conquests are staying at the Amis/Kilmarnock residence in Regent's Park Road, which Bob described to V as a great improvement on Kentish Town. Kingsley's son Philip, with pregnant girlfriend, was evicted to accommodate the Conquests (possibly a good excuse) on arrival from US. Kingsley is so utterly unable to travel alone these days that, when going to Swansea for the trip on which Paul Fussell accompanied him recently, his daughter Sally had to accompany him in train. Mentioned I had enjoyed Martin Amis's *Money*, to which Kingsley replied he found all Martin's novels unreadable, but would have to try the next one, as it is dedicated to him. I wonder if Martin is planning an Amis *Father and Son*, which might not be bad theme. Kingsley gave an uproarious imitation of someone singing a Celtic song (which Celtic nation unspecified) at a Hampstead party. Enjoyable day.

Friday, 19 September

Jamie Camplin sent a Thames & Hudson mock-up for *The Dance Album*. This seems well done, in fact some of the pictures brilliant in their ingenuity, even if one or two minor adjustments are required in both pictures and explanatory text. It is always difficult to judge an illustrated book when plates are only xeroxed. Apart from that the general impression is most satisfactory. In the afternoon Peter Mumford came to see me about felling trees by the lake, also the repair of the Stoney Lane gate recently broken by itinerant vandals. Mumford took V and John down to see what needed done, as I find myself rather stiff in the joints these days. Two or three trees must come down, including the one discussed earlier with the fissure beneath, which will shoot again.

I reread *Decline and Fall* (not done for long time). There is notable originality in first fifty pages, the way things go with a swing (as with *Lucky Jim*, the latter keeping up élan slightly longer). When the butler Philbrick (name of an Oxford undergraduate contemporary Waugh disliked) appears, a vein of silliness begins to be struck, from then on pure fantasy taking over with varying success. It should be added that when a film was made of the novel (a film which received an undeservedly poor reception) Philbrick was funny when acted. Grimes always good in the novel, realistic or fantastic, in general good at everything to do with school, masters, funny. An interesting point about *Decline and Fall* is that almost every first novel of that period has the theme of a young man, probably disastrously, trying to get girl. Cyril Connolly (*Enemies of Promise*) even made a chart of the anti-heroes from different schools (in practice, Eton, Clongowes) to whom this was a problem.

Waugh does not tackle this matter at all, chiefly, I think, because it did not bulk at all large in his emotional life at that period: perhaps never largely at any period, as such. On the contrary, a rich promiscuous older woman falls in love with Paul Pennyfeather, Waugh's anti-hero, almost to his own embarrassment, if unexpectedly enjoyably. She at once plans to marry him. Until this happens Pennyfeather seems totally untroubled by girl (or any other sex) question, sex playing no part in his own ambitions. When *Decline and Fall* first appeared, readers accepted its (truly appalling) vulgarity in gloating over the modish wedding preparations for Pennyfeather's wedding as satire; now, in the light of Evelyn's later social tastes, it is to be seen as yearnings towards all he aspired to, publicity, grand guests, general display.

.   In fact all his future preoccupations, including RC leanings, are to be found in this first novel, as well as his extreme ability to handle prose. Fantasies of latter half, prison, return to Oxford as obscure don, come off much better than Philbrick as East End gangster, etc. Finally, one agrees with Connolly that *Decline and Fall* is remarkable for the manner in which narrative is sustained at all costs (no concession to perfectionism), a fairy story, yet full of food for thought about its author; Paul Pennyfeather, for example, abandoned by his bride, takes it all in most philosophical manner imaginable, far from what happened in real life.

Sunday, 28 September

I slept badly, still feeling effects of gastric upset begun some days ago. Hilary and John Spurling brought down the Moynihan portrait. We then placed it on the dining-room wall over the sideboard, the Augustus John drawing moved to righthand of the south-facing window. All this was already prepared for with help of John (Powell). Subsequently, the light proving bad for displaying oil-painting over the sideboard, these two pictures were exchanged again. The Spurlings arrived rather late for luncheon, having with characteristic energy, walked up the hill to examine at close quarters the White Horse when approaching Westbury. The portrait looks better here than either in Rodrigo's studio or on wall of RA, surrounded by fairly second-rate stuff.

The Stockwells came up from The Stables to see it hung. At luncheon we drank a couple of bottles of Tom Rosenthal's Château Kirwan '71, excellent, definitely improved by keeping, in spite of being now relatively old. Hilary is going to Tulsa, Oklahoma, to read 6000 letters of Paul Scott's (apparently Scott kept copies of almost every letter he wrote). She is finding Scott's biography deeply interesting. Hilary is rather put out by the circumstance of Roland Gant retiring to France. Roland having been a close friend of Scott's, she had hoped he would prove chief source of information. In fact I am not sure myself that Roland might not have proved a bit cagey, holding strong views about Scott's 'image'. I met Paul Scott only once, when he was standing in for my agent David Higham, where he worked for ten years, doing it well people said. Scott seemed nice, sensible, no suggestion of drink, or general oddities, which seem to have lain under the surface, nothing more than might be expected from a reasonably intelligent stray publisher or literary agent, at last of which he appears to have been distinctly able.

The Spurlings went round the lake together in the afternoon (the battle-school walk), and would have called on friends near Warminster on way back had these been at home. Pondering on Hilary's adumbration of a portrait by Rodrigo Moynihan as my Eightieth Birthday present, I worked out this took just ten months from incubation of idea to picture hanging on dining-room wall.

Tristram's TV programme on Hitchcock was well received. Discussing this, Tristram remarked that Hitchcock was fond of talking of 'the Plausibles', ie. critics who always objected that some characters or episodes in his films were not 'plausible'. This also not uncommon aspect of novel-reviewing, eg. John Gross on *The Fisher King* (in principle favourably) for the *New York Times Book Review*, remarked that Lamont was 'weirdly implausible'. Roland Gant, reading the typescript, at once asked if Lamont was modelled at all on Harold Evans. This was to some extent true, so far as type was intended, combined with having met Evans only once and knowing nothing of his private life. Another *Fisher King* reviewer complained that saying a firm was 'flush of cash' (spoken by an adman) was the author's old-fashioned idea of business phrases. It had in fact been culled from a column in the *Financial Times* of six months before. Enjoyable day, if pretty tired at end of it.

Wednesday, 1 October

At Dr Rawlins's recommendation, owing to intermittent rectal bleeding, saw Mr Southwood at the Bath Clinic, who reported all well so far as potential polyp concerned. John Bayley's Introduction to *The Dance Album* arrived. Good, indeed, excellent, if concentrating rather less than might be wished on actual pictures involved in sequence. Also John will insist that Sillery is modelled on Sligger, true only so far as F. F. Urquhart, the Oxford don known as 'Sligger', had faint remnants of an undergraduate salon at Balliol when I was up. This can be put right by inserting a sentence to effect that, although Sligger is often thus identified, Sir Ernest Barker, a Cambridge don (encountered on the politico-military course there) is much closer, if again far from a portrait, or even a caricature. Several Cambridge papers did, in fact, suggest a Cambridge figure was intended when book appeared.

Barker (utterly unlike Urquhart) was keen on poor-boy-who-made-good angle on himself, which suggested that characteristic in Sillery, also the physical ebullience entirely unlike Sligger's devitalized manner. Bayley assumes Maurice Bowra to some extent also represented. If so such a thought never crossed my mind when writing. I can see now that has a certain force. Hugh Lloyd-Jones too mentioned some of Sillery's phrases ('golden opinions') as favourite Bowra ones. The great thing is to have Introduction written. It has all John Bayley's acuteness, individual style. On rereading I see, in fact, there are at least a dozen references to matter specifically illustrated in *The Album*.

Thursday, 2 October

V to London to attend Osbert Lancaster's Memorial Service at St Paul's, Covent Garden. Only a week ago I fully intended to be present, but felt too mouldy when it came to point to attempt the whole business. V said the music was splendid. Afterwards a wake took place at the Garrick Club. There V talked to various people. St Paul's Covent Garden emphasizes Osbert's Theatre rather than social side, but is reasonably appropriate. Constant Lambert, for instance, is commemorated by a tablet there.

I often used to walk back through its attractive precinct when at Duckworth's. Returning one afternoon I encountered, coming from opposite direction, journalist called Beccles Wilson, who frequented the outskirts of the Augustus John world (possibly his wife had been a John model). At one moment Beccles Wilson was involved in a row with the Sitwells. He was tall, fair, good-looking in a vacuous way. I asked if he had been visiting a publisher. 'No,' he said, then lowering voice apologetically, 'Just at times when I pass this church I drop in to slip up a shy prayer.'

V to Sussman in the afternoon, to whom she took my damaged lower plate. He cannot deal with this without my presence so another visit for luncheon down here with Mrs Sussman is planned.

Wednesday, 8 October

Dr Rawlins rang saying he wanted to look in after dinner, bringing with him another doctor with the wonderful name of John Reckless, calling up every sort of adventure story. It appears from blood tests recently taken that I have lost a lot of blood, and am now ticking over at less than half what normal blood strength should be, in short suffering from severe anaemia. This accounts for my feeling in extremely poor shape for some little time. Reckless examined me, then arranged I should go to Bath Clinic the following day. During the most serious moment discussing matters with the two doctors, Trelawney, who had secreted himself in the room, jumped on my knee.

Thursday, 9 – Tuesday, 14 October

This period spent in Bath Clinic. X-ray (downward) by Dr Roberts, bearded figure, who X-rayed me before; X-ray (upwards) Dr Emerson, quiet, grave, middle-aged. These revealed no troubles beyond suspected [subsequently confirmed] duodenal ulcer, also one in the oesophagus. I am now linked night and day to a contrivance from which blood (whose?) is dripped into me, and taking various pills. All this is under general superintendence of Dr Reckless, a nice chap, full of enthusiasm, who had even read one or two vols of *Dance* (but uncertain which).

His surname is apparently Huguenot (Reclès), family emigrated at Edict of Nantes Revocation, and started silk business in Macclesfield. Some went to the US, where formerly (now no more) was a Reckless Town, Massachusetts. The name is a good one for a movie serial, in which Reckless himself, good-looking, dashing, could play a hero. Much as I dislike being in these places, the Bath Clinic is better than most, pleasant nurses, efficient atmosphere, even if food, as usual, to be treated with caution. Items like potatoes baked in their skins are safer than dishes with names like *Entrecôte Gogol, sauce Toulouse-Lautrec*, etc.

While incarcerated I am reading (for review) Vol 1 of Martin Stannard's biography of Evelyn Waugh. Stannard (an academic) seemed quite a nice young man when he came to see us perhaps seven or eight years ago at the time of starting this book. I don't want to carve him up too savagely, but it is pedestrian to a degree, full of actual mistakes, not to mention lack of the faintest conception of handling titles correctly. It remains a mystery why persons writing books in which titles occur don't spend half-an-hour (at most) to learn all that is necessary. Indeed one cannot understand why someone like Stannard wanted to write about Evelyn (who would repay really intelligent treatment) at all, as he has no glimmering of the sort of social life to which Waugh aspired. Christopher Sykes, otherwise not very bright, did at least understand that, indeed belonged to it. The trouble is, I think, that Evelyn's knockabout humour is mistaken for simple good nature (which in a sense P. G. Wodehouse's humour was, whatever the depths of Wodehouse melancholy). This is shown by the public's shocked reaction to Waugh *Diaries* and *Letters*, when published, both remarkably skilled writing, but revealing a far from genial personality.

Sunday, 19 October

The Sussmans arrived about 11.30 am. Sussman & I at once adjourned to the Green Room, where I sat in the early Victorian chair with sloping arms (*bergère* chair?), while he fixed my lower plate. Then I gave place to V, who had developed some minor trouble since her last visit. It was a really wonderful convenience to manage both of us in this manner, even if luncheon was a bit late. Myra Sussman brought an enormous confection of chocolates wrapped in gold foil, held up on a golden dish, under which a golden Cupidon peeped out, like the final gasp of Art Nouveau decoration in a house of ill fame. One can't imagine where she acquired this splendidly generous gift.

I thought her more ebullient this time, V not sure of that. V sees her as necessary foil to set off her husband's almost too perfect performance as a social being, modify its narcissistic elegance. Eggs in aspic; roast beef; meringues & apple; Château Navarro '81, last not too bad, if unexciting. Sussmans set off home in pelting rain. It now appears that my ulcers may have been irritated by the Naprosyn produced by Dr Rawlins for an arthritic leg (which immediately improved), characteristic of a drug to do good in one direction, cause harm in another.

Friday, 24 – Tuesday, 28 October

The Stockwells at The Stables. They dined with us on Saturday; we with them on Monday, when we drank two bottles of the claret Virginia bought with my birthday present (Château Mallet? '78), excellent; both enjoyable occasions. I have been put on a regime of Vitamin B12, Tristram says that is now fashionable, injection by my pretty nurse (Sister Liz Carter) frequency perhaps gradually scaled down, otherwise probably for rest of my life.

I reread *Antony & Cleopatra*, one of my favourites. I had forgotten how long the play continues after Antony's death. It is a good moment when Cleopatra attempts to swindle Octavian in assessment of her property. After she is caught out, Octavian (cf. the Unjust Steward) agrees she was right to try and preserve something for herself (construction much used 17th century, now objected to by pedants ignorant of past phraseology, which avoids repeated preposition). Rereading *Macbeth*. Typical piece of donnish rubbish that Shakespeare did not write the Witches passages, when they were probably the bits of the play he enjoyed writing most ('Paddock calls, etc'), tho' of course un-Shakespearian in the sense that 'To be or not to be' might be called Shakespearian. One would agree Hecate may be an interpolation.

Wednesday, 29 October

V and I watched a TV programme about women photographers in the 1920s, which included Barbara Ker-Seymer. Barbara, a year older than me, must be coming up for eighty-three, the surviving friend I have known longest (if one excludes Henry Bath, at my prep school, never a friend in the same sense), as Barbara and I met when I was about twelve. Barbara's family knew Miss Evelyn Newton, who belonged to the Christian Scientist world which represented a section of my mother's life, the Ker-Seymers being, I suppose, Christian Scientists, at least involved to some similar extent.

My mother & I visited them in a large block of flats in West Kensington with extensive garden at back, in which Barbara and I, both about twelve, walked. There was some Ker-Seymer American connexion, expressed by Barbara giving me popcorn from a paper bag. She was the youngest of several sisters (who married sailors, I believe), said to be the favourite of her relatively rich grandmother. Barbara always had a little money of her own, which people who knew her well alleged she was pretty close with. On this West Kensington occasion Barbara also presented me with little coloured drawing she had done of a small girl in a gingham frock with a big bow in her hair. I possess it to this day.

The Ker-Seymer family (who appear in early vols of Burke's *Landed Gentry*) at some stage lost their money, possibly as recently as Barbara's father's generation. I met her again in the Twenties party world, I am not sure if those earlier occasions were ever referred to. John Heygate had rather a fancy for Barbara, a passion never consummated. His description of taking her home one night, her father then returning full of a party of his own he had been attending, gave birth to Mr Nunnery in *Afternoon Men*, depicted from Heygate's description, whether at all truly represented I do not know. This fact seems worth recording as good example of how a novelist sometimes 'creates' characters, ie. someone else's words working on the imagination. Barbara (now very deaf) is quite unchanged, the TV programme bringing back vividly not only her own diction, demeanour, but that of 1920s, of which she was so typical a specimen.

In early days she set up as lesbian, in spite of two husbands and a long list of lovers (Wogan Philipps, David Garnett). Her son, by John Rhodes, is now a successful businessman in the US. In the collection of lovers adumbrated in the TV programme, a black one appeared rather ostentatiously. I remember Barbara once remarking how one never got used to a jet black head beside you on the pillow on waking up in the morning. Barbara said as a child she was bored by pictures, then her mother lured her into Tate Gallery, saying it was a big shop, whereupon she fell in love with Henry Wallis's *Death of Chatterton* (the model is said to be George Meredith, whose wife subsequently ran away with Wallis). I always liked Barbara, found her attractive, and I think she liked me, but some sense of self-preservation preventing running into trouble with her (probably her colossal egotism), which could have happened in early party days. We sent her a postcard saying we had enjoyed her performance, Petrus Christus's *A Young Lady*, not unlike one of Barbara's own sitters in photographic days.

Monday, 3 November

I wrote congrats to Kingsley Amis for winning the Booker Prize with *The Old Devils*, now read twice. A second round obligatory, first requiring making of list of characters' names, with those of wives, otherwise, owing to similarity of Welsh surnames, impossible to remember who is who. In any case some difficulty in differentation between a group of individuals almost all of whom are retired, living in the same area, mainly occupying their days in drinking together. If a shade sentimental at the end (Kingsley possessing a distinct vein of sentimentality), a work of considerable originality, not least in the social level dealt with. The background is of persons who feel intensely Welsh, while at the same time loathing Welsh nationalism, professional Welshmen, especially the Welshness of the media hack such as Wynford Vaughan-Thomas.

The last's prototype appears as one of *The Old Devils* characters, returning from London to settle locally. Vaughan-Thomas collaborated in *The Shell Guide to Wales*, a reference book riddled with historical and other inaccuracies, reviewed by me in the *DT*. I was fairly rude, and should have been even ruder had it not been year of the Prince of Wales's inauguration at Carnarvon Castle, for which the *Guide* had evidently been hurried out. Vaughan-Thomas, said to have appreciated his projection at Kingsley's hands, died soon after its publication. I never met him so he may have been a better man than an historian or intermediary of Wales.

The technical difficulty which Kingsley lets himself in for is description of thoughts of the various different characters concerned, which (as naturally they are, in fact, author's thoughts) inevitably makes them all seem much alike. Probably no avoiding this, while up to a point no doubt they *were* alike, as a local group constantly meeting each other. Nonetheless it is a problem for the reader sorting them out as individuals. Such is an endemic difficulty with a certain kind of novel, where the author is faced either with this objection, or (as Kingsley in other novels has on the whole chosen) sees everything through the eyes of its author. Kingsley's own immediately recognizable tastes and prejudices inevitably rub off on these retired South Welsh (mainly) small businessmen, who have to be represented as far more consciously articulate, mentally analytical, than likely in real life. Again, a perennial author's problem even with the cowboy in Westerns.

This is, however, a professional criticism, written with professional knowledge of the extreme difficulty of surmounting certain technical hurdles, not likely to worry the general public, for that matter the professional novel-reviewers, whose ignorance of the techniques of novel-writing is generally fathomless. Martin Stannard wrote a long, almost embarrassingly humble, letter about mistakes in the Waugh biography, unavoidably complained about when I reviewed it: to mention only a few howlers, muddling up the two Duggan brothers; saying Gerald Duckworth, one of the grumpiest of men, was 'garrulous'; and wrongly identifying two guests in a wedding photograph, at least some of which could have been easily avoided by reading my own Memoirs with a little more care. (As H. G. Wells said to George Orwell: 'Read my early works, you shit.') Stannard's ignorance of the use of titles leads to indescribable confusion, notably in relation to Asquith/Herbert families. V has just finished book, finding yet further errors, so I sent him probably a far from exhaustive list of these.

When I was a child the housemaid or gardener would have known the difference between Lord Snooks and Lord John Snooks, which today professional gossip-writers, not to mention *The Times* and *Daily Telegraph*, get wrong. It is not a matter of snobbery, but correctness, failure to understand Lord Snooks is a peer of the realm with a seat in the House of Lords (nowadays as likely to be Trade Union boss or academic go-getter, as an hereditary aristocrat, nonetheless theoretically an eminent figure); Lord John Snooks, holder of a merely courtesy title, probably without money of his own, at best a modest settlement, having to earn a living, which younger sons in this country always had to do. It is like thinking, say, Deputy-Editor and Sub-Editor, can be used interchangeably.

Reflecting on Stannard's book, Evelyn's opinions, goings-on, and grey bowler, all left one with a dreadfully unnourished feeling. Obviously Evelyn had very considerable talents, immense will-power, but what a waste of time so much of it all was. I find the same unnourishing feeling in most of his books, except *Pinfold*, some of *Decline and Fall*, passages in the novellas, occasional sentences scattered about everywhere. On the other hand the *Diaries* and to a lesser extent the *Letters* (when not showing off to the Lygons and others) are absorbing. Former are perhaps the outstanding things Evelyn accomplished. In fact if *Pinfold*, so close to life, is looked on as his best fiction the conclusion seems to be that he was most gifted when writing autobiographically, not, as would almost universally be assumed, in a vein of fantasy or farce. He is a writer entirely without 'poetry', although one would at once admit that to be a tricky critical term to apply to any novelist. Could it be said of Kingsley Amis, a professional poet (quite a different thing)? On the whole I would say not. There is a certain 'poetry' about the background of *The Old Devils*, for instance. Nor is it at all true of, say, Wyndham Lewis (in spite of savagery), D. H. Lawrence (tho' also at his best in *Letters*), Virginia Woolf (better in *Letters*, immeasurably better in *Diaries*). Proust, Dostoevsky, Dickens, all of whose Letters are not on the whole outstandingly interesting, have much poetry in their novels; Joyce, too, tho' not in his *Letters*, nor for that matter poems. All rather interesting.

Monday, 10 November

Tessa Davies to tea after WI meeting at The Stables. She is on the board of Butler & Tanner, printers of *The Old Devils*, now thinking in terms of 90,000 after Kingsley won the Booker. Tessa said nowadays correct assessment of sales is of immense importance. To some extent always true, of course, large contemporary circulations no doubt adding to the desirability of guessing right. I heard from Roland Gant, who is suffering the usual tribulations of new house, collapsing floors, nothing working, etc. Roland sounded a bit isolated, out of the world away in French Alps, but they like the place and are planning to come over at Christmas.

Tuesday, 11 November

Lees & Mary Mayall to luncheon. They had been in Florence and said the whole Tuscan countryside was infected with British-inhabited villas. Not so long ago they visited Adrian Daintrey in The Charterhouse (for whom I ordered a case of wine for Christmas) and gave him lunch in an Italian restaurant nearby, where Adrian & I lunched. Adrian got so tight the Mayalls had some difficulty in getting him back to base. I asked if they all drank a lot. Lees said no, only Adrian, who insisted on consuming three or four Grappas, a lethal drink, at end of meal. Shades of Colonel Newcome staggering back to answer 'Adsum' in the setting sun. Odd telephone call in evening. Edward Greene rang to ask if I could tell him anything – absolutely *anything* – about the late Earl of Lovelace, who, as Viscount Ockham, was slightly senior to me at Goodhart's.

Greene, himself an Etonian, apparently is a crammer by profession. He seems to have mainly educated the present Lord Lovelace, Ockham's son.

Ockham (after succeding his father as Lovelace) died in 1964, having married a first wife in 1939, she dying about eighteen months later with no issue. He then married a second wife in 1951, Danish, widow of Baron Karl Gustav Blixen-Finicke, one presumes a relation, probably brother or nephew of the writer Karen Blixen's husband, Bror Blixen. This second wife gave birth to the present Lord Lovelace, who, knowing literally nothing about his father, is making these enquiries and anxious for information of any sort whatever. He himself is described in books of reference as 'educ. privately', so perhaps Greene undertook all his schooling. Ockham, as a boy, was not without a certain dissipated charm of an infinitely languid decadent kind, concerned with nothing but (so far as those could be brought about) dodging work, games, the Corps (last of which I believe he managed to get out of). He had not smallest intellectual interests, tho' quite funny sometimes in conversation.

Ockham, with two schoolfellows, Derek Erskine and Jo Aird, had to see Goodhart about something in the private part of the house on Sunday morning, where they found Goodhart's elevenses, a glass of milk and slice of cake on a plate. One of them drank the milk; one ate the cake; and one broke the plate. I don't remember just what eventually happened, but there was a corking row.

Ockham belonged to a group of boys a shade above me in the house, which at the time included Hubert Duggan. Ockham left Eton comparatively young, and did not go to university. I believe he was in Germany for a time, bought an aeroplane, crashed it, immediately bought another one. That must have been after he inherited. I told Greene this last, who said it was just the sort of thing the son wanted to hear as building up picture of his father and would fascinate him. My impression is that Ockham ended up in Kenya (where Derek Erskine settled, and was eventually knighted). This is to some extent borne out by the Blixen connexion, tho' how close Ockham's second wife was to Bror Blixen is purely conjectural. I can't quite see why the present Lovelace never asked about his father from his mother. Possibly he developed his interest only after she died. I told Greene, who sounded quite agreeable (fiftyish indicated by OEA list), about the Kenya possibilities, which could explain why it was difficult to trace Ockham in this country.

Friday, 14 November

I reread *Salammbô* (tr. W. Powys Mathers. Powys Mathers was an odd fish, fat, bearded, inarticulate, an oriental scholar, met by me with Varda in ancient days). What extraordinary stuff *Salammbô* is. Like Henty's *The Young Carthaginians*, which I read at my prep school, rewritten by Sade and Wilde, then turned over to an American academic for historical and sociological additions, the whole poured out incoherently, almost in manner of Burton's *Anatomy of Melancholy*. Maurice Bowra used to say that Billa Creswell (widow of Roy Harrod) combined the roles of Flaubert's two famous heroines, Emma Bovary and Salammbô (in appearance). There is indeed some resemblance between these two ladies in the respective novels. Salammbô essentially a nineteenth-century Frenchwoman like Emma. Billa undoubtedly has a slightly African look, and was concerned in early days about being rescued from provincial life in Norfolk. Flaubert wasn't much good at plots as such; his narratives, characterization are immensely monotonous, if not without a certain force deriving, one feels, from author's own acute misery.

At 9.30 am, Richard Ingrams rang, saying he was doing an article on Claud Cockburn for the *Dictionary of National Biography*, had I any information to give him on this subject. Apparently the *DNB* piece was to have been written by Malcolm Muggeridge, nowadays perfectly well physically, but incapable of handling any work of that kind. I replied to Ingrams that I knew nothing material about Cockburn, although we had met on and off since Oxford (Claud was up at Keble, three or four years senior to me) until within comparatively short time before his death.

Although I found Claud a pleasant drinking companion (he was a very considerable absorber of alcohol), I believed him to have been to the end of his days a most sinister brand of Stalinist Communist. When Cockburn edited *The Week*, one of many fabrications circulated by that (naturally covertly Communist) publication was that at George V's funeral (last really tremendous show of that kind, which I watched) King Carol of Rumania had such a hangover his masseur had to be included close to him in the procession to render assistance if required. There was indeed a somewhat strange figure in the cortège, dressed rather like a Greek evzone with white kilt, but wearing the jacket of apparently an ordinary lounge suit. He was in that party of foreign notabilities marching well behind the royalties following the coffin. He could not possibly have done anything for Carol, even had the latter fainted.

I learnt what had happened later from Freddy Packe, Welch Regiment contemporary of my father and lifelong friend. Packe became a courtier after retirement so was in the know. He explained that the white-kilted figure was a former Rumanian Prime Minister wearing national dress. Just before the procession set out, it looked like rain and an order was issued 'Greatcoats to be worn'. Having no greatcoat for that particular outfit, the Rumanian ex-Prime Minister, wishing not to disregard regulations, put on the jacket of his ordinary pinstripe suit.

I was responsible for suggesting Claud Cockburn to Malcolm as a potential writer for *Punch*, both of us, of course well aware of Cockburn's Communist proclivities. Malcolm regarded himself as perfectly well equipped to guard against any such propaganda in *Punch*. This led to Malcolm seeing much more of Claud than formerly, falling for him utterly, as he did for certain men who amused him, almost as if he were in love. In a sense he was. Cockburn, I think, had a thoroughly bad influence on Malcolm, exciting him into rages against everyone and everything, just when he needed to be calmed down. Cockburn, by *métier*, was always anxious to spread dissatisfaction with all existing institutions.

One exceedingly funny incident in the Cockburn/Muggeridge friendship was when Claud was staying with the Muggs in Albany. On leaving, Claud's bag remained there to be picked up by him on his way to the train after a visit to Fleet Street. In course of the morning Kitty Muggeridge noticed a bottle of their whisky had disappeared from the sideboard. Kitty had a pretty good idea where it had gone. Claud had not yet returned. She opened his unlocked bag, and found the whisky there at once. Kitty accordingly replaced the full bottle with an empty one. So far as I know the matter was never later referred to by either party. Ingrams, who is under Cockburn sway, is wholly unsuitable to do CC in the *DNB*.

Saturday, 15 November

V, noticing a lump under her arm, consulted Dr Rawlins, who arranged for her to see Mr K. Lloyd Williams, surgeon, at Frome Hospital, yesterday afternoon. She will have to have this lump removed; accordingly going into Bath Clinic on Thursday the 30 November, where Lloyd Williams is one of the consortium. I knew nothing of this until just before she saw Rawlins. It is worrying, to say the least.

Monday, 17 November

V, reading *Sunday Times*, said: 'Didn't you know a Cambridge don called Gow?' She then recited allegations by the journalist art-critic Brian Sewell (who belonged to the traitor Anthony Blunt's artistic circle) to the effect that Gow was Blunt's KGB 'controller' as a Soviet spy. A. S. F. Gow (d. 1978, age ninety-one, not 1975, as stated in my Memoirs), was a beak at Eton (he briefly taught me Greek), then he became a don at Trinity, Cambridge. I saw something of Gow during the politico-military course there. Andrew Gow was the friend and biographer of A. E. Housman. He was also George Orwell's 'classical tutor' at Eton. When I wrote somewhere that Orwell consciously tried to avoid a 'public school' accent, Gow sent postcard to me saying Orwell 'croaked discordantly' when he arrived at Eton in 1917.

I think Gow saw something of Orwell after he left school, possibly even helped him financially when things were difficult. That would have been during Orwell's most revolutionary period. It would have been almost inconceivable afterwards when George and I were seeing quite a lot of each other and Orwell was very anti-Communist, that he would not have said at one moment or another something like: 'You'd never guess it, but Granny Gow had Marxist leanings.' I could well imagine George saying that, had there been the least reason to suppose Gow was at all orientated to the Left.

Gow, as a considerable connoisseur of pictures and drawings, would certainly have known Blunt in the latter's capacity as an authority on Poussin and a figure in art world generally, but one cannot imagine anything less probable than that this Jamesian personality should have been a Russian agent. Gow and I, at his invitation, sometimes took walks together at Cambridge, during which Gow never mentioned the war, or public events of any kind. For him to turn out a sinister figure would be like the most implausible end to a bad detective story. As a rule I find the ever rolling stream of spy journalism beyond words tedious. I shall, however, await developments about Gow, even if evidence is doubtful. It turned out that the character called Brian Sewell was simply having his leg pulled in a big way.

Wednesday, 19 November

I decided to follow up *Salammbô* with a reread of *Madame Bovary* (tr. J. Lewis May, an edition with awful John Austen illustrations bought by my father). Feeling that I had read the novel once in French I thought I could let myself off that time. [I used to think I preferred *Education Sentimentale*, an opinion now reversed.] The difficulty with books like *Madame Bovary* that have made overwhelming impression on literature, is to put oneself in place of a reader familiar only with novels previous to its publication, so immense has been *Bovary*'s influence. The same is true of Stendhal's novels in quite a different way. Flaubert does rather pile on the agony at the end. Also one wonders why Bovary himself, having been impervious to all that happened before Emma's death, should not (in Flaubert's realistic manner) have been represented as still impervious, rather than become utterly broken down by circumstances, becoming an almost Dickensianly sentimental figure. Bovary might, for instance, even have been allowed to marry again, in a sense quite in keeping with the studied banality of the earlier part of the narrative.

Perhaps Flaubert felt there were limits to what even his public would stand, accordingly was prepared to make a few concessions. One notes several themes subsequently endemic in the French novel: for instance, priest and atheist chemist contrasted, in this case arguing while drinking and closeted together over Emma's corpse. The Catholic/Communist antitheses of this kind have been imitated in innumerable subsequent books, and films, Graham Greene among others, tho' he probably did that by way of his more recent novel called, I believe, *Don Camillo*, which I never read.

Alick Dru used to say that all the best jokes in French were about priests and doctors, which are never made in this country. French jokes about doctors, of course, date back to Molière at least, possibly one should say Rabelais, yet they are almost unexplored here. Clergymen might be said to provide an occasional comic theme, doctors feel hurt at once if mildest fun made of them here. Interesting to know why. The only time I made a little light fun of a doctor in *Dance* I received a pained letter from Sir Henry Bashford, the King's physician, who said he was a great fan, but that doctor I had described would never have said the things he was represented as saying. In point of fact it was all pieced together from what doctors had actually said in my presence. I therefore (as I always do when criticised by experts for inaccuracy), asked Sir Henry to put it right for future editions where I had erred. This he agreed to do. His corrections, as it turned out, were absolutely minimal.

Thursday, 20 November

A letter from Bibsy Colt (*née* Mizener) saying her mother, Rosemary Mizener, died earlier this month. Bibsy enclosed the Service Paper for Rosemary's funeral, headed with reproduction of Poussin's *Dance to the Music of Time*. This gave me odd feelings. I was much touched that the sequence should have played so large a part in the Mizeners' personal life, never having quite realized they were so conscious of it.

Arthur Mizener is in poorish shape these days and Rosemary's death is likely to cause problems about looking after him. Arthur was one of my earliest fans in the American academic world. We used to see quite a lot of them both when they were over here, or when we were in the US. The Mizeners were overwhelmingly kind to John when at Cornell. Rosemary, always a little severe in manner, behaved with great courage during her last years, when things were becoming difficult with Arthur, who was losing his grip on things, and her own health was in a rocky state. Although both Mizeners were intensely keen on what might be called the moral side of being American, this very intensity of feeling set them a little apart even from most other Americans. One felt Arthur, both intellectually and as a personality, was cut above the majority of other dons at Cornell, yet he never quite lived up to what was (looking back) a brilliant opening with the biography of Scott Fitzgerald, later a subject so interminably written about.

At that date Fitzgerald was relatively unknown in this country, and altogether out of fashion in US. Fitzgerald's essentials were, in truth, never explained beyond the Mizener biography. Rosemary (Swiss origins, I think) had been brought uρ in Europe as child, and took on her husband's American patriotism (Arthur was about a fifth generation from an emigrant German pastor). Patriotism is not quite word for this attitude, a personal sense of Americanism, which always fascinated me by its difficulty of definition, something quite different from nationalism of European countries, including Great Britain. Arthur would always say things like: 'Americans have baths, not tubs.' One would then immediately read in next half-a-dozen American books about someone having a tub.

This afternoon John drove us to the Bath Clinic, where I had check-up with Dr Reckless (satisfactory). V remained for her operation.

Sunday, 23 – Monday, 24 November

John & I visited V in Bath Clinic. She was still recovering on Sunday, obviously knocked out, very white. Monday she was a better colour and greatly improved. John has nobly taken on the cooking here, which he does very well. I reread *Macbeth*. There is much to be said for Empson's view that Macbeth is already planning the murder when he came on the Witches; also that it *is* important how many children Lady Macbeth had (Macbeth was her second husband) owing to Macbeth's obsession with the question of succession.

Tuesday, 25 November

John and I visited V. We go up to her room one by one, otherwise there is not a great deal of space to sit down. While I was there today Mr Lloyd Williams appeared. The report had come through. Naturally one hoped for complete clearance; that was probably over optimistic, but it was good, short of that. She is to have hormone treatment. Lloyd Williams is not particularly young, and wholly different in demeanour from either Southwood or Reckless. He has rather the air of a genial old-fashioned doctor on the stage, which is quite sympathetic. Tristram rang in the evening. He cheered me by pointing out that far more drastic treatment would have been ordered had things been anything but satisfactory in the circumstances.

Wednesday, 26 November

John and I had visited V in the Bath Clinic. It is now agreed that she should leave on Friday. Pat Naipaul rang in the evening. Vidia is in New York at the moment, on the way back from receiving the Ingersoll T. S. Eliot Prize in Chicago. Pat said Vidia was anxious we should all meet so that he could describe his American adventures, which one longs to hear. I explained to Pat that we had both been involved in medical troubles, and arranged that we would meet the Naipauls when these had been straightened out. She said Wednesday was a good day for them, as soles were delivered on Wednesday (Vidia not eating meat).

Mr Millard rang reporting the back door of The Lodge is past repair. I ordered a new one with glass panels, to give more light in the kitchen (about £300).

I reread *The Last Tycoon* (reflecting on the Mizeners bringing Fitzgerald to the surface). I don't think, even if completed, it would ever have been a first-rate novel. All the same, something about Fitzgerald's mature writing always carried one on. When his earlier novels were published over here (the Grey Walls Press) soon after war I read them all as a duty, something no longer manageable. The main objection to *The Last Tycoon* is the awfulness of Stahr, more or less its hero, whom Fitzgerald seems genuinely to have admired. Stahr would have been unspeakable in real life, indeed was that, in so far as his character modelled on Irving Thalberg, much sentimentalized in the novel, gradually merging into Fitzgerald himself. Thalberg, among other undesirable acts, destroyed all Stroheim's unshown films out of sheer spite.

Latterly in the novel, when Stahr turns into Fitzgerald, he gets drunk, and tries to beat up the Communist, with whom he has especially arranged a meeting for political discussion. Fitzgerald is always fatuous when attempting to deal with political matters, for which he had no instinct whatsoever. He also lands himself in various technical difficulties by telling much of the narrative through the eyes of a woman. This is more often than not to be avoided by male novelists. Thoughts attributed to the Danish Prince Agge are equally unconvincing. Various unusual incidents in the life of Sheila Graham (with whom Fitzgerald was living at the time of his death), even if true, are quite pointless when tacked on by Fitzgerald to his heroine. These eventualities had been brought about by the very special circumstances of Sheila Graham's career, and were not in the least applicable in general bearing on England at that period.

This habit of taking some unusual aspect in real life for labelling a character in a novel is quite often done by novelists, thereby merely false-carding the reader. Nonetheless, I can't say I was bored. I am always struck by the absolute acceptance of life on the part of Americans, something utterly different from European novelists, especially English ones. Few of the last could have prevented themselves from satirizing at least some of the Hollywood characters, all taken by Fitzgerald (in a sense rightly from his point of view) with absolute naturalistic seriousness. One method is not necessarily better than the other, merely the difference is so marked.

Alan Bell, Librarian at Oxford, wrote a book about Sydney Smith (I suspect an impossible man to be entertaining about) and is an amusing reviewer. I had been corresponding with him not long ago about Evelyn Waugh's *Diaries*, which he appears to be re-editing. In the course of these was mentioned Tony Wood, a good-looking Wykehamist, who won many hearts at Oxford, whom Evelyn Waugh records himself in his *Diaries* as whipping. Subsequently Tony Wood formed a lifelong ménage with Wyndham Lloyd, the medical brother of John (The Widow) Lloyd. Tony Wood dcd earlier this year, which I missed in the paper at the time. Alan Bell (to whom I had pointed out that in the *Diaries* the 'Tony' whipped by Evelyn was Wood, rather than me) obligingly sent the obit of Wood appearing in *The Journal of the Society of Archivists*. This I was glad to see.

After blossoming as an Oxford beauty, Tony Wood (descended from inventor of Crompton's Mule, or whatever it was) looking after records at Warwick. His family, the Woods, very comfortably off, he an only son with a couple of sisters, owned Bruern Abbey, where later we stayed once or twice after house was bought by Michael Astor. There were many stories about Tony Wood (two or three years older than myself), who, when I knew him at Oxford (New College), still looked like a pretty schoolboy. I believe he grew fat in later life. It was said that when playing billiards with his father, who was about to make a stroke, Tony suddenly stated: 'Father, I don't think I'm sexually normal', at which Wood *père* is alleged to have cut the cloth.

On some occasion invited to large country house, Tony forgot to pack his pyjamas, accordingly slept in his silk (perhaps artificial silk) dressing-gown of elaborate design. He had a wet dream in the night, resulting in a Turner landscape all over sheets. I can't remember how he dealt with this contretemps. When V and I stayed at Bruern under the regime of Michael Astor (whom we never knew at all well) Roy Jenkins, then Home Secretary, was among the guests. At one moment we were sitting in main part of drawing-room, alone except for some invisible pianist playing *Love is the Sweetest Thing* in the back part of the room. At close of this recital, the unseen player arose, passed through our end of the room, and glancing in our direction with a slight bow, exited through the door. It was the detective always in attendance on the Home Secretary.

Thursday, 27 November

Denys Sutton, who, in spite of having in theory retired from *Apollo*, continues to edit paper until Christmas, sent the last number, in which his editorial deals with the Art Museum at Los Angeles (which I regret to say we never visited when in those parts). One illustration from that gallery shows picture by the Napoleonic painter Baron Gros of a young French cavalryman, Sous-lieutenant Legrand, posed in front of his charger. John, looking through *Apollo*, pointed out the drawing I gave him for his twenty-first birthday appears to be a study for this portrait. The drawing, specifically described as by Gros, came from O'Nians Gallery, Ryder Street, St James's. I had forgotten the Gros attribution. The drawing shows two figures, one wearing a helmet, both of which appear to be Sous-lieutenant Legrand. Denys Sutton, to whom I sent a postcard about this was much interested. He is just back from New York.

Friday, 28 November

John brought V back from the Bath Clinic in time for luncheon. I had made a curry. Tristram came down for the night, arriving rather later for dinner, at which we drank a bottle of Bollinger '79 to celebrate V's return. Dinner was cooked by John with great success.

Saturday, 13 December

V saw Mr Lloyd Williams for check-up after the operation, all found satisfactory. She is looking decidedly better. She says there was a moment last week when she suddenly began to feel like a human being again. E. Ralphs, who seems to be writer of fairly mature age, fluent knowledge of Russian, after reading my Memoirs sent copy of the current Soviet translation of Lermontov's *A Hero of Our Time*. It is, in fact, a modern pocket edition of the (American) translation of a former edition from Soviet State publishing house put on market here. It is wonderfully old-fashioned in format, illustrations of lithographic type, embossed cover, embroidered marker, like books produced here in 1880s.

The translation by Martin Parker not at all bad, certainly just as good, if not better than Vladimir Nabokov's. Nabokov says in his Introduction to his own that all other translations into English of *A Hero of Our Time* are merely 'versions'. This is rubbish. I took the trouble when Nabokov's translation appeared to go through it with Parker's (at least one other). The only difference is that frequent use of a narrator is sometimes ignored by Parker, eg., 'The old captain said' is sometimes omitted, so that once in a way the story runs straight on. Occasionally 'blouse' used instead of 'laced shirt', etc. Hard to find better example of the pretentious nonsense Nabokov was in the habit of putting over (I also hold the lowest possible opinion of *Lolita*).

The new Soviet edition of *A Hero* is much smaller in format, generally modernized, with an Introduction and Notes, explaining that Lermontov's book is perfectly safe for Soviet readers to admire. It also contains some interesting coloured illustrations, mostly by Lermontov himself, an unusually competent amateur artist (an Hussar officer at that). They are landscapes of the Caucasus, where most of the action of book takes place. I found myself reading *A Hero* again from cover to cover and felt all its old fascination, which I cannot altogether explain. Lermontov writes with extraordinary force, economy and sense of character. Technical flaws are that the smuggling episode, vivid in itself, gives no hint of Pechorin's character to be later unfolded. That could have been done in a sentence, linking the incident with the rest of book. No doubt the Tamin episode is more or less straight autobiography, possibly bit of drama added. Two of illustrations show the little Black Sea port itself, where a girl tried to drown Pechorin because he had accidentally happened on the local smuggling gang's activities.

A similar linking of Pechorin's character seems required, if less so (as we already know a lot about him) in the last story about a fatalist Serb officer. At several moments throughout the narrative information is heard through open windows, etc, which one accepts as a nineteenth-century convention, simply a quick way of explaining that some news was discovered. Less acceptable is a Doctor not knowing how to load a pistol, inconceivable, one would think, in an Army Surgeon, which he appears to be. Even if true, as Pechorin's Second, the Doctor would have made some show of supervising loading for the duel. That was the first of a Second's duties, especially if he knew, as he did, that dirty work was on foot. I think (as one so often feels about novels) a bit more trouble on the author's part might have devised some more convincing method by which the same result could equally well have been attained. Nonetheless I was as entranced as ever by *A Hero*.

I could not help thinking, during a current reread of *King Lear*, that in writing 'O'er moor and fen, o'er crag and torrent till/The night is gone', Newman had running in his head Poor Tom's 'through ford and whirlpool, o'er bog and quagmire'.

Friday, 19 December

Georgia rang this evening to say she had passed into Oxford (Univ). I found myself very pleased about this.

Sunday, 21 December

My eighty-first birthday. Woke rather early, buzzed all over, my usual reaction to frost, otherwise felt not too bad later. V gave me a nice shirt, chosen by John. In the course of the morning the Stockwells rang, also Lees Mayall, who saw the birthday in the paper. Lees had been staying with in-laws at Southampton Water. Kingsley Amis rang, thanked for congrats on winning the Booker Prize, chiefly wanted to confirm what I had once told him that Whistler (rather than Orson Welles or Graham Greene) initially made joke about the Swiss having invented the Cuckoo Clock as chief fame in their cultural achievements. This I corroborated (Whistler's *Ten O'Clock*, 1885), so joke just over century old.

Monday, 22 December

Virginia, as advance party at The Stables, to dinner. She talked of Tristram playing tennis at the Vanderbilt Club, Shepherd's Bush, with Harold Pinter, Antonia, and others. Harold is furious if any untidiness at Club, people leaving their trousers about.

Christmas Day

V, John, I, lunched at The Stables; Archie, Georgia, suffering from high temperatures, so they had their meal together in the sitting-room; we in kitchen. A splendid classical Christmas dinner; turkey, plum pudding, among other things for Birthday, Christmas, Tristram gave me Kipling's *Uncollected Poems*. They go back to his schooldays, and I look forward to reading them.

Boxing Day

Party given at The Stables by Tristram & Virginia. Georgia by now has retired to bed with flu. Guests: Lees, Mary, Alexandra, Cordelia, Robert Mayall. Also Robert's current girlfriend Mrs Cavanagh, little plump leather-bound volume, top-booted, like something out of a Twenties party. Robert is now huge. He said the bookshop was doing all right. Cordelia looking after alcoholic women, and does not drink herself. Alexandra was very full of beans; Peter & June Luke, who left at Railford Mill the son and granddaughter by the Estramadura hairdresser (opera *Le Barbier d'Estramadura*); Joff, Tessa, Lucinda Davies; Giles Waterfield, who looks after the Dulwich Art Gallery, with his mother; Georgia Tennant, Silvy Thynne; Michael Briggs.

Sunday, 28 December

Tristram, Virginia, Georgia, Archie, John, lunched here: Welsh pie, made with turkey. We dished up The Stables party. Mary Mayall told Tristram that Red Lion House, where David Cecil lived at Cranborne, is now owned by an ex-hippy called Fripp, who lives there with an actress/pop star. Fripp says his family is much older than the Cecils, the latter jumped up in the neighbourhood, and takes a great interest in the history of the place.

Tuesday, 30 December

A letter from Freddie Bradnum (who did the radio adaptation of *Dance*) saying he had been suffering from resurgence of old war wound. BBC turned down *The Fisher King* as a radio play, in spite of Bradnum, Graham Gauld, and others, recommending it strongly. Tessa Davies came to tea. We talked of the new newspaper the *Independent*, from which I have already received one or two cuttings, but haven't yet seen.

Wednesday, 31 December

A fan letter from George ('Dadie') Rylands, saying he had once more read *Dance* with the greatest enjoyment. I remember he sent a congratulatory postcard when the sequence was finished. Rylands was in Sixth Form (KS) when I was a Lower Boy, he must now be in about his eighty-fifth year. He has combined academic/stage/social success, also regarded as a great Cambridge beauty, moved on outskirts of Bloomsbury. He always kept his head about things, and never associated with the sillier side of what he was mixed up in. He appears, so it is said, in Rosamond Lehmann's *Dusty Answer*. When we met a year or two ago at Anthony Hobson's I reminded him that I saw his performances of Viola in *Twelfth Night* at early moment of my school career. He is always a competent Shakespearian critic. He wrote 'Dear Powell'; I replied 'Dear Rylands', adding I hoped this was not too intimate. Certainly a form of address nowadays used only by old-fashioned social equals, while Public Relations girls, others one has never set eyes on, sign, indeed sometimes open, their letters with christian names. This attention from an old hand on the last day of the dying year, together with several references in leaders etc, to the announcement of the CH in Honours, is flattering.

Index